S0-CFB-616

SECOND EDITION

JOINT CUSTODY
AND
SHARED PARENTING

SECOND EDITION

JOINT CUSTODY

AND

SHARED PARENTING

Edited by

JAY FOLBERG

THE GUILFORD PRESS
New York   London

WSU Vancouver
Library

© 1991 The Guilford Press
A Division of Guilford Publications, Inc.
72 Spring Street, New York, NY 10012

All rights reserved

No part of this book may be reproduced, stored in a retrieval system,
or transmitted, in any form or by any means, electronic, mechanical,
photocopying, microfilming, recording, or otherwise, without written
permission from the Publisher.

Printed in the United States of America

This book is printed on acid-free paper.

Last digit is print number: 9 8 7 6 5 4 3 2 1

Library of Congress Cataloging-in-Publication Data

Joint custody and shared parenting / edited by Jay Folberg. — 2nd ed.
    p.   cm.
    Includes bibliographical references.
    ISBN 0-89862-768-0 (hardcover). — ISBN 0-89862-481-9 (pbk.)
    1. Joint custody of children—United States.   2. Parent and child
(Law)—United States.   3. Joint custody of children—Canada.
4. Parent and child (Law)—Canada.   I. Folberg, Jay, 1941–
KF547.J64   1991
346.7301′7—dc20
[347.30617]
                                                            91-20289
                                                            CIP

Preface to the Second Edition

When the first *Joint Custody Handbook* was published by the Association of Family and Conciliation Courts in 1979, the modest goal was to gather together all the writing, law, and research on joint custody. At that time there were only a few statutes and cases dealing with joint custody and little published research. In 1984, *Joint Custody and Shared Parenting* was published for the purpose of presenting in one volume diverse perspectives, as well as of making available in usable form the expanding literature relating to shared parenting following divorce. Sales of both books exceeded expectations. Rather than reprint the contents of the 1984 volume to meet ongoing demand, it was decided to revise and update this popular resource in light of the wealth of new writing, research, and law on the subject of joint custody.

This new volume represents the next generation of experience and development. During the past seven years, shared parenting has moved from a debatable alternative to a generally accepted option. The debate has shifted from the wisdom of joint custody as a concept to the circumstances in which it is most likely to work and the extent to which parental responsibility should be shared.

In this book we bring together the collected experience and knowledge of child developmental experts, therapists, court connected mediators, researchers, economists, and lawyers to examine the questions and issues presented by joint custody. Our intent is to provide information to parents and to the professionals who help parents decide on parenting arrangements following marital dissolution. The key chapters in Part I that place joint custody in perspective and a couple of the chapters in Part II are retained from the 1984 edition. The remainder are new and reflect developments since the 1984 edition was published. Some of these new chapters were written specifically for this book; others have been adapted from professional journals.

Part I provides a historical overview of child custody and the child-focused pros and cons of joint custody. Part II examines the factors central to choosing joint custody, when it is most likely to work, how to structure a successful parenting plan, some of the obstacles to acceptance of joint custody, some concerns, including those of female dependency and inequality, and the economic considerations.

The previous edition set forth an agenda for research on the effects of joint custody and contained some preliminary data from small samples. Now in Part III we have the benefit of research findings on the results of joint custody for children and parents. This research draws from larger samples over longer periods of time following marital dissolution and provides helpful comparisons between maternal, paternal, and joint custody in both the United States and Canada. Important descriptive data are presented comparing post-divorce parenting in a large sample 18 months following separation. Also provided is information from another longitudinal study that assesses successful, stressed, and failed joint custody 12 months following mediation, and then assesses the children at approximately 30 months after the conclusion of mediation. A longitudinal study of preschool children in joint custody draws distinctions between age groups. Next we look at whether joint custody and frequent access make a difference for parents who continue to contest custody following their divorce. Another research chapter helps answer the question of whether the form of custody is linked to the level of child support paid.

In Part IV the law of joint custody is discussed, beginning with a comprehensive look at current legal issues and emerging trends. An attempt is made in one chapter to reconcile the conflict between the preference for joint custody, the preference for a primary caretaker, and the law's distrust of preferences. Shared parenting can affect eligibility for Aid for Dependent Children, as explained in a separate chapter. A retrospective look at the still evolving California joint custody statute, which many other states have used as a model, is instructive. The final chapter sets out the Canadian legal perspective on cooperative parenting after divorce.

Two appendices are contained in the back of the book. Appendix A is a chart of all statutory enactments on joint custody and shared parenting, along with citations to significant appellate decisions interpreting the legislation. Appendix B contains a joint custody agreement, with many alternate provisions that may be adapted for use in a parental plan, settlement agreement, or court decree. The list of references following Appendix B also serves as a bibliography on joint custody.

Each of the authors has generously allowed the works selected for this volume to be printed here without personal compensation or royalties, all of which have been designated for the Association of Family and Conciliation Courts. The authors have allowed the editor discretion to adapt their writing to the format of this book. In many instances this has meant the deletion of introductory comments and material that, though unique in some ways, duplicated areas previously discussed. Original footnotes or references have been condensed or omitted from some articles, and chapter references have been merged into a master list located in the back of the book. In all instances, deletions have been made for editorial brevity and easier reading, not in criticism or censorship of the author's work.

There has been no attempt to edit the language of joint custody for consistency of use. Some authors refer to joint custody, others to shared custody or shared parenting, and still others coin descriptive designations that best fit their own writing. Although some statutes, such as Florida's Shared Parental Responsibility Law, purposefully incorporate language selected to avoid interpretations based on previous joint custody statutes, all appear to strive for increased parental cooperation and involvement following divorce. The choice of terms appears more a matter of history and semantics than of meaning. Although we have chosen both Joint Custody and

Shared Parenting as the title of this book and use the terms interchangeably through-out, we share the concern expressed by Dr. Richard Gardner in an addendum to his chapter. He comments that disagreement over false issues could be obviated by avoiding the use of all traditional custody terms, which imply possession and restraint. A more general designation in custody decrees, such as "residential and decision-making arrangement," would be more appropriate and less controversial. This is the approach taken by the State of Washington in its parenting legislation.

Finally, it must be noted that any opinions, findings, conclusions, or recommendations expressed in this book are those of the named authors and not the Association of Family and Conciliation Courts. The editor takes sole responsibility for all editorial decisions and editing in this volume.

JAY FOLBERG

Acknowledgments

The original *Joint Custody Handbook* was conceived and edited by Ann Milne, whose work and ideas inspired the subsequent two volumes. The Association of Family and Conciliation Courts (AFCC) and its former executive director, Stanley Cohen, encouraged and prodded me in the editing and preparation of this book. All royalties are donated directly to AFCC.

The manuscript for this book was prepared with the facilities and staff assistance of Lewis and Clark Law School. The manuscript was processed by Lenair Mulford, whose skill, patience, and dedication are legendary. Sharon Pack also provided valuable word-processing assistance. Final editing was accomplished with the assistance of staff at the University of San Francisco School of Law.

Several law students helped keep the book on track and attended to the details. Special thanks go to Sue Ann Trzynka, then a law student at Lewis and Clark, and to Claire Solot Cohen, a law student at the University of San Francisco. Valuable research assistance and updating was provided by Lee Ryan, reference librarian at the University of San Francisco School of Law.

Finally, I wish to gratefully acknowledge the patience and generosity of the contributing authors. The preparation of this volume has been agonizingly slow in coming to print; the authors have graciously tolerated frustrating delays that were beyond their control. They have each allowed their chapters to be included here as a gift to the Association of Family and Conciliation Courts without any compensation for themselves. For this we are particularly thankful.

Contents

SECOND EDITION

JOINT CUSTODY

AND

SHARED PARENTING

I
Joint Custody in Perspective

1

Custody Overview

JAY FOLBERG

> This first chapter introduces the concept of joint custody, places
> custody approaches in a historical perspective, defines custody
> terms used throughout the book, and constructs a framework for
> subsequent chapters. The chapter concludes with a discussion of the
> role of law and professional attitudes in setting norms of parental
> behavior following divorce.

Child custody following divorce is being recast in state legislatures and courtrooms throughout the United States, as well as by parental agreement. Prompted by evolving parental expectations and roles, the law is changing to reflect new post-divorce family patterns and sensitivity to issues of gender equality. The dramatic changes in the law of custody are part of a second wave transforming family law. The first wave was centered on the no-fault divorce movement, in which the grounds for divorce were reshaped to comport with the reality of marital breakdown (see Glendon, 1989).

Historical Perspective

A review of the history of custody approaches and court decisions illustrates how the law and philosophy concerning custody have changed to accommodate changing times (see Jacob, 1988). New theories of child development and changing family structures have in the past led courts to reexamine custody preferences (Schepard, 1985). A historical review is helpful at the outset to better understand and place in perspective the current interest in joint custody.

Jay Folberg, Dean and Professor of Law at the University of San Francisco School of Law, was President of the Academy of Family Mediations and a past President of the Association of Family and Conciliation Courts. Most case citations have been omitted from this overview in the interest of brevity. Case citations can be found in Folberg, "Joint Custody Law—The Second Wave," 23 Journal of Family Law 1 (1984–85).

In England, the common law regarded children as their father's property. The presumption that the father was the person entitled by law to the custody of his child was irrefutable (Foster & Freed, 1978c). The English rule of parental preference does not appear to have been so strictly applied in nineteenth century America (Mnookin, 1975).

The dramatic social and economic upheavals of the nineteenth century reshaped the dynamics of the family. Industrialization changed rural, agrarian societies into urban societies. Accompanying the transition to wage labor was the separation of the home and workplace which placed fathers in factories and shops, while mothers generally remained at home as the primary nurturers of the children (Roman & Haddad, 1978b). The specialization of parental function and the smaller economic units fostered by the industrial revolution helped create the concept of the nuclear family as the foundation of society (Stack, 1976).

The nineteenth century also saw significant changes in the status of women and children. The early women's rights movement brought women greater political power, enfranchisement, and laws granting them the right to own property rather than to be property. Concurrently, the nineteenth century brought changes in the attitude of society toward children (Aries, 1965). Society's acceptance of child development theories that viewed children as evolving human beings led to placing a higher value on the importance of maternal care, which undermined the paternal custody assumption (Derdeyn, 1976a; Mnookin, 1975).

Consequently, the preference for fathers in custody disputes gave way to a preference for mothers as custodians, particularly of young children (Schepard, 1985). Most courts, at one time or another, adopted a judicial presumption favoring mothers as custodians of their children (Roth, 1975). Although early cases extolled the father–child relationship, the pendulum's swing in favor of mothers elicited even more lyrical extremes of judicial bias. Judges began to speak of the child's needs as the paramount consideration in awarding custody. The resulting "best interest test" was not so much a fixed formula as it was a general approach to custody decisions. The "best interest of the child" has become the cornerstone of most custody statutes. Later case law and more recent statutes seek to define the best interests approach by listing specific factors courts should consider in awarding custody. Although many statutes direct that the factors be given equal weight, courts appear to give their greatest attention to the child's need for stability and continuity of relationships and environment (Folberg & Graham, 1979). The interpretation of "stability and continuity" attributed to the influential book *Beyond the Best Interests of the Child* (Goldstein, Freud, & Solnit, 1973), frequently referred to in the chapters of this book and discussed here by one of its authors, slowed acceptance of alternative forms of custody.

Just as the early women's rights movement influenced family structure and custody considerations, the contemporary equal rights movement has again altered the balance (Morgenbesser & Nehls, 1981). The movement's emphasis on equality in the marketplace, greater independence for women to pursue professional goals, and less sexual stereotyping has led to greater participation by fathers in the parenting function in intact families (Quinn, 1976). With fathers more likely to have been involved in the day-to-day care of their children (McCready, 1975;

Young & Willmot, 1973), there is less reason to assume that upon divorce an award of custody to the mother will give the child greater continuity and stability than an award to the father.

While early research on child development stressed the maternal role, recent research has emphasized the importance of the role that fathers play in their children's development, as well as the importance of both parents being involved with and available for the child (Roth, 1975). In the past, courts usually granted an award of custody to the father only on a showing that the mother was unfit (Oster, 1965). More recently, courts have indicated a willingness to award custody to fathers when the facts of the case appear to make such an award appropriate (Solomon, 1977).

Fathers, perhaps encouraged by what they perceived as a more friendly judicial climate, began seeking custody in greater numbers in the 1970s (Quinn, 1976). In the United States, they also began challenging the constitutionality of the tender years presumption, and other obstacles to fair judicial treatment in custody decisions. Fathers began uniting to support one another's custody battles and to press for legislative changes (Morgenbesser & Nehls, 1981).

Convenient presumptions, first for the father, then for the mother, were no longer available as a shortcut to courts in arriving at the most appropriate custody determination. Where parents disagreed about custody, judges found themselves in the perplexing bind of trying to predict, with limited information and no existing consensus, which of two fit parents would best guide a child toward adulthood (Mnookin, 1975).

In 1957 North Carolina passed a statute allowing for the joint custody of children after divorce if it was clearly in the best interest of the child. Twenty-two years later, California statutorily declared a public policy of encouraging parents to continue to share their parenting rights and responsibilities after dissolution of the marriage. During the past decade, there has been an explosion of public interest in joint custody legislation. Over 40 states have enacted joint custody or shared parenting laws. Many of these statutes were inspired by the early California legislation (Jacob, 1988), although some stopped short of the California approach, while others have gone beyond it and California has again amended its statute. In all but a couple of states without joint custody legislation, shared parenting is authorized by case law in limited circumstances. These statutes, as well as key cases, are collected and charted in Appendix A.

Custody Definitions

The statutes and case law, as well as the psychological literature, sometimes describe the forms of custody following divorce in vague and overlapping terms. The lack of standard definitions may create confusion. Arguments that might validly be advanced against one form of custody are occasionally misdirected to discourage a different custody form. We will attempt to define here the basic custody arrangements, recognizing that some of our authors may take exception to these definitions or may further clarify definitions as used in their chapters which follow. The four forms of custody discussed and compared here are sole custody, split custody, divided custody, and joint custody (or shared parenting).

Sole Custody

The most commonly approved form of custody upon dissolution remains an award of sole custody to one parent with visitation rights to the noncustodial parent. The noncustodian, by informal agreement, may have a voice in important decisions affecting the child, but ultimate control and legal responsibility rest with the custodial parent.

Split Custody

The distinguishing factor in split custody is a custody award of one or more of the children to one parent and the remaining children to the other (Lindey, 1982). The policy of the law has generally been to keep siblings together because "a family unit is struck a vile blow when parents divorce; and is struck an additional one where children are separated from each other" (*Ebert v. Ebert*, 38 N.Y.2d 700, 704, 346 N.E.2d 240, 243 (1976)). Courts, therefore, often refuse to grant split custody absent compelling reasons. Severe competition or hostility between siblings may be one such reason. Another reason may be the inability of either parent to care for all of the children at once.

Divided Custody

Divided custody allows each parent to have the child for a part of the year or every other year. This form of custody may also be referred to as alternating custody. Each parent has reciprocal visitation rights under this arrangement, and each exercises exclusive control over the child while the child remains in his or her custody.

Although courts routinely divided custody upon parental request until the beginning of the twentieth century, divided custody has generally been disapproved in this century. Courts will most often award divided custody which provides for residence with one parent during the school year and the other during vacations. There is no clear line between "sole" custody with visitation rights for the entire summer and "divided" custody. When parents' homes are widely separated, making frequent visits impractical, courts have sometimes approved divided custody. On the other hand, some courts have justified divided custody on grounds that both parents live in the same area. In these cases, the court viewed the proximity as minimizing the strains that divided custody might place on the children (Folberg & Graham, 1979).

Joint Custody

The term "joint custody" as used in this book goes beyond the concept of "divided custody," although the terms have been used interchangeably in other publications. Joint custody may also be referred to as shared parenting, joint parenting, co-custody, concurrent custody, shared custody, co-parenting, or joint managing conservators. Although there may be some legislative differences when a statute refers to shared parenting or joint managing conservators, rather than joint custody, that difference is derived from the wording of the rest of the statute, not from the choice of a descriptive custody term. We will use joint custody interchangeably with shared parenting and other similar co-custody terms throughout this book, except in our descriptions of statutes.

The distinguishing feature of joint custody is that both parents retain legal responsibility and authority for the care and control of the child, much as in an intact family. Joint custody upon divorce is defined here as an arrangement in which both parents have equal rights and responsibilities regarding major decisions and neither parent's rights are superior. Joint custody basically means providing each parent with an equal voice in the children's education, upbringing, religious training, nonemergency medical care, and general welfare. The parent with whom the child is residing at the time must make immediate and day-to-day decisions regarding discipline, grooming, diet, activities, scheduling social contacts, and emergency care.

Some writers and some statutes distinguish between joint physical custody and joint legal custody. The definition offered above is one of joint "legal" custody. Joint "physical" custody refers to the sharing of residential care of the child or, in other words, regularly switching with whom the child lives.

Some believe that the term "joint physical custody" should be reserved for near-equal residential time arrangements (Roman & Haddad, 1978a). Some statutes establish "substantial physical care" with each parent as the criteria for determining the existence of joint physical custody. Persia Woolley (1984) rejected the distinction between joint physical and joint legal custody and instead viewed the distinguishing trait of joint custody as allowing each parent to interact with his or her child in everyday situations rather than "visiting" them.

Joint Custody and Control During Marriage

The least disruptive custody arrangement following divorce is likely to be the one most resembling the custody and control exercised before divorce. Custody and control between parents during marriage has received little judicial and clinical scrutiny because courts and professionals have been reluctant to intercede in such matters during marriage. Historically, the intact family had been viewed as a self-governing unit, with parental control vested primarily in the father. The modern legal trend has been to equalize parental rights. In the intact family the father and mother generally have joint and equal rights to the custody, care, and services of their children (Foster & Freed, 1978).

Parental "custody" during marriage is seldom defined in statutes or cases (Clark, 1988). Where it is defined, it embraces a bundle of rights and obligations. The parents have an obligation to protect and care for their children, to control and discipline their children, to provide necessary medical care, and to make decisions regarding the education and religious training of their children (Folberg & Graham, 1979).

The authority and responsibility regarding children are generally not differentiated between the parents. Although fathers were primarily responsible for supporting children at common law, modern case law and statutes have tended to make the parental support obligation joint and several (Freed & Foster, 1977). Reciprocally, the parents jointly have a right to share the children's services and earnings. These rights are not unrestricted. The state will intervene in the affairs of an intact family unit to protect the children's welfare. This state power is explained as stemming from the Crown's prerogative as *parens patriae* to protect subjects unable to protect themselves (Clark, 1988).

Joint Custody Following Divorce

When a marriage ends, the courts have the task of determining the future care and custody of any minor children. At this point, they must sort out and assign the bundle of parental rights and obligations that have probably been undifferentiated in the intact family (Schepard, 1985). The belief that a court must award custody to one of two fit parents complicates the task. In most jurisdictions the mother and father, by statute, are equal contenders for custody of their children (Foster & Freed, 1978b). Even though the parent awarded "custody" usually has less than exclusive control and parental power, the noncustodial parent generally ceases to have authority to make significant decisions or to engage in long-range planning for the children (Clark, 1988). The noncustodial parent retains authority over day-to-day decisions made during visitation periods while the children are in that paren.'s care (Gaddis, 1978).

De Facto *Joint Custody*

Even if the formal marital settlement agreement or the custody decree may indicate sole custody to one of the parents, there may be an informal joint custody arrangement. Following divorce, some parents informally agree to share their parental responsibility much as they did prior to divorce. Often this *de facto* joint custody comes as a gradual development (Woolley, 1978a). The parents may then ask the court to give legal sanction to the ongoing arrangement. A circuit court judge in Oregon summed up what must be a common judicial experience:

> "We have had joint custody . . . forever. Not because the court thinks it is necessary to decree joint custody, but because parents went ahead despite what the decree said and did what was best. . . . I've had a number of cases in court where they wanted a final stamp of approval, but for a number of years they had gone ahead and done what was best for the children and the best thing for themselves without paying too much attention to what the court decree said." (Blanding, 1977)

Stipulated *Joint Custody*

Joint custody is most often decreed when the parents present an executed separation agreement to the court for approval and include within their agreement a plan for joint parenting. There are few published statistics on the incidence of joint custody decrees, and even less information on the number of families operating under some sort of *de facto* joint custody arrangement. The number of reported appellate cases summarized in Chapter 16 is not an accurate indicator of the incidence of joint custody because the reported cases only arise from the litigation and appeal of continuing disagreements—the antithesis of cooperative parenting. Current statistical information on custody arrangements do not accurately document the number of joint custodial families, but the number is increasing, as indicated in the research findings contained in Part III of this book. Information about the alternative of joint custody is becoming more widespread, statutes are increasingly encouraging it, and court-connected counseling and mediation are becoming more readily available to assist in achieving cooperative parenting following divorce.

Court-Ordered Joint Custody

In addition to *de facto* joint custody and to joint custody granted pursuant to a separation agreement, courts in some states may award joint custody when neither party, or only one party, has requested it. Court-ordered joint custody, however, remains controversial (*see* Mummery, 1987). Some of the newer statutes discussed in Part IV are intended to counter judicial resistance to the ordering of joint custody. These legislative enactments run the gamut from simply recognizing the legality of joint custody orders to creating a strong presumption favoring joint custody whether or not the parents agree and requiring judicial findings if joint custody is not decreed.

Conclusion

Much of the research described and summarized in this book supports the conclusion that the best interest of the child is served by the continued involvement of both parents in the post-divorce life of the child. Put another way, it appears that divorces having the least detrimental effect on the normal development of children are those in which the parents are able to cooperate in their continuing parental roles. Parental cooperation cannot be easily ordered or legislated, but it can be professionally, judicially, and statutorily encouraged and endorsed. "Winner take all" sole custody resolutions tend to exacerbate parental differences and cause predictable post-divorce disputes as parents try to strike back and have the last word. Joint or shared parenting following divorce is an appealing alternative.

Joint custody is, however, not for everyone, as explained in Chapter 8. The indiscriminate use of joint custody as a judicial "cop out" or way to avoid hurting one parent would only substitute one evil for another (*see* Singer & Reynolds, 1988). For some, the anger and frustration surrounding divorce is too great an immediate obstacle to the cooperation required to make joint custody work. Family violence is increasingly a matter of great concern and the topic of research (*see* Ohlin & Tonry, 1989). Domestic violence or abuse against children or the other spouse is a clear indication that joint custody is inappropriate and a warning signal of the possibility of further abuse or violence.

For those whose divorce was precipitated by severe differences over how the children should be raised or who have, in fact, harmed their children by consciously using them as weapons in their private war, joint custody may be only a perpetuation of unacceptable and damaging parental conduct. There are, sadly, some parents who do not care for their children and others who are incapable, because of pathological disturbances or marginal capacities, of participating in reasoned decision making for their children. In many cases joint custody may be contraindicated because the divorce may have been marked by one parent's lack of involvement in caring for and making decisions about the children. A majority of divorcing parents, however, are capable of joint custody. It defies reason, research findings, and what we know of human potential to think otherwise.

Therapists, judges, attorneys, and researchers are coming to recognize that parents themselves can best decide the most appropriate arrangement for the care and custody of their children upon divorce. Custody policy and professional attitudes should provide a standard of expected behavior to guide parents following divorce. We too often forget that one of the most noble functions of law is to serve as a model of expected behavior. Past custody policy and professional skepticism have helped create a model of one-parent families and parental hostility following divorce. Joint custody provides a model of cooperation and continuing parenting. Shared parenting is a positive and reasonable standard of expected parental behavior.

2

Joint Custody: In the Best Interest of the Family

MEYER ELKIN

*Meyer Elkin, as the senior statesman of the conciliation courts'
movement and as founding editor of the* Conciliation Courts
Review, *has helped develop and foster the concept of cooperative
parenting following divorce. We asked Mr. Elkin to help set the
stage for this book by distilling the thoughts in his many editorials
on joint custody. Here he presents a summary of the benefits of joint
custody and the criteria for determining when it is appropriate. Mr.
Elkin concludes with a moving call for us to reexamine our traditions and biases in light of changing times.*

Joint custody is a recent attempt of the law to reduce the trauma of divorce for the
child and to avoid further fragmentation of an already fragmented family. It is also the
law's attempt to adapt to the reality of social change which has resulted in new and
diverse lifestyles and social values rejecting the nuclear family model as the only
desirable model of the "American Dream."

As is to be expected with a new concept, the opponents and proponents of joint
custody argue with much heat and often without an awareness of new knowledge in
social science research. The new findings suggest that joint custody, as an alternative
to sole custody, is worthy of rational consideration. Although not a panacea nor
applicable to all families, it can be used for more families than are currently opting
for it. For those who are chained to tradition and are opposed to joint custody, it is
worth noting that sole custody has not worked very well and that it seems to work
best when, in fact, it is akin to joint custody.

Meyer Elkin, M.S.W., is the former director of the Los Angeles Conciliation Court.

11

Benefits of Joint Custody

Joint custody offers many benefits and advantages to parents and children. Joint custody affirms that *parents are forever*. A divorce ends the legal relationship between husband and wife, but it does not end their roles as parents, their responsibilities to the child, and their parent–child relationships. Ideally, both parents should continue to be involved with their children. This is more easily accomplished when courts, lawyers, and society give parents permission to do so. The message now being given is that parents should not have contact with each other, that it is OK to hate each other. Research findings conclude that it is important for the parents to maintain an amicable parenting relationship, not only for the sake of the children but for their own sake as well.

Joint custody helps create two homes and reinforces the concept that *families are forever*. A divorce ends a marriage but not the family. The relationships among the family members are rearranged in a variety of ways, depending on the family's needs and lifestyle. The law should recognize that the nuclear family model is only one of the many family lifestyles available to families. Two separate but interrelated homes can emerge from the original family following divorce.

Joint custody tends to *equalize the power and authority* between the parents. Unequal power and authority in any relationship engenders ongoing frustration and hostility. Unequal power in divorce creates a "winner/loser" relationship which is a barrier to personal and familial growth and development. Additionally, unequal power may result in a parent "kidnapping" the child and in more post-divorce litigation.

In the research related to children of divorce, there appears a consensus regarding two essential conditions necessary to ensure a good post-divorce adjustment for children: (1) easy access to both parents and ongoing parental involvement and (2) cooperating parents who are able to make joint decisions for the child's welfare, no matter what their feelings are about each other. This requires an ability to separate the marital roles from the parental roles. Joint custody helps create these conditions.

Research also tells us that the father plays a very important part in the child's life, from the first day of birth. Joint custody ensures ongoing father–child contact. By its very nature, joint custody eliminates the demeaning, alienating concept of "visitation" from the divorced family's vocabulary and feelings. The child has two functioning homes—not one home and a visitor. Custody and visitation cannot be separated; they are always interrelated.

In sole custody, children often have the problem of divided loyalty. Joint custody reduces this conflict. Sole custody divides the family; joint custody integrates it. The fear of "shuttling" children between two homes may be more a function of the anxiety of adults than the children's ability to integrate parental roles and adjust to joint custody.

When parents develop a joint custody plan, the children may feel less rejected and abandoned. Children may perceive such a plan as evidence of the ongoing concern and love of both parents for the children and the family as a whole. The fearful question of the child, "Who will take care of me?" is answered twofold. The fear of losing a parent is diminished. Joint custody protects the child's right to the involvement of two parents in the child's life.

Children of divorce need family stability and continuity of contacts. Joint custody, more than sole custody, fulfills this need. A joint custody plan that is successfully implemented also reduces the risk of the children losing contact with their kinship network, particularly the grandparents who are able to provide love, support, and connection with the family's roots.

Joint custody is a more flexible approach than sole custody. It encourages parents to personalize and tailor a plan to fit the family's unique needs rather than forcing the family to fit into a general fit-all plan as in sole custody. Joint custody also reduces the child's fantasies about the qualities of each parent. Reality is often less frightening than fantasies.

In joint custody, both parents have more time for themselves and new relationships. They do not feel "trapped" with no relief from rearing the children. There is less likelihood of having "overburdened" mothers and "underburdened" fathers.

In a dysfunctional marriage, the ego is torn to shreds and self-esteem reaches new lows. It is important for divorced parents to experience success through their own accomplishments. Despite the initial problems of implementation, joint custody, according to recent research findings, can increase self-esteem. It is well known that if we expect more of people, they usually rise to the occasion. Joint custody creates greater expectations of parents and addresses itself to their strengths rather than their weaknesses.

Criteria for Joint Custody

If joint custody is to become an acceptable alternative to sole custody, there is an urgent need to develop criteria that will suggest success. The following positive parental criteria are offered as a beginning:

- Parents who are both committed to making joint custody work because of their love for their children and desire to be involved in their lives.

- Parents who have a good understanding of their respective roles in a joint custody plan and are willing and able to negotiate differences.

- Parents who are able to give priority to their children's needs and are willing to arrange their lifestyles to accommodate their children's needs.

- Parents who are able to separate the husband/wife roles (where the anger started) from their parental roles.

- Parents with a reasonable level of communication and willingness to cooperate.

- Parents who have the potential flexibility to make changes in the joint custody arrangement as the developmental needs of their children change.

Criteria Against Joint Custody

Joint custody is not for every divorced family. If the following negative factors are present, joint custody is contraindicated:

- A history of addiction by one or both parents.

- Family violence, including child abuse (emotional, physical, sexual).

√ - Child neglect.

- Mental pathology.

- A family history indicating inability of the parents to agree regarding the rearing of children.

- Parents who are unable to differentiate between their needs and their child's needs.

- Children who are likely to be unresponsive to joint custody arrangements or rebel against joint custody.

- Families with a severe history of disorganization.

- Families in which both parents are unalterably opposed to joint custody.

- Logistics mitigating against a joint custody plan.

Conclusion

A custody determination should involve more than merely establishing a residential address for the child. Whenever possible, the overall goal of a custody plan should be shared parenting, an approach which supports the idea that parents and families are forever. Joint custody, as presented in this book, promotes the idea of shared parental rights, responsibilities, and empowerment. Sole custody too often results in the father feeling disenfranchised and divorced from his child and the mother being overwhelmed by having to assume most of the parenting responsibilities. The frustration and anger on both sides creates a family that is constantly in a state of disequilibrium and too often back in court.

Sole custody has had center stage for over a hundred years; now there is a growing concern among knowledgeable people in the law and behavioral sciences that present practices and procedures in custody matters are in need of review, fresh analysis, and change. It is not possible to conclude at this time that the best interests of children are being served under sole custody. We must focus on the interests of the family as a whole, not just the child's interests, for the two are interrelated.

There is no consensus as to the desirability of joint custody in the law or the behavioral sciences. There is great need for research to learn if joint custody is a workable concept for meeting human needs. We should all carefully examine the research findings presented in this book. If eventually the research findings as well as our own professional experience tell us that joint custody works, we may very well have discovered one of the most important missing links in the divorce process with resulting benefits to parents and children of divorce as well as to the society of which they are a part. Every link in the divorce process must be considered in relation to all others.

Joint custody emerges at an appropriate time in the history of divorce because of concurrent examination of other important links in our divorce traditions. There are more requests by fathers for custody and growing interest in the concept of mediation, which is closely linked to joint custody and self-determination. It is of vital import-ance that court counseling and mediation services be available in all jurisdictions to facilitate joint custody. Each of these new concepts, when considered only on the basis of professional experience with divorcing and divorced families, is difficult for the traditionalist (judge, lawyer, mental health professional) to accept, because they view matters through the prism of failure. Professionals most often see families when collective weaknesses have overcome individual strengths. In each of these new approaches, we are increasing our expectations of parents and are addressing ourselves to their strengths, not their weaknesses.

Joint custody is as much an attitude as anything else on the part of the law and behavioral sciences as well as the parents. For the parents it is an attitude of commitment, cooperation, and trust; for the law and behavioral sciences it is an attitude of willingness to let go of inappropriate traditions and false assumptions that close the mind to the positive part that joint custody can contribute to the divorced family as it strives to meet its needs as an ongoing and viable reorganized family.

The concept of joint custody is designed to avoid continuous fragmentation of the divorced family by eliminating the common hazards of sole custody. Within the context of joint custody, the primary concern is meeting the needs of children of divorce in a reorganized family. In the past, we have not always heard the silent cries of these children for two parents. Let their cries always ring in our ears so that we do not allow our unexamined traditions and biases to stand in the way of their needs in these changing times.

3

In Whose Best Interest?

JOSEPH GOLDSTEIN

> *Two books*, Beyond the Best Interests of the Child *and* Before
> the Best Interests of the Child, *both by Goldstein, Freud, and
> Solnit, have been frequently cited and most influential in early
> policy discussions about joint custody. The importance of continu-
> ity of care for children and the limited capacity of the courts in
> ordering custody arrangements have been much debated since raised
> by these authors. Here Professor Goldstein clarifies their theories,
> including the concept of continuity and limited court capacity, and
> applies them to joint custody.*

The law ought to and does presume that children are entitled to the joint care and
custody of their parents. Indeed, it is generally in the best interests of a child to be in
the joint custody of his or her parents—whether or not they are now or ever have been
married. That is certainly what the continuity guidelines of *Beyond the Best Interests
of the Child*[1] is all about. In that book Anna Freud, Albert J. Solnit, and I explained
how important continuity of relationships is to a child's normal development. We
observed:

> Physical, emotional, intellectual, social, and moral growth does not happen without
> causing the child inevitable internal difficulties. The instability of all mental processes
> during the period of development needs to be offset by stability and uninterrupted

Joseph Goldstein, Ph.D., LL.B., is Sterling Professor of Law, Yale University Law School.
An earlier version of this chapter appeared in *Family Law: Dimensions of Justice*, Rosalie S. Abella and
Claire L'Heureux-Dube (Eds.) (Toronto: Butterworth & Co. (Canada) Ltd., 1983).

1. The text of this chapter rests heavily on and directly incorporates passages from J. Goldstein, A. Freud,
and A. J. Solnit, *Beyond the Best Interests of the Child* (copyright 1973, 1979 by The Free Press, A Division of
Macmillan Publishing Co., Inc.) and J. Goldstein, A. Freud, and A. J. Solnit, *Before the Best Interests of the
Child* (copyright 1979 by The Free Press, A Division of Macmillan Publishing Co., Inc.). Direct quotations
and modified passages are reproduced by permission of the copyright holder and Burnett Books (London).

support from external sources. Smooth growth is arrested or disrupted when upheavals and changes in the external world are added to the internal ones.[2]

Thus it is important for the law to facilitate the establishment and continuation of what we call "psychological" parent–child relationships ". . . to maintain the family unit in domestic peace . . . [t]o repair the family unit where there is a breach; [and] to reinforce the remainder of the unit where the breach is irreparable."[3]

Joint custody and, indeed, access or visitation are buttressed, if not justified, by the continuity guideline. That is true, but not past the point where the breach between parents threatens the maintenance, reinforcement and continuity of the remainder of the family unit. When the authority of the court becomes a substitute for shared understanding between separated parents, or when the authority of the law is used to impose the will of one parent over another by enforcing visitation and joint custody orders, the continuity of relationships within the newly organized family unit(s) is undermined. At that point joint custody is no longer joint. In the eyes and the life of the child it becomes split or divided custody and visitation or access becomes transportation—forced attendance. At that point only lip service is paid to continuity; the continuity of the tie to both parents is placed in jeopardy. If the continuity guideline is correctly understood, it should enable the court to recognize when the law becomes an interrupter rather than a reinforcer of the remainder of the family unit—when it ceases to protect and instead undermines the psychological bonding between child and parent.

Thus, from the vantage point of a child's well-being, the presumption in favor of joint custody is not without qualification. It is valid only so long as both separated parents remain in agreement about continuing together to be directly responsible for the custody and care of their children. The word "agreement" in the context of the child's best interest does not mean a legally enforceable agreement or a token agreement camouflaging the coercive force of the state. It means real, and probably rare, agreement on the part of both parents to share in the care and custody of their child and to cooperate with one another in fulfilling their parental roles despite their inability to find a satisfactory basis for living together.

How we come to take the stand we do about the limits and limitations of the law and of judges in determining custody for children of separating parents may best be explained first by reviewing what was said in *Beyond the Best Interests of the Child*, and secondly, by discussing in some detail its implications for determining:

1. what ought to be established before the "best interests of the child" can be invoked over the right of separating parents to decide who shall be responsible for the custody and care of their children;

2. the role of law with regard to visitation or access; and

---

2. Goldstein, Freud, & Solnit, *Beyond the Best Interests of the Child*, new ed. (1979), at 32 [hereinafter cited as *Beyond the Best Interests of the Child*].
3. From remarks of Chief Judge Andrews of 7 January 1980, quoted by Judge Karswick in *Re C.* (1980), 14 R.F.L.(2d) 21, at 25 (Ont. Prov. Ct.).

3. the role of law with regard to joint custody.

The guidelines developed in *Beyond the Best Interests of the Child* rest on two convictions. First, we believe that a child's need for continuity of care by autonomous parents requires acknowledging that parents should generally be entitled to raise their children as they think best, free of state interference. This conviction finds expression in our preference for minimum state intervention and prompts restraint in defining justifications for coercively intruding upon family relationships. Second, we believe that the child's well-being—not the parents', the family's, or the child care agency's—must be determinative once justification for state intervention has been established. Whether the protective shell of the family is already broken before the state intrudes, or breaks as a result of it, the goal of intervention must be to create or recreate a family for the child as quickly as possible. That conviction is expressed in our preference for making a child's interests paramount once his care has become a legitimate matter for the state to decide.

So long as a child is a member of a functioning family, his paramount interest lies in the preservation of his family. Thus, our preference for making a child's interests paramount is not to be construed as a justification in and of itself for intrusion. Such a reading would ignore the advantages that accrue to children from a policy of minimum state intervention. The goal of every child placement, whether made automatically by birth certificate or more deliberately following direct intervention by administrative or court order, is the same. With the possible exception of the placement of violent juveniles, it is to assure for each child membership in a family with at least one parent who wants him. It is to assure for each child and his parents an opportunity to maintain, establish, or reestablish psychological ties to each other free of further interruption by the state.[4] That is what continuity is all about.

With these convictions and that common purpose in mind, in *Beyond the Best Interests of the Child* we proposed and explained the following guidelines for determining the placement and process of placement for children whose custody becomes the subject of legal action:

Placement decisions should safeguard the child's need for continuity of relationships.

Placement decisions should reflect the child's, not the adult's, sense of time.

Child placement decisions must take into account the law's incapacity to supervise interpersonal relationships and the limits of knowledge to make long-range predictions.[5]

These guidelines were designed to pour content into the best interests standard—or what we call the least detrimental available alternative standard.[6]

---

4. Goldstein, Freud, & Solnit, *Before the Best Interests of the Child* (1979), at 4-5 [hereinafter cited as *Before the Best Interests of the Child*].

5. *Beyond the Best Interests of the Child*, at 31, 40, 49.

6. *Before the Best Interests of the Child*, at 6.

In the eyes of the law, to be a child is to be at risk, dependent, and without capacity or authority to decide free of parental control what is "best" for oneself. To be an adult is in law to be perceived as free to take risks, with the independent capacity and authority to decide what is "best" for oneself without regard to parental wishes. To be an adult who is a parent is therefore to be presumed by law to have the capacity, authority, and responsibility to determine and to do what is "good" for one's children, what is "best" for the entire family.[7]

Freud refers to "the long period of time during which the young of the human species is in a condition of helplessness and dependence."[8] He explains how this "biological factor" on the one hand burdens the parents with the full weight of responsibility for the survival and well-being of their offspring and, on the other hand, assures that the day-to-day ministering to the child's multiple requirements will turn the physical tie between them into a mutual psychological attachment. Such constantly ongoing interactions between parents and children become for each child the starting point of an all-important line of development that leads to adult functioning. Helplessness requires total care and over time is transformed into the need or wish for approval and love. It fosters the desire to please by compliance with a parent's wishes. It provides a developmental base upon which the child's responsiveness to educational efforts rests. Love for the parents leads to identification with them, without which impulse control and socialization would be deficient. Finally, after the years of childhood comes the prolonged and in many ways painful adolescent struggle to attain a separate identity with physical, emotional, and moral self-reliance.

These complex and vital developments require the privacy of family life under guardianship by parents who are autonomous. The younger the child, the greater his or her need for them is. When family integrity is broken or weakened by state intrusion, the child's needs are thwarted, and the belief that parents are omniscient and all-powerful is shaken prematurely. The effect on the child's developmental progress is invariably detrimental. The child's need for safety within the confines of the family must be met by law through its recognition of family privacy as the barrier to state intrusion upon parental autonomy in child rearing. These rights—parent autonomy, a child's entitlement to autonomous parents, and privacy—are essential ingredients of "family integrity."

Two purposes underlie the parents' right to be free of state intrusion. The first is to provide parents with an uninterrupted opportunity to meet the developing physical and emotional needs of their child so as to establish the familial bonds critical to every child's healthy growth and development. The second purpose, and the one on which the parental right must ultimately rest, is to safeguard the continuing maintenance of these family ties—of psychological parent–child relationships—once they have been established. The two purposes are usually fulfilled when the parental right is assigned at a child's birth simply on the basis of his biological tie to those who produce him.

Beyond these biological and psychological justifications for protecting parent–child relationships and promoting each child's entitlement to a permanent place in a

---

7. *Ibid.*, at 7.
8. Freud, *Inhibitions, Symptoms, and Anxiety* (1926), Standard Edition, vol. 20 (1959), at 154-55.

family of his own, there is a further justification for a policy of minimum state intervention. It is that the law does not have the capacity to supervise the fragile, complex interpersonal bonds between child and parent. As *parens patriae* the state is too crude an instrument to become an adequate substitute for flesh and blood parents. The legal system has neither the resources nor the sensitivity to respond to a growing child's ever-changing needs and demands. It does not have the capacity to deal on an individual basis with the consequences of its decisions, or to act with the deliberate speed that is required by a child's sense of time. Similarly, the child lacks the capacity to respond to the specific rulings of an impersonal court as he responds to the demands of personal parental figures. Parental expectations, implicit and explicit, become the child's own. However, the process by which a child converts external expectations, guidance, commands, and prohibitions into the capacity for self-regulation and self-direction does not function adequately in the absence of emotional ties to his caretakers.

A policy of minimum coercive intervention by the state thus accords not only with our firm belief as citizens in individual freedom and human dignity, but also with our professional understanding of the intricate developmental processes of child-hood.[9]

What are the implications of the convictions and guidelines of *Beyond the Best Interests of the Child* for (1) state intervention to determine custody when parents separate, and (2) if intervention is justified, making custody joint or subject to visits or access with the noncustodial parent?

1. Divorce or separation of married parents would no longer in and of itself automatically give the court authority to review or decide custody. Judicial intervention would only be justified when one or both separating parents, whether married or unmarried, bring to the court their disagreement, if they have one, about the custody of their child. Children of unwed parents would be regarded no differently than the child of married parents who divorce or separate. In accordance with the continuity guidelines, the courts would be restrained from forcing parents who separate to abdicate their role as exclusive (but joint) representatives of their children. They, the parents, would remain free to work out for themselves, if they can, the custody and care arrangements that they believe will best serve the interests of their child and their now divided family. They would continue to have joint custody and care of their children, even if one parent with the support of the other assumes full responsibility for day-to-day care.

But when they fail to find their own way of resolving their disagreements about custody, separating parents, in effect, temporarily give up an important part of their autonomy. By turning to the court, they open up the otherwise "private realm of family life which the state cannot enter." They declare themselves unfit to decide custody; they significantly alter the parent–child relationship; they deprive their child momentarily—until the court decides which one will have custody—of insulation from direct contact with the law. The child is exposed, for as short a time as possible, to the impersonal direction and coercion of the court. Since there is

---

9. *Before the Best Interests of the Child*, at 8-12.

little possibility of the child's entering into any intimate relationship with the court, there is also no likelihood that he will identify with the attitudes and rulings of the new authority over his life. Therefore, the court's discretion at the disposition stage should be limited to deciding *who* shall have custody, and as little time as possible should elapse before the child's position under a personal parental authority is fully restored.[10]

2. Courts and commentators most frequently question our conclusion that it is in the best interest of the child for the custody award to be as unconditional as a child's assignment at birth to his parents—as unconditional as we believe it ought to be when parents remain together or remain in agreement about their children despite their separation.

Too often judges confuse their *authority* to do, with their *capacity* to do. They fail to realize that the *who* and *how* of custody are and must be separate. It is the *who* which judges must and can decide. It is the *how* which is beyond any judge's competence. But judges often fail to see what is obvious once said—that the intricate and delicate character of the parent–child relationship places it beyond their constructive (though not beyond their destructive) reach. Familial bonding is too complex and too vulnerable a process to be managed in advance or from a distance by so gross and impersonal an instrument as the law. In rejecting this guideline as simplistic, judges become the oversimplifiers.

Were judges able to put themselves in the skin of a child who is the subject of a custody dispute, they would restrict their activity to answering the one question that they really can and must answer, which is *who* shall have custody and not *how* or *under what conditions* the custodian and child are to relate to one another and to others. But, like the well-intentioned, over-protective, and often destructive parent who does not know when to let go, such judges decide not only who is to be parent, but also give in to the temptation of deciding *how* the child ought to be raised.

Too frequently judges behave as if the function of placement decisions is to provide a child with autonomous judges, not autonomous parents. They act as if the *parens patriae* doctrine and the best interests standard granted them the competence to be good, albeit absentee, super-parents with a veto power. Courts, administrative agencies, and the experts upon whom they rely must learn to reject such simplistic remedies for the harm and hurts children may suffer when their parents separate. Judges can no longer deny what their own experience should make obvious to them, which is that they have the time and capacity to damage but not to nurture or manage the healthy growth of familial bonds. In their professional roles they cannot be parent to someone else's children. The best informed and most sensitive family court judges, singly or rolled into one, do not a parent make. At best and at most, the law can provide a new opportunity for the relationship between a child and at least one of his parents to unfold free of coercive meddling by a judge. This is not to say that the law should preclude the development of a cooperative arrangement over time between the parents in conflict. But it is to say that no such arrangement can be forced or enforced by law and still serve the child's interests.

---

10. *Ibid.*, at 31-37.

Our conclusion that noncustodial parents should have "no legally enforceable right to visit" their children continues to be the most misunderstood, most controversial, and most resisted aspect of our suggestion that all but emergency and other truly temporary placements should be unconditional. Since we hold the same view about court enforceable joint custody agreements, what we have to say about access or visitation applies as well to joint custody.[11] Our view on visitation has been misread to mean that we oppose the continuation of contact between a child and his noncustodial parent. It has been challenged with the argument that our position (1) conflicts with the least detrimental alternative standard, especially with the continuity guideline; (2) deprives a child of his basic right to maintain his ties to the noncustodial parent; and (3) places an instrument of revenge in the hands of the custodial parent (usually pictured as an angry mother) who will use it to spite the noncustodial parent (usually pictured as a thwarted and well-motivated father).

We reasoned, always from the child's point of view, that custodial parents, not courts or noncustodial parents, should retain the right to determine when and if it is desirable to arrange visits. We took and continue to take this position because it is beyond the capacity of courts to help a child to forge or maintain positive relationships to two people who are at cross-purposes with each other; because, by forcing visits, courts are more likely to prevent the child from developing a reliable tie to either parent; and because children who are shaken, disoriented, and confused by the breakup of their family need an opportunity to settle down in the privacy of their reorganized family with one person in authority upon whom they can rely for answers to their questions and for protection from external interference. After all, the goal of every placement decision, whether made at birth by certificate or later by more direct state intervention, is to provide each child with an opportunity—unbroken by further intrusion—to establish or reestablish and maintain psychological bonds to those to whom he is entrusted.

A child develops best if he can have complete trust that the adults who are responsible for him are the arbiters of his care and control as he moves toward the full independence of adulthood and gradually comes to rely upon himself as his own caretaker. A court undermines that trust when it subjects the custodial parent to special rules about raising him, for example, by ordering (even scheduling) visits with the noncustodial parent. In the child's eyes, the court, by directing him to act against the express wishes of the custodial parent, casts doubt on that parent's authority and capacity to parent. It damages, particularly for the younger child, his confidence in his parent's power to shield him from threats from the outside. It invites the older child to manipulate his parents by invoking the higher authority of the court rather than to learn to work things out with the custodial parent. We formulated the continuity guideline in direct response to such considerations. We urged, therefore, that the already handicapped relationship between child and custodial parent not be plagued by the never-ending threat of disruption by the impersonal authority of the court.

---

11. *Beyond the Best Interests of the Child*, at 113-16.

However, we did not and do not oppose visits. Indeed, other things being equal, courts, in order to accord with the continuity guideline, could award custody to the parent who is most willing to provide opportunities for the child to see the other parent. And—even though we do not believe that a noncustodial parent can play the same significant role in a child's life as a parent in an intact family—we usually encourage custodial parents who seek our advice to facilitate the maintenance of the relationship between the child, particularly the older child, and his noncustodial parent. But such advice can and should be nothing more. Custodial parents must remain free to accept or reject our notions about the importance of continuity. The guideline cannot be pressed any further in favor of the child's now secondary relationship to the noncustodial parent. As time goes by and as circumstances change, the child needs a parent who can work out with him ways of resolving his wishes to see and not to see the other parent, as well as of dealing with his joys and sorrows following visits, and his hurts when noncustodial parents refuse to maintain contact or fail to show. Meaningful visits for the child can occur only if both the custodial and the noncustodial parents are of a mind to make them work. If so, a court order is both unnecessary and undesirable. If not, such orders and the threat or actual attempt to enforce them can do the child no good.[12]

We favor contact between a child and his noncustodial parent so long as neither parent can use the courts to enforce the other to arrange visits. Even if requested by both parents, we would object to courts making a visitation or joint custody agreement a part of its decree. If mere registration were to give both parents a greater sense of commitment to make visitation or joint custody work, a certificate of recognition of the agreement with no more than symbolic force might be issued to them. As an alternative, it might not be inappropriate for judges to add to their unconditional custody awards a paraphrase of the state's warning to cigarette smokers:

> DENIAL OF VISITS OR FAILURE TO COOPERATE IN
> MAKING YOUR JOINT CUSTODY AGREEMENT WORK
> MAY BE DETRIMENTAL TO YOUR CHILD

Out of concern for equalizing the bargaining strength of separating parents, Mnookin and Kornhauser argue that visitation and joint custody agreements should be specifically enforceable in law.[13] Their faith in the law's capacity to implement such contracts in situations where the law has already proved powerless to enforce meaningful marriage relationships by contract seems ludicrous. The marriage contract is now generally construed to mean "till divorce do us part."[14] When the fad for joint custody agreements fades, we will begin to recognize how costly it, like other magic formulas, has been to children. Strangely, our reasons for objecting to court-enforceable visits seem to be more easily recognized by courts resolving disputes about "joint" custody. For example, in reversing a lower court order that had awarded to the parents

---

12. *Ibid.*, at 116-19.
13. *See* Mnookin & Kornhauser, "Bargaining in the Shadow of the Law: The Case of Divorce," 88 *Yale Law Journal* 950, at 980-84 (1979).
14. *See Beyond the Best Interests of the Child*, at 185-86, n.8.

joint custody of two sons aged six and seven-and-a-half to spend weekdays with the mother and weekends with the father, Chief Judge Breitel of the New York Court of Appeals said:

> Entrusting the custody of young children to their [divorced] parents jointly, especially where the shared responsibility and control includes alternating physical custody, is insupportable when parents are severely antagonistic and embattled. . . . [I]t can only enhance familial chaos. . . . It would, moreover, take more than reasonable self-restraint to shield the children, as they go from house to house, from the ill feelings, hatred, and disrespect each parent harbors towards the other.[15]

After observing that the court must "recognize the division in fact of the family" and that "there are no painless solutions," Judge Breitel said:

> In the rare case, joint custody may approximate the former family relationships more closely than other custodial arrangements. It may not, however, be indiscriminately substituted for an award of sole custody to one parent.[16]

What the court fails to recognize is that no parent has sole custody so long as he or she is subject to rules of visitation, and that courts are as powerless to forge affection by a visitation order as they are by decreeing any other form of "joint," "divided," or "split" custody.

Finally, courts and commentators, blinded by the specter of spiteful custodial parents denying visits or opposing joint custody at the child's expense, have rejected our position with the misleading assertion that visitation or access is a right of the child, not of the parents. In fact, by subjecting an award of custody to an order imposing visits, the court does not protect the child's "basic right" to see his noncustodial parent. It merely shifts the power to deprive the child of his "right" from the custodial parent to the noncustodial parent. Visitation orders make the noncustodial parent—rather than the parent who is responsible for the child's day-to-day care—the final authority for deciding if and when to visit. Even if the court orders visits because it believes they will serve the child's best interest, the noncustodial parent remains free not to visit, to "reverse" the court without risk of being in contempt. The court is powerless, as it should be, to order noncustodial parents to visit their "waiting" children. But the court has the corrosive power to have a child forcibly removed from a custodial parent who refuses to allow visits, or to imprison that parent for contempt.[17] When it exercises such power, the court disrupts, not ensures, continuity of parent–child relationships. It establishes for the child—and indeed for other children in the family who are not themselves subject to visitation orders—that the custodial parent cannot be trusted and is powerless to protect them. Courts obscure the real issues when they say what they cannot mean—that access or visitation, or indeed joint or divided custody, is "a basic right of the child rather than a basic right of the parent."[18]

---

15. Braiman v. Braiman, 378 N.E.2d 1019, 1021 (1978).
16. *Ibid.*, at 1022.
17. *Beyond the Best Interests of the Child*, at 120-21.
18. *Ibid.*, at 121.

Briefly—and from the child's vantage point—the right of decision about the child's care and wishes must be vested in someone. Common sense and psychoanalytic notions about child development confer it upon the custodial rather than the noncustodial parent. However parental fitness is defined, separated parents in disagreement about joint custody or access become unfit for their child when forced to "cooperate," even though each individually could be a fit parent for that child. Changed circumstances and changing needs in the life of a child are best dealt with by a functioning family, by the family's decision *at the time*. The court's enforcement, or even the threat of enforcement of a prior agreement about joint custody or access, becomes an obstacle to the integrity of the new family, an invitation to the invasion of its privacy, and a violation of parental autonomy. Courts and legislatures must not allow their good intentions to obscure the harm they do to children.

II
Factors Influencing the Choice of Joint Custody

4

A Guide to Decisions about Joint Custody: The Needs of Children of Divorce

DONALD T. SAPOSNEK

Legal and clinical practitioners have refined their initial question, "does joint custody work?", to a more focused inquiry, "for whom does joint custody work?" Saposnek answers this question by identifying the parental characteristics and children's characteristics which are associated with successful joint custody arrangements. He then provides practitioners with a series of recommendations to be used in helping divorced couples consider and develop parenting arrangements that will be in the best interests of their children. The chapter concludes with a discussion of the benefits and drawbacks of imposed joint custody.

In the past decade, there have been two major, widely recognized views on the needs of children of divorce. An early influential perspective was offered by Goldstein, Freud, and Solnit (1973) in their classic *Beyond the Best Interests of the Child* (discussed by Goldstein in Chapter 3). These authors first acquainted us with the concept of the "psychological parent," of which they suggest most children only have one. They told of the devastating effects on children of breaking or disrupting the attachment of the child to this parent. Extrapolating from situations of foster placement and adoption,

Donald T. Saposnek, Ph.D., is a clinical psychologist in Santa Cruz, California. He is Director of the Family Mediation Service of Santa Cruz and of Mediation Training, Santa Cruz. In addition, he is on the faculty of the University of California, Santa Cruz.

This is a revised version of a chapter published as: Saposnek, D.T. (1987). Recent developments in joint custody: Definitions, issues, and recommendations. In P.A. Keller and S.R. Heyman (Eds.), *Innovations in Clinical Practice: A Source Book* (vol. 6). Sarasota, Florida: Professional Resource Exchange.

they suggested that child custody disputes are best settled by using the standard of the least detrimental alternative and by giving sole custody to "the psychological parent." The parent holding sole custody then would have total say as to whether, and in what fashion, the noncustodial parent would have contact with the child.

The findings of Wallerstein and Kelly (1980b) generated new perspectives. Their longitudinal research found that children of divorce did better when they had regular and continuing contact with both parents after the family split up, and when their parents either ceased fighting upon separating or never commenced fighting. More-over, Wallerstein and Kelly found that children in their study experienced emotional attachments to *both* parents. The children reported that they ". . . considered the term 'one-parent family' a misnomer. Their self-images were firmly tied to their relationship with both parents and they thought of themselves as children with two parents who had elected to go their separate ways."

In an attempt to bridge the gap between the two major views on the best custody arrangements for children of divorce, Samis and Saposnek (1986) developed a syn-thesis of the views of Goldstein et al. (1973), with those of Wallerstein and Kelly (1980b). We view the notion of the "psychological parent" as valid but in need of expansion and we present the argument that while children of separating parents may in fact have only one psychological parent, they may also have two, or even three or more, or they may have none. By assessing the quality of attachments to the major caregivers, the mediator or clinician can facilitate (and actively steer) a custody arrangement that can most effectively buffer the child from the inevitable stresses of divorce. Such stresses arise, minimally, from all the changes he or she undergoes, and are oftentimes significantly increased to the point of "overburdening" (Wallerstein, 1985b) with poor quality post-separation parenting.

Does Joint Custody Work?

Until very recently, we have had little else beside popular opinion to go by for documenting the effects of joint custody arrangements on divorced families. Interest-ingly, even court mediators in California, who have now mediated tens of thousands of cases, have largely assumed that the joint custody arrangements which they helped arrange have been working out wonderfully. The evidence for this is the fact that these cases mostly have not returned to court for litigation. Although some return to mediation to modify their agreement, most do not. Behind this conviction is the belief that if parents do not return to court or to mediation, they must have resolved their conflicts with each other, and their child must be getting along just fine. Thus, this seems to satisfy the second of Wallerstein and Kelly's criteria for a successful post-di-vorce custody arrangement—reduced parental conflict. However, as recent research (Irving, Benjamin, & Trocme, 1984b; McKinnon & Wallerstein, 1986; Phear et al., 1984; Saposnek, Hamburg, Delano, & Michaelsen, 1984; Steinman et al., 1985) is beginning to indicate, such is not necessarily the case.

In many ways, to ask whether joint custody works is similar to asking whether psychotherapy works. For countless years, therapists searched and researched the answer to this question, until we realized that the issue was far more complex. Only upon realizing this complexity did we begin to ask the right questions in an appropriate multi-leveled form: "Which clients, with which kinds of problems, presented at which times, do best with which therapist, using which techniques, for which length of time, and with which goals?" (Saposnek, 1984, p. 1061).

Joint custody, like psychotherapy, certainly can and does work out well in many cases, although the evidence to date has been mostly based on professional and personal opinion, rather than on systematic research. However, to really understand such findings, we must ask the parallel multi-leveled question: Which divorcing families, with what kinds of marital histories, with what specific kinds of pre- and post-separation disputes, with what age children, with what coping styles, temperament styles, and qualities of parent–child relationships, presented at which times in the divorcing process, can handle what specific kinds of decision-making patterns and time-sharing schedules within a joint custody arrangement? Answers to some of these questions are beginning to unravel, as presented and discussed in the research section of this book. This chapter will focus on the nature of the co-parental relationship and the coping abilities of the child in helping to determine if joint custody will work.

Parental Characteristics

Steinman et al. (1985) found in their study of outcomes of joint custody that parents could be categorized into three major types: successful (27%), stressed (42%), and failed (31%). The "successful" group had parents with the following qualities:

1. Maintenance of respect and appreciation for the bond between their child and former spouse despite the anger and disappointment from the failed marriage.

2. A psychological make-up that allowed them to step back and maintain some objectivity through the divorcing process, at least in relation to the children.

3. An ability to empathize with the point of view of the child and the other parent.

4. An ability to shift emotional expectations from the role of mate to that of co-parent.

5. An ability to establish new role boundaries.

6. Generally high self-esteem, flexibility, and openness to help.

In contrast, the "failed" group had parents with the following qualities:

1. Intense, continuing hostility and conflict that could not be diverted from the child.

2. Overwhelming anger and the continuing need to punish the spouse.

3. A history of physical abuse and substance abuse.

4. A fixed belief that the other is a bad parent.

5. Inability to separate their own feelings and needs from those of the child.

The fixed belief that the other is a bad parent was a major predictive factor that separated the "successful" group from the "failed" group. "Failed" group members rigidly and persistently blamed the ex-spouse for the divorce, for their problems, and for difficulties the children were having. They were unable to separate the role of spouse from the role of parent.

The kinds of parents who comprise the "failed" group were the subjects of a recent study reported by Johnston, Kline, and Tschann (Chapter 15). In their longitudinal study sample of 100 highly litigious families entrenched in custody and visitation disputes, they found consistent evidence that children in court-ordered joint custody arrangements (characterized by more frequent access to each parent) were more emotionally and behaviorally disturbed than those in court-ordered sole custody arrangements. Specifically, children who shared more days each month with both parents were significantly more depressed, withdrawn, and uncommunicative, had more somatic symptoms, and were more aggressive, as reported by their parents. These researchers relate their findings to the fact that increased parental conflict was generated when children had more frequent access arrangements. Hence, joint custody that involves frequent transitions is contraindicated when the parents are in protracted high conflict following divorce. These children are more caught up in the disputes, and "are passively used as weapons or are active agents in the disputes. . . . A vicious cycle emerges in which the child's distress and symptomatic behavior fuels the parental fight over the custody and access arrangements" (Johnston & Campbell, 1988, p. 174).

The observation that interparental conflict bodes poorly for children and is related to a variety of emotional and behavioral disturbances in intact, separated, and divorced families has been well-documented in the literature (see reviews by Emery, 1982; Clingempeel & Reppucci, 1982). And, it is clearly the conflict, and not the separation or divorce per se that is related to these disturbances. Moreover, Felner and Terre's (1987) review of the existing literature "failed to support the contention that joint custody will reduce post-divorce conflict. Indeed, it may do just the opposite" (p. 141). They further point out, quite aptly, that the studies in the past that were supportive of the notion that joint custody could minimize conflict were conducted on couples who had unusually low levels of conflict and high degrees of cooperation, as compared with other divorced couples. Hence, they were able to voluntarily enter into joint custody arrangements in an amicable fashion.

Of most interest in Steinman et al.'s (1985) study is the "stressed" group, which is the largest and the one that most often comes to the attention of clinicians and mediators. Parents in this group continued to have very intense and ambivalent feelings toward each other. They were not able to distance themselves from the marital issues as well as the parents in the "successful" group. The "stressed" parents manifested strong feelings of guilt and of missing the ex-spouse. These parents must struggle harder to contain the intensely ambivalent feelings that are stirred up through contact around the children. It is likely that for this group, a legal structure which encourages or even forces joint custody has the potential to convert many of its parents to accept such an arrangement. Having not yet lost all trust in the other spouse, there may be the potential for developing quality shared parenting over time, even if reconciliation is not possible.

I believe that the adversarial system can convert members of the "stressed" group into members of the "failed" group. And, it also seems clear that mediation and counseling approaches can bump "stressed" members up to the "successful" group. Education about how to make joint custody work and well-timed strategic interventions can make a particularly great difference for these divorcing parents. The "successful" group will very likely make joint custody work by themselves; interventions can be straightforward and primarily educational. The "failed" group will not be able to carry out a joint custody plan, and requires intervention by the court (although a very promising alternative approach has been described by Campbell & Johnston, 1986, and Johnston & Campbell, 1988). However, members of the "stressed" group, with a skilled mediator's or mediation-oriented counselor's intervention, has potential to protect children from the longer-term psychological loss of a parent, by arranging a joint custody plan. Steinman (1984, p. 119), though, appropriately warns us:

> We should not assume that parents are prepared to undertake joint custody simply because they have technically agreed or compromised through mandatory mediation. A legal agreement does not necessarily mean parents have settled their disputes, or have the resources to implement joint custody . . . [it] is at greatest risk of failure when . . . [court] ordered in the hope that it will end a battle and parents will learn to cooperate.

Children's Characteristics

Research also suggests that there are certain types and ages of children for whom joint custody orders may work well, and others for whom such an order could spell disaster. Among very young children (under age three), those who did well did so in spite of the particular schedule of time-sharing. As long as the conflict between the parents was contained, and the motives for and quality of parenting were good, most children under the age of three were able to handle the many transitions of the joint custody arrangement. However, the three-to-five-year-old group generally had more difficulty coping, even when parenting quality was good. McKinnon and Wallerstein (1986) note that it is difficult to determine clearly which of the many stresses in the life of a child of divorce account for their distress and regression. They speculate, though, that this age group had more complexity to their lives and awareness of (and resistance to) the changes in their families than did the children under three. The changes included increased demands of pre-school, introduction of step-parents into their lives, birth of siblings, geographical moves, and so forth.

Among older children (through age 15), most were able to keep their complex schedules clear and demonstrate a sense of mastery over switching between homes. However, 25% of the children "were anxious and insecure about switching homes. They worried about themselves, their parents, possessions, and exhibited an overall sense of instability" (Steinman, 1984, p. 116). These children fell into two age groups: four-to-five-year-old girls, and seven-to-nine-year-old boys with learning problems at school who had a great deal of difficulty keeping track of things. Hence, certain cognitive and emotional factors in children may preclude adjustment to joint custody arrangements, even when the parents provide a sound base for it. For example, if a child is always tense and anxious because he cannot remember where he left his things or which house he is to go to, the benefits of joint custody may be overshadowed by the chronic confusion and resulting deterioration of self-confidence and self-esteem. Moreover, if the child manifests certain temperament characteristics, such as low adaptability to changes, and withdrawal from new situations, the changes required in joint custody may overload the child's system (Saposnek, 1983a).

For all the children in Steinman's study, continuity of school life and friendships was found to be very important, particularly to latency-age and adolescent children. They valued the stability of remaining in one school and used school as an anchoring place. Teenagers' involvement in social and school activities and their strivings for independence from their parents, made two-home arrangements contrary to their needs as adolescents. Clearly, continuity of school and of peer relationships are important considerations in developing joint custody arrangements.

Steinman poignantly summarized her findings about the needs of children in joint custody plans by concluding, "It may be that a cooperative, smooth running co-parenting relationship is a *necessary* but not *sufficient* condition for children to do well. In other words, we need to consider not only which *parents*, but also which *children* make good candidates for joint custody" (p. 117).

Recommendations to Practitioners

Steinman (1984, p. 126) suggests that "Joint custody is a philosophy, not a legal formula." She further writes, "The philosophical premise that distinguishes joint custody is threefold: (1) parents cooperate and share authority and responsibility for their children after divorce, (2) mothers and fathers are viewed as equally important to their children, and (3) the children alternate living in both parental homes" (Steinman, Zemmelman, & Knoblauch, 1985, p. 554). Moreover, notes Steinman (1984, p. 127), "Joint custody is a process, not a panacea." Achieving a workable joint custody arrangement requires each parent to make a lengthy commitment to be continually rational, to cooperate, to trust, and to compromise, and to adjust to innumerable life changes which divorced families go through over the years of child-rearing (e.g., changing developmental needs of the child, entrance into school, adolescence, remarriage, birth of a new baby, geographical moves, illnesses, and adjustment problems of the child). It is this commitment and flexibility of attitude upon which workable joint custody agreements are based.

In helping divorcing couples consider and develop a co-parenting arrangement that will be closest to being in the best interests of (or of the least detriment to) their child, the following recommendations are offered to the practitioner:

1. Respect the status quo. This means looking at the nature and quality of the pre-separation relationships and respecting the kinds and numbers of attachments the child has manifested with his or her caregivers. Dramatic changes in time-sharing based on what might seem "fair" for the divorcing parents, or aesthetically nice for a family (i.e., the "ideal" of 50/50 joint custody), may increase the stress of the child and negate the intended beauty of the plan. It is important to help the parents understand the significance of these attachment bonds to a child's further development, while working on a plan to increase the range of the child's attachments to at least both parents, if possible.

2. Consider the sincerity of the parents' motives in requesting their particular plan. (These motives are elaborated at length in Saposnek, 1983a.) Reasons for the request that are not conducive to the child's needs should not be overlooked in the interest of "getting an agreement," for the agreement developed may make things worse for the child. Contrary to our assumptions when we began doing mediation, it now appears that *any* agreement is not always better than *no* agreements. While it takes courage for a mediator or clinician to refuse to participate in the development of an agreement that to the clinician's mind does not serve the interests of the child, it is well advised. Sometimes it is better for the clinician acting as mediator to refer the case back to the court with a request that a thorough evaluation of each parent be done than to condone an agreement which may be destructive to a child.

3. Spend quality time interviewing the children. Children do not respond honestly or helpfully if they are rushed. Take enough time to develop good rapport, and to help the child feel safe and comfortable. Always be honest but soft and sensitive with the children about why you want to talk with them. For example, a good explanation is the following: "As you may know, your mommy and daddy need my help for them to make good decisions for you about how you are going to share your time with them when they live in two different houses." After such a content opener, you may explore the child's different feelings of comfort or discomfort while with each parent, and so forth. It helps for the clinician to be knowledgeable about normal child development and about the typical responses that children of divorce give, to accurately interpret their responses. Give the parents constructive and helpful feedback of your impressions of the child's needs. Do not assume that they will automatically know what to make of your feedback, but help them to understand the implications of the feedback for their co-parenting plan.

4. Assess and help the parents to respect the child's perceptions of time, the child's need for predictability, and the *child's* sense of attachments to various family members (which are sometimes different from a *parent's* experience of the child's attachments!). Also help the parents to appreciate the importance of the child's relationships with friends, and his or her feelings about his or her school and neighborhood. This is particularly important with latency-age children and adolescents.

5. Develop a schedule which proceeds with gradual shifts in time-sharing, rather than, for example, suddenly plunking a young child into the middle of an alternate-week sharing plan when he or she has never spent any time alone with his or her father, but has always been very deeply attached to his or her mother. Easing the child more gradually into a schedule of increasing time shared with his or her father can significantly reduce the child's stress.

6. Develop a plan for closely monitoring the child's responses to all schedule changes, especially during the first year or two after the marital separation. Moreover, a format should be developed from the start for modifying whatever plan is put into effect as the needs of the child and parents change over time. The monitoring and modifications can be dealt with between the parents, or with a mediator or therapist if necessary. It is significant to note that McKinnon and Wallerstein (1986) found that schedules, once established, were likely to be inflexible and extremely difficult to change, even with cooperative and caring parents. Hence, with less cooperative parents, it becomes even more important to build into any agreement the method for revising the plan as the family members' needs change, because constructive revisions are not likely to happen on their own.

7. If a joint custody plan seems feasible, educate the parents about how to make joint custody work. This can include discussions about the spirit of co-parenting, practical tips on logistics, cautions about things to avoid (e.g., such as assuming that stepparents and stepchildren will easily accept each other), and hints on preventative measures to avert future conflicts (e.g., keep phone conversations brief and focused only about the children). Suggestions of practical books and articles to read that inform parents about the pragmatics of joint custody can be of considerable help. Several good books to recommend (and to read yourself) are: Galper (1978), Woolley (1979), Ricci (1981), Ware (1982), Newman (1981), Goldzband (1985), and Adler (1988). Also, learn if there are any joint custody support groups for parents available in your area. Some are for mothers, most are for fathers, and some are mixed groups. These groups are very helpful to parents in learning practical skills and in sharing tips for making joint custody arrangements work optimally. If it seems advisable, refer one or both parents to such groups.

8. Become informed and skilled at basic custody mediation concepts and techniques, by reading books and journals articles (see Saposnek, 1983a, 1983b), by attending conferences, and taking training courses (contact the Academy of Family Mediators, or the Association of Family and Conciliation Courts for training courses available), and by sitting in with a skilled child-custody mediator in your area. It cannot be stressed enough how important it is that the practitioner dealing with custody matters be knowledgeable about children, about family dynamics, about divorce dynamics, and about applicable legal rules (which determine the actual climate regarding permissible custody arrangements). With a well-informed background and well-learned skills, the practitioner can competently guide a divorcing family into a co-parenting

arrangement that will be least destructive to the child. If a case seems too difficult for one's level of competence, one should not hesitate for a minute to refer it to someone more skilled in this area. Custody disputes that are not settled skillfully will often persist interminably, with the unfortunate but common consequence being the devastation of the child.

With these recommendations, the practitioner can more comfortably assess the feasibility of joint custody for a given family and facilitate its development, in light of the current state of knowledge about the effects of joint custody on children.

Should Joint Custody Be Imposed on Divorcing Families?

Most professionals writing on joint custody have maintained that court-ordered joint custody for a post-separation family in which one or both parents do not want it is destined for failure. These authors stress that a fundamental necessity for joint custody to work well is cooperation and trust between the parents. However, when we first began working under California's mandatory mediation law (in 1981), we saw over and over again that with the structure of mediation available and legally supported, and with a systematic educational/strategic approach for mediating (see Saposnek, 1983a, 1983b), couples who initially resisted joint custody arrangements would reach agreement and begin to implement a co-parenting plan. In our follow-up studies, most of these families continued to carry out their shared parenting without returning to court or demanding modification, albeit with varying degrees of difficulties. Moreover, when asked how their children were doing with the co-parenting arrangements, most reported that the children were doing fine. While there were inconsistencies in how each parent from a given family reported the degree of well-being of the children, for the most part the children reportedly seemed to be doing better than the parents. Hence, we concluded that joint custody can be ordered by the court (often via the influence or pressure of a mediator) and that such an arrangement can hold up and work out well for the children.

However, in our initial zeal to prove the potency and humane nature of these radical changes in state law (regarding joint custody and mandatory mediation), we appear to have overlooked, or perhaps been merely unaware of, several important issues. For one, parents often seriously distort their perceptions of how their children are coping with the divorce process, at least during the "crazy times"—the year or two after separation (Campbell & Johnston, 1986; Saposnek et al., 1984; Steinman, 1984). So, when mediators would ask parents about the children, usually at least one of the parents (most often the parent who at the time of being asked was satisfied with the custody arrangement) would report that the children were doing fine. Second, most mediators do not interview the children, and even if they do it is often for too short a period of time for the children to get comfortable enough to open up their often painful or scary feelings. Hence, because the data on how children were actually doing have been either absent or possibly distorted, many of us appear to have prematurely gloried in our conviction that joint custody arrangements are successful for almost all children. Moreover, as mediators, we have felt somewhat self-righteous in asserting the rights of *both* parents to be involved in a significant way with their children, as if such a fair balance for the parents would assure a fair arrangement for the children (i.e., that their needs would be met). Unfortunately, we have looked at the "fairness" of the arrangement as if it were clearcut, rather than the complex issue that it is (Saposnek, 1985).

Looking with a more sober view, though, we now find the emerging research suggesting that joint custody is quite problematic for a substantial number of divorcing families. Atwell, Moore, Nielsen, and Levite (1984), in their study of children's reactions to various joint physical custody arrangements, suggest that parental custody agreements often ignore the needs of the children and may be detrimental to them. They stress the importance of assessing the effects of parental agreements on the children. Noble (1983) contends that there is no clear evidence as to which custody arrangement is most beneficial, but meanwhile families are arranging custody on the basis of what they can do to survive separation rather than on the rational judgment of the most desirable long-term effects for their children. Judith Wallerstein, whose research with Joan Kelly pioneered the rapid rise in joint custody arrangements, more recently writes:

> when the annals of the 1980s are examined at some future time, the extraordinarily rapid spread of joint custody as a preference for children in divorced families will undoubtedly be a subject of interest. . . . The trend to establish two separate homes for the child that requires that the child move back and forth flexibly, especially when instituted by parents who remain in conflict over the children, has occurred with hardly any examination of the motivation of the parents, the processes of their interaction over time, and most of all the outcome for the children. (Wallerstein, 1985a, p. 516)

To gain a broader perspective for answering the question about the effectiveness of forced joint custody, consider the outcomes of studies on *voluntarily* developed joint custody arrangements. In one study, of 32 children from four-and-one-half to 15 years of age, most of whom had been living in joint custody arrangements for over half of their lives, Steinman (1984) found that one-third of them were unhappy and had significant adjustment problems. Although it was not possible to understand fully the extent to which the dual-home arrangement contributed to their difficulties, they were clearly overburdened by the demands of the arrangement and were unable to achieve a feeling of mastery and security within their post-divorce living situation, even after a number of years. This was the case for these children even though the sample of families had parents who were committed to a joint custody plan and were generally satisfied with it.

In another study reported in this volume (McKinnon & Wallerstein, Chapter 13), one of very few that investigated the effects of joint custody on very young children, 25 families with children aged 14 months to five years were followed for up to four years. All of the parents in this study chose joint custody voluntarily, not as a result of a court order or of court-ordered mediation. Though the desire to nurture the child in continuing close contact with both parents is the primary motivation assumed for making joint custody arrangements, these researchers found this to be the main driving force among only one-third of their sample. Other motives of parents for wanting joint custody had roots in self-interested practical and economic considerations, and in unconscious as well as conscious needs at the time of separation, such as in the service of denying the divorce, to limit one's care-giving responsibilities after separation, and so forth. Unfortunately, the only young children who clearly did well in joint custody were those whose parents' central motive was a deep commitment to the child. These parents provided genuine, loving, and close relationships for their child after the separation and held co-parenting as a high value in their lives. A genuine attachment existed between the children and both parents, "and the parents were willing to inconvenience themselves greatly to put their children's needs ahead of their own" (p. 156). McKinnon and Wallerstein further point out that the cooperation and collaboration necessary for divorcing partners to make joint custody work well for a child "is rare" (p. 159). Moreover, because the child's prognosis is determined largely by the parent–child relationships, the motives of each parent for wanting joint custody become a significant factor in the outcome for the child. As these authors point out, joint custody does not necessarily preclude parental neglect. When the arrangement reflects limited interest in the child by one or both parents, the child is unlikely to receive adequate care.

Of particular interest is McKinnon and Wallerstein's observation regarding parents who sought joint custody as a way to avoid full responsibility for care-giving. The preschool teachers of their children would notice emotional distress signs in the children's behavior and would automatically attribute this distress to the time-sharing schedule ("It's caused by this kid having to shuttle back and forth between her parents!"), rather than to the inadequate quality of parenting received by these youngsters at both homes. Such conclusions frequently feed naive, preexisting, and unsubstantiated beliefs that no child can handle a joint custody arrangement.

The motives of parents for wanting joint custody may also include the desires to reunite, to assert power over the other parent, to get revenge, or to retaliate (Saposnek, 1983a). Hence, forcing or pressuring a couple into a joint custody arrangement when the quality of their commitment to, or caretaking of, the child is suspect may do the child more damage than benefit. McKinnon and Wallerstein also found, contrary to their hopes, that joint custody did not protect young children from experiencing the grief and anxiety of the family rupture. Instead, they found that children in joint custody are indistinguishable in their initial distress and early responses to the family breakup from children in sole custody arrangements. Overall, these researchers found that the young children who did best in joint custody were those whose parents were highly committed and sensitive to the needs of their child for a quality relationship with both parents, and whose parents insulated them from any parental conflicts. Short of this, there was no evidence that joint custody per se protected the young child from the stress of divorce. However, there was also no evidence that a sole custody arrangement would have been any better.

These conclusions found further support in even more recent research reports. In a study of 93 children between the ages of 3 and 14 years of age, a two-year, post-divorce follow-up found no evidence that joint custody arrangements promoted child adjustment any better than did sole custody arrangements (Kline, Tschann,

Johnston, & Wallerstein, 1988). Wallerstein and Blakeslee (1989) further report that, in this study, the custody arrangement per se had but a minor influence on the psychological adjustment of the children. Factors that had more significant effects included the parents' emotional functioning at separation, their degrees of anxiety and depression, the age, sex, and temperaments of the children, and the amount of conflict between the parents a year later.

In considering, then, whether imposed joint custody is beneficial, the research suggests that the question is more complex. A number of factors needs to be considered regarding the nature of the co-parental relationship and the coping abilities of the child.

Conclusion

Without a doubt, as more data come in, we will have to revise our ideas and approaches concerning parenting after divorce. We are participants in a massive social experiment . . . raising a whole generation of children of divorce, an event that is unprecedented in our history, and unknown as to its eventual outcome. As we continue to learn, skillful applications of our budding knowledge of joint custody can serve many children well, if indeed we view it merely as an option, not a panacea.

5

Shared Parenting: What It Takes to Succeed

ALISON TAYLOR

Alison Taylor, a staff member of a public, court-connected service that offers mediation to parents before, during, and after divorce, provides us with her observations of when shared parenting can succeed. She sees shared parenting as not simply a division of time, but a mutual agreement to respect and comply with each other's rules. Taylor offers suggestions regarding the formation and evaluation of successful shared-parenting agreements. Substantive areas for consideration include determination of what decisions are to be made jointly as well as mutual agreement on appropriate activities and acts. Procedural aspects of such agreements include parental recognition and incorporation of children's needs, not deferring responsibility for choices to the children, scheduling regular times for review and revision of the agreement, and implementation of appropriate modes of communication. Taylor concludes that shared parenting may be an adaptive response of families to meet societal demands and pressures.

This chapter is not intended as a rigorous exercise in scientific method or as a review of the professional literature, but, rather, it is a collection of observations and their implications for shared parenting from my point of view as a staff member of a public, court-connected service that offers mediation to parents before, during, and after divorce. Because I am constantly exposed to parents in all stages of separation and

Alison Taylor, M.A., is a mediator working for the Family Court Service, Oregon City, Oregon.

This chapter is a revision of an article appearing in *Family and Conciliation Courts Review*, Vol. 27, No. 2, Dec. 1989 (pp. 7–16). The article won the first annual Meyer Elkin Award from the Association of Family and Conciliation Courts.

divorce and at all levels of conflict from slight to severe, I am in a position to see common patterns and isolate generalizable themes that may be of interest to those considering joint custody. While it is true that most of the population I deal with express difficulty with some aspect of their separation and/or the parenting system— creating a biased or skewed perception—I believe that many of their patterns are reflections of "generic issues," issues that face all parents in our society, regardless of socioeconomic standing, divorce status, or their desire and ability to be good parents.

Premises

"Shared parenting" is the new jargon for post-divorce parents who attempt to maintain an active, involved relationship with their children, despite the hazards of different work schedules, new household rules and structures, and, often, leftover feelings regarding the demise of the marital relationship. This new jargon seems preferable to the current legalistic phrase of "custody." Custody implies possession, as if children were neutral objects to be passed back and forth. "Visitation" implies that the parents who do not "own" their child through custody are limited to "visiting" with them, rather than relating to them and parenting them. "Shared parenting" at least implies some understanding of the underlying philosophy—that is, in order to maintain this post-divorce arrangement, the parents must cooperate and share.

But what, really, must they share? Time? Energy toward listening to and learning with their children? Money? Weekends, recreation and unscheduled time—or week-day hours after work, with its hurried task orientation and the need for active overseeing of homework and chores? What about involvement with others, such as grandparents, siblings, step-parents, aunts, and cousins? And more important, *who* is sharing? Is it the biological parents who are sharing their children by making complex schedules, or is it really the children who are now sharing their lives with those parents, and perhaps new people, in new ways?

Sharing can be done in many ways. It can mean taking turns, or it can be done by dividing the items in question (in this case, the children's time, energy, interests, and future). I sometimes use the analogy of sharing an apple—you can pass the apple back and forth, each taking bite after bite, or you can take a big knife and slice it in half, or one of you can keep it whole but have it for a specific amount of time, then change and let the other one have the whole apple. One of the primary issues is what effect any of these ways of sharing is going to have on the integrity and stability of the item in question. All of the above are ways of sharing, but from whose perspective are shared-parenting arrangements being developed, the child's or the parents'?

It is my proposition that all parents, both in "intact" or in divorced family structures, have a set of rules and expectations about fundamental issues regarding the raising of children. This view is based on the sociological perspective outlined by Babbie (1977), that all relationships are sets of agreements. Parents "share parenting" to the extent that they each agree with one another's rules and expectations and are willing to comply with those views. Because these agreements are often covert and implicit rather than explicitly stated, there are many families, intact or divorced or blended, that are not aware of their parenting rules, the *quid pro quo* of daily life ("I'll take Melissa to daycare on my way to work, but you need to share in the responsibility of picking her up").

Some intact families do not, by design or default, actively share the parenting of their children, or do so in a very limited way. Sometimes the father does not take an active role in dealing with the children's feelings, activities, or learning, or has assigned those tasks to the woman, effectively cutting out the biggest parts of sharing the children. Sometimes this is a matter of learned, culturally determined role behavior. In some parts of our culture the man's role is defined in terms of economics alone. He is expected to provide the financial support while the woman is expected to assume the rest of the child-rearing responsibilities. They share parenting only insofar as they have defined what each parent is to do without the other. Some women prefer to be the active parent, even undermining the man's attempts at involvement by negating his attempts to have individual relationships with the children or by not allowing the father to have time to pursue these relationships due to crowded schedules that leave him out.

In families that have not experienced divorce and those that have, the sharing of parental responsibilities is often determined more by time availability than by natural inclination or conscious agreements about how each parent would like to parent. Parents of pre-school children often must work out schedules of caring for the children based on when they are not working, hoping that the other parent is providing the children with what they need when "on duty." As Feldberg and Kohen (1976) pointed out, most families must parent in an anti-family setting imposed from the outside. Often, parenting systems evolve over time without a lot of discussion about the implications.

What I have found important in working with families before, during, and after divorce, is to ask concrete questions regarding the actualities of the parents' unique parenting style, financial contribution, relationship with each child, set of responsibilities, and expectations for themselves and the other parent. These factors must be assessed before you can get a true picture of whether any family has an active "shared-parenting" arrangement that balances the tasks with the rewards. The sum of these factors gives each family its unique definition of "shared parenting."

No matter what family structure or custody pattern is in place, the following questions are necessary to determine the past and present realities:

1. How did this system get built, and who designed it?

2. How did everybody react to it initially, and how are they each reacting to it now?

3. Does it meet everybody's needs and wishes?

4. Under what circumstances would this change?

Shared does not always mean equal, and unequal does not always mean unfair. If you ask the above questions to parents in private caucus away from the other parent, you might find entirely different answers, yet the caretaking goes on and the parents may or may not define it as a problem. For example, if one parent is a busy professional, the other parent may need to be the sole care provider for the children during peak family hours such as evenings, weekends and school recesses and holidays, when other families share child-based demands. While this parent may also have a part-time job, there may be an implicit agreement that he or she can only work if the child-care responsibilities are met. Both parents might state that this inequality and lack of mutual sharing is not a problem, since the children's need to have a parent available is being met very well, and their needs to share their time and energy between work and family have a balance or a division of labor with which each parent is comfortable. These unequal partners do not necessarily feel that their system is wrong simply because all aspects of parenting are not equal. As Steil (1983) points out, there is a difference between equality and equity.

In the ebb and flow of family life cycles, as so clearly defined by Carter and McGoldrick (1980b), this balance may shift when the children get older. For example, Mom may have started to progress in her career and needs more time to devote to it, and Dad may now be able to relax a little since he has found his niche and has seniority with its privileges. The children may need less direct supervision, or more. They may require less weekend involvement because of activities and friendships, or more time by parents chauffeuring them to and fro. If the parenting system cannot change to meet these changed needs, then one or more of the members of this family will become dissatisfied and will break agreements, expectations, and rules, on the basis of this unfairness.

It has been my experience that if you ask a family during or after divorce the same four questions to determine their parenting system, the parents now in two separate households may, like non-divorced families, give different answers. However, unlike non-divorced families, these differences will be seen as a problem. It seems that when parents divorce, they focus on their rights as a way to assess their situation and move toward a perceived vision of what is fair. Inequalities that had been tolerated in the implicit or explicit marital agreement are now relabeled as unfair and unacceptable.

Post-divorce fathers often start to demand equal time in the allocation of child-rearing, yet many have the same job-related constraints they had before the divorce. The children's need for parental availability may not have changed, but because divorce implies two parties who are equal under the law (if not in the marketplace), the power balance between the parents has now changed. Their expectations and abilities to be physically and emotionally available to the children may also have changed.

Mediators and counselors working with divorcing and post-divorce parenting systems need to augment the above four basic questions about parenting structure by looking at the concrete ways the parents are currently coping with the everyday issues of life. I believe that all parenting systems must, and do, have an implicit or explicit, planned or spontaneous, *de facto* way of dealing with the following items, each of which should be addressed to gather working detail from each parent, and perhaps from step-parents:

- Communication (parent–parent; parent–child)

- Organization of responsibilities (who does what?)
- Scheduling (where is the child, when?)
- Substitute care providers (who's acceptable, how often?)
- Decision making (who decides what?)
- Discipline/enforcement of rules (consistent?)
- Contingencies/unusual events (what should we do if . . . ?)

My further premise, based on working with people who are struggling with these issues, is that a good understanding about the expectations for each parent's role and function in regard to each of these questions, and a consensus about acceptable ways to deal with them, leads to cooperative and successful "shared parenting." In other words, the parents' (and step-parents') individual and collective opinions regarding the sum of these issues determines whether shared parenting will work to the satisfaction of both parents. Whether cooperation was talked about beforehand or has simply grown out of the situation, the level of congruence between expectation and reality about these topics is a gauge of how successfully, and in what way, the parenting system is truly shared.

When Shared Parenting After Divorce Works

The major advantage of many shared-parenting arrangements during and after divorce is that these arrangements can meet each parent's need for time off from parental responsibilities—often better than their original, idealized expectations. "Quality time" has been the catch words of a generation of parents who are both struggling to meet societal and work demands and still have something left at the end of the day to give to their children. Often, these needs are met at the expense of the parents' own needs for some quality time for themselves as individuals and their relationship as a couple. Parents can become disillusioned and distressed, blaming the other person if this lack of attention to personal needs continues, creating a reevaluation of their commitment to the relationship. When answers for reconstruction or revitalization of the current structure of the original relationship do not readily present themselves, divorce may look like a better solution.

In the best shared-parenting plans, an alternation of parental duty allows each parent active child supervision during times when each is not distracted by other responsibilities, and each parent has defined times when no parenting responsibilities are required. This gives each parent some time and energy to pursue personal interests and to engage in adult activities and new relationships without having to ask permission—and without having to combine or confine activities to only those which can be done with children present. Both time to parent *and* parental roles are more clearly defined. For many divorcing parents, that role has been defined by the court as 100% parent, every other weekend.

While some parents regret that divorce means that both parents cannot tuck their children into bed every night, some may be pleased to have time on the nights they do not have the children to read, think, go out, or make love without interruptions or complex planning, even if this is not publicly acknowledged. For many, post-divorce life is a study in contrasts: spontaneity increases while schedules become more rigid. If they have had schedules imposed upon them, parents lose choices over what they can do at particular times, yet they gain the freedom to do anything they want at other times. Since each person has a different toleration level for each of these poles of the continuum, shared-parenting plans work best when they meet the needs of each parent for flexibility and spontaneity, while also providing for family-specific needs for stability and predictability.

Although divorce statistics have flattened, there is still a high probability that divorce will occur for any given marriage. Divorce followed by shared-parenting arrangements may be a new social structure of choice that fits better with the realities of two parents in the workforce than the traditional models of marriage and parenting. It may be an adaptive response, and in that way may be a new evolutionary phase of social structure.

Problems in Shared Parenting

Many recent studies in the professional literature have tried to compare different post-divorce family structures to determine which pattern seems to minimize negative effects on children. Many of these studies are based on observable behaviors of the children, and self-reports of satisfaction by the parents. While this line of inquiry is a valid approach, I believe that it is more useful for mediators, judges, and others who are working with divorcing parents to look at the specific agreements and understandings that parents must have in any given family structure in order to meet everyone's needs.

To some degree, the professional community may have been approaching this subject in the wrong sequence. We have been asking parents, both in the courts and in mediation, to create systems and structures for which we have names (sole custody, joint custody, split custody, alternating custody) before we have asked or analyzed what component parts will work for this particular set of parents and children. We have been forcing people into pigeonholes because we have felt that it was more expeditious, yet, they return post-divorce, trying to deal with the component issues. Before we get the parents to articulate their needs for the items listed above (communication patterns, scheduling mechanisms, disciplinary policies), we try to get them to tell us their position on the type of general structure into which all of this must fit. We, as advisors and facilitators, have been asking parents to start with the end result, instead of going through the process of building agreements step by step.

The situation of divorce is analogous to that of the needs of special education students. Legislation (Pub. L. 94-142) requires educators to first *evaluate* the needs of the student, then *create a special program* for that student that would address the student's needs, and only then, as the final step, *determine the placement*. In other words, the parents and educators together must choose the particular structure for the student's program from options that are, or could become, available only after they know what answers must be provided.

What I am suggesting is that we, as helpers, have complicated the problems of divorce decisions by making divorce a win–lose, either–or situation, or by obfuscating the situation by calling a rose by other names. As Bruch (1988) has pointed out, the shades of difference between the placement categories become meaningless, since a parent who has "visitation" from Friday through Sunday may have as much, or more, actual parenting time as another parent who has "joint custody" but who only parents the children on Saturdays. We have been focusing on the question of "what is it?" instead of "what is it made of?" or "how does it work?" Instead of arguing semantics, parents need to know how they are going to be expected to parent.

The needs of the parents and the children should be evaluated first through interviews, family studies, tests, etc. Then agreement should be reached on what could help, what must be included, what cannot be done, and the actual parenting program that meets primarily the children's needs and secondarily the parents'. Then, as a third step, finally reach a decision as to what structural type of custody arrangement could provide those components best.

The recent Washington state legislation (Gaddis & Sooter, 1988) throws away the terms "custody" and "visitation," and replaces them with the requirement that all divorcing couples must develop an individualized parenting plan that outlines very specific roles, responsibilities, and consequences for non-compliance. The Washington legislation is a valiant attempt to have parents, with the help of their attorneys, counselors, and mediators, build a parenting "program" rather than negotiate only on the basis of the ultimate "placement" decision.

Beyond this essential problem of what comes first—the components or the structure—there are additional problems in some shared-parenting plans. Grouped below are a number of options that may illustrate the components that are problematic, with some suggestions for what can make the shared-parenting situation better.

Inability of the Structure to Meet Changing Needs

Parental satisfaction that leads to cooperation with the parenting plan most often leaves out the important factor of the *child's* perception of the success of the system. If the parents are happy enough with the arrangement, it will continue, whether or not the children are happy with it, whether in fact it meets their current needs and matches their abilities to carry it out. Since most families are not structured as true democracies, but rather as oligarchies of adults, a child has few legal rights, and often even less "clout" or power to persuade the adult decision makers concerning the most basic issues of life.

Parental expectations regarding the normative patterns of family structure following divorce are often inappropriate when viewed from the context of recent child development research. As Hodges (1986) and others point out, the needs of younger children can contraindicate overnight stays or extended periods of time without contact from the other parent, and older children need the flexibility of not being tied to a rigid alternation so that they have time available to pursue their own developmental stage of remaining loyal in relationships and preparing to leave home. This is especially true for children under three and those over 16, whose needs for immediacy of contact, continuity of care, flexibility, or total time spent with each parent varies considerably from the standard court prescribed, "every other weekend from Friday at 6 p.m. through Sunday at 7 p.m." or the totally undefined "reasonable and seasonable." Even a scrupulously equal bargain of "six months in one household, six months in the other" may fly in the face of the changing needs of the children.

Parents have come to expect these parenting system options, and see them as normative outcomes of the divorce condition, because the courts so routinely select these systems and because many attorneys advise their clients that this is the best solution they can expect, not because they are necessarily the best for any particular family. They may accept these options because they were the best they could negotiate at the time. Once selected or imposed upon a family, these standardized options tend to stay in place, whether they are working well or not.

Once parents have an agreement in place—either one of the standard parenting options mentioned above, or a self-created plan that initially did take the children's ages and needs into consideration—what happens if the children's needs change or are not being met? Children are often put into an extremely difficult position at that point and are forced to make a painful choice. They can just live with the untenable situation and cope as best they can, or they can restart "divorce wars" (which may have only recently de-escalated) by registering their discontent with one or both parents. What a terrible burden of responsibility falls to the child who is placed, often for the second time, in an avoidance–avoidance internal conflict with all its guilt and frustration.

For many children, this kind of situation requires that they must begin or remain acting out in increasingly strong and self-defeating ways, until they are tagged by a system that indicates in ways the parents cannot ignore that there is some sort of problem. Unfortunately, many times the children are then labeled as "the problem," and end up making the rounds of school personnel, counseling agencies, juvenile justice, or even mental health systems. These resources most often cannot or do not address the underlying issues of the inherent conflicts in the parenting system. Even if these agencies recognize that it is a structural, not a personal problem, they have no direct authority to create the needed changes, especially if the parents prefer to blame the child, the other parent, or deny the relevancy of the structure to the problems.

To me, one of the most obvious problems with most divorce agreements concerning the children, and even the best designed shared-parenting plan, is that the agreements and decisions on the court order only reflect realities at the point in time when they are made. Most divorces have no expectation or process for change. Worked out by attorneys and ratified through judges who may not be aware of family and individual lifecycles and predictable points of change, shared-parenting plans only reflect what made sense, or could be negotiated, at that time.

Children, however, do have predictable points when their lives will change no matter whether they are in one kind of divorced family structure or another—they move from grade to grade, school to school. All divorces involving children, and shared-parenting plans especially, should require reevaluation of custody, visitation, and shared-parenting responsibilities and schedules with enough lead time so that parents could make a change. Such agreements to review the structure and schedule should be done in such a way that everybody has enough time to adjust to the new schedule before it is implemented. Changes should be based on the very predictable progression through school. This concept of review and revision based on or coordinated with predictable events and utilizing specific criteria makes so much more sense than the "one-size-fits-all" approach. It would remove the burden of responsibility for bringing the issues to everyone's attention from the children, and the adults, by making the calendar responsible for instigating the review.

Currently, a parent or other adult who tries to spare the child this burden of internal conflict by pointing out a changed need, or takes on the role of advocate for the expressed needs or desires of a child, is often viewed suspiciously by the other parent. Even the professionals trying to work with the case can start with automatic assumptions based on their background of theory and philosophy that may or may not be correct about that parent's hidden agendas, self-interested motivation, or supposed unhealthy "enmeshment" with the child.

It is difficult for most parents to upset the uneasy balance of prior agreements or court orders, to willingly throw the situation back into conflict. Often parents avoid taking this role of advocate even when the need is very apparent, simply because they are afraid that their motivation and goals will be misinterpreted. While it is a valid and necessary parental responsibility to monitor a child's progress, to protect the child against potentially harmful situations, and to steer them toward things that will contribute positively to their lives, post-divorce parents in some shared-parenting configurations are often unable to perform this function because of a lack of adequate information and communication patterns between the parents. They may also hesitate for fear that their intervention may make the situation worse for the child.

Since few court-connected mediation programs address these parental post-divorce conflicts, the parent's fear may be justified, since the only recourse is to enter the legal arena. Motions for modifications often miss or hide the real issues because they limit the kinds of conditions that must be present in order to bring the matter before the court. For example, if a parent is concerned about post-divorce parenting issues such as discipline or step-parent roles, but no "change of circumstances" has occurred, and the situation is not severe enough to start intervention by the protective services, that parent may not be able to bring the matter to the courts for conflict resolution, and may not have access to court-connected services that can promote conflict management. If requirements are met to bring the matter before the court, the judge is often forced by legal restrictions to recommend remedies that may not solve the problem.

For example, a post-divorce parent in a joint custody situation may see that the weekly alternation of the children between parental households is inhibiting the junior and senior high school children from forming the kind of friendships and social contacts that are so important at that age. If the parent approaches the other with these concerns, they may be suspected of trying to undermine the joint custody agreement. The shared-parenting plan that met the small children's need for close and regular contact with both parents is now hindering their age-appropriate activities. Short of an open and positive responsive agreement by both parents, the concerned parent must now go to an attorney and restart a legal battle for custody, or attempt to get the children some relief and document their need by having them go to a counselor or therapist who may not recognize these as parenting concerns, but rather individual psychological issues of the children.

Changed needs come in two varieties—the children's needs for change, and the parents'. An adult's need for more time away from, or more time with, a child fluctuates due to the fluid nature of the divorce situation and the adult's need to reestablish a new identity and household. Studies show that the majority of men and a large percentage of women return to a stable continuous relationship or marital state within a few years of the divorce. This means children gain step-parents who may or may not be willing to parent them, who may or may not have other children to deal with and other parenting schedules to keep. Time constraints and life logistics in a "blended family" make changes and often leave little time for the parents to be a couple and to do the important work of boundary definition and shared identity that is necessary in the early stages of a relationship. The parents' emotional and physical presence may also change. While a parent may have the intention of parenting the children the same as before the divorce (or even better), the reality may not allow it. Shared-parenting plans may now impinge on weekend time that needs to be allocated to the new family's solidarity and bonding.

The parent with the new need or changed response to the shared-parenting structure may be reluctant to bring up the issues, partly because it may be interpreted negatively by the former spouse, and partly because it threatens the status quo and creates much uncertainty. However, not dealing with the changed needs, abilities, and circumstances leads to resentment and further problems, as the gap widens between the expectation of what should be going on and the reality of what really is happening.

If this potential for changed needs and abilities, temporary or permanent as they may be, has not been legitimized and planned for, if there is no positive way to approach the subject without making the other parent more angry, then each of the parents is placed in an avoidance–avoidance internal conflict. To do nothing brings problems, but to do something brings problems. As pointed out earlier, displacing the conflict on the children to do something about it does not work either.

The best solution to this set of problems with shared-parenting plans is to plan for them by setting an expectation for change before it happens. Contingency planning, or asking the parents to imagine, "what if . . ." can go a long way in setting a more positive stage when future changes occur. This may require mediators, attorneys, and others to write into the original divorce action a set of mutually acceptable agreements regarding the time frames for review of the original agreements, or a set of objective criteria that would be sufficient to start such a review. The original agreement should reflect that a change based on the children's or parents' current needs is not a failure of the original parenting plan, but simply growth and evolution of a living agreement over time. If shared-parenting plans have a mechanism for spotting and responding to the kinds of conditions mentioned above, the shared parenting will work not only in the immediate present, but in the long-term future.

Parents Deferring Responsibility for Choices to Children

I have often heard parents who are trying to reach agreements regarding shared physical custody deny, distort, or try to mitigate the power deficit of the children by announcing that, "Wherever Johnny wants to live is fine," or, "I know that the courts let a 15-year-old decide which parent they want to stay with and that's fine with me." While these statements make the parent appear to be cooperative and in touch with the child's expressed wishes, it is my opinion that they are often uttered by parents who unconsciously are avoiding the responsibility for making difficult parenting decisions, and who are making the child determine what is fair, appropriate, and workable. While seeming to bend over backwards to meet the child's needs, these parents are shifting the burden of choice onto the children. They are attempting to reduce their own conflict by displacing it.

Seen from a structural family perspective, such responses by parents who are trying to create a shared-parenting plan are inappropriate because they place the child above the parent in the family hierarchy. Letting the child decide undermines the important social message that, despite the divorce, parents are forever, and both father and mother have roles that are important enough to be mandatory. Seen from a legal perspective, such responses hold no legal basis, since the child is not an active decision maker regarding his or her own custody. While judges may want to hear what older teenagers have to say, it is only one part of the input the judge must evaluate. In reality, the children must adhere to the parents' agreement, or to what the court imposes if the parents can't agree.

Parents should be aware of these reality factors and the common urge to relieve the conflict by allowing children to decide. Such responses minimize the importance of the parents and set an uncomfortable precedent in the child's mind about his or her relative power with each parent.

Evaluation by Components

It appears that there are several component parts of any shared-parenting plan that is going to work. The most basic understanding that parents must have is who makes what decisions about the child. Because of the differing definitions and interpretations under the law, the terms "joint custody," or "shared custody" may mean entirely different things to each parent, and it would be natural for parents to incompletely understand what is expected of them and what they are, and are not, entitled to do under the arrangements worked out for them by attorneys or those imposed by a judge. It is important for those who are negotiating the divorce agreements, and the parents, to understand completely who is responsible for the major types of decisions parents must make, such as medical and educational services, permission to sign contracts, get a job, marry, or enlist in the armed services.

There is more to parenting than these large decisions, and the usual post-divorce disputes arise from decisions or actions that are not covered under these understandings. Does a parent who is sharing the physical custody of the child have the right, or obligation, to have the child's hair styled in a way that would or would not be offensive to the other parent? Who's going to help the child select appropriate clothes, and what if each parent has a different interpretation of what is appropriate? What about discipline techniques that range from not enough to borderline abusive? The concept that mom's house can be vastly different from dad's house and that the child will adapt to the inconsistencies, is fine until the child must be entirely different in one place as opposed to the other. Daily decision making is the stuff of life, and post-divorce parents need to be clear with each other and the children about what the limits are. They must have a process already in place when the child tests those limits. Having parents really set forth what their decision-making process is and how differences of opinion will be handled will go a long way in preventing the usual type of post-divorce disputes.

No matter what structure is selected or evolves, post-divorce parents need information about their children in order to make good decisions and maintain an active and involved relationship that is more than superficial. This need is particularly great for those parents trying to maintain some consistency for the child's sake, or those who have made mutual decisions about parenting and are trying to implement them in separate households. How can a parent effectively monitor what's going on in the other parent's environment without inappropriately involving the children, snooping, or infringing on the other parent's personal freedom?

No person in business, scientist, or other professional would ever try to make important decisions that have lasting consequences and profound effects without adequate information. Yet the courts routinely send parents out with divorce orders that are silent on this issue of post-divorce communication, leaving them to make important parenting decisions without adequate channels of communication between them. For example, parents who are trying to evaluate a child's educational progress so they can implement appropriate strategies of support in their household rules, or those who have concerns about how effective the other parent is in advocating for the child, must have the best information available. Although new education laws allow all parents access to the child's full school record, many post-divorce parents feel awkward or meet resistance by school staff when they attempt to get adequate information upon which to base decisions.

Unless they have agreed to this communication system ahead of time, parental calls to gather or give information can be interpreted as meddlesome, intrusive, and controlling. Parents who want to provide such necessary information may find a deaf ear from a parent who is so active in screening out the former spouse that they screen out child-related information too. Legitimate parental concerns are often misinterpreted based on former marital issues and conflicts. While using written notes and letters would seem like a good way to make sure that important information gets conveyed, most parents react poorly to written communication, stating that it is too time-consuming, tedious, and formal. They resent having to parent by paper, since they find it cold, impersonal, and unworkable. Instead, they often leave important information to pickup and delivery times. Parents cannot calmly and rationally make good, mutually acceptable decisions over the heads of their children while they are changing from one household to another. Using the same analogy as before, would a professional be able to clearly see patterns or offer constructive suggestions to a colleague if given information while trying to get out the door to attend another appointment?

Because avenues for direct communication are often threatening, blocked, or non-existent, a parent who has concerns about the child in the other parent's environment often tries to elicit information and help, overtly or covertly, from the children, thus using them as information conduits and placing them back in the middle between parents who are not doing business effectively. This puts the children in the role of tattlers, whistleblowers, accomplices, even conspirators. It returns the children to a situation of uncertainty and loyalty conflicts.

If parents in shared-parenting plans really want to adequately supervise their children, they will develop a communication plan that provides a routine, scheduled, and open forum for discussion. Adequate communication for post-divorce parents can be set up in the beginning, with expectations on the part of both parents that they will stockpile concerns until they can have a "parents' meeting." This should happen at least once a month so that the concerns are still fresh, but also so that they are looking at patterns and issues, not just immediate reactions to temporary situations. The exception to this is any problem that either parent would define as an emergency. It is helpful to have the parents define for each other what might fall under that category. The parents need to come to their own understandings of how often and in what way issues can be discussed, what setting will be used, who should attend, who will set it up, and who will pay any costs involved.

Substitute care of children during each parent's time to have the parenting responsibility is also a major topic to consider discussing if shared parenting is going to work. Most parents are reluctant to have the children go to the other parent if that parent is not truly available due to work schedules or need for time off; most parents would rather be seen as the first recourse before a babysitter or other substitute care provider is used. Parents often have strong feelings about step-parents, live-in partners, and other relatives being used for childcare during the parent's time with the children. Again, what is important is that the parents themselves define what they would expect of the other parent, how often a parent can be away from the children and still have the system work, and who they consider acceptable substitutes.

Summary and Interpretation

All parenting systems, both in intact families or those restructured by divorce and subsequent remarriage, have a set of agreements about how to parent. They may be implicit or explicit and they may or may not be mutually perceived. The more concrete and mutual they are, and the more the actual parenting reflects the mutual agreements, the more an observer would say that the parenting system is "working."

"Shared-parenting" arrangements after divorce can be structured many different ways and the legal system, in an attempt to create clarity, has defined different custody patterns. The definitions, and the implications of these options differ considerably, often leaving parents unsure of their actual rights and responsibilities. It is unfortunate that we often force parents into decisions about which structure or system they want before we help them analyze what components are involved and which structure would be the best one to provide those components.

In order to evaluate the current or proposed shared-parenting plan, the helper (mediator, attorney, counselor, or judge) should ask some basic questions about the structure to both parents and any step-parents. These will give the helper some ideas about the structural conflicts that are built into the system. The most important components that contribute to a "working" or mutually acceptable, effective shared-parenting plan for all family members are: Decision making, communication, task delineation, scheduling, substitute care, discipline and enforcement of rules, and contingency and emergency planning.

Certain hazards seem inherent in some shared-parenting structures and in some approaches to shared parenting in general. There are three major categories of problems: the inability of shared-parenting agreements to meet the changing needs of either children or parents, parents abdicating their role and deferring inappropriate choices to the children, and parents minimizing their own losses by displacing them onto the children. These hazards can be overcome with awareness on the part of the helpers and parents, and with specific modifications that can be built into the agreements.

I have suggested that shared parenting, when structured to avoid these pitfalls, can not only "work," but may in fact be an appropriate, adaptive response and a new evolution of the family system to meet new societal demands and pressures. It is up to us as helpers to guide parents and to individualize the parenting plan and parenting structure to fit as closely as possible the current and future needs of the children and the parents.

6

Examining Resistance to Joint Custody

JOAN B. KELLY

Joan Kelly, who has devoted much of her professional life to examining the effects of divorce on children, here examines professional attitudes toward joint custody. Resistance on the part of judges, lawyers, and mental health professionals may stem not from clinical data or psychological theory, but from the unconscious attitudes and feelings of the professional. This important contribution may help us guard against making judgments based on unconscious, irrational, or irrelevant factors.

In the past two decades, the divorce rate in the United States has tripled, and since 1972, more than one million children each year have had their lives affected and substantially changed by their parents' divorce. During this period, our society has seen enormous social and economic change. Women with children of all ages have entered the workforce in unprecedented numbers, not only in response to considerable economic need but to address the need felt by many women to create for themselves an additional source of psychological satisfaction and self-esteem other than full-time parenting. At the same time, there have been substantial changes within the family as men and women have redefined their parental and marital functioning in ways which have begun to blur traditional roles. The most visible result has been the increasing numbers of fathers who occupy a central, if not equal, role in the nurturing and care of their children.

In the wake of such dramatic social change divorce laws have been reevaluated and public policy regarding custody and visitation for families in the midst of divorce

Joan B. Kelly, Ph.D., is the Director of the Northern California Mediation Center, Corte Madera, California.
This article is a revised version of a paper presented at the Association of Family and Conciliation Courts meeting, "Patterns and Perspectives: The 21st Century Family," in San Francisco, May 1982.

has been reexamined. The no-fault divorce, and new statutes defining joint custody as a viable (and in some instances preferable) alternative to sole custody, are the most significant and far-reaching results of this reexamination. The joint custody statutes evolved not only in response to the foregoing societal changes and increased parental activism, but also as a result of an accumulating body of divorce research which focused on the short- and long-term responses and adjustment of parents and children to divorce. Among the findings were: (1) children's intense dissatisfaction with the traditional pattern of twice-a-month visitations and their expressed desire for more liberal contacts with the noncustodial parent (Kelly, 1982; Wallerstein & Kelly, 1980a); (2) the significant relationship between frequency and amount of post-divorce contact with the father and the child's psychological and social adjustment (Hetherington, 1979; Hess & Camara, 1979; Wallerstein & Kelly, 1980a); (3) the father's negative psychological reactions to his reduced parenting opportunities post-separation and divorce (Greif, 1979a; Jacobs, 1982; Kelly, 1982; Keshet & Rosenthal, 1978; Wallerstein & Kelly, 1980a, 1980b, 1982); and (4) the mother's need for relief from the psychological and economic stress from being a full-time, single parent (Kelly, 1982; Wallerstein & Kelly, 1980a; Weiss, 1979b).

The trend in the direction of increased acceptance of joint custody in law and in practice has been accompanied by an unusual level of controversy among those professionals within the fields of mental health and law dealing with divorce-related issues. The concept of joint legal custody has been troublesome to some, but it is the joint physical custody issue, in particular, which has been the focus of impassioned debate. Attitudes regarding shared parenting after divorce range from outright and total opposition to wholehearted acceptance of joint custody for everyone.

It is ironic, and of some interest, that we have subjected joint custody to a level and intensity of scrutiny that was never directed toward the traditional post-divorce arrangement (sole legal and physical custody to the mother and two weekends each month of visiting to the father). Developmental and relationship theory should have alerted the mental health field to the potential immediate and long-range consequences for the child of only seeing a parent four days each month. And yet until recently, there was no particular challenge to this traditional post-divorce parenting arrangement, despite growing evidence that such post-divorce relationships were not sufficiently nurturing or stabilizing for many children and parents.

Why does the concept of joint custody or shared parenting after divorce arouse such passion? This paper seeks to examine the resistance seen in mental health and legal practitioners to the concept of joint custody after divorce. It should be stated that joint custody is not herein defined as an equal 50/50 sharing of the child's time, although it may include that, but rather a post-divorce parenting plan which goes beyond traditional visitation to include each parent at least 30 percent of the time, or more, in the child's ongoing life.

In examining the potential sources of resistance to the changes in post-divorce parenting arrangements, it would appear that there are several important influences to consider: (1) the larger cultural tradition of which we are all a part; (2) the psychological theories that influence our thinking and our decision making; and (3) the more elusive but important unconscious attitudes which shape our reactions and thinking.

In examining resistance to joint custody, the author's intent is not to make a statement favoring presumptive joint custody. Rather, the intent is to identify some of the less recognized factors influencing the decision making of judges, lawyers, mediators, and mental health evaluators which are not relevant to the particular family under consideration, but nevertheless are powerful legal and psychological contributors to the final decision regarding post divorce parenting.

Cultural Tradition

Cultural tradition is strongly embedded in our lives and, regardless of our level of education or sophistication, has an important influence on our reactions to social/psychological events and issues. We have assimilated within our societal and personal fabric many decades of precedent for mothers having primary responsibility for their children. Because women were the primary caretakers a half century ago, mother–child relationships became the focus of attention of psychoanalytic theory and practice, and of child development research. This resulted in a deemphasis of the viability and importance of the father–child relationship. Over time, mother–child relationships achieved a special type of sanctity within our society, and today we see mothers who feel they own their children. As a result, when divorce occurred, judicial decisions and laws reflecting society's views ensured that women were awarded custody of their children almost routinely. As the divorce rate spiraled and women moved into the workforce, little thought was given to changing the prevailing practice until the massiveness of the social change within our society was inescapable.

There is no need to be continuously aware of the pervasive and strong role that cultural tradition has in determining our values, our thinking, and therefore our decision making. A California Superior Court judge demonstrated this influence when he summarily rejected a father's recent proposal for a larger role in the child's life, saying: "Children belong with the mother." A Missouri senator was, perhaps, representative of the American mainstream when he stated: "I believe that a mother is more important than a father. Fathers should not be granted rights equal to those of mothers." For lawyers, mediators, and mental health professionals, the extent to which cultural tradition continues to dominate our thinking can be measured by the inner suspicion we hold that fathers *cannot* be as committed to parenting their children as can mothers, or that men must *prove* their parenting skills to us whereas we assume that with women those same skills are already in place and need not be challenged or examined. The result of such thinking in making decisions about divorcing families may be to deny many children the opportunity of a continuing and meaningful relationship with both parents.

Psychological Concepts and Theories

It is essential that we examine the psychological theories and concepts that govern our thinking and decision making with regard to divorcing parents and children. Many of these theoretical constructs are valuable and have been serviceable in our understanding of the traditional intact family. But some of these concepts appear to lose coherence in their translation to the needs of children in the divorced family. The child's need for stability in his daily life has been long identified as important in the ongoing development of the child. Within the intact family, stability implied stable care and routine, consistent caretakers, and some protection from erratic, capricious parenting. Yet, with divorce, the concept of stability underwent a transformation and became defined by many mental health professionals as one house, one toothbrush, and one primary parent. This *geographic definition* of stability took precedent in our thinking and decision making over the equally (if not more) important aspect of stability that is provided by a continuing relationship with a loving parent who no longer lives in the child's home. The geographic definition of stability was invoked to argue that youngsters could not successfully integrate the regular and frequent experience of visiting father's home into their ongoing development. Yet we observed young children in the intact family successfully integrating the experience of daily child care, pre-school, and overnights with grandparents and friends. It is important to examine developmental and psychoanalytic concepts such as stability, not only for their applicability to the developmental needs of the child in the divorced family, but because they can become loosely applied and ill-defined clichés which may actually obscure our thinking about the child's real needs.

The concept of separation anxiety has also been important in post-divorce decision making, particularly in discouraging overnight visits between infants and toddlers and their fathers. Several decades ago, infant research focused entirely on mother–child interactions, and discovered that infants and toddlers in specific stages reacted to the absence of the primary caretaker, usually the mother, with anxiety. But when developmental researchers discovered fathers in the past decade, they learned that fathers, too, were identified early in life by infants as special, and that separation from fathers, as well, created anxiety and unhappiness. Our body of child development knowledge would suggest, in fact, that infants and toddlers with a bond to a nurturing father must have more overall contact, including some overnights with their fathers, rather than less time. The young child is hampered by a very primitive sense of time, a paucity of language, and immature cognitive and memory faculties. Thus, the child is not sure when or if a next visit will occur. He or she may experience considerable anxiety in the absence of the "absent" parent if the interval between visits is too long, and parent and child may lose significant ground in the closeness of the relationship if the contacts are not sufficiently frequent and with enough time at any given contact to really "know" each other. Therefore, if one of our goals after divorce is to enhance the child's ability to build permanent relationships, we must reevaluate our thinking in this regard and expend more effort on developing creative and productive arrangements which will serve the child's need. In addition to mid-week and weekend overnights, for example, many infants and toddlers have benefited from their father or mother visiting the daycare or nursery school for lunch, or occasionally assisting with the program.

As the joint custody concept has flourished, more concern has been expressed about children's ability to cope with differences in personality, style, and attitudes of their parents after divorce. The psychological concepts of identity formation and identity confusion underline these concerns. The child's ability to cope with and successfully integrate these parental differences within the intact marriage has not been, however, a major parallel issue. There is as yet no research data confirming the disruption of identity formation after divorce due to such differences, except in cases where parents have extreme differences which create conflict for the child. For the most part, it is parental anger about the other parent's differences which can create problems for the child rather than the actual differences themselves.

Another concept contributing to resistance among lawyers, judges, and mental health professionals to joint custody has been the belief that parents who divorce are unable to cooperate about anything, including their parenting after the divorce. This concept actually draws upon two somewhat erroneous and simplistic notions about divorce. The first is that a marriage that fails has done so in every regard, and that the conflict that led to the termination of the marriage permeated child-rearing issues and parental decision making as well. While this is clearly true in some marriages, there is evidence that substantial conflict regarding child-rearing practices is not present in a majority of marriages (Ahrons, 1980a; Kelly, 1984a; Wallerstein & Kelly, 1980a). Lawyers, in particular, seem to share the belief that if parents could cooperate regarding their children, they would not be divorcing in the first place. Adults divorce for many reasons related to adult needs and dissatisfactions, but dissatisfaction or conflict stemming from the spouse's parental behavior is not among the more prevalent reasons expressed for obtaining a divorce (Bloom & Hodges, 1981; Kelly, 1982; Kitson & Sussman, 1982). The second notion is that the anger which attorneys and mental health professionals observe during the divorcing period will remain undiminished during the years following divorce. However, there is evidence that the intense anger between parents diminishes within the first year post-divorce, particularly if litigation is completed (Ahrons, 1984; Wallerstein & Kelly, 1980a). After two years post-separation, only a small percentage of parents (close to 15%) remain intensely or pathologically enraged. Therefore, we must avoid making policies and decisions based upon the small minority of parents who thrive upon the aggression permitted and unleashed within the adversary system. While these individuals are the most frequent and difficult clients of the conciliation courts, they are not representative of the average divorcing parent whose anger, bitterness, and disappointment run a briefer and often more contained course.

A further resistance to joint custody is expressed in the widely held belief that joint custody should never be awarded unless both parents agree. Proponents of this view state that it is not in the "best interest" of the child to be involved in such a shared parenting arrangement because the hostile environment between parents will be perpetuated. While there are clearly some cases in which parental opposition to joint custody is warranted, it is instructive to examine the reality and outcome of this common view more closely. First, this position seems to ignore the finding that parents with sole custody orders also experience a period of intense conflict to which the children are witness. There is not yet evidence available that, on a daily basis, children in unilaterally desired joint custody arrangements experience *more* hostility, or that the hostility they initially experience would not be balanced by the opportunity to continue their relationship in a meaningful way with both parents. And, in denying joint custody *solely* on the basis of one parent's opposition, the child's wishes and developmental needs are not even being considered as a relevant factor in decision making. Therefore, there is a need to assess parental opposition to shared parenting on a case-by-case basis.

Further, it is important to recognize that men are almost always the supplicants in the process of obtaining either joint legal or physical custody, unless presumptive joint custody statutes exist. As discussed earlier, it is still presumed in our society that women will keep the children in their care, and therefore, men must either ask, negotiate, or litigate for both the legal right and the physical time with which to remain centrally involved in their children's lives. To the extent that public policy or legal statutes specify that both parents must agree to a joint custody order, women continue to have enhanced power with regard to the children's future, without regard to the parenting capacities of each parent.

An additional psychological theory contributing to wariness about joint custody is that parents who enter into joint custody arrangements are still "emotionally married." Here, joint custody is viewed as a mechanism for avoiding the reality of the pending divorce and the demise of the marital relationship. In short, seeking joint custody is defined as evidence of pathology, rather than what may be a healthy desire to continue parental involvement post-divorce. And if, for some, joint custody does have elements of a continuing or transitional emotional attachment to a spouse or the overall family structure, it is not apparent how this might be detrimental to the child unless such a parent actively fosters the hope of reconciliation in the child. This seems generally not to be the case.

As indicated earlier, each of the psychological constructs discussed above have a valuable contribution to make in understanding the developmental needs of the child. We must continue, however, to examine them for their applicability to the child within the divorced family. There is some evidence that in our well-meaning efforts to save children in the immediate post-separation period from anxiety, confusion, and the normative divorce-engendered conflicts, we have set the stage in the longer run for the more ominous symptoms of anger, depression, and a deep sense of loss by depriving the child of the opportunity to maintain a full relationship with each parent.

Unconscious Responses to Joint Custody Arrangements

In addition to cultural tradition and psychological concepts guiding our thinking, there are other complexities which contribute to professional resistance to shared parenting. Perhaps the most difficult to identify and change are those unconscious attitudes and reactions in the lawyer or therapist which shape their thinking regarding post-divorce custodial arrangements. It is important to be aware of a few forms which these unconscious attitudes take, and the potential hazards posed for professionals if they are not recognized.

Women in the legal and mental health fields are particularly vulnerable to unconscious, dimly understood reactions if they have children of their own. When a father seeks assistance in obtaining frequent visiting, joint custody, or sole custody, professional women may feel profoundly threatened by what this represents to the security or stability of their own mothering role. If so, a likely response is one of hostility which may have nothing to do with the merits of the particular case. Further, if professional women are themselves divorced with sole custody of their children, they are potentially more vulnerable to the hostility aroused by such requests. The result of such unrecognized hostility or suspicion may be, for the male client, either a subtle or more outright attempt by the professional to discourage the father from pursuing his goal of meaningful parenthood, a devaluation of the material presented by the father supporting his interest in shared parenting, or a very lukewarm or shoddy pursuit of his request as reflected in psychological reports or legal strategy. When women lawyers or mental health evaluators are hired by angry women clients whose goal is to exclude the father from any continuing role in the child's life, the reverse may be true. There may be indiscriminate belief in the mother's reasons for denying shared parenting, and hyper-aggressive legal strategy or biased psychiatric reports which lean heavily on psychological clichés and theory rather than data.

For men, there are comparable hazards. When a father seeks a rich and continuing relationship with his children after divorce, male lawyers, judges, and psychotherapists may react with suspicion, derision, or hostility. The father's request for considerable parental involvement may bring to the surface doubts or regrets about the quality of fathering the professional male is providing, or has provided, to his own children. The potential for rejecting, or treating lightly, the father's attempts to seek a shared parenting arrangement is especially great if the attorney or mental health evaluator has failed to maintain a gratifying relationship with his own children after divorce. And similarly, when embittered women wish to severely limit the father's opportunities to see his children and seek the guidance and support of lawyers or therapists, the male professional may not adequately challenge the client's views because they, themselves, have been excluded from their children's lives either by choice or by default.

The impact of unconscious attitudes in family law, mediation, and divorce counseling work is insufficiently understood and seldom discussed. Yet it is clear that such attitudes and feelings are present in all of us who assist parents in making decisions, and that they play a key role in the various post-divorce arrangements which are made regarding the children of divorce. Our responsibility is to fully recognize and accept that there are men and women who have no interest in their children within the intact marriage or the divorce, there are men and women who are inadequate parents, and there are men and women whose own narcissistic needs take precedence over the needs of their children. And there also are men and women who love their children and genuinely want to be responsible loving parents. To be equally responsible participants in the divorce process, professionals should bring to the surface and clearly understand their own attitudes, feelings, and biases. If we are fully conscious of where we stand in this arena, then we can assist parents in decision making with integrity.

Meeting Children's Needs

The task of assisting parents in developing post-divorce arrangements which meet the developmental and psychological needs of their children is a complex one. The needs of divorced children are no different than the needs of children in the intact family, but it may be harder to meet youngsters' developmental needs after divorce because divorce, unlike marriage, does not exist for the purpose of nurturing children. Parents rarely seek divorce to enhance their children's development, but rather to enhance or improve the quality of their own adult lives. Sometimes divorce automatically removes a barrier to good psychological development, for example, by separating a child from daily contact with a cruel parent. But for the most part, there is no assurance that divorce will benefit children unless specific attention is paid to their particular psychological and developmental needs, and decisions are made based on the recognition of these needs.

The problem is that in divorce, more so than in marriage, children's developmental needs may be in competition with each other. As mentioned earlier, the preschool child needs a degree of structure and stability to maintain and enhance his psychological functioning and ongoing development, and in divorce, this is often interpreted as indicating a need for one custodial home, not two. But the youngster also has a *competing* need to maintain a nourishing relationship with a loved parent that will sustain itself in a meaningful way. To accomplish this goal, or fulfill this need, the preschool child needs a considerable amount of time with that parent, at regular intervals. Thus, the need for stability and the need for a good relationship compete with each other, and our dilemma is to arrange things to satisfy both important needs. Complicating our task is the recognition that some situations or post-divorce arrangements fulfill short-term developmental needs, while compromising longer term psychological needs. Returning to the preschool child, the moves back and forth between homes may initially create some confusion and anxiety, but this must be balanced with the knowledge that the child may later struggle with painful feelings of disappointment and longing because his father is essentially a stranger. It is important to adopt a frame of reference which includes assessing all the alternatives which might arise from the post-divorce arrangements. We must look at short- and long-term problems, and short- and long-term gains.

Increasingly, we are seeing before the courts two adequate parents of reasonable psychological health, both of whom want to parent full time. Such cases have the potential to push counselors and clinicians beyond the limits of current psychological knowledge and predictive capacity. In these instances, we are more likely to make judgments based primarily upon unconscious, irrational, or irrelevant factors. The turmoil and angers of divorce often make it difficult for us to remain honest, objective, and nonaligned. In fact, where each parent is deemed to be a "good enough parent," and each supports and encourages the child's relationship with the other, there is *no* basis in either psychology or law for making a rational choice between parents. In these families, the lawyer, judge, and mental health professional can most effectively address the child's interests by encouraging each parent to take an active post-divorce role in the child's life, by expecting that they will share both parental responsibility and gratification on an ongoing basis, in two separate homes.

7

Joint Custody, Feminism, and the Dependency Dilemma

KATHARINE T. BARTLETT
CAROL B. STACK

This chapter explores women's dependency and its ramifications within the context of child custody. The anticipated benefits of joint custody to both men and women appear great, yet as theory transforms into practice, women may discover dangers in joint custody arrangements. Although lessening dependency for some women, for others joint custody may increase dependency between women and their children, women and their former spouses, and women and the courts. In an attempt to remedy the dangers for women, Bartlett and Stack suggest that by an assertive restructuring of current custody laws, existing norms and expectations can be changed and the ideals of shared parenting can be reached. They caution that implementation of joint custody must be done in such a way as to avoid inequalities.

Katharine T. Bartlett is a Professor of Law at Duke University School of Law.

Carol B. Stack, Ph.D., is the Director of the Center for the Study of Family and the State in the Department of Public Policy and Anthropology, Duke University.

Many friends and colleagues made critical comments on earlier drafts that were helpful to us in revising this article. We thank especially the participants in the Feminism and Legal Theory section of the Women and Dependency Conference held July 22–26, 1985, by the Institute for Legal Studies, University of Wisconsin–Madison Law School that was organized by Martha Fineman; we also thank David Chambers, Linda Girdner, Bell Hooks, Allison Jagger, Herma Hill Kay, Michael Livesay, Martha Minow, Elizabeth Minnich, Sandra Morgen, Deborah Rhode, Tom Rowe, Kevin Stack, and Nadine Taub.

A version of this chapter, with different footnoting, appeared in 2 *Berkeley Women's Law Journal*, Fall 1986 (pp. 9–41).

Dependency is a dilemma for women. Women's dependency, which arises largely from their status as caregivers, can be both a strength and a source of vulnerability and exploitation. The dependent relationships which women form are often coercive and degrading, but at the same time they may satisfy the needs of women for affirmation and influence. Efforts to overcome the oppressive aspects of dependency, while successful in some respects and for some women, may exacerbate the problem in other ways.

The issue of joint custody illustrates the contradictory nature of women's dependency. Joint custody has the potential both to help women develop more independence and to aggravate the problematic aspects of dependency in women's lives. Although joint custody was expected to help women, it has had mixed effects, benefiting some women, hurting others, and for still others, helping and hurting at the same time.

This chapter examines joint custody as an example of the complicated nature of women's dependency. In the first section, we set the movement toward joint custody in the context of the egalitarian goals of women's rights groups in the 1970s. We then describe the emergence of the feminist critique of this movement in the 1980s.

In the next two sections, we explore the shortcomings of the joint custody critique. In the first of these, we examine different areas of women's dependency, including the relationships of women to men, to children, and to the state. Within these areas, we analyze differences in the experience and consciousness of situations of dependency in which women find themselves. These differences, based on race, social class, and generation, may affect how women respond to changes in custody rules. We conclude that in assuming a single yardstick for evaluating the effects of joint custody on women, the feminist critique of joint custody is incomplete and inconclusive, overlooking the differences which structure women's relationships to the state, to the courts, to public and private patriarchy, and to race and social class.

In the second of these sections, we examine the relationship between custody norms and ideology,[1] emphasizing both the importance of law in forming ideology and the importance of ideology in changing social attitudes and practices. We conclude that the critique of joint custody errs in ignoring or underestimating both of these factors and that joint custody is ideologically a desirable alternative to sole custody.

Finally, in the last section, we explain that much of the detriment suffered by women under joint custody statutes is attributable not to joint custody statutes themselves, but to the holdover of traditional attitudes and practices about child custody. We argue that we should direct our efforts toward improving the circumstances for women within which custody decisions are made and toward purging the stereotype-bound premises which continue to pervade the resolution of these disputes, rather than rejecting joint custody altogether.

---

1. We use the term "ideology" in this chapter in a number of different senses, all described in R. Geuss, *The Idea of a Critical Theory* (1981). Here, we use it in the descriptive sense, to describe the beliefs, attitudes, and habits, actually held. *Id.* at 4-12. It is used elsewhere to mean the "approved models of action, goals, ideals and values," which "are most likely to enable the members of the group to satisfy their wants and needs and further their interests" (ideology in the "positive" sense), *id.* at 22, and still elsewhere, to mean a consciousness based upon mistaken assumptions (ideology in the "pejorative" sense). *Id.* at 12-22.

We note that the effect of joint custody upon women is not the only, or even the most important, focus in evaluating joint custody. A more complete approach would necessarily examine the effects of joint custody and other custody alternatives on children. There is already some evidence supporting the view that joint custody offers substantial benefits over other alternatives for many children.[2] Further studies may offer more guidance in this area, but they are unlikely to resolve the debate over the impact of joint custody on the interests of women. The results of studies designed to ascertain the welfare of children are rarely, if ever, conclusive.[3] Moreover, they take place in a political and social context which affects both an assessment of the evidence[4] and what we might say about the primacy of the child's best interests.[5] Thus, how we interpret the interests of children inevitably will be influenced by how we evaluate the interests of mothers and fathers as well.[6] This chapter focuses on the interests of mothers.

Joint Custody, Dependency, and the Feminist Critique

The women's rights movement has long emphasized the price paid by many women for allowing their identity, status, and financial security to be tied to their predominant position as mothers. In the 1970s, joint custody offered promise as a way to make motherhood less costly to women. It appeared to be a means of counteracting traditional gender roles that confine women to the home and men to the workplace. It implied a rejection of the stereotypes that women are suited to nurturing children and that men are not. These stereotypes had been reinforced by the fact that under then existing custody norms, women obtained exclusive custody of their children in most cases.[7] Joint custody also promised to facilitate greater emotional and economic

---

2. Clingempeel & Reppucci, *Joint Custody After Divorce: Major Issues and Goals for Research*, 91 Psychological Bull. 102 (1982). See, e.g., Abarbanel, *Shared Parenting after Separation and Divorce: A Study of Joint Custody*, 49 Am. J. Orthopsychiatry 320 (1979); Greif, *Fathers, Children, and Joint Custody*, 49 Am. J. Orthopsychiatry 311 (1979). *See also* D. Luepnitz, *Child Custody* 150 (1982) (joint custody at its best is better than sole custody at its best).

There is considerable additional authority that children who continue to have regular and frequent contact with both parents after divorce do better in terms of their social, cognitive, and academic development than children who do not. The best known of these is J. Wallerstein & J. Kelly, *Surviving the Breakup: How Children and Parents Cope with Divorce* 218-19 (1980) (the child's relationship with the noncustodial father is critical to the child's adjustment to the parents' divorce, even when the child has a good relationship with the custodial mother).

3. For a review of research pertaining to the welfare of children and an analysis of the limited, usually inconclusive, findings of this search, see Chambers, *Rethinking the Substantive Rules for Custody Disputes in Divorce*, 83 Mich. L. Rev. 477, 503-41, 550-57 (1984).

4. Mnookin, *Child-Custody Adjudication: Judicial Functions in the Face of Indeterminacy*, Law and Contemp. Probs., Summer 1975, at 226, 258-61.

5. *Cf.* Sugarman, *Roe v. Norton: Coerced Maternal Cooperation*, in *In the Interest of Children* 365, 444-47 (R. Mnookin ed. 1985) (the children's interests were used as a cover for the interests of others in litigation over the coercion of welfare mothers to name their children's fathers).

6. Our argument, here, is an empirical one—that consideration of the interests of adults in child custody disputes is simply unavoidable. For a principled analysis of why we *should* take parents' interests into account, in addition to the interests of children, see Chambers, *supra* note 3, at 499-503.

7. *See* L. Weitzman, *The Divorce Revolution: The Unexpected Social and Economic Consequences for Women and Children in America* 257, Table 23 (1985) (about 90% of custody awards were made to the mother).

independence for women, who could pursue work, career, or personal goals without disproportionate responsibility for child care.

The positive consequences of joint custody were anticipated during a period of optimism that social and political momentum towards gender equality would continue, creating autonomy and independence for women. In this period, joint custody was also advocated by fathers' rights groups seeking equal rights for fathers to their children and by children's advocacy groups who sought the advantages for children of having two parents actively involved in their lives after divorce. As a result of support from these diverse groups, joint custody has become a vigorous national trend.[8]

For many women, the trade-offs made in this period have come to seem inequitable. While fathers sought and obtained rights to equal custody, the goals sought by women were anchored to changes in social institutions and to changes in the consciousness of those who interpret the law, and of fathers themselves. These changes have not kept pace with the success of men in obtaining equal rights. Women's earning power still lags considerably behind that of men.[9] Structural changes in employment, such as comparable worth, affirmative action, parental leave and day care options, and other steps to counteract occupational segregation and associated wage inequities, have made only minimal headway for women over the past decade. Further, despite the perception of raised consciousness toward equality in the household, women, even working women, continue to bear primary responsibility for care of the household and children. As a result, many women remain in low-wage jobs while continuing to bear the bulk of childrearing responsibilities.

The feminist critique of joint custody stresses the gap between the ideals underlying equal parenthood and the reality. As a result of their increased custodial rights, fathers have attained greater economic leverage in the bargaining process surrounding custody decisions. Thus women wishing to retain satisfactory custody arrangements with their children have found themselves more vulnerable at divorce, often needing to negotiate away economic for custodial rights. This may create a situation in which women are unable to make ends meet, unable to pursue potential employment possibilities, and trapped in a choice between poverty and economic dependency.

Further, in making custody decisions and enforcing the rights of fathers, courts have tended to be too easily impressed by the good intentions of fathers and have exaggerated the credit due them for their new-found willingness to assume some active role in parenting.[10] Courts are also quick to assume that if custody of a child is evenly

---

8. While there is no recent, broad study on the incidence of joint custody, there is general agreement that joint custody is on the rise. *See, e.g.,* Folberg, *Joint Custody Law — The Second Wave*, 23 J. Fam. L. 1, 1 (1984-85); Steinman, *Joint Custody: What We Know, What We Have Yet to Learn, and the Judicial and Legislative Implications*, 16 U.C.D. L. Rev. 739, 740 (1983); Kelly, *Examining Resistance to Joint Custody*, in *Joint Custody and Shared Parenting*, 39, 40 (J. Folberg ed. 1984); Schulman & Pitt, *Second Thoughts on Joint Child Custody: Analysis of Legislation and Its Implications for Women and Children*, 12 Golden Gate U.L. Rev. 539, 539 (1982); Scott & Derdeyn, *Rethinking Joint Custody*, 45 Ohio St. L.J. 455, 455-57. Two California studies of divorce cases, one of divorce cases in Marin County, the other in Santa Clara County, found joint custody being awarded in 18% and 13% of cases, respectively. *See* L. Weitzman, *supra* note 7, at 251.

9. The latest figures show that women in full-time employment earn on an average only 66.5% of what men earn. *See* Mellor, *Weekly Earnings in 1983: A Look at More Than 200 Occupations*, Monthly Lab. Rev., Jan. 1985, at 54, 55.

10. *See, e.g.,* Dick v. Dick, 147 Mich. App. 513, 383 N.W.2d 240 (1985) (in changing the physical custody of the children from the mother, who was moving out of state, to the father, the court emphasized the "extraordinary relationship" of the father with his children—a relationship based upon the father

shared, the father's child support payments should only reflect expenses incurred while the child is in the mother's physical custody, even though some expenses are fixed year-round and children may suffer a significant decline in their standard of living when living with the mother.[11] At the same time, many courts have been unable to adjust their expectations about the proper role of mothers in employment and in raising children. Courts easily ignore the career interests of mothers in making custody orders restricting the geographic location of the children to the place of the father's current employment.[12] And mothers may be penalized in custody hearings if they have not acted (or intend not to act) like dependent, full-time mothers.[13]

Where joint custody statutes lead courts to give fathers greater access to their children, some men use the opportunity to have more frequent contact with their former spouses to continue to control, and even abuse, them.[14] Such continued contact may disable some women from emerging from destructive and dependent relationships with their former husbands.

These and other unexpected consequences have propelled some feminists to attempt to win back or retain traditional female prerogatives in child-custody matters. Our purpose in this chapter is to examine the basis of this counterswing in feminist thinking. We shall look particularly at the connection between joint custody and the problem of women and dependency, a connection which is at the heart of the recent feminist critique of joint custody.

In an important sense, our focus on dependency as a problem for women regretfully reinforces a certain dominant hierarchy of values within relationships in which traits such as autonomy and domination are valued over vulnerability and interconnectedness. In fact, many of these qualities should be revalued rather than viewed as a problem for women. We nevertheless use the simplified terms, "independence" and "dependency," because they are familiar and because they capture some important aspects of women's subordination in our society. We assume that within the context of our present society, the aspect of a woman's dependency referring to her relationships that involve compulsion, even though assented to at some level by the woman and even though meeting a perceived need, is on the whole undesirable; conversely, we assume that the aspect of independence referring to the capacity and inclination of individuals to make choices unconstrained by such compulsion is desirable.[15] The definitions and normative meanings we give to these terms should become clearer as the chapter develops.

---

visiting every Wednesday and on alternating weekends, being a Cub Scout leader and Little League coach, taking his children to hockey practices and games, and participating in the children's religious instruction).

11. Hortis v. Hortis, 367 N.W.2d 633, 635-36 (Minn. Ct. App. 1985); Esposito v. Esposito, 351 N.W.2d 608, 610 (Minn. Ct. App. 1985).

12. *See generally* Spitzer, *Moving and Storage of Postdivorce Children: Relocation, the Constitution and the Courts*, 1985 Ariz. St. L.J. 1.

13. *See, e.g.*, Gulyas v. Gulyas, 75 Mich. App. 138, 254 N.W.2d 818 (1977) (In awarding a child to the father, the court notes the mother's career ambitions as a factor against her); Masek v. Masek, 89 S.D. 62, 228 N.W.2d 334 (1975) (a mother who lost custody to the father slept until 9 a.m. on Saturdays, failed to prepare breakfast for her husband who left for work at 7 a.m., and on occasion ran out of jam and cookies).

14. *See* Schulman & Pitt, *supra* note 8, at 555.

15. Albert Memmi carefully distinguishes dependency from subordination, stressing the consent of the dependent and the benefits received from dependency. A. Memmi, *Dependence: A Sketch for a Portrait of the Dependent* 5-6, 75-76, 80 (1984). We focus on dependency to take in those aspects of consent and benefit which are missing from the concept of subordination, but we emphasize the compulsory aspects of

Women, Power, and Dependency: Three Contexts

In this section, we examine three dependency relationships that are implicated by legal rules about child custody: (1) the relationship between women and their children; (2) the relationship between women and the men to whom they are or were formerly married; and (3) the relationship between women and the instruments of the state, notably courts, upon whom women may come to depend for enforcing their rights or interests against others. In each case, we find that the issue of women and dependency is more complicated than recognized by either traditional women's-rights analysis or the recent feminist critique of joint custody. Our analysis brings social class, ethnicity, and other variables into the debate and refocuses prior attempts to gener-alize situations of dependency. Once the debate is enlarged, it is apparent that custody rules that appear to create or enhance situations of dependency in one context may enhance the independence of women in other contexts. Moreover, even under similar circumstances, custody rules may have effects that simultaneously magnify and mini-mize the phenomenon of dependency.

Women and Children

One of the most salient aspects of women's dependency concerns their relationships to their children. Women attain self-definition, self-esteem, and power through their children. In so doing, however, women confine themselves to roles which deprive them of other sources of power and gratification. They become dependent upon those who are their only source of independence. Seeing the extent to which children are both a source of women's oppression and a source of their autonomy is pivotal to understanding the larger social context of the joint custody debate.

The nature of dependency relationships between women and children may vary widely between and across boundaries of class and race. Mothers and children who live in working-class ethnic neighborhoods or in many black urban and rural commu-nities, for example, are likely to be surrounded by a complex network of kin.[16] A long and well-documented history provides a portrait of a dynamic and large kinship unit, including both kin and fictive kin who assume responsibility for children.[17] Since the slavery era, black women have depended extensively on the energies and abilities of kin to care for and nurture their children while others were active participants in the workforce.[18] The elderly and young people—men as well as women—were primary caretakers for the babies and young children. A consciousness has developed from this experience which accepts both men and women as able parents and nurturers of children.[19] Although gender oppression exists in black communities, this conscious-

---

dependency relationships. It should be recognized, as Memmi does, that consent is often a highly problematic, strategic response to an oppressive situation. *Id.* at 4, 94-95. Memmi captures well the deep ambiguities in the concept of dependence, composed as it is of both compulsion and satisfaction, and bringing both happiness and misery. *Id.* at 80, 91, 99.

16. C. Stack, *All Our Kin: Strategies for Survival in a Black Country* 90-107 (1974).

17. *See* H. Gutman, *The Black Family in Slavery and Freedom, 1750-1925*, at 213-15; *see generally* E. Martin & J. Martin, *The Black Extended Family* (1978).

18. C. Stack, *supra* note 16, at 63, 88.

19. *Id.*

ness has prompted a relatively egalitarian view of the capability of both genders to raise young children.[20]

In their extended families, black women and other women of color do not necessarily depend on their children for their identity and security. Children and extended family life are more often seen as resources. This is partially because black children in extended families are not especially situated in a one-on-one relationship with their mothers. Further, many black women see the family as a refuge from institutional racism. It is part of a "culture of resistance"[21] in which family and community members across the lifecycle share resources, responsibilities for children, and access to them. Joint custody, for these women, would recognize patterns of childrearing that are already quite familiar.

By contrast, in the middle-class family model, childrearing is centralized in the nuclear family and monopolized by the mother. Mothering in middle-class nuclear families tends to isolate women and children from fathers, other kin, and the elderly.[22] This isolation is enhanced by divorce. For the middle-class mother, joint custody can dramatically reduce the role of children as a resource by lessening her control over family life and the bases for her identity. Here the dependency issue is very complex. Family life and children are a source of women's identities, and control over children in the home sphere may be the only meaningful power that some women experience.[23] Yet it is just this confinement to the home sphere that perpetuates women's dependence upon children, as well as upon the men that support them. Women whose economic, social, and psychological security is embedded in their children's dependency become in turn dependent upon their children. This kind of dependency can be a source of joy and exhilaration for women, but it can also be a source of their confinement and anger.

Joint custody may force women to give up some of the control and power they exercise over their children, and some of the autonomy and self-definition derived from their status as mothers, but it may also free them from a dependency which may stifle women as well as their children.[24] Joint custody may allow women, who during marriage were full-time mothers, to resume or commence job training, thereby attaining a new sense of identity and self-esteem. Employment is likely to make women more economically self-sufficient, at least in the long run.[25] At divorce, when

---

20. See Farkas, *Education, Wage Rates, and the Division of Labor Between Husband and Wife*, 38 J. Marriage & Fam. 473, 481 (1976) (younger black husbands spend more time at housework than do white husbands, and the presence of children induces an increase in the husband's housework).

21. This term is borrowed from M. Caulfield, *Imperialism, the Family and Cultures of Resistance*, in *Capitalism and the Family* 73 (1976).

22. E. Janeway, *Cross Sections from a Decade of Change* 65-67 (1982).

23. A. Rich, *Of Woman Born* 38 (1976); Ehrensaft, *When Women and Men Mother*, in *Mothering* 41, 49 (J. Trebilcot ed. 1984). See also R. Weiss, *Marital Separation* 171-72 (1975) (found that mothers perceive children as critical to their sense of value as a person after divorce).

24. Children after divorce may become victims of their mothers' dependency. For example, a child may be discouraged by the mother from spending a year with the father because of the impact such a change would have on the mother's financial situation. Children may also become power brokers in their mothers' lives, mediating relationships with others in the family with whom the mother may depend for emotional or financial support, or acting as spies or weapons in parental conflicts.

25. See Weitzman, *The Economics of Divorce: Social and Economic Consequences of Property, Alimony and Child Support Awards*, 28 UCLA L. Rev. 1181 (1981). Using statistics from Los Angeles County, Weitzman found that of the women who had sole custody of their children and depended completely on court-ordered support, 93% fell below the poverty line following divorce. Of the men who fully paid their child support obligations, 61% maintained an above intermediate-level income. *Id.* at 1239-40.

mothers typically are suffering from increased stress and responsibilities, joint custody may also be liberating psychologically, especially if implemented within a social ideology that treats joint custody as an acceptable alternative and not an expression of inadequacy on the part of women. Joint custody can enable women to pursue other interests and goals, which men have been able to do to a greater extent than women under traditional sole-custody arrangements.[26]

Women perceive a need to hold on to the sense of value derived from their traditional identity as nurturant and responsible mothers. Yet women's independence may rest on their ability to pursue other identities as well. On the one hand, giving up control over and dependency on children involves giving up what advantages women may have. On the other hand, not to give up constraining and self-limited relationships of dependency perpetuates a situation in which women obtain power and gratification only through these dependencies.

Women and Men

It is women's dependency on men that is the focus of the feminist critique of joint custody. Critics argue that joint custody statutes increase men's rights at divorce and their bargaining strength with respect to women, making women more vulnerable to claims and threats made by men.[27] Underlying this critique are the assumptions that women take more responsibility for their children than do men, love their children more than men do, and are more willing than men to sacrifice in order to retain custody of their children.[28] As a result, women will sacrifice their own financial rights, and even those of their children, in negotiations at divorce in order to preserve maximum custody of their children.[29] This distortion in bargaining at divorce occurs,

---

Women in different income classes may experience this drop in income more or less acutely. A study of divorced women in the Northeast showed that after divorce, the family income of women from the lowest income families fell 19%, while the family income of women from the highest income families dropped 60%. Koen, Brown, & Feldberg, *Divorced Mothers: The Costs and Benefits of Female Family Control*, in *Divorce and Separation* 234 (G. Levinger ed. 1979). In terms of relative economic disparity, which substantially affects the imbalance of power relationships, see Maret & Finlay, *The Distribution of Household Labor Among Women in Dual-Earner Families*, 46 J. Marriage & Fam. 357, 357 (1984), women from middle and higher income families may actually experience divorce from a greater position of dependency than women from lower class families.

The result of financial distress on divorced women and their children is dramatic. Women must often move to a less expensive neighborhood and accept low-paying jobs before being able to improve their skills. Weitzman, *supra*, at 1261-63.

26. See Hetherington, Cox, & Cox, *Divorced Fathers*, Fam. Coordinator, Oct. 1976, at 417, 420-22 (two months following divorce, fathers spend more time at work, in household maintenance, in solitary activities, and with friends than do mothers; one year after divorce, fathers are involved in programs of self improvement and in greatly increased social activity; there was a decline in later activities two years after divorce); Gasser & Taylor, *Role Adjustment of Single Parent Fathers With Dependent Children*, Fam. Coordinator, Oct. 1976, at 397.

27. See Schulman & Pitt, *supra* note 8, at 549, 554-55; Scott & Derdeyn, *supra* note 8, at 478.

28. Another way to articulate this assumption is that women are more risk-adverse than men about custody of their children. For a fuller discussion of the bargaining dynamics that would follow if one were to assume that women value custody of their children more highly than men, see Mnookin & Kornhauser, *Bargaining in the Shadow of the Law: The Case of Divorce*, 88 Yale L.J. 960, 979 (1979).

29. Schulman & Pitt, *supra* note 8, at 554-56, 559-60. In many cases, the competition for custody of the children may mask a continuing struggle for power within the marriage, whereby parents seek to protect themselves from the distress caused by the deteriorating relationship and to cast blame on each other for the divorce. See Scott & Derdeyn, *supra* note 8, at 493.

it is claimed, even if men do not really want joint custody of their children or do not intend to exercise their joint custody rights.[30]

Particular forms of joint custody provisions may disfavor women still further. For example, a "friendly parent" provision operates in sole-custody disputes to favor the parent who demonstrates the greater willingness to allow the other parent access to the children.[31] This rule may make it too risky for a woman to oppose a father's request for joint custody, even in justifiable circumstances, for to do so might imply that the mother is unwilling to permit the child the greatest access to both parents and thus is less suitable as a custodian. To avoid this implication, the woman may accept joint custody even when she feels it is in neither her nor her child's best interests.[32]

Some joint custody statutes relax the usual rule requiring a "substantial change of circumstances" when one party seeks to modify an exclusive custody order to one for joint custody.[33] Critics point out that with a lower standard for modifying sole-custody orders, a woman's former husband has more opportunity to intrude in her life. Potentially, the former husband could repeatedly challenge the woman's custodial status, perhaps ultimately wearing down her ability to defend that status.[34]

Joint custody awards themselves have additional implications for the dependency of women. Major decisions affecting the child must be made jointly by both parents who have joint legal custody, requiring discussion and collaboration between parents and creating opportunities for manipulation and the exercise of power by the stronger parent over the weaker. Where physical custody is equalized, frequent contacts between parents are likely, as children are transferred from one parent to the other. This contact permits the continuation of abusive entanglements, which may have been the reason the divorce was initiated. Thus, a spouse who was manipulated during the marriage will continue to be subject to influence and power after divorce. It is for this reason that some of the most vociferous opposition to joint custody legislation has come from representatives of battered women's groups.[35]

30. In fact, the greater the disparity in the value placed by the parties on custody, the greater is the bargaining advantage given to the party who values it less highly. *See* Scott & Derdeyn, *supra* note 8, at 477-80.

31. *See, e.g.,* Cal. Civ. Code § 4600(b)(1) (West Supp. 1986); Colo. Rev. Stat. § 14-10-124(1.5)(f) (Supp. 1985); Iowa Code Ann. § 598.41.3.e (West Supp. 1986); La. Civ. Code Ann. art. 146.A(2) (West Supp. 1986); Me. Rev. Stat. Ann. tit. 19, § 752.5H (Supp. 1986); Mich. Comp. Laws Ann. § 722.23(j) (West Supp. 1986); Mont. Code Ann. § 40-4-223(1)(b) (1985); Nev. Rev. Stat. § 125.480.3(a) (1985); 23 Pa. Cons. Stat. Ann. § 5303 (Purdon Supp. 1986).

32. Schulman & Pitt, *supra* note 8, at 554-56.

33. *See, e.g.,* Cal. Civ. Code § 4600.5(j) (West Supp. 1986); Colo. Rev. Stat. § 14-10-131.5(4) (Supp. 1985); Haw. Rev. Stat. § 571-46.1(d) (Supp. 1984); La. Civ. Code Ann. art. 146.F (West Supp. 1986); Nev. Rev. Stat. § 125.510.3 (1985); 23 Pa. Cons. Stat. Ann. § 5310 (Purdon Supp. 1986). As Schulman and Pitt point out, these provisions may apply only to modifications which seek joint custody, not those attempting to modify a joint custody order which is not working. Schulman & Pitt, *supra* note 8, at 563, *citing* Haw. Rev. Stat. § 571-46.1(d).

34. Schulman & Pitt, *supra* note 8, at 562-63.

35. *See, e.g.,* the veto message of Governor Carey, disapproving joint custody legislation requiring court approval of joint custody if agreed to by the parents, and requiring courts to consider joint custody if joint custody is in the child's best interests. According to then-Governor Carey, groups opposed to the legislation included the New York State Chapter of the National Organization for Women, the Women's Bar Association of the State of New York, the Coalition for Abused Women, Inc., the New York State Coalition Against Domestic Violence, Inc., the Center for Women's Rights, Inc., the New York Chapter of the American Academy of Matrimonial Lawyers, the Committee on the Family Court of the New York County Lawyers' Association, the Committee on Matrimonial Law of the Association of the Bar of the City of New York, the National Center on Women & Family Law, the Legal Aid Society, and the New York City Commission on the Status of Women. 8 Fam. L. Rep. (BNA) 4067 (Sept. 28, 1982).

This critique reflects an important social reality for women. Untold numbers of women are both financially and emotionally dependent upon their husbands. Women still bear the primary responsibility for care of the household and children. Many women with children are battered women; their children may also have been abused by their fathers. Moreover, untold numbers of women have been emotionally dependent upon their husbands. The gap between the knowledge that they must separate themselves from overbearing, manipulative, or abusive husbands and their ability to do so widens if custody arrangements force them to have continuing, sometimes frequent, contact with their former spouses.

This reality does not, however, reflect the social, economic, or cultural experience of all women. Analogous to the effects of race and class on women's dependency on children, women's dependency on men rests in part upon the particular contexts in which women find themselves. Women who envisaged a life devoted to childrearing and homemaking, with little or no labor force participation outside the home, whose identifies are entirely bound up in their primary caretaking functions, may be vulnerable to rules that lessen their chance of sole custody at divorce. Even these women, of course, may later come to believe that they have benefited from the consequences of joint custody. Moreover, women who have worked outside the home during marriage are already accustomed to some degree of sharing of familial tasks, including child care, by both parents.[36] Still other women may wish to become more independent or to pursue educational or professional interests after divorce, a goal facilitated by social networks and joint custodial fathers.[37] In communities where responsibility for raising children has been lodged in the immediate and extended kin group, including the father's kin, mothers already benefit from shared custody, functional through informal arrangements.[38]

The level of financial dependency on male support influences the subjective and objective experiences of women following divorce.[39] Low-income black women have historically participated in the labor force and assumed a provider role in their families.[40] Buttressed by extended kin and employment, however low-paying, they are less affected by divorce. However, low-income and middle-class women who were solely dependent on male providers during marriage suffer a substantial drop in income

---

36. Maret & Finlay, *supra* note 25, at 360; Pleck, *Men's Family Work: Three Perspectives and Some New Data*, Wellesley College Center for Research on Women Publications, vol. 2, art. 9, 15-17 (n.d.).

Not surprisingly, the most important variable in predicting wives' home responsibility is their relative economic contribution to the household. Kotkin, *Sex Roles Among Married and Unmarried Couples*, 9 Sex Roles 975, 980 (1983); Maret & Finlay, *supra* note 25, at 362. On the basis of their findings, Maret and Finlay conclude that "as men and women approximate equality in the workplace, they will move toward more egalitarian sharing of domestic responsibilities." *Id.*

Race was another significant correlate of household responsibility in the Maret and Finlay study, with working women in black families having relatively lower levels of home responsibility than white women. *Id.* at 361.

37. McKinnon & Wallerstein, *Joint Custody and the Preschool Child*, 4 Behav. Sci. & Law 169, 182 (1986).

38. C. Stack, *supra* note 16, at 50-54, 87-89.

39. Newman, *Symbolic Dialects and Generations of Women: Variations in the Meaning of Post-Divorce Mobility*, 13 Am. Ethnologist 230, 237-40 (1986).

40. B. Hooks, *Ain't I a Woman: Black Women and Feminism* 75, 82-83 (1981). It should be pointed out that the accord between the informal practice of joint custody in many black communities and the goals of joint custody is disrupted by the rules and regulations of our public welfare system.

following divorce,[41] which is often accompanied by a low rate of child support payments after the first year of divorce.[42] These women, despite their previous social positions, may find themselves more dependent on ex-husbands than their low-income counterparts who are embedded in the social networks of ethnic communities. Generational differences also explain differences in the subjective experiences of women following divorce.[43] All of these differences have been largely ignored by the generalized critique that joint custody harms women.

In sum, there is much that is valid in the critique of joint custody. However, joint custody has different consequences for women depending upon their particular situations of dependency. For many women, joint custody can have a liberating effect. In the last section we discuss how the oppressive aspects of joint custody may be limited without doing away with the beneficial role that joint custody might play in the lives of women.

Women and the State

The final piece of the dependency puzzle that we will address concerns women's dependency on the state. There are many aspects to this relationship, but the most important one in the recent critique of joint custody focuses on the role of courts in making and enforcing child-custody orders. It is argued that joint custody statutes abrogate the authority and integrity of courts by usurping their authority to make custody decisions in the best interests of children.[44] As we will show, however, this critique ignores the implications for increasing the dependence of women upon institutions and rules that perpetuate a hierarchical social structure in which women are confined to subordinate roles.

It should be noted first that most joint custody statutes merely provide joint custody as an explicit alternative to other more traditional forms of custody.[45]

---

41. Weiss, *The Impact of Marital Dissolution on Income and Consumption in Single-Parent Households*, 46 J. Marriage & Fam. 115, 126 (1984).

42. *See* Weitzman, *supra* note 25, at 1253-56 (Only one-third of one sample of divorced women reported regularly receiving the full amount of child support that they had been awarded). Even in Michigan, a state which has one of the best child support enforcement mechanisms, only 47% of fathers paid 90% or more of their support awards over a seven-year period ending in 1973. D. Chambers, *Making Fathers Pay* 77-78 (1979). Percentages vary along racial and ethnic lines. Reece, *Joint Custody: A Cautious View*, 16 U.C.D. L. Rev. 775, 781 (1983), *citing* U.S. Bureau of the Census, Current Population Reports: Divorce, Child Custody, and Child Support, Series P-23, Nos. 106-107 (1979). *See also supra* note 25.

43. Newman, *supra* note 39, at 246-48.

44. Schulman & Pitt, *supra* note 8, at 552. *See also* Lemon, *Joint Custody as a Statutory Presumption: California's New Civil Code Sections 4600 and 4600.5*, 11 Golden Gate U.L. Rev. 485, 498 (1981) (Quoting from the testimony of Professor Herma Hill Kay during consideration of joint custody legislation in California, who opposed a presumption in favor of joint custody unless both parents agreed to joint custody, because otherwise consideration of the children's best interests would be eliminated in favor of joint custody).

45. *See, e.g.*, Alaska Stat. § 25.20.060 (1983); Colo. Rev. Stat. § 14-10-124(5) (Supp. 1985); Haw. Rev. Stat. § 571-46.1 (Supp. 1984); Ind. Code Ann. § 31-1-11.5-21 (West Supp. 1986); Ky. Rev. Stat. Ann. § 503.270(3) (Michie/Bobbs-Merrill 1984); Mass. Gen. Laws Ann. ch. 208, § 31 (West Supp. 1986); Mo. Rev. Stat. § 452.375 (1986); N.C. Gen. Stat. § 50-13.2(b) (Supp. 1985); Okla. Stat. Ann. tit. 12, § 1275.4(B) (West Supp. 1987); Or. Rev. Stat. § 107.105 (1984); Tenn. Code Ann. § 36-6-101(a) (Supp. 1986); Wis. Stat. Ann. §§ 767.24(1)(a), (b) (West 1981).

In most states, a court must make specific findings indicating that joint custody is appropriate before it may be ordered. *See, e.g.*, Cal. Civ. Code § 4600.5(c) (West Supp. 1986); *In re B.T.S.*, 712 P.2d 1298 (Mont. 1986); N.M. Stat. Ann. § 40-4-9.1(I) (1986).

These statutes do not diminish, but, if anything, enlarge the scope of judicial authority.[46] Statutory joint custody preferences and presumptions limit the discretion or open-ended custody exploration of courts in certain ways. Statutes establishing a preference for joint custody require courts to consider joint custody;[47] others require courts to give reasons if joint custody is not awarded.[48] These statutes, however, do not prevent courts from reviewing custody agreements and ensuring that the interests of the child are best served. Even joint custody presumptions do not destroy the court's ability to protect children. Most presumptions in favor of joint custody operate only when parents have agreed to it[49] and even then may require courts to make findings in support of it.[50] Only Louisiana,[51] Florida,[52] and Idaho[53] have statutory presumptions in favor of joint custody which operate even if the parties have not agreed to it or if neither party requested it, and these presumptions can be overcome with evidence that joint custody is not in the child's best interests.[54]

It is puzzling that feminists argue that joint custody preferences or presumptions usurp the power of courts, for this argument assumes courts should be given more discretion, rather than less, to decide what is in the best interests of the child. This argument is inconsistent with the widely prevailing view of feminists that our courts already bring too much white, middle-class, male bias into custody deci-

---

46. In most states, the enactment of joint custody option statutes actually had little if any effect on the extent of judicial authority, for courts were free to order joint custody even in the absence of the express joint custody provision. See, e.g., Colo. Rev. Stat. § 14-10-124 (1973); Haw. Rev. Stat. § 571-46 (1976); Me. Rev. Stat. Ann. tit. 19, § 214 (1981); Minn. Stat. Ann. § 518.17 (West 1969). But see Ind. Code § 31-1-11.5-21 (1980), construed in Cradic v. Cradic, 544 S.W.2d 605 (Mo. Ct. App. 1976) (Mandated that custody be given to one parent or the other).

47. See, e.g., Ill. Ann. Stat. ch. 40 ¶ 602.1(b) (Smith-Hurd Supp. 1986) (upon application of either or both parents); Iowa Code Ann. § 598.41.2 (West Supp. 1986) (upon application of either parent); Mass. Gen. Laws Ann. ch. 208, § 31 (West Supp. 1986).

48. See, e.g., Cal. Civ. Code § 4600.5 (West Supp. 1986) (if either parent requests joint custody); Conn. Gen. Stat. Ann. § 46b-56a(b) (West Supp. 1986) (where parents have agreed); Idaho Code § 32-717B (1983); Iowa Code Ann. § 598.41.2 (West Supp. 1986) (if either parent has made application for joint custody); Kan. Stat. Ann. § 60-1610(a)(4)(A) (West Supp. 1985); Me. Rev. Stat. Ann. tit. 19, § 752.6 (Supp. 1986) (if parents have agreed to joint custody); Mich. Comp. Laws Ann. § 722.26a(1) (West Supp. 1986) (if either parent has requested joint custody); Mont. Code Ann. § 40-4-224(1) (1985) (if either or both parents has requested joint custody). See also Mass. Gen. Laws Ann. ch. 208, § 31 (Supp. 1986) ("Where the parents have reached an agreement providing for the custody of the children, the court may enter an order in accordance with such agreement, unless specific findings are made by the justice indicating that such an order would not be in the best interests of the children").

49. See, e.g., Cal. Civ. Code § 4600.5(a) (West Supp. 1986); Conn. Gen. Stat. Ann. § 46b-56a(b) (West Supp. 1986); Me. Rev. Stat. Ann. tit. 19, § 752.6 (Supp. 1986); Miss. Code Ann. § 93-5-24(4) (Supp. 1986); Nev. Rev. Stat. § 125.490 (1985). See also Mont. Code Ann. § 40-4-224(1) (1985) (presumption in favor of joint custody if either or both parents apply for it); N.H. Rev. Stat. Ann. §§ 458:17.II(a), (b) (Supp. 1985) (if both parties have agreed or upon application of either party); N.M. Stat. Ann. § 40-4-9.1(A), (D) (1985) (in an initial custody determination or when both parents agree).

50. See Cal. Civ. Code § 4600.5(c) (West Supp. 1986).

51. La. Civ. Code Ann. art. 146.C (West Supp. 1986).

52. Fla. Stat. Ann. § 61.13(2)(b)2 (West 1985).

53. Idaho Code § 32-717B(4) (1983). See also N.M. Stat. Ann. §§ 40-4-9.1(A), (D) (1986) (presumption either where both parents agree or in initial custody determination).

54. See, e.g., Turner v. Turner, 455 So. 2d 1374, 1380 (La. 1984) (when parents "lack completely any spirit of cooperation, and a continued joint custody arrangement would serve only to stunt the development of these children," the presumption in favor of joint custody has been rebutted); see also Elebash v. Elebash, 450 So. 2d 1268, 1270 (Fla. Dist. Ct. App. 1984) (holding that "shared parental responsibility statute does not eliminate, or limit, the trial court's discretion to provide for the best interest and welfare of children," including overturning parental agreement on joint custody).

sions,[55] a more particularized version of the generally accepted understanding that the unfettered "best interests" test gives too much play to the predispositions of individual judges and allows them to make findings based solely upon their own experience and bias.[56]

It seems apparent that the judicial integrity objection to joint custody springs less from a concern with preserving judicial discretion per se than from an objection to the particular limitations being imposed on that discretion. At least in this century, women have generally expected and have obtained sole custody of their children at divorce. The assumption of the judicial integrity argument is that women need the special protection of the state, acting through the courts, to protect their interests. This objection, which is revealed most starkly in recent efforts to resuscitate the gender-based "tender years" or "maternal preference" doctrine,[57] seems to suggest that women should be left dependent upon the courts to apply rules and standards that give women an advantage over men in custody proceedings.

Many efforts have been made to define the best interests test so as to give child-custody decisions some coherence and consistency. Thus, in applying the best interests test, courts within a state have tended to agree on a composite of narrowing criteria that are considered relevant to a child's best interests. It is generally accepted, for example, that a child's best interests are served more by a nurturing than by a cold, unfeeling caretaker;[58] by one who uses reasonable discipline more than by one who lets the child do just as she pleases[59] or who physically abuses the child;[60] by one who is mentally stable more than by one who is mentally unstable;[61] by one who has time to spend with the child more than by one who does not;[62] by one who has cared continuously and regularly for the child in the past more than by one whose contact

---

55. *See, e.g.,* Sheppard, *Unspoken Premises in Custody Litigation,* 7 Women's Rts. L. Rep. 229, 233 (1982); Uviller, *Fathers' Rights and Feminism: The Maternal Presumption Revisited,* 1 Harv. Women's L.J. 107, 121-26 (1978); P. Chesler, *Mothers on Trial: The Battle for Children and Custody* 239-68 (1978). Examples of such bias include custody decisions in which economic resources (which tend to be higher for males) and remarriage (which is also higher for males than for females) have been influential. Polikoff, *Why Are Mothers Losing: A Brief Analysis of Criteria Used in Child Custody Determinations,* 7 Women's Rts. L. Rep. 235, 237-39, 241 (1982). To further her claim of male bias, Polikoff states that while women are discriminated against in custody decisions for having fewer economic resources, they are also penalized when they leave the home to take jobs to improve their economic positions, since they are then not as accessible to their children as it is thought they should be. *Id.* at 239. Whether or not this bias exists, or would exist without the built-in momentum in favor of custody to women, women continue to obtain custody in the large majority of child custody cases. L. Weitzman, *supra* note 7, at 501-05. This appears to be the case even where men contest custody. The Phear study showed that maternal requests for sole custody were realized twice as often as paternal requests. Phear, Beck, Hauser, Clark, & Whitney, *An Empirical Study of Custody Arrangements: Joint Versus Sole Legal Custody,* in *Joint Custody and Shared Parenting* 144, 152 (J. Folberg ed. 1984).

56. *See* Mnookin, *supra* note 4, at 263. *See also* Reece, *supra* note 49, at 777 (Judges decide custody cases on basis of personal bias or conviction).

57. *See, e.g.,* Klaff, *The Tender Years Doctrine: A Defense,* 70 Calif. L. Rev. 335 (1982); Uviller, *supra* note 55.

58. *See, e.g., In re Marriage of Bowen,* 219 N.W.2d 683, 689 (Iowa 1974).

59. *See, e.g., Leo v. Leo,* 213 N.W.2d 495, 497 (Iowa 1973).

60. *See, e.g., In re Marriage of Cotton,* 103 Ill. 2d 346, 469 N.E.2d 1077 (1984); *Miller v. Parker,* 53 Ala. App. 312, 299 So. 2d 754 (1974).

61. *See, e.g., Huehn v. Huehn,* 103 A.D.2d 884, 477 N.Y.S.2d 1010 (1984).

62. *See, e.g., Modling v. Modling,* 232 So. 2d 673, 675 (Ala. 1970); *Lovett v. Lovett,* 164 N.W.2d 793, 803 (Iowa 1969).

with the child has been intermittent or irregular;[63] by one who offers the child a stable home life more than by one who moves frequently or whose home life is chaotic.[64] Each of these preferences is an expression of, and a limitation on, the best interests test.

A joint custody preference, similar to criteria used to select who is the better sole custodian, helps to better define what is in the child's best interests by creating a non-arbitrary priority as to the type of custodial arrangement. A custody presumption further narrows the otherwise open-ended best interests standard. Specific criteria will always limit the influence of the judge's individual predispositions; the question is whether these limitations faithfully translate into a sound policy.[65]

Critics also point to the higher likelihood that joint custody preferences will coerce women into accepting custody arrangements that are unsatisfactory to them and not beneficial to children.[66] This criticism also seems misdirected. Even if it was shown to be true that women settle more custody disputes out of court because of statutory joint custody preferences, there is little basis upon which to conclude that courts make better child-custody decisions for women, even after full and fair hearings, than the parties can make for themselves. On the whole, we should expect that negotiations are superior to court hearings. Parties know their circumstances far better than courts can discern after lengthy hearings. Moreover, the now-traditional wisdom that parents and children suffer a heavy toll from litigating custody disputes in adversarial hearings has not been seriously challenged.[67] Resolution through negotiation does permit behind-the-scenes manipulation, but this manipulation is not absent from costly courtroom proceedings,[68] nor is it limited to cases involving joint custody.[69] Finally, as we explain in the following sections, manipulation and other

---

63. *See, e.g.*, Garska v. McCoy, 278 S.E.2d 357 (W. Va. 1981) (establishing primary caretaker presumption); Van Dyke v. Van Dyke, 48 Or. App. 965, 618 P.2d 465 (1980); Commonwealth *ex rel.* Jordan v. Jordan, 302 Pa. Super. 421, 426, 448 A.2d 1113, 1115 (1982); Weatherly v. Weatherly, 330 N.W.2d 890, 892 (Minn. 1983).

64. *See, e.g.*, McCann v. McCann, 270 Pa. Super. 171, 174-75, 411 A.2d 234, 236 (1979); Durrette v. Durrette, 288 S.E.2d 432, 434-35 (Va. 1982). *See generally* Uniform Marriage and Divorce Act 402, 9A U.L.A. 197-98 (1979) (requiring courts to consider all relevant factors, including: "The interaction and interrelationship of the child with his parent or parents, his siblings, and any other person who may significantly affect the child's best interest . . . the child's adjustment to his home, school, and community . . . and the mental and physical health of all individuals involved").

65. Scott and Derdeyn evaluate child custody laws according to their "definition costs" (the costs associated with the application of a criterion that does not faithfully promote the underlying legal objective), and their "application costs" (costs associated with the difficulty of applying a particular criterion). Scott & Derdeyn, *supra* note 8, at 463-71. They conclude that joint custody preferences have low definition costs, but high application costs when joint custody is given a favored legal status. *Id.* at 469-77, 496-98.

66. *See* Schulman & Pitt, *supra* note 8, at 555, 559; Scott & Derdeyn, *supra* note 8, at 474-77. *But see* Reece, *supra* note 42, at 776 (criticizing joint custody presumption because it intrudes on private decision making); Neely, *The Primary Caretaker Rule: Child Custody and the Dynamics of Greed*, 3 Yale L. & Soc. Pol'y 168 (1984) (Individualized rules of decision making prompt "sinister bargaining").

67. *But see* Melton & Lind, *Procedural Justice in Family Court: Does the Adversary Model Make Sense?*, in *Legal Reforms Affecting Child and Youth Services* 65, 73-77 (G.B. Melton ed. 1982) (argued that the divorce rather than the adversary process is what upsets children, and that children may benefit from the adversary process).

68. *See* Neely, *supra* note 66, at 173-74, 186 (Described sham battle of experts in custody disputes that are really about money).

69. *See* L. Weitzman, *supra* note 7, at 228-29, 242-43 (described manipulation of children and of parties in disputes under the former sole-custody regime in California); Foster & Freed, *Law and the Family: Politics of Divorce Process—Bargaining Leverage, Unfair Edge*, N.Y. L.J., July 11, 1984, at 1, col. 1, 6, col. 1.

abusive practices can be more directly attenuated by means other than eliminating joint custody preferences.

Critics of joint custody have shown that women's rights advocates were naive in believing joint custody would revolutionize gender roles in parenting. Yet the argument that joint custody should be rejected because it aggravates the dependency and oppression of women is incomplete and unsatisfactory. It assumes a "common oppression" of women which, as Bell Hooks puts it, "disguis[es] and mystif[ies] the true nature of women's varied and complex social reality."[70] Because differences in race, social class, generation, and other background factors all affect how women view family and kin ties and the degree to which women accept oppression and dependence as a natural occurrence, any analysis of the effects of joint custody laws based solely upon its impact on women is necessarily inconclusive.

An alternative, or supplementary, approach to analyzing joint custody laws focuses on ideology. At the heart of how women respond to their various situations of dependency are the ideologies they acquire as they do so. Ideologies are also important in how men define their own roles with respect to their children and to the women in their lives. These ideologies emerge from the experiences of men and women and are as various as these experiences can be. In addition, these ideologies become the filter through which experiences are interpreted. Thus, insofar as law influences ideology, it may not only have specific, concrete effects on a woman's life, but also provide input into the ideological framework that affects how she interprets those concrete effects. In the next section, we turn from our examination of the more immediate, and varied, effects of joint custody laws to the more long-range, and perhaps predictable, ideological consequences.

Law, Ideology, and Social Change

Feminist critics of joint custody have focused on the concrete and immediate effects of joint custody laws. These critics have ignored another critical feature of the law: its expressive or symbolic power to alter social expectations and norms.[71] If meaningful social change is a goal, the messages conveyed within the law about how men and women should participate in the raising of their children cannot be overlooked. Women, in the long run, cannot depend upon the enforcement of laws to ensure that those with whom they share intimate relations deal with them fairly. They must depend ultimately upon changes in attitudes about social and family roles.

The power of the law to reinforce existing norms and expectations that lie at the root of social reality is widely accepted.[72] The dynamics of law in changing social

---

70. B. Hooks, *Feminist Theory: From Margin to Center* 44 (1984).

71. Gusfield, *Moral Passages: The Symbolic Process in Public Designation of Deviance*, 15 Soc. Probs. 175, 177 (1967); Ball & Friedman, *The Use of Criminal Sanctions in the Enforcement of Economic Legislation: A Sociological View*, 17 Stan. L. Rev. 197, 220-21 (1965).

72. In invalidating state laws and practices that were based at least in part on assumptions about proper sex roles, courts have recognized the power of law to perpetuate stereotypes. *See, e.g.*, Mississippi University of Women v. Hogan, 458 U.S. 718, 730 (1982); Orr v. Orr, 440 U.S. 268, 283 (1979); Califano v. Goldfarb, 430 U.S. 199, 217 (1977); Stanton v. Stanton, 421 U.S. 7, 14-15 (1975).

ideologies are more complicated and far from clear.[73] There is empirical evidence linking legal reforms to changes in behaviors and, ultimately, social attitudes. In a number of areas, it has been shown that as certain behaviors are compelled, they become routine and institutionalized until individuals who were initially resistant to the compelled behavior become psychologically committed to the assumptions underlying it and develop attitudes and beliefs in support of the behavior.[74] This process is far from complete in the area of race relations, and some of the same factors explaining resistance to nondiscriminatory racial attitudes exist with respect to gender-role attitudes as well.[75] This does not mean, however, that meaningful changes in these attitudes are not possible. It may begin with the most blatant stereotyped attitudes about appropriate gender roles in childrearing. More gradually, the deeper, internal beliefs and assumptions upon which more subtle attitudes are based hopefully will be affected.

We do not mean to overemphasize the yield from legal reform. Changes in the law, alone, are not likely to produce gender-based equality.[76] However, an end to the

---

73. A number of factors appear to affect the relationship between law and social change, including the type of law, Chambliss, *Types of Deviance and the Effectiveness of Legal Sanctions,* 1967 Wis. L. Rev. 703; the nature of the habits and customs sought to be changed, Zimring & Hawkins, *The Legal Threat as an Instrument of Social Change,* in *Law, Justice and the Individual in Society* 60, 62-63 (J. Tapp & F. Levine eds. 1977); and the extent to which the new law is consistent with prevailing public norms, Rose, *Sociological Factors in the Effectiveness of Projected Legislative Remedies,* 11 J. Legal Educ. 470, 472-73 (1959); H. Rodgers & C. Bullock, *Law and Social Change: Civil Rights Laws and Their Consequences* 185-86 (1972); Zimring & Hawkins, *supra* at 64. Other factors include the extent to which the law is seen to be violated, Berkowitz & Walker, *Laws and Moral Judgments,* 30 Sociometry 410, 422 (1967); and the extent to which the law is seen to be unfair, Ball, *Social Structure and Rent-Control Violations,* 65 Amer. J. Soc. 598 (1960), *reprinted in Law and the Behavioral Sciences* 198-99 (L. Friedman & S. Macaulay 2d ed. 1977). Personality differences may account for differences in people's reactions to legal control, Berkowitz & Walker, *supra* at 419, 422, as do their particular life situations, Andenaes, *Deterrence and Specific Offenses,* 38 U. Chi. L. Rev. 537 (1971).

74. S. Vago, *Law and Society* 261-62 (1981); T. Pettigrew, *Racially Separate or Together?* 278-81 (1971); Ball & Friedman, *supra* note 92, at 220-21. This phenomenon is explained in psychological theory as a response to "cognitive dissonance," whereby people's attitudes adjust to conform to behaviors that are compelled in order to eliminate the dissonance between the two. *See* Festinger & Carlsmith, *Cognitive Consequences of Forced Compliance,* 58 J. Abnormal Psychology 203 (1959); *see also* W. Muir, *Prayer in the Public Schools: Law and Attitude Change* 7-8 (1967) (describing the "conversion hypothesis").

Motivations for initially complying with the law vary, some people responding to the threat of punishment or social disapproval, others to a general belief that the law ought to be obeyed. *See* T. Pettigrew, *supra* at 280; S. Vago, *supra* at 253-56. In some cases, individuals are let "off-the-hook" by laws which require of them conduct towards which they themselves may have been inclined but which was discouraged by conflicting social norms. T. Pettigrew, *supra* at 280; W. Muir, *supra* at 8-9 (describing the "liberating hypothesis" of the effect of law on social change).

75. Thomas Pettigrew has concluded that while gross stereotypes and blatant race discrimination have been eliminated in accordance with these patterns, changed behavior has not been accompanied by full internalization of nondiscriminatory attitudes, in part because inadequate interracial environments exist to reinforce the new behavioral expectations. Pettigrew, *New Patterns of Racism: The Different Worlds of 1984 and 1964,* 37 Rutgers L. Rev. 673 (1985). This observation suggests that the institutionalization process attempted by legal change has not been entirely successful in the area of race relations. *See also* S. Vago, *supra* note 74, at 262. In a thoughtful essay, Sally Lloyd-Bostock questions both the process of movement from responses to imposed law to internalization of norms, and the relationship between ·internalized norms and actual behavior. Lloyd-Bostock, *Explaining Compliance with Imposed Law,* in *The Imposition of Law* 9, 13, 15 (S. Burman & B. Harrell-Bond eds. 1979). To an important extent, however, her observations point to the subtlety and complexity of the process of internalization rather than to the conclusion that the phenomenon does not actually occur. One does not need to believe that the process of internalization is ever complete, to believe that attitudes may shift as a result of behaviors, and that behaviors may become more automatic as a result of attitude shifts.

76. *See* Law, *Rethinking Sex and the Constitution,* 132 U. Pa. L. Rev. 955, 956 (1984) ("The judicial enforcement of constitutional norms, even when broadly conceived and applied, is not likely to produce sex-based equality"); Williams, *Equality's Riddle: Pregnancy and the Equal Treatment/Special Treatment*

law's complicity in inequalitarian norms may be a precondition of reform[77] and even a catalyst for it.[78]

Even if it could be assumed that the state can influence social norms through its custody laws, one might question whether it is appropriate for the state to try to do so. Does not this effort suggest imposing a majoritarian social order in the most "private" of spheres that will contribute to a conformity at least as repressive as the current dominant social ideology of gender-differentiated roles? We generally prefer to think of the state as neutral in these matters, allowing parents the freedom to choose diverse lifestyles, including the allocation of childrearing responsibilities. Will custody rules designed to promote shared parenting harm our tradition of social and cultural diversity and individual lifestyle choices?

Underlying these questions is an assumption that somehow the state *can* be neutral. This assumption is highly questionable. Custody questions, in particular, involve standards that may imply judgments about previous parental conduct or predictions about what will be in the best interests of the children in the future. These standards necessarily involve judgments about the desired qualities of parents and the kind of upbringing children should have. Whatever these particular judgments might be, they can hardly be "neutral."

A number of custody rules have been advanced on the basis of their supposed neutrality. Some critics of joint custody, for example, have urged that custody decisions be made on a case-by-case basis, whereby each party has the burden of demonstrating that the particular custody arrangement she or he advocates is in the best interests of the child.[79] This approach is neutral on its face. However, in its application it would operate within the well-entrenched norms under which parenting roles are assigned by sex. Judges applying this rule would be inclined to reflect dominant social norms, which assume that women are the more appropriate primary guardian of their children, at least so long as they continue to act as mothers should act.[80]

A feminist might attempt to justify a best interests, case-by-case approach on the grounds that an approach that helps women win custody battles is better than another approach that does not.[81] This argument responds directly to the concern about the

---

Debate, 13 N.Y.U. Rev. L. & Soc. Change 325, 374 (1984-85) (anti-discrimination provision sets parameters of operation but cannot do "the basic job of readjusting the social order").

Berkowitz and Walker report studies showing that peer opinions are more responsible for modifying moral judgments than changes in the law. Berkowitz & Walker, *supra* note 73, at 418.

77. *Cf.* Taub & Schneider, *Perspectives on Women's Subordination and the Role of Law*, in *The Politics of Law* 117, 124 (D. Kairys ed. 1982) ("Because the law purports to be the embodiment of justice, morality and fairness, it is particularly effective in performing [the ideological function of camouflaging the fundamental injustice of existing sexual relations]").

78. Levine, *Methodological Concerns in Studying Supreme Court Efficacy*, 4 Law & Soc'y Rev. 583, 592 (1970).

79. *See, e.g.*, Schulman & Pitt, *supra* note 8, at 551-53; Scott & Derdeyn, *supra* note 8, at 496-98; Testimony of Edith Swerdlow, Joint Custody and Child Support, Hearing of California Assembly Committee on Judiciary, Oct. 14, 1981, at 72-77 (copy on file).

80. *See* Polikoff, *supra* note 55; cases cited *supra* note 13.

81. *Cf.* C. MacKinnon, *Sexual Harassment of Working Women: A Case of Sex Discrimination* 117 (1979) (policy or practice should constitute unconstitutional sex discrimination if it "integrally contributes to the maintenance of an underclass or a deprived position because of gender status"); Olsen, *Statutory Rape: A Feminist Critique of Rights*, 63 Tex. L. Rev. 387, 430 (1984) (urged a direct call "for what we really want" instead of trying to fit goals into rights arguments); Freedman, *Sex Equality, Sex Differences, and the Supreme Court*, 92 Yale L.J. 913, 961-64 (1983) (sex equality should be defined on the basis of an "explicitly normative theory").

short-term costs of joint custody to some women who would have gained sole custody under former custody rules, but it is highly problematic as an approach that is "good for women." As we stated earlier, women's interests cannot be collapsed into one formula. In the short term, a near guarantee of custody of one's children may be thought to be victory for women, but in supporting an ideology that mothers more than fathers should devote themselves to the care and custody of their children, this approach itself draws on traditional stereotypes that are easily perpetuated by sole-custody decisions. These stereotypes confirm that women usually will (read, *should*) take primary responsibility for the caretaking of children. Neutrality in this context is a facade, describing how things are regardless of what better state of affairs one might imagine.[82]

Other commentators have urged adoption of the primary caretaker presumption, which seeks to give the parent who has had primary caretaking responsibilities for the child exclusive custody at divorce.[83] This presumption also illustrates the folly of attempted neutrality. It makes no assumptions about the gender of the family childrearer and for that reason appears to be a neutral child-custody rule. However, in accepting unaltered the norm that there be *one* primary caretaker and *one* primary breadwinner, it leaves untouched a non-neutral and discriminatory reality. Thus, while a few men may win custody under the standard, traditional family patterns and expectations (which are unaffected by the presumption) for the most part will continue to assure that the woman is the caretaker. A primary caretaker assumption thereby plays into and perpetuates patterns by which one parent (read, *the mother*) continues to be primarily responsible for the care of the children.

The choice, then, is not between joint custody and a neutral rule but between custody rules that reflect different ideologies and have different effects. Evaluating effects is difficult, as we have shown above, because of differences in the contexts in which custody rules are applied; but it is certainly not clear that the effects of rules favoring joint custody, applied in appropriate circumstances, are appreciably harder on women than those that follow from the application of traditional custody rules.

From the point of view of ideology, rules favoring joint custody seem clearly preferable. Joint custody stakes out ground for an alternative norm of parenting. Unlike the "neutral" best interests test or a primary caretaker presumption, these rules promote the affirmative assumption that both parents should, and will, take important roles in the care and nurturing of their children. This assumption is essential to any

---

82. *Cf.* Gordon, *New Developments in Legal Theory*, in *The Politics of Law*, *supra* note 101, at 281, 286 (described Antonio Gramsci's concept of hegemony, in which the oppressor maintains control by successfully projecting his view of social reality on the oppressed, assisted by principles of neutrality, so that "both the dominant and dominated classes believe that the existing order, with perhaps some marginal changes, is satisfactory, or at least represents the most that anyone could expect, because things pretty much have to be the way they are").

The conclusion that a "simple" best interests standard perpetuates custody by mothers was borne out in the California experience when the maternal presumption rule was changed to a best interests standard in 1973 with virtually no effect on the incidence of awards to mothers. *See* L. Weitzman, *supra* note 7, at 231-32. Professor Weitzman in her study of the effect of changes in custody law on custody awards found that even after the change in the law, judges still considered mothers to be, as a general matter, the best custodians of children. *Id.* at 235-36.

83. *See, e.g.*, Chambers, *supra* note 3; Neely, *supra* note 66; Polikoff, *supra* note 55, at 237. *See also* Garska v. McCoy, 278 S.E.2d 357 (W. Va. 1981).

realistic reshaping of gender roles within parenthood. Only when it is expected that men as well as women will take a serious role in childrearing will traditional patterns in the division of childrearing responsibilities begin to be eliminated in practice as well as in theory. Only with this transformation in the attitudes of men and women about parenting roles will it be possible to say that parents make a genuine choice in how they allocate childrearing responsibilities.

What about the father who has not had his consciousness reformed and who has not played an active role in raising his children during the marriage? If we support custody laws that allow men to "win" joint custody at divorce when they have played only a minimal role in their children's lives before divorce, will we not unfairly reward "undeserving" fathers? Will we not miss an opportunity to give them an incentive to participate more in childrearing during marriage? Is not exactly the wrong message conveyed to parents if the "rights" of fathers to their children at divorce are not contingent upon having been active as parents during marriage?

These troubling questions bring us back to a consideration of the alternative approaches to understanding the effect of law on social behavior. If one views the relationship between law, social norms and practices as one of incentives and rewards, carrots and sticks, and sees the results of the application of legal rules solely in terms of legal entitlements or "rights," it might seem as if fathers who have not assumed equal parenting responsibilities should not have equal custodial rights at divorce. Even from this perspective, it is doubtful that "incentives" to share equally in parenting responsibilities would work in the context of marriage where, despite statistics to the contrary, couples rarely contemplate that they themselves will divorce and disagree about the custody of their children.

If one is concerned with changing attitudes as well as behavior, however, there are good reasons to emphasize the expressive function of law over its coercive function. To change legal consciousness—that body of accepted principles around which ordinary people conform their conduct, usually voluntarily—the law should be a more powerful force when it expresses the ideal and assumes desired conduct, than when it attempts to create incentives to coerce behavior that is assumed to be involuntary. Arrangements such as joint custody may be coerced, nudging parties who would not otherwise have chosen it to implement it. But the attitudes that make it work depend on more subtle influences.

The message, "You, father, will not have joint access to your children after divorce if you have not functioned as a father before the divorce," focuses on the rights of the father, clearly informing him that his entitlements as father are contingent upon his prior conduct. Co-parenthood, under this formulation, will depend upon having earned it.

In contrast, the message, "You, father, have a role to play in your children's lives which is to participate actively in their upbringing and assume day-to-day responsibility for them jointly with their mother, and you will do so after the marriage even if you do not do so during the marriage," creates a norm which is not contingent. This message asserts a moral imperative of nurturing responsibility for children, not a set of "rights" that can be earned (or declined). The desired norm is strengthened by its lack of contingency and by the fact that desired role redefinitions persist despite participants' not "deserving" the benefits of co-parenthood.

Another reason for favoring a strong, non-contingent norm concerns the attitude parents bring to the custody battle itself. A rights-oriented "I deserve it" mentality often infects custody battles, encouraging parents to turn their focus away from their commitment to their children. De-emphasis of earned "rights" subordinates individual entitlements to the needs of others for commitments of responsibility. This de-emphasis, which is consistent with some of the positive values of the women's tradition, ultimately benefits both women and children.

To summarize, the structure of law matters in the formation of ideologies relating to gender roles, in how women confront these situations of dependency, and in how others in turn respond to women who resist playing the roles established for them in the dominant ideologies. The law cannot remain neutral in deciding what ideology to promote. The law may either support hegemonic ideologies or help to reshape them, and the role it adopts is significant in shaping people's expectations and how they approach their relationships with other people. Changes in the law may become part of a reformed legal ideology, and such reform is essential to true and persisting social change.

In urging laws that favor women, feminists necessarily confront some of the fundamental ideological dilemmas of feminist theory and politics, including the dilemma of dependency. Women seek the removal of barriers imposed upon them in order to become equals but sometimes feel they need "special treatment" in order to reach this goal. Egalitarian norms such as those represented in joint custody statutes enhance a climate in which attitudes about parenting may move in the direction of greater sharing, but they make women in some situations of dependency not more equal but more vulnerable to increased exploitation. Another aspect of the dependency dilemma relates to the normative contradictions in the concept of dependency. Women seek independence and the freedom to direct their destinies freed from the traditional roles that have been thrust upon them. Yet they do not want to shed entirely those "female" traits traditionally associated with the ability and inclination to act as the primary, nurturing parent.[84] It would be a shame if greater "independence," such as that which may follow from shared parenting norms, causes women to move from dependency on men and dependency *within* male ideologies, to dependency *upon* male norms of independence and autonomy.

In assessing the issue of joint custody, the dependency dilemma must be faced head-on and resolved for our time; it cannot be resolved by simply ignoring half of the dilemma. Social justice cannot be achieved either by pretending that men and women are already equals in society or by assuming that they never can be. Moreover, efforts to achieve these ideals should not be wholly abandoned because of the risk of absorbing some of the undesirable characteristics associated with "male" values of independence and autonomy; we must have some optimism that feminist values,

---

84. *See generally* Karst, *Woman's Constitution,* 1984 Duke L.J. 447; C. Gilligan, *In a Different Voice* (1982); Feral, *The Powers of Difference,* in *The Future of Difference* 88 (H. Eisenstein & A. Jardine eds. 1980).

rather than inevitably succumbing to more powerful and sinister forces, are strong enough to transform those influences.

Implementing Joint Custody

Critics of joint custody have pointed to a number of inequities in how joint custody has been implemented. For the most part, these inequities are not inevitable and can be alleviated, if not eliminated, by adopting implementation rules that take account of circumstances of abuse or unfairness.

Custody rules that force a choice between able parents perpetuate the current role identification of women and childrearing. We favor the promotion of joint custody even when both parents do not at the outset agree to such an arrangement. Although it cannot be said that court-initiated joint custody will alone reverse the negative attitudes parents may have toward one another or the rights-oriented mentality described above,[85] there are some indications that parents who are initially resistant to a joint custody arrangement will adjust to that arrangement if ordered to do so by a court. Several experts suggest that shared-custody arrangements ordered by courts in highly acrimonious divorces are often eventually worked out reasonably well to the benefit of the children.[86] Improved models for and availability of custody counseling may lead to even more promising results in this area.[87]

Where certain circumstances make joint custody impractical or put women at an unfair disadvantage, rules should exist which direct judges to reject that alternative. For example, joint custody ordinarily should not be ordered where physical abuse has taken place or is threatened. The threat of violence is not only harmful to the woman

---

85. The link between court-initiated joint custody and cooperative attitudes needs further study. Studies of comparative relitigation rates between cases where joint custody is awarded and cases where sole custody is awarded, while promising on the surface, fail to control for sufficient variables to support the conclusions of the researchers. Ilfeld, Ilfeld, & Alexander, *Does Joint Custody Work? A First Look at Outcome Data of Relitigation*, 1983 Ann. Progress Child Psychiatry & Dev. 545; Phear, Beck, Hauser, Clark & Whitney, *supra* note 55, at 151, 153-55.

Similarly, authority establishing that fathers involved in custody arrangements involving frequent contact with their children are far more likely to pay child support than those who are not, does not support the existence of any causal link between custody arrangements and child-support compliance. *See, e.g.,* Wallerstein & Huntington, *Bread and Roses: Nonfinancial Issues Related to Fathers' Economic Support of Their Children Following Divorce,* in *The Parental Child Support Obligation: Research, Practice and Social Policy* 135, 143-45 (J. Cassetty ed. 1983); Furstenberg, Nord, Peterson, & Zill, *The Life Course of Children of Divorce: Marital Disruption and Parental Contact,* 48 Am. Soc. Rev. 656, 665 Table 7 (1983); D. Chambers, *supra* note 42, at 127-29. Pearson and Thoennes, in their study, found specifically that although fathers with joint custody do a better job of paying child support than those without joint custody, these differences diminish when controlled for employment problems and father's current marital status and new family obligations. Pearson & Thoennes, *Child Custody, Child Support Arrangements and Child Support Payment Patters* 13 (1985) (copy on file).

86. *See* McKinnon & Wallerstein, *supra* note 37, at 177; Greif, *supra* note 2, at 318; M. Roman & W. Haddad, *The Disposable Parent* 116-21 (1978); Woolley, *Shared Custody,* Fam. Advoc., Summer 1978, at 6, 7, 33; J. Wallerstein & J. Kelly, *supra* note 2, at 130-31, 218. *But see* Scott & Derdeyn, *supra* note 8, at 495; Reece, *supra* note 42, at 778-79; Steinman, *supra* note 8, at 759.

87. *See, e.g.,* Charnas, *Joint Child Custody Counseling — Divorce 1980s Style,* 64 Soc. Casework: J. Contemp. Soc. Work 546 (1983) (presented a model of joint custody counseling that stresses resolution of parent-oriented rather than marriage-oriented problems, and reinforces the message that the parents have no choice but to cooperate with one another).

but will almost certainly negate the benefits of joint custody for the child.[88] A few statutes make specific provisions regarding custody in spousal abuse situations,[89] and some courts have shown that they are able and inclined to take this factor into account.[90] Courts can be made much more sensitive to this problem. Evidence of one party's manipulation of the other should also be treated as an indication as to whether joint custody is in the best interests of the child.[91]

Further, parents should not be penalized under "friendly parent" provisions for opposing joint custody in good faith, either inside or outside of court. Such a penalty provides too great an incentive for taking unfair advantage of joint custody preferences in custody proceedings. Only if a court finds bad faith in opposing joint custody should such opposition be relevant to the determination of a parent's willingness to allow the other parent access to the children.[92]

In many cases, problems or difficulties with joint custody are actually inequities that have been carried over from the legacy of sole custody. For example, parents with sole custody who wish to relocate have frequently been prohibited from doing so, unless they are willing to give up custody of their children.[93] In some decisions, it seems clear that courts assume that the careers and educational opportunities of mothers are less important than those of fathers.[94] If joint custody rules inherit the same restrictions placed on the geographical mobility of custodial mothers, then they also will incorporate gender-based discrimination that reinforces the economic dependency of women.[95] Although special arrangements may have to be made, families

---

88. In fact research has shown a positive correlation between domestic violence and the failure to sustain a joint custody-relationship. *See* Steinman, Zemmelman, & Knoblauch, *A Study of Parents Who Sought Joint Custody Following Divorce: Who Reaches Agreements and Sustains Joint Custody and Who Returns to Court*, 24 J. Am. Acad. Child Psychiatry 554, 561 (1985).

89. Florida combines a statutory presumption in favor of joint custody with such a special provision. *See* Fla. Stat. Ann. § 61.13(2)(b)2 (West 1985). *See also* Alaska Stat. § 25.20.090(8) (1983); Cal. Civ. Code § 4608(b) (West Supp. 1986); Ill. Ann. Stat. ch. 40 § 602(a)(6) (Smith-Hurd Supp. 1986).

90. *See, e.g.*, Edelin v. Edelin, 457 So. 2d 171 (La. Ct. App. 1984); Bishop v. Bishop, 457 So. 2d 264 (La. Ct. App.), *cert. denied*, 460 So. 2d 1048 (La. 1984); In re Marriage of Hickey, 689 P.2d 1222 (Mont. 1984); Heard v. Heard, 353 N.W.2d 157 (Minn. Ct. App. 1984). *See also* Falls v. Falls, 52 N.C. App. 203, 278 S.E.2d 546, *pet. denied*, 304 N.C. 390, 285 S.E.2d 831 (1981).

91. *See, e.g.*, Emerick v. Emerick, 5 Conn. App. 649, 502 A.2d 933 (1985); Huffman v. Huffman, 50 Ill. App. 3d 217, 365 N.E.2d 270 (1977); Dodd v. Dodd, 93 Misc. 2d 641, 403 N.Y.S.2d 401 (1978); In re Marriage of Handy, 44 Or. App. 225, 605 P.2d 738 (1980).

92. *See, e.g.*, Kline v. Kline, 686 S.W.2d 13, 15-16 (Mo. Ct. App. 1984); Rolde v. Rolde, 12 Mass. App. Ct. 398, 403, 425 N.E.2d 388, 391 (1981); Mastropole v. Mastropole, 181 N.J. Super. 130, 139, 436 A.2d 955, 960 (1981). *See also* Wilcox v. Wilcox, 7 Fam. L. Rep. (BNA) 2197 (Mich. Ct. App. 1980) (Beasley, J., dissenting) (disputed the court's award of joint legal custody, and strongly disagreed with the trial court's penalty against a mother for contesting joint custody in good faith and for refusing "to cooperate in a plan that requires her to maintain a constant, close, continuing relationship with her ex-husband"). Numerous cases have awarded sole custody to a mother despite her opposition to joint custody. *See, e.g.*, In re Marriage of Weidner, 338 N.W.2d 351 (Iowa 1983); In re Marriage of Heinel and Kessel, 55 Or. App. 275, 637 P.2d 1313 (1981).

93. Sheehan, *Post-Divorce Child Custody and Family Relocation*, 9 Harv. Women's L.J. 135 (1986).

94. *Compare* Bennett v. Bennett, 228 Wis. 401, 280 N.W. 363 (1938) (a father was permitted to remove the minor children to New York for employment at a larger salary), *with* Fritschler v. Fritschler, 60 Wis. 2d 283, 208 N.W.2d 336 (1973) (a mother was not permitted to relocate with the children out of state despite what she considered, among other things, to be better job opportunities). *See also* Spencer v. Spencer, 132 Ill. App. 2d 740, 743, 270 N.E.2d 72, 74 (1971) (a mother was allowed to relocate with the children to follow her new husband); Bezou v. Bezou, 436 So. 2d 592 (La. Ct. App. 1983) (by moving to Washington D.C. to take a job, a mother, a successful attorney, lost custody of the child to the father, a successful doctor).

95. *See, e.g.*, Dick v. Dick, 147 Mich. App. 513, 383 N.W.2d 240 (1985) (a joint custody award under which a mother had primary custody was modified to a sole-custody award to the father when the mother

(and thus joint custody) can and often do function in two locations. In our highly mobile society, there is little sacred about the particular city, state or geographical area of residence of a family at the time of divorce. Indeed, decisions to relocate have long been justified by parents who claim that the best interests of children are inseparable from both the economic well-being of the family and the personal career trajectories of the parents. A few courts have shown that joint custody need not preclude relocation by one parent.[96] Where joint custody is impracticable because of relocation, rules should not be applied based on discriminatory assumptions about the greater importance of the father's career.[97]

Joint custody has also been applied with a continuing, unrealistic view of the respective economic positions of the parties. Genuine imbalances still persist between male and female incomes.[98] Divorce is particularly devastating to the income levels of women, which are unlikely to rise so long as women remain single parents.[99] Support provisions should take account of the differences in ability of parents to support their children to an extent at least as great as current law now provides under sole-custody arrangements. Child support should not be eliminated on the assumption that parents who have joint custody are equally able to support themselves and their children. Further, child support should not be determined by a formula which takes into account the respective parents' needs only when they have physical custody of the children;[100] the cost of maintaining a home appropriate for a joint custody arrangement should also be considered.[101] If economically feasible, women and children should not have to pay for joint custody by accepting a standard of living considerably below what the parties enjoyed during the marriage. In the long-term, of course, the greater economic opportunities for women allowed by joint custody should work to reduce the income disparities that give rise to the obligation of men to continue as primary providers.[102]

Joint custody as it has been implemented has been detrimental to many women. Many of the shortcomings attributed to joint custody, however, are inherited from precedents set and habits learned in sole-custody disputes. The solution to these problems, if joint custody is found to be otherwise desirable, is not to reject joint custody but to examine possibilities for improving its implementation that do not perpetuate or worsen the effects of traditional gender-role arrangements.

---

moved out of state, because of the father's "extraordinary relationship" to the children, which was based on his participation in athletic activities, boy scouts, and religious instruction of the children).

96. See Scott v. Scott, 124 Mich. App. 448, 335 N.W.2d 68 (1983); Hornbeck v. Hornbeck, 702 P.2d 42 (Okla. 1985).

97. Neither should joint custody be ordered simply to help a court avoid making a difficult but necessary custody decision. See, e.g., Korf v. Korf, 221 Neb. 484, 378 N.W.2d 173 (1985); In re Boone, 75 Or. App. 413, 706 P.2d 205 (1986).

98. See supra note 9.

99. Weiss, supra note 41, at 116-17. See also supra note 25.

100. See, e.g., Hortis v. Hortis, 367 N.W.2d 633, 635 (Minn. Ct. App. 1985) ("We recognize some of those expenses [attributable to the needs of the children] are year around"); Esposito v. Esposito, 371 N.W.2d 608 (Minn. Ct. App. 1985).

101. See, e.g., Colo. Rev. Stat. § 14-10-123.5(2) (Supp. 1985).

102. Other rules may also be appropriate to address the concerns of women whose particular situations of dependency allow easy frustration of the legitimate goals of joint custody. Likewise, state policy should not create economic incentives for women to prefer sole custody, as it does under current AFDC regulations. See supra note 40.

Conclusion

Dependency is a complicated dilemma for women. Dependent relationships subordinate women to others, but in so doing, they fulfill the needs many women perceive for support, affirmation, and power. The element of consent is often corrupted in relationships of dependency, but efforts to overcome dependency may degrade women's positive values of nurturance and interconnectedness. Such efforts may leave women more exposed to exploitation by others, aggravating the conditions that have made dependency oppressive for women in the past.

Recent feminist arguments for sole custody appear to be self-protective, short-term reactions to a gender revolution in which women have given away an historical custodial preference in their favor in order to acquire other benefits. At this moment in history, some women experience that they have given away more than they have gained. However, in assuming the need of women for custodial preferences and the near inevitability of male domination over women, these arguments ignore—indeed, seem to abandon—the effort for elimination of predetermined gender roles. The feminist critique of joint custody recognizes "reality," but only part of it, and perpetuates antiegalitarian norms that contribute to the continuation of this reality.

Women have traditionally provided extraordinary resources to working husbands and fathers, who as breadwinners could count on women to provide the support structures that enabled them to have both families and careers. Learning from models of morality that emphasize relationships and obligations over fairness, rights, and rules,[103] women have typically placed responsibilities to others first in their lives. Yet, in order to expand their own opportunities, be they social, political, or economic, women too need resources. Joint custody offers the resource of shared parenting and shared responsibilities.

Even more important, joint custody preferences in law may contribute to a transformation of both male and female values, as men through parenting learn nurturance and cooperation in their intimate relationships and women learn independence without abandoning their values of caretaking.[104] As a resource that builds upon feminist values, joint custody offers hope in restructuring gender roles that alternative rules do not. Joint custody may in the end help accomplish the transition from dependency based on connived consent to reciprocal and truly voluntary relationships.

Much of the ideal, long-term social, economic, and political progress initially expected by women has not been realized. Likewise, women's good faith expectations of short-term benefits from revisions in family law, such as joint custody, have been disappointed. Nonetheless, joint custody may remain a promising vehicle for desirable

---

103. *See* C. Gilligan, *supra* note 84, at 19, 151-60.
104. *See* Hoffman, *Increased Fathering: Effects on the Mother*, in *Fatherhood and Family Policy* 167, 178 (M. Lamb & A. Sagi eds. 1983).
   The increased role of fathers in parenting may also break the cycle by which male characteristics are defined in the context of having had a female primary caretaker. *See* N. Chodorow, *The Reproduction of Mothering* 180-90 (1978); *see generally* D. Dinnerstein, *The Mermaid and the Minotaur* (1976).

change, one which we cannot afford to throw away on the basis of incomplete or narrow analyses. This legal reform is not an answer for women if it masks or mystifies traditional gender-role assignments, but it may not be wise to allow our initial frustration with the application of joint custody to cause us to abandon it altogether. The challenge of any legal reform is to ride out the dilemmas it poses without allowing them to paralyze movement toward our vision of a better world.

8

Joint Custody Is Not for Everyone

RICHARD A. GARDNER

There are undeniable advantages to joint custody, but they may never be realized if joint custody is imposed on people who lack the maturity and commitment needed to make shared parenting work. This chapter highlights attributes of couples who will benefit from joint custody and identifies traits which make some couples poor candidates for shared custody. This highly regarded and much published child psychiatrist notes circumstances which may arise later to cause problems in joint custody arrangements. He concludes that when joint custody works, it can be the best of all possible custody plans, but it should not be recommended indiscriminately. In an addendum written for this book, Dr. Gardner advocates the use in court decrees of a general semantic designation other than "joint custody," such as "residential and decision-making arrangement."

Here's How to Spot Whether It Will Work for Your Client

When I use the term "joint custody," I envision a custodial arrangement that attempts to approximate as closely as possible the flexibility in the original two-parent home.

Richard A. Gardner, M.D., is Professor of Clinical Psychiatry at the Columbia University College of Physicians and Surgeons. He has written many books and articles on a wide variety of subjects related to child psychiatry. Many attorneys know him from his *Boys and Girls Book About Divorce* and *The Parents Book About Divorce*. His most recent book is *Family Evaluation in Child Custody Mediation, Arbitration and Litigation* (1989).

Reprinted with permission from the Fall 1982 issue of *Family Advocate*, Volume 5, Number 2, p. 7, published by the American Bar Association Family Law Section. Copyright 1982 American Bar Association.

In such an arrangement, both parents have equal rights and responsibilities for their children's upbringing, and neither party's rights are superior. Neither parent is designated as the sole or primary parent. There is no structured visitation schedule; the children *live* in *both* homes. They do not *live* in one home and *visit* the other. This distinction separates joint custody from traditional custodial arrangements and offers several psychological advantages to both children and parents.

From a psychological point of view, joint custody is probably the healthiest and most desirable of the various custody plans available to divorced parents and their children. As a result, it has become quite popular—perhaps too popular. Joint custody often is recommended indiscriminately, but not every divorced parent is a good candidate for it. It is important, therefore, for family law practitioners and judges to study the psychological advantages and disadvantages of joint custody and to be aware of the type of parents who can make it work to the benefit of their children and themselves.

Advantages of Joint Custody

Of all existing custodial arrangements, joint custody most closely approximates the original marital household. It is free from artificial schedules that are totally unrelated to the vicissitudes of life. There is a free flow of involvement with both parents—obviously a more natural lifestyle. This offers children (especially older ones) more input into what happens to them, and they are less likely to suffer from the sense of impotence that a primary custody arrangement with strict schedules can create.

A drawback of this flexibility is that the children may attempt to manipulate their parents: "If you make me turn off the television set, I'm going to go to Daddy's house!" But knowledgeable parents are unlikely to allow such manipulation or to acquiesce to these threats. Parents with joint custody arrangements should consider the child's wishes, but they also should use their own adult judgment. They should not allow a child's input to be used to flee from difficult situations, but should recognize that, at times, a transfer to the other home may help decompress a conflict-laden situation.

Another advantage of joint custody is that it may avoid some of the tensions of sole-custody arrangements. Specifically, in sole-custody arrangements one parent is placed in a position of authority over the other, which is bound to produce resentment. The fact that the noncustodial parent's opportunities to be with the children are reduced often creates conflict—much to the children's detriment. The children's greater accessibility to both parents in a joint custody situation lessens the likelihood of animosity.

Furthermore, a visiting father in a sole-custody arrangement is likely to resent the fact that while he may be the primary (if not total) child-support contributor, his access to the children is significantly restricted. In joint custody, however, the father may feel more motivated to contribute to his children's support.

With joint custody arrangements, each parent usually assumes both housekeeping and breadwinning roles. They therefore provide parental models that are more consonant with the direction in which family life is moving—families in which parents share homemaking and economic obligations. As a result, children are better prepared for the future by joint custody than by sole-custody arrangements modeled on the traditional family roles of the mother as sole homemaker and the father as the only breadwinner.

Joint custody also reduces the possibility of a father being viewed as a bearer of gifts and taker to circuses while the mother is seen as the disciplinarian. In joint custody, both parents play both roles.

Another major psychological advantage of joint custody is that each parent is protected against the terrible sense of loss that a noncustodial parent feels in a sole-custody arrangement. If one parent is awarded primary custody after litigation, the visiting parent cannot help feeling that he or she has been judged the *worse*, or at least the *less adequate*, of the two parents. A loss of self esteem is added to the loss of the children. This ego debasing experience is less likely to occur with joint custody.

This advantage for parents makes it tempting to recommend joint custody. I do not believe, however, that it should be a central consideration. The custody decision should be based on the children's best interests, not on protecting a parent's self-esteem.

When Joint Custody Is Harmful

Joint custody decisions enable judges to avoid a complex and difficult fact-finding task by offering a seemingly benevolent resolution. It certainly is easier for a judge to award joint custody than to deliberate about all the mind-boggling facts involved in a custody conflict. And judges who circumvent such challenges often justify their actions by considering themselves advanced and modern thinkers.

The main drawback of granting joint custody so frequently and automatically is that it may do many children more harm than good. For example, it increases the chances that they will be used as weapons or spies in parental conflicts; because no restraints are placed on noncooperating parents, such use of the children is likely. Certainly sole-custody arrangements cannot protect children from this situation, but it does reduce the opportunities for parents to involve their children in such manipulations.

Furthermore, automatic awarding of joint custody seldom takes into consideration the logistics of school attendance, and, therefore, it can cause problems in the educational realm as well. It is for these reasons that many family lawyers and psychiatrists are beginning to view joint custody as a judicial "cop-out."

Another frequent criticism of joint custody is that it may be confusing for a child to be shuttled between two homes—especially when there are different lifestyles, disciplinary measures, rules, and even socioeconomic conditions. Its critics claim that having two homes can give a child a sense of unpredictability and a lack of environmental continuity. Although this is detrimental for a child, it probably is not relevant to children older than three or four. They generally can adjust well to such transfers, and even younger children are not necessarily harmed by "shuttling. "

What is important is whether the children will suffer from the nature of the parenting, not the rooms in which the parenting occurs. Even if a young child experiences some mild degree of psychological harm from environmental discontinuity, the disadvantage would be more than outweighed by the advantage of the child's having access to both parents in a less structured, less artificial arrangement.

Who Should Have Joint Custody?

Joint custody is viable only when three provisions are satisfied:

1. Both parents are reasonably capable of assuming the responsibilities of childrearing—their involvement with the children and affection for them are approximately equal. When there is a significant difference between the parents in these areas, another custodial arrangement should be considered.

2. The parents must have demonstrated their capacity to cooperate reasonably and meaningfully in matters pertaining to raising their children. They must show the ability to communicate well and be willing to compromise when necessary to ensure the viability of the arrangement. The key words here are *cooperation* and *communication*.

3. The children's moving from home to home should not disrupt their school situation. Accordingly, the arrangement generally is possible only if both parents are living in the same public school district or reasonably close to a child's private school.

Recommending joint custody requires a certain amount of foresight. Although the first and third provisions may be satisfied by many parents involved in custody disputes, the second may not be. The greater the friction and animosity, the less likely it is that the second provision will be satisfied.

Because the animosity between parents may be greatest at the time of their divorce, that often is not a good time to recommend a joint custody arrangement. Also, if both parents are fighting for sole custody, they probably are poor candidates for joint custody. Unless the lawyer can reasonably predict that the hostilities will die down and cooperation will increase, joint custody should not be recommended.

This problem can be prevented to some degree by making joint custody arrangements temporary, and finalizing them only after the parents have had an opportunity to prove for six to nine months whether or not they truly can handle it.

Poor Candidates

Many types of parents are poor candidates for a viable joint custody arrangement. The family law practitioner or judge should watch out for people who fall into the following categories:

1. People who cannot communicate with one another. Parents living apart must be able to communicate well with one another if they are to provide their children with an optimum environment for dealing with the stress and special problems of divorce.

   Unfortunately, adversary proceedings, both inside and outside the courtroom, do not provide attorneys or judges with a chance to observe parental communication. In fact, the adversary system may worsen parental communication because messages are relayed through intermediaries—their attorneys. Responses often are delayed and the chances of inaccuracy increase. The adversary system may make a joint custody arrangement less likely to succeed.

2. Parents who cannot cooperate. As mentioned above, the parents must demonstrate a capacity for being able to cooperate with each other as well as communicate. Some psychotherapists believe that conflicts should be divided into issues that pertain to the children and those that do not. They hold that if there is basic agreement in the area of child rearing, lack of cooperation in other areas need not interfere with a joint custody arrangement. Joint custody, they say, still can be a viable arrangement if the parents can separate their marital problems from parenting conflicts.

   Although theoretically there may be such people, I have not seen any to date. Generally, disputing parents are involved in an all-out war which includes criticism of the other spouse in both marital and childrearing areas.

3. Parents who are actively litigating for sole custody of the children. The adversary system tends to polarize parents and reduces the chance that they will cooperate. Attorneys, therefore, should schedule conferences at which both the parents and their attorneys try to reduce animosities and work out marital difficulties in a nonadversarial setting. Divorce mediation, which is available in various forms today, also can lessen the likelihood that the legal system will reduce communication and cooperation.

   But not everyone agrees that parents who are actively litigating are automatically poor candidates for joint custody. Some argue that a joint custody arrangement might reduce hostilities by removing one area of conflict.

   My experience, however, has been that children more often are used as tools in fighting when there are no external limitations, such as a visitation schedule. Therefore, active litigation is more likely to increase than reduce animosity. Note that I am not totally against adversary proceedings in divorce and custody conflicts. I simply believe that adversary proceedings should be the last resort, not the first, for separating parents who are in conflict.

ㄴ

Other Danger Signals

There are many other situations that should set off a warning signal for family law practitioners whose clients are considering joint custody. For instance, one often sees a situation in which one parent wants joint custody and the other wants sole custody. Sometimes the parent asking for joint custody really wants sole custody but recognizes that he or she is unlikely to obtain it. That parent may then "fight" for joint custody as a compromise.

Joint custody is a terrible compromise for warring parents. When recommended in such situations, what may actually result is a *no-custody* arrangement that merely is called joint custody. Neither parent has power or control, and the children find themselves in a no-man's land exposed to their parents' crossfire and available to both as weapons. The likelihood of children developing a psychological problem in such a situation is practically 100 percent.

In addition, not all parents who want custody of their children are motivated by deep love and affection. Specious reasons often are operative. When these are present, they lessen the likelihood that joint custody will succeed.

A mother, for example, may welcome a joint custody arrangement because it gives her the opportunity to "dump" the children on the father more frequently, thereby allowing her to assume less responsibility for raising them.

Vengeance also can be a motive. The father, for example, may basically consider his wife to be the preferable parent. But he may also realize that by fighting for sole or joint custody, he can hurt his wife in a most effective way—threatening to deprive her of the children.

A parent also may request joint custody in order to reduce shame or guilt over the fact that he or she does not want custody at all. Essentially, that parent would much prefer that the other parent have sole custody. Instead, he or she asks for joint custody, hoping that the other parent will assume the major responsibility and assuaging any guilty feelings about wanting to reject the children.

For two parents who constantly shift the responsibility for their children to one another, joint custody may seem an easy way out. Under a strict visitation schedule in a sole-custody arrangement, there is a greater obligation to assume parental duties on the part of both the custodial and noncustodial parent. Joint custody provides flexibility for copping out.

The availability of each parent to assume childrearing responsibilities must also be considered before recommending joint custody. Granting joint custody to parents when one is intensely involved in a career and the other stays home means joint custody on paper only. The children cannot reasonably spend half their time with the parent who has a full-time job. The split in childrearing responsibilities will be unequal because one parent will be unavailable for frequent school vacations and holidays or for emergencies such as sickness and accidents that may require a parent to be home with a child. Parents in such a situation rarely are good candidates for a true joint custodial arrangement.

The Prognosis

A smoothly operating joint custody arrangement may run into trouble if one of the parents remarries. That parent must then assume many more obligations (especially if there are stepchildren on the scene) and may not be able to handle the responsibilities of joint custody.

In addition, a stepparent may cause problems if he or she cannot accept the ongoing cooperation and communication with the ex-spouse that joint custody requires. And if both parents remarry, the risk of a joint custody arrangement breaking down is even greater.

There are other life changes that can compromise, if not totally destroy, a working joint custody arrangement. If one parent takes a job with increased responsibility or travel, he or she may no longer have the flexibility necessary for joint custody. And if one parent moves out of the school district or far from the children's private school, joint custody may become impractical.

Parents who appear capable of cooperating and communicating well at the time of their divorce may find their relationship later deteriorates, precluding a successful joint custody situation. Divorced mothers generally are in a more vulnerable position with regard to picking up the pieces of their lives than divorced fathers. Fathers usually have greater opportunities to remarry and still have more earning power, the advances of the feminist movement notwithstanding.

As a result, divorced mothers may become increasingly frustrated with their lives. The resentment engendered by the disparity between the mother's own life and that of her former husband may contribute to a deterioration in the relationship with her ex-spouse. And this can wreck a joint custody arrangement that might once have worked smoothly.

Yet despite all the threats to its success, a joint custody arrangement, approximating as it does the original marital situation, is the most desirable and psychologically healthy of the various custody plans that have been proposed thus far. When it works, it can protect the children better than any of the alternatives from the psychological damage a divorce often causes.

Currently, the arrangement is much in vogue. It has a reputation of being egalitarian, nonsexist, and benevolent. Unfortunately, it is being indiscriminately recommended for people who are extremely poor candidates for joint custody. The criteria presented here can help family practitioners to define more specifically which families may profit from the arrangement and which may not.

Special Addendum Prepared for
Joint Custody and Shared Parenting

Since the publication of the preceding material, the author has had further thoughts on the joint custody concept which he hopes will be given serious consideration by both the legal and mental health professions. It has become apparent that joint custody is "sweeping the nation." At this point there is hardly a state that has not either passed legislation in which the joint custody concept in one form or another is incorporated or has seriously considered the passage of such statutes. In principle I am pleased by this turn of events. However, it has become apparent that the term is variously defined, not only in different states but by attorneys, mental health professionals, and clients. As a result, an element of confusion has been introduced—confusion that has resulted in unnecessary prolongation of litigation and time wasted on irrelevancies. The result has been further expense and psychological trauma to clients, most often avoidable.

Often, the conflicts are semantic ones. The parties involved in discussing a potential joint custody arrangement may each have a different concept of the meaning of the term—a situation that will predictably cause confusion and wastage of time. Or attorneys will haggle over the definition of the term and/or whether a particular client's custodial arrangement warrants the designation. In such conflicts the parties become sidetracked into issues that may be basically irrelevant to the decision. Furthermore, what has traditionally been called *sole custody* may be given the name *joint custody* because of the belief that such designation will protect the unfavored party from feelings of lowered self worth. Such utilization of the term may introduce an element of further confusion, especially in those who are reviewing the court rulings and possibly even using such rulings as an established precedent. Sometimes *joint custody* is essentially *no custody*, and what was designed to provide children with a flexible visitation program ends with their being in a no-man's land, equally available as weapons and/or spies to both of their warring parents. The problem may be further complicated by the term *joint custody* itself. In a sense, *joint custody* is a contradiction in terms. The word *custody* implies entrapment, possession, and restraint. The word *joint* connotes cooperation and flexibility of movement. When older children are involved, the joint custodial arrangement includes taking into consideration their wishes in any decision making. Accordingly, there is an internal contradiction in the term *joint custody*, especially when it applies to older children. Lastly, there are parents who *fight* for joint custody. If people are indeed litigating for joint custody, they are generally not likely to be good candidates for it.

I believe that the aforementioned problems concerning the joint custody arrangement could be obviated in a relatively simple way. The semantic problem could be eliminated by strictly avoiding the utilization of any commonly used term: joint custody, sole custody, alternating custody, shared custody, divided custody, split custody, etc. Rather, I would recommend that all arrangements be subsumed under a general rubric such as *residential and decision-making arrangement*. This is essentially what we are concerning ourselves with anyway. We want to decide where the children should be at any particular time and what powers the parent with whom they are shall have. All of the aforementioned terms are attempts to define a particular arrangement for the children's residence, visitation, and parental decision making powers. The use of this general term (or one like it) would enable us to avoid the time and energy wasted in arguing over which type of custodial arrangement would be most applicable to a particular family. Rather, we should focus on the particular *substantive* considerations that are relevant to the particular family.

One has to ascertain whether the parents are equally capable of parenting and whether they are equally available to assume parental obligations. One must determine whether they have demonstrated the capacity to cooperate well with one another and to communicate successfully. When these questions have been answered, then one directs one's attention to the question of whether or not the individuals need a court-imposed schedule or whether they can be relied upon to utilize successfully a nonscheduled arrangement. Generally, people who are equally capable as parents and who can communicate and cooperate can be trusted to utilize successfully a nonscheduled arrangement for visitation and place of residence. Those who cannot may need a court-imposed schedule.

The next question relates to decision-making powers. Are both individuals relatively equal with regard to decision-making capacity? If not generally equal, are there some areas in which one parent should be given priority and other areas in which the other parent should be given priority? To simply designate one parent as the only one to make primary decisions may not fit in well with the reality of the situation. Of course, considerations of cooperation and communication must also be attended to when deciding about decision-making powers.

When all of the aforementioned questions have been answered, a suitable program should be formulated. I would recommend that attempts to compare it to one of the traditional arrangements is not only a waste of time, but may be detrimental in that it may complicate the whole process. The only name that should be given should be *residential and decision-making arrangement* or an equally suitable name. This name circumvents the problems resulting from the use of the aforementioned traditional terms. It directs attention to the substantive issues with which we should be exclusively concerned. And it has the fringe benefit of reducing the likelihood of litigation because one cannot readily fight for it. One may choose to fight for sole custody, joint custody, and even shared parenting. But one is far less likely to fight for a residential and decision-making arrangement because one has it already. Without the win-or-lose element, without the opportunity for wresting something from the other spouse, the impetus to fight is reduced (but not completely removed, because one could still litigate for a particular kind of residential and decision-making arrangement).

I am recommending this arrangement primarily because it will reduce time and energy expended on irrelevant issues in litigation and thereby protect clients from unnecessary expense and grief. I am not recommending this plan to protect the self-esteem of the parent who was traditionally designated the noncustodial parent or the one who "lost" the custody battle. Self-esteem is far too complex an issue to be significantly affected by this relatively minor factor. The plan encourages our focusing on the concrete issues—those that are directly related to what will happen to the children—rather than abstractions which are often irrelevant and meaningless to them and a waste of time in the course of litigation.

9

Shared Physical Custody: Economic Considerations

ALICE MILLS MORROW

There are both economic benefits and costs when parents share physical custody of children in two households. This chapter examines those economic costs and benefits. The child-related items likely to require increased expenditures in shared physical custody situations are listed and discussed.

When parents divorce, their marriage relationship ends but their relationships with their children continue. The responsibilities of being a parent—including financial support—and the rewards and satisfactions of being a parent should continue after divorce. To this end, increasing numbers of divorcing parents attempt to set up custodial situations that insure that the children spend sufficient time with each parent to develop meaningful relationships with both.

The living situations that parents create to enable children to live with both parents take many forms. For purposes of this article "shared physical custody" is any living situation where children spend substantial time—one-third to one-half of their nights—with each parent.

While research on the economic aspects of shared physical custody is limited, there is some anecdotal evidence that it does not create increased money concerns. Woolley (1984) reported, "Interestingly, money was very low on the list of problems or considerations where sharing parents were concerned. . . . The father who has more contact with his children is less likely to resent paying for them, and the mother who knows she can rely on her ex-husband for more than just economic help is more apt to be understanding of the financial pinches everyone encounters" (p. 20).

Alice Mills Morrow is Extension Family Economics Specialist at Oregon State University. She is an attorney, a Certified Financial Planner, and a Certified Home Economist.

There is some statistical evidence suggesting economic benefits. Pearson and Thoennes (Chapter 16, this volume) found more regular and complete child support payments when there was shared physical custody. In addition they found that increased paternal contact with children resulted in financial contributions outside of regular support payments. Pearson and Thoennes remind us, however, that these benefits may be a result of the characteristics of parents who opt for shared physical custody rather than a result of shared physical custody itself.

In spite of the lack of definitive data, it appears certain that there are both economic benefits and costs when parents share physical custody of children. The more accurately parents predict these benefits and costs, the better able they are to make custody and financial decisions and to plan their financial futures.

Parental Expenses

Parents provide economic support to children in two ways: (1) monetary expenditures for the purchase of goods and services for the child, and (2) time expenditures on homemaking and parenting.

When parents divorce, the cost of supporting the two post-divorce households is more than the cost of supporting the pre-divorce household. When physical custody is shared, total costs are further increased because of the duplication of some major expenses. While the total time spent on homemaking and parenting probably does not increase, the sharing of custody probably results in a more equitable division of the time and energy costs. Economic changes must be anticipated as custody plans are developed.

Monetary Expenditures

About half of the money parents spend on children is for housing and transportation (Espenshade, 1984). These major expenses are the expenses most likely to increase in shared physical custody arrangements. The other half of the money parents spend is for food, clothing, recreation, medical care, child care, and education. These expenses will be unchanged or change only slightly. In some situations, custody arrangements may allow parents to coordinate their own work schedules and their children's schedules in such a way that they decrease child-care expenses. One additional expense category—not used by economists but used by parents—is what parents call "the other stuff" or unplanned expenses. Unplanned expenses could be included in the expense categories listed, but they are often overlooked and take parents by surprise. Shared custody is likely to result in a redistribution of unplanned expenses.

Housing—Housing costs increase when physical custody is shared. A residence for a parent living alone is less costly than a residence for a parent and her or his children. Both parents incur the cost of providing housing for children year-round, in order to have it available during the periods when the children are in the home. The more children in the family, the greater the increase in housing costs. In addition to increased rent or mortgage expense, the total cost of furnishings and appliances related to the care of the children increases because of the duplication of household items— beds, linens, dishes, etc.

Transportation—Transportation costs increase when physical custody is shared. Part of the increase is because of the cost of commuting between parents' homes. There are additional increases because each parent incurs some expenses year-round in order to have transportation available during the periods when the children are in the home. For families with teenagers who drive, there is a substantial increase in the cost of auto insurance if both parents have insurance for teenage drivers. For some families, cars insured for young drivers may be a luxury. However, such insurance may be a necessity for families living in rural areas where distances are great and there is no public transportation.

Unplanned Expenses—Any custodial parent can report numerous child-related expenses never contemplated during child-support negotiations. Children regularly announce unplanned expenses. "Tomorrow I have to pay for my cheerleading sweater." "Bobby sat on my glasses." "For the concert I am supposed to wear a white shirt, black dress pants, black socks, and black shoes." Ricci (1981) summarizes this as follows: "The parent with the lion's share of the child raising responsibilities also has the lion's share of the costs." When custody is shared, these unplanned expenses are also shared. While this does not reduce total costs, it results in greater equity of parental expenditures.

Time Expenditures

Time expenditures for homemaking and parenting must be considered as economic costs. Such costs are often expressed as "opportunity costs"—the income a parent forgoes because of time spent caring for children. Examples of opportunity costs include being unemployed (or less than fully employed) because of the time needed to care for very young or handicapped children, losing income because of lost time from work when a child is sick, or forgoing increases in income because overtime, promotions, or job transfers are not possible because of family responsibilities.

Parents spend a great deal of time and energy raising children. Increasingly, families—whether married or divorced—need two incomes to provide adequate financial support for their children. All parents, married or divorced, struggle to balance the time and energy needed for family and employment responsibilities.

The divorced working parent with sole physical custody of her or his children has one full-time job raising the children, another job that is paid work, and almost no time left for her- or himself. Divorced parents who share physical custody of their children share the time and energy costs of homemaking and parenting. They share the joys of parenthood along with the cooking, cleaning, disciplining, and caregiving.

Sharing the time and energy costs of homemaking and parenting is an economic benefit and facilitates the labor-force participation of both parents. When both parents are employed, each has the benefits of employment—present and future income, health, disability, and life insurance, and future retirement benefits.

Predicting Changes

There are no data on childrearing costs related to physical custodial arrangements. However, there is agreement that some monetary expenses increase. Changes in time expenditures, though less tangible than monetary expenses, are critical. As parents develop plans for sharing parenting responsibilities, they must predict economic changes. Record keeping and budgets will help parents better understand the monetary changes. The better understanding parents have of economic consequences, the greater the likelihood of a successful shared physical custody arrangement.

The Child-Support Obligation

Sometimes a parent believes that if the children spend equal time with each parent, all child-support obligations have been met and no further support payments are necessary. Most often, this is not true. The chances of a successful shared-custody arrangement are reduced if one parent wrongfully believes that the arrangement eliminates the necessity of him or her making child-support payments. Support payments are not eliminated unless two conditions are satisfied: (1) the parents have equal incomes, and (2) each parent pays half of the children's direct expenditures (Williams, 1987).

Parents contemplating shared physical custody of children cannot assume that the amount each parent spends on the children is proportional to the amount of time he or she spends with the children. For example, if a child spends one-third of her time with dad, dad may or may not pay one-third of her clothing expenses or one-third of her medical expenses. Expense records are the best way to determine how much each parent is spending on the children. If the financial plans assume that expenses are paid in proportion to time spent with each parent, expenses must be monitored to insure this happens.

Parents also cannot assume each parent is obligated to provide one-half the total support. States use one of three child-support models: the income-sharing model, the cost-sharing model, or the percent-of-income model. The amount of parental income is a factor in each of these models.

If one parent has more income than the other, he or she has a higher child-support obligation, and must contribute more toward the child's support than the parent with the lower income. Therefore, if the children spend half the time with father, and, in fact, he pays half the expenses, and if father's income is higher than mother's, his support obligation is more than mother's. Therefore, he will still be required to make a child-support payment to mother.

Summary

The decision to share physical custody of children should not be an economic decision. However, the economic consequences of the decision must be understood by, and be acceptable to, the parents. While there are some economic benefits to shared physical custody, shared physical custody does not reduce the cost of raising a child. To the contrary, shared physical custody increases the total cost of raising a child. Parents sharing physical custody of children must be realistic about, and willing to incur, these additional costs.

III
What Research Tells Us about Joint Custody

10

A Comparison of Maternal, Paternal, and Joint Custody: Understanding the Varieties of Post-Divorce Family Life

DEBORAH ANNA LUEPNITZ

Forty-three families with either maternal, paternal, or joint custody were studied, an average of 3.5 years after divorce. Most of the 91 children in the sample were not maladjusted, and their adjustment was independent of custody type. Children in joint custody retained filial relationships with both parents, as opposed to the avuncular relationships they developed with non-custodial parents in the single-custody situations. It appears from this study that joint custody at its best is superior to single-parent custody at its best. However, the author cautions against a legal presumption for joint custody, and discusses some contraindications to its use.

Few topics in social science have provoked as much debate in the past decade as that of child custody. The contributing historical events to this controversy have included: (1) the divorce rate, which now affects one in five American children, (2) the feminist movement, which has spurred thinking about the reorganization of the family (Stack, 1976; Chesler, 1978; Chodorow, 1978; Dinnerstein, 1976; Ehrensaft, 1980), and (3)

Deborah Anna Luepnitz, Ph.D., is a Clinical Psychologist on the staff of the Philadelphia Child Guidance Clinic, Philadelphia, Pennsylvania. This chapter is reprinted with permission from the *Journal of Divorce*, Vol. 9(3), Spring 1986.

a culture which is increasingly child centered, and therefore inclined toward finding ways to protect children from divorce and other traumas.

Clinical opinion on the issue of joint custody ranges from the most disapproving stance of Goldstein et al. (1973) to the opposite of Roman and Haddad (1978b), who believe that judges ought to begin with a presumption for joint custody. The proponents of joint custody have had some impressive successes in affecting the law. In California, for example, judges must now begin with a presumption for the joint award—and must explain why single custody is preferable, should they decide against it (Ilfeld et al., 1982).

Research on joint custody is still in its beginning stages. The books by Galper (1978) and Ricci (1981) proved to be tremendous tools for parents and clinicians in learning how to implement the joint award, but neither work was based on a systematic investigation.

The earliest systematic studies were limited either by sample size (i.e., Abarbanel's 1979 study examined only four families) or by the absence of in-depth exploration of the families (i.e., Greif, 1979a). Wallerstein and Kelly's benchmark study (1980b) did not focus on custody, although their conclusions about the importance of continuing contact with both parents provides some support for the idea of joint parenting.

Steinman (1981) performed one of the most complete studies of joint custody to date. She studied a "normal" sample of 24 joint custody families with 32 children, ages four-and-a-half to fifteen. She concluded that the children—with the exception of some of the very youngest—were not confused about their joint custody schedule, and had adapted fairly well to it. Steinman found, however, that these children exhibited a "hyper-loyalty" to their parents; they showed extreme concern that both parents would get equal time and affection from them. Although several children stated that joint custody was better than single-parent custody, most of them preferred their intact family. Steinman's study provides us with very useful information, but did not employ a comparison group of single-custody mothers and fathers. The research to be described in this chapter is unique in that it involved the examination of a sample of parents with all three types of custody.

Purpose

The goals of the present investigation were: (1) to compare children's adjustment in maternal, paternal, and joint custody, (2) to explore the advantages and disadvantages of each form of custody for both parents and children, and (3) to compare parental conflict in maternal, paternal, and joint custody families.

Sample

Forty-three families participated in the study (i.e., 16 with maternal, 16 with paternal and 11 with joint custody), including their 91 children. In each case the final separation had occurred at least two years prior to the interview. Children in the three groups were matched by age and sex. The sample is a "normal" one, in that families were not recruited from clinics or hospitals. Instead they were solicited from lawyers, singles' groups, and newspaper ads.

The eleven joint families maintained a variety of living arrangements. In one case, the children spent half the day with each parent. In another case, the children split the year between parents, and in still another case, the child alternated years between parents. The model arrangement, however, was some form of split week, i.e., three days with father and four with mother.

The joint families were comparable to the single-custody families in terms of income. Median income for both joint- and single-custody *mothers* fell in the $4,000–$9,000 bracket. Median income for joint- and single-custody *fathers* fell in the $14,000–$20,000 bracket.

In only 54% of the joint cases had parents agreed from the outset on some form of shared custody. In the remaining cases there was conflict over the question of custody initially.

Measures

Each family was interviewed for four to six hours. Measures included:

1. The Piers-Harris Self-Concept Test for Children.

2. Parents' ratings of the child's self-esteem, psychosomatic problems, and behavior problems.

3. A family interaction task, in which the parent and children responded collaboratively to five TAT cards. An independent rater coded the tapes for "emotional climate," i.e., the levels of supportiveness and non-supportiveness which characterized their interaction, according to an adaptation of Alexander's (1973) coding scheme.

4. A structured interview with the parent alone and with each child alone, focusing on how family functions were performed before and after divorce, and how each person felt about the custody arrangement.

Results and Discussion

1. The sample as a whole was not maladjusted. Only eight of the 91 children (11%) exhibited symptoms that might require psychotherapy. These children tended to score lower on the Piers-Harris Self-Concept Scale than the other children. This finding contrasts markedly with the findings of Wallerstein and Kelly (1980b) who found massive maladjustment in their children. The contrast between the two studies will be discussed later in this chapter.

2. Child adjustment (as measured by Piers-Harris scores) was independent of custody type.[1]

3. Child adjustment (as measured by parents' ratings of children's self-esteem and psychosomatic and behavior problems) was independent of custody type.[2,3,4]

4. The family's "emotional climate" was independent of custody type.[5]

5. Children in families with continuing parental conflict (determined by a score on a self-report inventory) scored significantly *lower* on the Piers-Harris,[6] and were rated by parents as having *more* psychosomatic problems[7] and *more* behavior problems than children in low-conflict families.

6. Both joint custody and single-parent custody hold powerful advantages and disadvantages for both parents and children.

Advantages of Joint Custody

Two Filial Relationships—The children in this study who had joint custody appeared to have retained two psychological parents in their lives. Whereas half of the children in single-parent custody never saw the other parent at all, all of the joint custody children had regular contact with both parents. Moreover, the interviews with them elicited descriptions of their lives in both houses which revealed that "business as usual" went on with both parents. In the single-custody families, in contrast, a visit with the non-custodian was more likely a holiday or a "date." Furthermore, contrary to the warnings about children having to "serve two masters," the vast majority of children in joint custody were pleased and comfortable with the arrangement. Only three children expressed some confusion about following two sets of rules, or feeling that their parents had conflicting expectations. Here is an example of a nine-year-old girl caught in such a conflict:

> It is confusing. Suppose I ask mom to go skating and she says "yes" and then I tell dad and he says "Your friend is sleeping over tonight." And it makes me disappointed. Also, when my mother lets me have cookies my dad yells at me for not telling mom "no." He feels you'll live longer if you eat certain things. She says, "Enjoy life while you have it."

Problems such as these can escalate if the parents are not vigilant, and serious symptoms can result.

---

1. ANOVA yielded: $F_{(2,66)}$ = .25; $p > .10$.
2. ANOVA yielded: $F_{(2,85)}$ = .423; $p > .10$.
3. ANOVA yielded: $F_{(2,85)}$ = 1.16; $p > .10$.
4. ANOVA yielded: $F_{(2,85)}$ = .433; $p > .10$.
5. ANOVA yielded: $F_{(1,66)}$ = 4.15; $p > .05$.
6. ANOVA yielded: $F_{(1,85)}$ = 11.62; $p > .001$.
7. ANOVA yielded: $F_{(1,86)}$ = 9.70; $p > .001$.

Not only were the majority of children not confused or tormented by the joint arrangement, however, but most (75%) considered having two houses to be advantageous, i.e., as "more fun," "more interesting" or because it allowed them a time and place to have a wholesome relationship with each parent. For example, one fifteen-year-old boy said:

> In some ways, it is better to live this way than to be living together. My relationship with both my parents is better than before. I can talk with them separately instead of dealing with them at the same time. I don't like them as much together. They're totally different people, and I like each of them for what they are. And they can be theirselves when they're alone.

Parental Conflict—A most compelling finding from this study was that the joint custody families engaged in much less relitigation than the single-custody families. In fact, none of the joint families had relitigated, whereas 56% of the single-custody parents had returned to court at least once to battle over money and visitation. These findings are corroborated in a study by Ilfeld et al. (1982) who followed 414 custody cases in California in order to investigate relitigation patterns. They found that joint custody parents resorted to relitigation only half as often as parents with single-parent custody. Moreover, their study included a subset of 18 families in which one parent had opposed joint custody. Even in these families, the relitigation rate was no higher than the single-parent custody rate.

These findings are significant because a common criticism of joint custody is that it will lead to continued conflict between spouses, who, after all, divorced because of their differences. This criticism is given weight by the fact that in this study, as in several others, continued parental conflict correlates positively with poor adjustment in children (Raschke & Raschke, 1979; Wallerstein & Kelly, 1980b). One could justifiably argue that any custodial arrangement which ensured more battles between divorced parents ought to be considered at odds with the best interest of children. However, the present study showed that joint custody parents had *less* conflict than single-parent custodians with the ex-spouse. This was shown not only in the absence of relitigation, but also by lower scores on a self-report inventory of conflict. It is not that joint custody parents did not disagree with each other; they did disagree, and often needed to change the logistics of their arrangement. However, they were able to disagree in a more civil manner than their single-parent-custody counterparts. (The possibility cannot be ruled out, however, that the joint custody families were self-selected for the ability to negotiate reasonably.)

Money—A third advantage of joint custody has to do with money. Only half of the single-custody mothers in this study reported that they had received child support reliably from their ex-spouse. The remaining half received either partial, erratic support, or none at all. These data are corroborated by findings from other studies. Lenore Weitzman (personal communication) has found similarly grim statistics on child support nationally. She also maintains that a father's compliance with child support is *not* related to his financial ability to do so! In this study, the joint fathers, in contrast to the single-custody fathers, supported their children reliably. None of the joint custody mothers had to return to court to fight for child support, although several of them felt they would have liked more of it. It is possible that joint custody fathers continue to support their children because they feel fully involved in other ways, and not as though they lost the children to their ex-spouses. The financial plight of mothers after divorce is extremely serious (Luepnitz, 1982) and thus financial support is a major apparent advantage to joint custody.

Child Care—A fourth advantage of joint custody has to do with child care. Over one-third of the joint custody families said they relied on the other parent almost exclusively for substitute care. The single-custody parents, in contrast, cited substitute care as one of their greatest problems. The single mothers, especially, because of their low incomes, were often forced to rely on their families of origin for child care while they worked, which often overburdened the grandparents. Two of the single mothers, in fact, had been forced to move in with their parents because the burden of working and sending children to sitters was unmanageable. In contrast, it was a great advantage for joint parents always to know that their children had a place to be when they themselves were at work or socializing, and that no cost was involved.

Burn-out—A fifth advantage to joint custody has to do with time-off from parenting. All of the single-custody parents reported feeling overwhelmed at times by the pressure of solo-parenting with no one to consult with and no time off. Joint custody parents have a built-in break. Without asking for it or making special plans, they have part of the week (or the day or the year) to be free of parenting.

The results of this study clearly reveal several advantages of joint custody over single-parent custody. However, there are also several serious disadvantages to joint custody which make single-parent custody seem preferable in some cases. These will be described next.

Advantages of Single-Parent Custody

Protection of Abused Wives—Three of the 16 single-custody mothers mentioned that their ex-husbands had physically abused them, and it was essential for their safety that they avoid contact with them. Having sole custody allowed them to be free of these battering men in a way that joint custody would not. The issue of spouse abuse is very important in evaluating the concept of mandatory joint custody, and will be explored at the end of this chapter.

The two other advantages of sole custody most often cited in this study had to do with geographic mobility and remarriage.

Mobility—A number of single-custody mothers and fathers stated that joint custody would have seriously constrained their ability to move out of a particular neighborhood, county, or state. The ability to move had allowed them to find better jobs and to feel the exhilaration of "starting over" with new friends, without having to remain in close contact with their ex-spouses.

Remarriage—Single-custody mothers and fathers were aware that remarriage brings with it all of the new issues of the so-called "blended family." A child who is in joint custody with two parents, where even one of whom remarries, must then deal with new issues of authority and loyalty. Who comprises the unit responsible for making and enforcing day-to-day rules? Is it still biological mother and father, or is it now mother and stepdad, and to what degree? These problems are not insurmountable; joint custody parents do remarry and they often can turn this relational complexity to advantage (Ricci, 1981). Nonetheless, it is undeniable that from the point of view of a parent, it seems preferable in many cases not to have to confront this complexity at all.

These Findings Compared with Those of Wallerstein and Kelly

In contrast to the findings of Wallerstein and Kelly (1980b), the children in this study as a group were not maladjusted. In the Wallerstein and Kelly study, five years after the divorce, 37% of the children were "moderately to severely depressed." The authors clearly believe that divorce is an egregious experience for children. The parents in the present study reported that their children had had emotional reactions to the divorce conforming closely to those described by Wallerstein and Kelly, but not with the same intensity or duration. One major difference between the studies is that in gathering their sample, Wallerstein and Kelly promised counseling to their families as an incentive to participation. This may have elicited a group that represented the most distressed portion of the divorcing population (Luepnitz, 1981). In contrast, the sample in the present study may also represent an extreme group—those who are extraordinarily resilient to crisis. Both ends of the spectrum, of course, are important to investigate. What is objectionable about the Wallerstein and Kelly bias, however, is that their apocalyptic cries about the effects of divorce tacitly imply that the "intact family" is a wholesome structure, beyond serious philosophical reproach. In order to understand how two studies could produce such different conclusions, let us consider the reality of the contemporary intact family—which is the source of all divorced families. The structure of the model American family is that father is peripheral and mother is overly burdened with child care, and sometimes emotionally over-involved with the children (Lasch, 1979). The family is not typically very connected with the community. After divorce, things can get better or worse. The father may become even more removed, failing to support the children financially and often not even visiting them. Mother may become more overwhelmed, and even closer to the children. Because of her poverty and her exhaustion, she may withdraw from social functions and the family may become more isolated from the community than before the divorce. This structure can lead to depression and behavior problems in children, such as those described by Wallerstein and Kelly.

The post-divorce family can also be an improvement. When both parents retain their commitment to raising their children, the father may be more responsible than he was during the marriage. Mother, being freed of the total burden, may begin to work outside the home or return to school. Each parent may learn to rely more on relatives, neighbors, and support groups in the community. Thus, divorce can actually be corrective to the problems of the "intact" family structure. This description fits many of the families in the present study.

The Erosion of the Presumption for Maternal Custody

Over millennia of human history, fathers have been the legal custodians of their children (Luepnitz, 1982). Not until the late 19th century did women begin to receive custody of minor children in some cases. From the 1920s until the mid-1960s, the judicial presumption for maternal custody has been called into question by people at diverse points on the political spectrum. It is essential to look at whose interests will be served by changes in custody practice—particularly by the practice of mandatory joint custody.

This study has revealed many advantages to both children and parents in families where joint custody works well. An important question remains, however: if a presumption for the joint award were to become more firmly entrenched in the law, would women lose some of their ability to protect and separate themselves from violent men? This is of particular concern since, in California, for example, a judge in ordering single-parent custody, is required to take into account which parent will be more likely to grant access to the children to the other parent. What does a mother do who has suffered physical abuse from a spouse who decides that he wants joint custody? He might be very willing to share parenting, but her position might (justifiably) be that she wants no sharing at all. This woman would have to choose between losing her children entirely and continuing to place herself in danger. It is important to keep in mind that up to "50% of all women will be battered at some time in their lives by men who love them" (Walker, 1980). If a man is abusive to his *children*, judges will often take this into account when granting or denying visitation rights. However, judges do not always believe that wife abuse makes a father unfit. Indeed, in a recent case in Illinois, a father *convicted* of murdering his wife was granted custody of their six-year-old son.[8]

Changing the law in such a way as to ensure fewer single-mother custody awards is a very complicated issue for progressive thinkers. On the one hand, it is a goal of nearly all feminists to involve men more in child care. The necessity of men learning to "mother" will be a wholesome change for men themselves who will develop ways of being and feeling which civilization has forced them to deny. Many feminists also believe that if men became more involved in primary child care, that the misogynist history of our species would begin to change. Chodorow (1978) and

---

8. *In re* Abdullah, 80 Ill. App. 3d 1144, 400 N.E.2d 1063 (1980). On appeal, custody was removed from the father and the child was adopted. *See In re* Abdullah, 85 Ill. 2d 300, 423 N.E.2d 915 (1981).

Dinnerstein (1976) have written eloquently on this subject. They believe that the universal oppression of women is related to the fact that *women*, as the primary caretakers and first love objects, have been and continue to be the focus of humanity's infantile rage and dependency. All of our terror of being abandoned, our fear of being overwhelmed, and our ambivalence about being born into a mortal body—these most profound and ineffable of human feelings are directed towards women. It is reasonable to hope that the universal devaluation/idealization of women will be attenuated when both men and women become the objects of the infant's most primitive emotions. Thus, it is of extreme importance to involve men with children and child care. Many feminists have leapt from these beliefs and hopes to the position that more paternal and joint custody will represent the progressive alternative to single-mother custody.

The results of the liberal push for custody alternatives have been more complicated than some of us originally anticipated. One result was that 15 states passed bills explicitly ensuring men's rights to custody after divorce. This legislative coup was occurring at the very same time that Congress failed to pass the Equal Rights Amendment to the Constitution. It occurred at the same time that states such as Pennsylvania were unable to pass laws prohibiting a man to rape his wife. The author's own clinical experience is that, although women still receive custody in most cases, almost all women going through divorce now suffer the anxiety of losing their children—an anxiety created precisely by the new liberal laws and *zeitgeist* concerning custody. Some of those women *will* lose custody—even very traditional mothers who never would have lost custody 20 years ago. This painful fact has led some authors (Chesler, 1986) to advocate *no* mandatory joint custody, and even a legal presumption for mother custody. It is not the purpose of this chapter to propose a solution to the ethical and legal dilemmas of changing custody laws. It is essential, however, that in becoming the advocate for any particular solution, that all of the political, as well as psychological, angles be considered.

Conclusions

Both joint custody and single-parent custody have advantages and disadvantages. In this study, the joint custody families engaged in no relitigation, while the single-custody parents did so in over half the cases. In addition, the joint custody children retained two psychological relationships with their parents, whereas half the single custody children saw their non-custodians not at all. It is reasonable to conclude that joint custody at its best is superior to single-parent custody at *its* best.

The author does not endorse mandatory joint custody, however, because it may result in single mothers—an extremely disenfranchised social group—having less protection from abusive ex-husbands.

Finally, the author views divorce not as the demise of the completely wholesome nuclear family, but instead as an instance of painful upheaval—which can prove either destructive to the individuals involved, or corrective to the alienation and inequities intrinsic to the contemporary American family.

11

Shared and Sole-Custody Parents: A Comparative Analysis

HOWARD H. IRVING
MICHAEL BENJAMIN

The Toronto Shared Parenting Project sought to overcome some of the methodological problems associated with earlier research on shared parenting. This study compared the experience of 201 shared and 194 maternal sole-custody parents. The results indicate that satisfied shared parents experienced a range of benefits not available to their sole-custody counterparts. The findings are explored in terms of their implications for legal policy and clinical practice.

Concern with the adversarial system has resulted in major changes in the way divorce is managed across North America. This includes the reduction or elimination of fault grounds, the increasing use of mediation services, and the creation of a new form of child custody variously known as joint custody or shared parenting. This is a custodial arrangement in which care and control of the child(ren) is the responsibility of *both* parents, either legally and/or physically (Irving et al., 1984a). While shared parenting recently accounted for only about 3% of custodial children (Furstenberg et al., 1983)—more in specific regions (Weitzman, 1985)—available evidence suggests that this proportion is rapidly increasing (Folberg, 1984b; Furstenberg & Nord, 1985).

Howard H. Irving, Ph.D., is a Professor, Faculty of Social Work, University of Toronto, Toronto, Ontario, Canada.

Michael Benjamin, Ph.D., is a family sociologist who works as a research consultant and professor, and is research coordinator of the Student–Environment Study Group at the University of Guelph, Guelph, Ontario, Canada.

Since its inception, much of the debate about the desirability and efficacy of shared parenting has been ideological in character. Consequently, much of the extant literature consists of the rhetorical efforts of shared-parenting proponents[1] and critics.[2] While these efforts have enriched the literature conceptually, the credibility of the debate is limited insofar as it continues largely in the absence of empirical data (Clingempeel & Reppucci, 1982).

Initially, this was justified, since relevant data were largely absent, and the data that were available were seriously compromised by various methodological flaws, including small and unrepresentative sample sizes, the use of unreliable measures, the absence of first-hand child data, the scarcity of comparison group designs, and so on (Steinman, 1983; Benjamin & Irving, 1985).

Increasingly, purely rhetorical argument cannot be justified in the face of a research literature that, while still small, is rapidly expanding (Coller, 1988; Folberg, 1984a). Indeed, our reading of recent reviews of this literature (Benjamin & Irving, 1985; Coller, 1988; Clingempeel & Reppucci, 1982; Derdeyn & Scott, 1984; Irving & Benjamin, 1986, 1987; Richards & Goldenberg, 1985; Steinman et al., 1985) suggest general support for three conclusions: (1) most empirical studies demonstrate that, across a range of dimensions, shared parenting is a positive custody choice for the majority of the families involved; (2) methodologically, recent work has seen steady improvement in the quality and quantity of available data; and (3) available studies remain methodologically problematic, both in general, and particularly, with regard to the handful of studies that have directly compared shared-parenting and sole-custody samples (Ahrons, 1980b; D'Andrea, 1983; Ilfeld et al., 1982; Luepnitz, 1982, 1986; Phear et al., 1984; Pojman, 1981; Shiller, 1986a; White & Bloom, 1981; *see* Weitzman, 1985: Ch. 8). With regard to the latter, for example, comparative studies have confined their observations to group-level findings; while a proportion of dissatisfied shared parents are now routinely noted (Irving & Benjamin, 1987), no study to date has explored in any detail the basis for the satisfaction or the dissatisfaction of shared parents (*see* Benjamin & Irving, in press).

To overcome some of these deficiencies, we initiated the Toronto Shared Parenting Project.[3] To date, only partial accounts of the results have been published (Irving et al., 1984; Irving & Benjamin, 1986; Benjamin & Irving, in press). In what follows, we present a comprehensive summary. Beginning with a brief statement of the Project's methodology, presentation of the findings will be divided into four parts: (1) shared parents, (2) satisfied and dissatisfied shared parents, (3) simple comparison of shared and sole-custody parents, and (4) complex comparison of shared and sole-cus-

---

1. A partial list includes Alexander (1977), Bodenheimer (1977), Clawar (1983), Cook (1980c), Cox & Cease (1978), Eder (1978), Elkin (1984, 1987), Ernst & Altis (1981), Foster & Freed (1979), Green (1983), Greif & Simring (1982), Grote & Weinstein (1977), Miller (1979), Kelly (1983, 1984b), Morgenbesser & Nehls (1981), Nehls & Morgenbesser (1980), Robinson (1983), Roman & Haddad (1978b), Salfi & Cassady (1982), and Schreiber (1983).
2. A partial list includes Allen (1984), Benedek & Benedek (1979), Caroll (1982), Gardner (1982b), Goldstein et al. (1973), Hagen (1987), Hagen & Hoshino (1985), Patterson (1982), and Weitzman (1985).
3. During the period 1983–1986, this research was funded by the Social Sciences and Humanities Research Council (Ottawa, Canada), Grant 498-83-0017.

tody parents. We conclude by exploring the implications of these findings for sociolegal policy and clinical practice.

Method

Sampling—In Canada, there is no simple way of discovering the current incidence or distribution of shared-parenting couples (*see* McKie et al., 1983). Random sampling by means of the public record is precluded and we did not have the resources to undertake random sampling on a household basis. The alternative involved snowball sampling targeted on several specific sources, including appeals in the media (newspaper and radio), personal contacts, and a letter sent to more than 20 child-care or parenting groups.

Sampling criteria included: (1) residence within metropolitan Toronto (population: 2.5 million), (2) English language proficiency, and (3) the perception that they and their former spouse shared care and control of their child(ren). The last criterion was intended as the rough equivalent of legal joint custody in the United States (*cf.* Steinman, 1981); the proportion of couples with joint physical custody was left an empirical matter.

The final sample consisted of 395 respondents. This included 201 shared parents (75 couples [75% of the subsample] and 51 individuals) and 194 (maternal) sole-custody parents (42 couples [43% of the subsample] and 110 individuals). Both subsamples contained equal numbers of men and women. In addition, limited resources meant that data were restricted to adult respondents; children were not queried directly.

Instrumentation—All data were gathered by means of a questionnaire specifically designed and pretested (n=24) for this study. This consisted of 114 items which combined Likert-type questions with open-ended or probe questions. The final data base encompassed 268 mostly ordinal variables with additional variables derived from the open-ended items. In all cases, the questionnaire was administered by a trained interviewer in the respondents' own homes, with interviews lasting 1.5–2.0 hours.

Data Analysis—Classification of respondents into "satisfied" and "dissatisfied" subgroups relied on a 12-item satisfaction index.[4] Derivation of the satisfaction index used principal component analysis. This involved three steps. First, principal component analysis was applied to generate a scale incorporating the common elements of constituent items—the weight of each component a function of how much it shared with the other items. In addition, missing values for each

---

4. Constituent items were as follows: satisfaction with the process of shared parenting (V124); parent satisfaction with the visitation schedule (V171); child satisfaction with the visitation schedule (V172); the effect of shared parenting on the children (V173); change in the level of satisfaction among parents (V174); change in the level of satisfaction among children (V175); satisfaction with the shared-parenting arrangement (V179); the quality of the shared-parenting experience (V180); time to a smooth working shared-parenting arrangement (V181); parent satisfaction with shared childrearing responsibilities (V251); child satisfaction with shared childrearing responsibilities (V252); and, recommend shared parenting (V268).

item were replaced by their mean score so as to maximize the number of respondents included in the analysis.[5] Next, intercorrelations were run between each item and the scale which, together with the principal component analysis, revealed a high degree of consistency and thus good internal validity.[6] Finally, the scale was collapsed into two categories—"satisfied" and "dissatisfied"—based on the distribution of responses to its constituent items. On inspection of this distribution, the cut-off point was set at 3.59 (on a scale of 1 to 5).

Turning to the qualitative data, the responses to all open-ended or probe items were transcribed and then inspected for patterns, regularities, or themes. Limited resources precluded formal content analysis.

Finally, all quantitative data were key punched, checked, and cleaned, and then analyzed using SAS. Analysis relied on chi square. Unless noted otherwise, all comparisons reported below have met or exceeded a standard alpha of 0.05 and a gamma (a strength coefficient) of 0.20.

Findings

As noted above, we will report the findings in four parts: (1) shared parents, (2) satisfied and dissatisfied shared parents, (3) simple comparison of shared and sole-custody parents, and (4) complex comparison of shared and sole-custody parents.

Shared Parents

Sociodemographic Profile—The majority of shared parents were in their 30s (68%), with most male respondents working full-time (81%). On the basis of male modal income ($21-30,000 [26%]), education (university [63%]), and occupation (service, technical, or teaching professionals [75%]), shared-parenting respondents were classified as either "middle-" (65%) or "working-" (35%) class. Shared parents typically had two children between the ages of one and 12 in what was the first marriage for both partners (79%). The largest proportion were non-practicing Protestants (49%).

Marital Separation—In the largest proportion of cases, the wife initiated the marital separation (48%) which had been in place at the time of testing for nine or more years (65%). Value differences and communication problems were the major basis for the separation, with most respondents describing the level of marital conflict as "mild" to "moderate" (57%). One-third of these respondents were remarried or living common-law; while the remainder lived "alone," 65% reported involvement in a new intimate relationship which had been in place for anywhere from six months

---

5. The first principal component analysis accounted for 45% of the variation among the 12 items comprising the scale.
6. Correlations between the scale and its constituent items (i.e., first principal eigenvector) were as follows: V124 0.22; V171 0.34; V172 0.32; V173 0.27; V174 0.26; V175 0.19; V179 0.37; V180 0.31; V181 0.26; V251 0.29; V252 0.30; and V268 0.30.

to three years. The majority of former spouses resided less than five miles from each other (78%), many only a "short walk" away.

Initiation of Shared Parenting—Shared parenting was usually suggested by one or the other spouse (85%). Most couples reported little previous knowledge of it and most selected it for one of three reasons: it best reflected their mutual investment in childrearing; it was thought best for the child(ren); or it appeared the best way to minimize the trauma of the divorce for the child(ren). Friends and relatives were perceived as hostile to this custodial arrangement. Among a majority of couples (60%), a lawyer was directly involved in drafting their separation agreement. Lawyers were typically seen as supportive of a shared-parenting arrangement, although less than half actually recommended it. Overall, 60% of lawyers were rated "helpful."

Shared-Parenting Schedule—At the time of testing, just over half of all respondents had been involved in a shared-parenting arrangement for three years or less. Among the largest proportion of couples (50%), care and control of the child(ren) was mutual and in 40% no primary residence was cited. This was related to the distance between spouses' residences ($p<.02$): among those who lived "close" together (i.e., walking distance or short ride), mutual care and control was typical (42%) whereas maternal control was more likely among those who lived "far" apart (i.e., long drive) (78%). Nevertheless, most shared parents saw themselves as having mutual responsibility for the children and nearly all (90%) perceived their arrangement as "different" from a sole-custody arrangement.

Once established, their shared-parenting agreement was usually (67%) maintained without disruption. In addition to shared responsibility for child care, this also stipulated their cost-sharing arrangement and their child-sharing schedule. As to costs, most respondents reported either a 50/50 (41%) or a 75/25 (38%) arrangement, with husbands bearing the major responsibility in the latter case. These arrangements were typically maintained (85%) without incident. As to child care, the largest proportion of respondents reported a weekly child-sharing schedule (41%) on the grounds that it was thought best for the child(ren). While both parents reported a high level of childrearing involvement prior to their divorce (85%), fathers were more likely than mothers to report a significant increase in such involvement following the initiation of shared parenting (63% vs. 37%; $p<.0001$). Despite such involvement, shared parenting worked out almost immediately for only a minority of parents (36%); the majority encountered some initial difficulties (52%). Thus, time to a smooth working arrangement varied: some achieved early success (42%); others took up to a year (32%); a minority were still struggling at the time of testing (13%).

Co-Parental Relationship—Co-parental relations were described by the majority of respondents as "friendly" (55%), with communication typically positive but restricted to childrearing issues. We also queried respondents concerning the impact of their involvement with a new intimate partner. In most cases, the involvement of former spouses in a new intimate relationship was seen as having a positive effect (76%) on their shared-parenting arrangement.

Satisfaction with Shared Parenting—Finally, 83% (n=167) of respondents reported satisfaction with their shared-parenting arrangement, and 88% recommended it to parents in a similar situation. Satisfaction was directly related to the length of time it took to achieve a smooth working relationship, with those who reached this state in less than a year significantly more likely to report satisfaction than those who took more than a year.

Satisfied and Dissatisfied Shared Parents

As noted above, 17% of respondents (n=34) reported dissatisfaction with their shared-parenting arrangement. This suggested the possibility that satisfied and dissatisfied respondents might differ across a wider range of variables. As the findings reviewed below demonstrate, this suspicion proved correct.[7]

Sociodemographic Profile—Satisfied and dissatisfied shared parents were entirely comparable across most sociodemographic indicators, with only a few exceptions. For example, satisfied shared parents had a narrower range of income ($20,000–$50,000) and more education (completed university) than their dissatisfied counterparts. Satisfied shared parents were also significantly *less* likely to report that their own parents had been divorced (11% vs. 27%, $p<.02$), and *more* likely to indicate that they lived a short distance from their former spouses.

Marital Separation—Satisfied shared parents were more likely than their dissatisfied counterparts to describe the relationship with their former spouses prior to their separation in "positive" terms (*e.g.*, "caring," "reasonable," "supportive" and "cooperative"). Similarly, satisfied parents were more likely to describe their degree of marital conflict as "mild" or "moderate" (23% vs. 12%, $p<.03$) compared to dissatisfied parents who were more inclined to use the descriptor "extreme" (39% vs. 64%, $p<.03$). Finally, satisfied shared parents were more likely to judge that their marital separation had *not* adversely effected the child(ren).

Initiation of Shared Parenting—For parents with children, marital separation is necessarily associated with the choice of a custody option. In this context, satisfied shared parents were more likely than their dissatisfied counterparts to have selected shared parenting jointly. Satisfied shared parents were also much more likely to have reacted positively to the suggestion of shared parenting (81% vs. 56%, $p<.005$) and were less likely to have experienced a change of heart with increasing experience. Indeed, of those parents who did report a change in their response to the notion of shared parenting, satisfied as opposed to dissatisfied parents were significantly more

---

7. For a more complete report of these data, see Benjamin & Irving (in press).

likely to indicate that their opinion had either become "more positive" or "much more positive" ($p<.005$).

Related differences were apparent on inspection of open-ended items concerning reasons for selecting shared parenting. Among satisfied parents, shared parenting was selected because it was in the best interests of their children or it normalized childrearing following divorce. By contrast, dissatisfied parents did so because they felt they had been coerced, in the interests of obtaining a cheap divorce, as a way of increasing the likelihood of reconciliation, as a way of avoiding another traumatic confrontation, or as a way of ensuring continued contact with the child(ren).

Returning to the quantitative data, while both groups had engaged a lawyer, for a larger proportion of satisfied as opposed to dissatisfied parents the choice of custody option and the creation of an agreement with respect this selection was made without the involvement of a lawyer. Satisfied parents were also more likely to rely on a verbal as opposed to a written agreement and to report satisfaction with the process of arranging their shared-parenting agreement.

Shared-Parenting Agreement—The resulting shared-parenting arrangement could be characterized in several ways, each of which differentiate between satisfied and dissatisfied parents.

First, satisfied as opposed to dissatisfied parents were more likely to have had an arrangement in which there was no primary residence (42% vs. 12%, $p<.001$); children simply moved between residences. Open-ended responses suggest that the existence of a primary residence was an important source of resentment and bitterness among dissatisfied parents, especially wives.

Second, satisfied as opposed to dissatisfied parents were more likely to have a formal, written schedule concerning the movement of children between homes. The creation of this schedule was less likely to have involved a lawyer among satisfied shared parents, and the resulting schedule was more likely to be a source of satisfaction among satisfied shared parents and their children. Consequently, not only were satisfied shared parents more likely to perceive shared parenting as having had a "positive" effect on their child(ren), but, among those whose level of satisfaction had changed, it was more likely to have become "more positive."

Again, these findings were reflected in open-ended responses. Among satisfied parents, there was sufficient congruence among husbands' and wives' descriptions that a coherent picture of their child-sharing schedule was not difficult to assemble. Such was not the case among the accounts of dissatisfied parents. Indeed, the lack of congruence was so striking and so consistent as to render their accounts typically incomprehensible. In turn, the child-sharing schedule was the single most frequent source of complaint among dissatisfied parents.

Third, satisfied as opposed to dissatisfied parents were more likely to describe shared parenting in terms of mutuality, both between former spouses as well as in terms of their relationship with their child(ren). Thus, satisfied shared parents were significantly more likely to associate shared parenting with joint decision making and shared responsibility (71% vs. 35%, $p<.0001$).

Fourth, satisfied as opposed to dissatisfied parents were more likely to adhere to agreed upon financial and child-sharing schedules. Concomitantly, return to court for purposes of adjusting their agreement was significantly *less* likely among satisfied shared parents.

These differences were reflected in open-ended responses. Many dissatisfied parents reported that their agreement had undergone numerous negotiated revisions since its inception and now bore little resemblance to its original form. Indeed, at the time of testing, a handful of these respondents were in the process of relitigation in an effort to secure a sole-custody arrangement. It was not surprising, then, that many dissatisfied parents identified the legal processes associated with obtaining and maintaining their shared-parenting arrangement as highly problematic.

The consequences of these various features of their shared-parenting agreement were twofold. On the one hand, satisfied as opposed to dissatisfied parents were able to establish a working arrangement much sooner; indeed, many dissatisfied parents were still struggling more than a year after the inception of their agreement. On the other hand, divergent descriptions of the advantages and disadvantages of shared parenting emerged. Satisfied parents reported advantages such as shared responsibility, a feeling of achievement, and the ability to remain flexible. By contrast, dissatisfied parents were more likely to highlight a range of disadvantages, including inconvenience, lack of time, and the feeling of being emotionally and physically drained (17% vs. 62%, $p<.0001$).

The Co-Parental Relationship—Shared parenting necessarily entails the maintenance of some sort of co-parental relationship. In this area too, satisfied and dissatisfied parents differed. The thrust of these differences concerned the greater degree of mutuality among the former as opposed to the latter. Thus, compared to their dissatisfied counterparts, satisfied parents were more likely to report that joint decision making was the norm, their former spouse could always be contacted when needed, and communication with their former spouse was "warm" and "friendly" (74% vs. 21%, $p<.0001$).

This impression was confirmed by respondents' qualitative remarks. Dissatisfied parents typically characterized their relationship with their former spouse in terms of poor communication and pervasive feelings of bitterness; indeed, several respondents stated that they could no longer tolerate any contact with their former spouse. Consequently, repeated contact between such spouses was experienced as highly problematic and was becoming increasingly so.

Turning to the children, much the same picture emerges. Satisfied parents were more likely than their dissatisfied counterparts to indicate that the child(ren) were rarely upset following shifts between homes. Further, satisfied shared parents were more likely to associate shared parenting with increased post-separation parenting involvement, with the result that they now felt closer to their child(ren) than ever before. They were also more likely to perceive that the child(ren) were satisfied with their current childrearing arrangement.

Finally, we explored respondents' feelings concerning the reciprocal effects of combining a new intimate relationship with a shared-parenting arrangement. Both subgroups agreed that shared parenting had little effect on any new romantic relationship. Satisfied parents, however, were more likely than their dissatisfied counterparts to indicate that involvement in a new intimate relationship had a "positive" effect on their shared-parenting arrangement.

Simple Comparison of Shared and Sole-Custody Parents

Data reported in this section are "simple" only in the sense that, like all comparative studies in the literature (see above), they compare shared and sole-custody parents at the group level.

Sociodemographic Profile—Across most sociodemographic indicators—including two out of three related to social class—there were no differences between shared and sole-custody parents. There were only two exceptions: shared parents were older, that is, more concentrated in their 30s (71% vs. 10%; $p<.0001$), and were more likely to report a university education.

Marital Separation—As regards their marital separation, the groups differed most with respect to the enmity which they continued to attach to it. Shared parenting as opposed to sole-custody parents, for example, were less likely to feel guilty over the breakdown of their marriage (46% vs. 61%; $p<.005$), more likely to indicate that the decision to separate was mutual (37% vs. 25%; $p<.01$), and that the level of pre-separation conflict was "low" (21% vs. 13%) or "moderate" (36% vs. 20%; $p<.0001$).

Initiation of Custody—The process of arriving at a custodial arrangement further distinguished the two groups. Shared as compared to sole-custody parents were more likely to arrive at a custody arrangement without the help of a lawyer (39% vs. 20%; $p<.0001$). This initially more positive view was supported by subsequent experience, with shared parents more likely to report a "positive" change in their reaction to custody (37% vs. 27%; $p<.04$).

Custody Arrangement—The positive view of shared parents was further reflected in the comparative reaction of their children. Thus, shared as opposed to sole-custody parents were more likely to perceive child satisfaction with their child-sharing/visitation arrangement (49% vs. 36%; $p<.01$). It was also reflected in the level of parent-child contact, with shared parents much more likely to report weekly child contact (40% vs. 8%; $p<.0001$) as well as greater consistency in child-support payments (85% vs. 72%; $p<.002$). Perhaps in consequence, shared parents were more likely to report that their custody arrangement had worked out well almost immediately (36% vs. 20%; $p<.0001$).

Co-Parental Relationship—Such relative concordance was also reflected in the co-parental relationship. Thus, shared as compared to sole-custody parents were more likely to describe their ongoing relationship as "friendly" (55% vs. 42%; $p<.03$), to note that parenting decisions were "often" made jointly (76% vs. 40%; $p<.0001$), and to report "very extensive" involvement in childrearing (65% vs. 49%; $p<.0001$).

In a similar vein, shared parents were more likely to judge that the effect of a new intimate relationship was "positive" (32% vs. 16%; $p<.002$).

Outcome Satisfaction—While the two groups did not differ in outcome satisfaction per se, shared as opposed to sole-custody parents were more likely to stress various sources of satisfaction (*e.g.*, child likes the proximity of both parents (77% vs. 35%; $p<.0001$), less likely to note sources of dissatisfaction (*e.g.*, high cost: 16% vs. 36%; $p<.0001$), and more likely to perceive that their children were satisfied with their arrangement (91% vs. 80%; $p<.003$).

A supplementary finding of note concerns gender differences. Across a range of variables, shared-parenting men and women recorded nearly identical responses. In contrast, among sole-custody respondents, men and women consistently differed (*e.g.*, child-support payments consistent: male 85%, female 61%; $p<.0004$).

Complex Comparison of Shared and Sole-Custody Parents

Apart from the substantive results, comparison of shared-parenting and sole-custody groups at the group level was extremely valuable for three reasons: first, it highlighted the large number of variables that either failed to distinguish between the two groups or were redundant; second, it helped identify six clusters encompassing a total of 22 variables which consistently distinguished between the two groups (*see* Appendix); and third, it suggested that the two groups differed fundamentally as a function of the interaction between three factors: custody status (shared parenting vs. sole custody), satisfaction (satisfied vs. dissatisfied), and gender (male vs. female).

The results reviewed in this section, then, are "complex" in two senses: first, they involve comparison of the groups in terms of the interaction of satisfaction and gender; and second, they are confined to the 22 variables noted above, a variable set we will call the "selected process profile" (SPPO, since they collectively refer to the manner in which child custody is enacted and maintained through time. Our large sample size made it possible to explore two such comparisons: Comparison 1 interacted custody status with either sex (A) *or* satisfaction (B), while Comparison 2 interacted custody status, sex *and* satisfaction. The results were as follows.

Comparison 1A: Custody Status x Sex—This analysis showed that shared parents consistently exhibited a more positive SPP than their sole-custody counterparts. This was largely expected *within* sex; we predicted that shared-parenting women would display a more positive profile than sole-custody women (*e.g.*, weekly child contact: 41% vs. 7%; $p<.0001$). What was surprising was that these findings held *across* sex: not only did shared-parenting women display a more positive SPP than sole-custody men (*e.g.*, satisfaction: 80% vs. 64%; $p<.01$), but the same was true for shared-parenting men relative to sole-custody women (*e.g.*, increased childrearing involvement: 56% vs. 28%; $p<.0002$).

Comparison 1B: Custody Status x Satisfaction—Here, while the same trends were evident as reported above for sex, the findings were somewhat more heterogeneous. Satisfied shared parents exhibited a more positive SPP than either satisfied (*e.g.*, positive effect on children: 86% vs. 67%; $p<.0003$) or dissatisfied sole-custody parents (*e.g.*, negative feelings re former spouse: 32% vs. 58%; $p<.03$). While there was no difference between groups when *both* were dissatisfied, dissatisfied shared parents still exhibited a more positive SPP than satisfied sole-custody parents (*e.g.*, weekly child contact: 17% vs. 8%; $p<.0002$).

Comparison 2: Custody Status x Sex x Satisfaction—Analysis of data with respect to Comparison 2 was restricted to *nine* subgroups of particular clinical interest. The findings of Comparison 1 (A and B) suggest that all custodial parents do not experience their arrangement in the same way; rather, their adjustment distributes along a continuum from highly positive (satisfied shared-parenting men and women) to highly negative (dissatisfied sole-custody men). The results of Comparison 2 yield a more complex picture involving three patterns of difference.

First, when both groups were satisfied, shared parents consistently exhibited a more positive SPP than their sole-custody counterparts, both among men (*e.g.*, positive effect on children: 86% vs. 64%; $p<.003$) and among women (*e.g.*, emotionally draining: 17% vs. 37%; $p<.005$).

Second, satisfied groups *always* exhibited a more positive SPP than dissatisfied groups irrespective of either custody option or sex. For example, dissatisfied shared-parenting men were less likely to report increased involvement in childrearing than satisfied sole-custody women (17% vs. 30%; $p<.0002$). Similarly, dissatisfied shared-parenting women were more likely to find their arrangement emotionally draining than satisfied sole-custody women (67% vs. 37%; $p<.02$).

Third, when both groups were dissatisfied, sex was a critical differentiating variable: there were few differences between dissatisfied shared-parenting and sole-custody men (*e.g.*, high cost: 15% vs. 53%; $p<.02$); however, among dissatisfied women, shared-parenting women displayed a more positive profile than their sole-custody counterparts (*e.g.*, children like the proximity of both parents: 39% vs. 9%; $p<.04$).

Discussion

In the majority of cases, shared parenting offered parents and children a satisfying arrangement which only improved through time. While this offered benefits superior to a smooth-working sole-custody arrangement, that too could be quite satisfying, especially for the women and children in question. Finally, while *both* shared parenting and sole custody could yield intensely troublesome and unhappy arrangements, shared parenting alone offered the solace of continued contact between the child(ren) and both their parents.

Thus, while shared parenting was not satisfying for all who chose it, it did offer a range of distinct advantages for the clear majority of shared parents. Choice of shared parenting appeared especially indicated among couples who exhibited some combination of the following attributes: (1) low to moderate levels of pre-separation conflict; (2) a "child-centered" orientation to parenting; (3) mutuality with respect both to the decision to end their marital relationship and to the selection of shared parenting; and (4) motivation among both parents to accept and overcome the day-to-day exigencies and complications invariably associated with enacting a shared-parenting arrangement.

As always, the strength of these assertions rests on this study's methodological strengths and weaknesses. In this sense, this study acts as a mirror, reflecting the research literature in which it is embedded. As regards strengths, five features of the present study stand out: the large sample size; the use of primary as opposed to secondary data; the comparative research design; the inclusion of data pertaining to a large array of variables; and, the complex comparative analysis. Turning to weaknesses, here five features are noteworthy: the absence of direct child data; the use of cross-sectional as opposed to longitudinal data; the use of a selected as opposed to a random sample of respondents; the absence of selection criteria to ensure matched subsamples; and the reliance on only one as opposed to multiple sources of data. Taken together, these ten attributes suggest the ideal course for future research in this area.

Implications: Policy and Practice

These findings hold a range of implications for both sociolegal policy and clinical practice. In closing, we selectively discuss a few examples which stand out for us in each category.

Sociolegal Policy

The policy implications of the present work center on changes to existing child-custody statutes and to the attitudes of lawyers and judges.

The first and most central is universal recognition of a general principle: following divorce, it is in the best interests of children that they maintain frequent, reliable, and ongoing contact with both their parents (*see* Isaacs, 1988).

The existing judicial preference for sole custody is rooted in an historical context which favors an adversarial approach centered on the individual. Both facets of this preference have become increasingly problematic. The adversarial system, with its emphasis on "winner take all," tends to promote protracted conflict rather than a spirit of compromise (Schwartz, 1984) crucial to solutions in keeping with the best interests of the child(ren). Similarly, the focus on individual rights, responsibilities, and obligations promotes a conception of the family seen as a collection of individuals, and too often transforms the children into pieces of property over whose ownership or control parents may struggle. This flies in the face of the family systems literature which holds, among other things, that: the organization of family systems is independent of the members taken one at a time; such systems shape the manner in which members perceive and experience both each other and the external world; and, the patterned relationships which constitute family life bond members together and create the context within which members' behavior are meaningful (Benjamin, 1983; Reiss, 1981).

From this perspective, the fact that sole custody disrupts the relationship between the children and the non-custodial parent (father) violates one aspect of their sense of self. On the one hand, given that concern for the best interests of the child is a universally accepted second general principle (Derdeyn, 1976a, 1976b), logic argues against any custody arrangement which disrupts the relationship between the child(ren) and both the parents. On the other hand, data from the present study suggest that, by comparison with sole custody, shared parenting seems to benefit the majority of child participants while promoting joint co-parental involvement, decision making, and fiscal responsibility, as well as encouraging maximum contact between the child(ren) and both parents. On both these grounds, we contend that child-custody statutes should rest on a rebuttable presumption of shared parenting (*see* Coller, 1988). Such a presumption assumes that parent's rights to care for their child(ren) and child(ren)'s rights to maintain their relationship with both parents should not be lost in divorce and then "won back" through the courts. Rather, these respective rights can only be lost or limited for just cause, with the burden of proof on those who would seek to avoid shared parenting. Accordingly, the onus would be on the judge to state explicitly why in a given case he or she refuses to honor a shared-parenting presumption (Everett, 1984). Moreover, as we have seen, shared parenting need not be a 50/50 split, either in time or in money, to be satisfying for all parties. Nor, in most cases, need distance or movement between residences prove insurmountable problems.

None of this is to suggest that shared parenting is necessarily suitable for all parents, hence the rebuttable nature of the presumption. In this regard, Coller (1988) suggests the following as likely grounds upon which to reject shared parenting: inability to parent the child; substance abuse; physical abuse of spouse or child; great geographical distance involving small children; intractable overt hostility over time between spouses despite mediation; and the expressed desire of a parent not to participate in shared parenting. While we agree in principle, for reasons that will soon become apparent, we take exception to Coller's final criterion.

The thrust of these remarks is to argue more generally that following divorce, the key issue before judicial personnel should not involve selection among divergent custody types (*e.g.*, Weitzman, 1985), but rather with creating a parenting plan which best matches the needs and interests of the children in question. Based on the present study, this suggests a preferred hierarchy of parenting arrangements or plans, with both physical and legal shared parenting first, legal shared parenting only second, and sole custody (with or without access) third. Application of a given option to a specific family should be guided by both the principles noted above, that is, the child(ren)'s best interest and maximization of parental involvement, parenting continuity, and mutual decision making with regard to child care.

Given the high level of mutuality among most shared parents, application of a parenting plan in the form of a presumption of shared parenting would likely pose few problems for parents who agree that shared parenting is best for them. But what if they do not, and child custody becomes a matter of contention between them? We still believe that shared parenting makes good sense. Our data show that even when shared parents are unhappy with their situation, there is still a greater degree of parent-child contact within a shared-parenting as opposed to a sole-custody arrangement. Recall, too, that shared-parenting fathers were far more likely than their sole-custody counterparts to become more actively and more extensively involved in parenting, despite the fact that both reported comparable levels of parenting prior to the divorce (*see* Kelly, 1983).

Accordingly, we suggest that imposing shared parenting on reluctant parents will, at worst, likely do no more harm than sole custody, while offering some of them an unexpectedly positive post-divorce custody experience. This said, it seems reasonable to expect that such couples will be at higher risk of running into difficulties than couples who enter into shared parenting voluntarily. This implies that shared parenting should *not* be applied on an all-or-nothing basis. Rather, we suggest that all couples enter into shared parenting for a trial period of between six and 12 months. At the end of that time, their experience with shared parenting would be reviewed and shared parenting either made permanent, modified, or abandoned altogether in favor of sole custody.

Such a trial period would provide the opportunity to adjust terms and conditions in response to parental complaints. While such adjustments would best be done informally or through the use of third party involvement (see below), the court would always be available to adjudicate intractable conflict. Given the principles set out above, the thrust of any parenting plan would be to adjust it to serve the children's best interest. In many instances, we suggest, this would likely be best served within a shared-parenting arrangement. However, with the exception of contraindicated couples, the state of our knowledge is such that we cannot predict with any degree of certainty which couples will succeed with shared parenting and which will not, hence our view that shared parenting should first be seen to fail before sole custody is regarded as an appropriate option. Such a view contrasts sharply with opponents of shared parenting (*e.g.*, Weitzman, 1985) who view problems with it (*e.g.*, the similarity of problems associated with legal shared parenting and maternal sole custody) as the basis for its rejection, an approach which appears to throw the baby out with the bathwater.

While we reject such arguments, they are valuable at least insofar as they call attention to the range of problems that may arise among shared-parenting families. This, in turn, suggests the need for the routine application of some mechanism intended to promote problem solving among shared parents and to reduce the likelihood that such problems will become insurmountable. Such a mechanism, we suggest, is encompassed by the role of third party support. While several possible forms of support immediately come to mind, our own bias would favor the involvement of family mediators (*see* Irving & Benjamin, 1987). The latter appear a particularly appropriate choice because of their increasing involvement with divorcing couples as an alternative to the adversarial system.

In this context, it is worth noting that divorce can be characterized as a family crisis. During this time, family systems may be more amenable to change than at any other time (Bross & Benjamin, 1983). The direction of change will depend in large part on the nature of the intervention(s) to which they are subject. Advice from a lawyer concerning a fight for or acquiescence to sole custody constitutes one type of intervention. Advice from a family mediator concerning involvement in a shared-parenting plan constitutes a different type of intervention.

While this way of characterizing the involvement of lawyers and family mediators will not apply in all instances, it is quite typical in our clinical experience (*see* Irving & Benjamin, 1987). It is salient in two respects. First, mediation may be useful not only in helping couples select a custody option, but also in terms of identifying underlying family problems, differentiating between appropriate and inappropriate reasons for making such a selection, and maintaining ongoing contact and thus assisting with problem solving as required. Second, there appear to have been a fair number of sole-custody parents in our sample who, if advised differently, might well have opted for shared parenting. Similarly, there appear to have been a small number of dissatisfied shared parents who might have avoided this outcome with appropriate intervention.

These findings speak to the potential usefulness of family mediation in the choice and maintenance of shared-parenting arrangements. Its use finds further support in a restricted literature which demonstrates the outcome effectiveness of this approach (Emery & Wyer, 1987; Irving & Benjamin, 1987; Sprenkle & Storm, 1983; Koopman & Hunt, 1988; Kressel, 1985). This implies that custody statutes which support shared parenting as a preferred option should simultaneously support the *routine* use of mediation services during the trial period.

As we envision it, with regard to shared-parenting couples, the mediator would serve three primary functions. The first would simply be to monitor the couple's progress during the trial period. The second would be to intervene as needed, for example, in order to teach couples communication or negotiation skills, or to help them work through conflict in particularly difficult areas. Finally, the mediator could be called on to prepare a report for the court describing a given family's experience with a shared-parenting plan and make recommendations as regards its continuation, modification, or abandonment.

Finally, we turn from statutory reform to attitudinal change among judicial personnel. While many lawyers have come to see the value of shared parenting (Miller, 1979), the present study demonstrates that substantial opposition still exists. Similar opposition among an equal proportion of judges seems likely (*see* Coller, 1988).

Like the statutes which they administer, their preference for sole custody (Fineberg, 1979; Scott & Derdeyn, 1984), we suggest, is rooted in adherence to an adversarial model of judicial action and an individualistic model of the family. Nothing is more symbolic of these perspectives than the very language of current custody law. "Petitioners" and "respondents," "contested" and "non-contested cases," "litigated settlements" and "judicial decrees": this is the language of combat, of opponents locked in a struggle, championed by their respective lawyers, in which the winner takes the child(ren) as the prize. Similarly, "custodial" and "non-custodial" parents, "visitation" and "access" rights, and "care and control" orders are all ways of conceiving of a family split into its constituent elements, with any remaining linkages between them formalized in legal ritual.

In our view, none of this is appropriate to the continuing relationship between parent and child. While one may choose to "visit" the hospital or the funeral parlor to see a sick or deceased friend or relative (Everett, 1984), it is entirely inappropriate to speak of "visiting" one's own child(ren), a point non-custodial fathers have been making for some time (Roman & Haddad, 1978b). In this context, the language of "shared parenting," of "negotiated agreements," "parenting plans" and "co-parental cooperation" does not merely involve a change of terminology; it represents a paradigmatic or "second order" shift (Watzlawick et al., 1974) from an adversarial to a cooperative model of judicial action and from an individualistic to a relational model of the family (Everett, 1984).

Given the rising incidence of shared parenting (Furstenberg & Nord, 1985; Weitzman, 1985) and accompanying statutory changes, such a shift seems to us inexorable. But change is a hard thing for most of us; we resist it because it is new and threatens long and sincerely held beliefs. Thus, the erosion of opposition to shared parenting among lawyers and judges may well be a long and gradual process. If, as this study demonstrates, shared parenting is in the best interests of many (but not all) children (*see* McKinnon & Wallerstein, 1987; Richards & Goldenberg, 1985; Steinman, 1981; Steinman et al., 1985), then some way must be found to accelerate its acceptance. The obvious answer is through education, including the widespread dissemination of current and ongoing research efforts in this area.

Clinical Practice

The second area to which our study speaks is that of practice. Practitioners in this area help parents and/or their child(ren) accept this change in their life and cope with the transition difficulties it inevitably brings (Beal, 1980; Charnas, 1983; Durst & Wedemeyer, 1987; Keshet & Mirkin, 1985). Increasingly, practitioners are coming to realize that divorce is not an anomalous event, but rather a normative one, much like birth, death, or leaving home (Carter & McGoldrick, 1980a; McCubbin & Figley, 1983). As such, they must become aware of the special exigencies and stresses which characterize this process in order that they be most helpful to clients who are going through it.

What the present study makes clear is that child custody appears to represent a discrete subphase within the larger process of divorce. This includes not only the interactional bases for selecting a shared-parenting option, but also the subsequent processes it sets in train as parents and children struggle to cope with the day-to-day problems and joys of living within a shared-parenting arrangement.

In short, shared parenting represents a new family form about which parents, children, *and* practitioners have much to learn if they are to survive. In turn, the present study calls special attention to four aspects of the shared-parenting experience.

First, while most divorcing couples appear well suited to the shared-parenting option, some are *not* and should be directed towards a sole-custody arrangement. The problem for practitioners is acquisition of the necessary assessment skills to differentiate between these two groups. Here, we can do no better than to reiterate those inclusion criteria noted already: mutuality, cooperation, circumscription, and motivation. Given some evidence of the presence of these attributes, the couple in question will likely be good to excellent candidates for shared parenting and should be so advised. Conversely, as the number of opposite attributes increases, shared parenting will increasingly be contraindicated.

Second, a commonly accepted clinical principle is that the better prepared one is for a given event, the better one will be able to cope with its demands and the less disorganizing its consequences. In this regard, practitioners can provide an important psycheducational service. For many clients, shared parenting will be totally new, its meaning and exigencies opaque. Recall, too, that for many satisfied shared parents, smooth adjustment was anything but automatic; it required hard work lasting up to a year in some cases. If a couple's choice of shared parenting is to be fully informed, practitioners will need to know all this and more so that they may pass on this information to the appropriate clients.

Third, as in any transitional period, the problems associated with it are most pressing while it is still new and strange. Here, practitioners will not only need to be vigilant of early difficulties, but will be most helpful in a support capacity. This study makes clear that the logistical and relational demands of shared parenting can be significant. We speculate that this is especially true in the initial period—say the first six months—when considerable adjustment is required to achieve a workable shared-parenting arrangement. However carefully a shared-parenting agreement is drawn up, it cannot possibly foresee all contingencies. Consequently, it is during this period that the family is most vulnerable to a "vicious cycle" of conflict and recrimination leading to outcome failure. By providing needed support during periods of particular stress and/or crises, practitioners may help ensure that client families derive the maximum benefits from their shared-parenting arrangement.

Finally, practitioners need sufficient knowledge of shared parenting so as to suggest practicable alternatives to the problems couples encounter. The present study indicates that scheduling, money, and co-parental decision making represent those areas in which conflict is most likely. Here, satisfied shared parents displayed no single best solution; rather, they were characterized by flexibility, willingness to compromise, and a single-minded focus on the best interests of their child(ren). In our clinical experience, it is the latter attitude that is the practitioners' most powerful lever for change, with vestiges of the "old" marital relationship the central underlying problem (*see* Irving & Benjamin, 1987). Thus, effective intervention with shared-parenting families not only requires generic clinical skills, but also in-depth substantive knowledge concerning the typical developmental course of couples who enter into a shared-parenting arrangement.

Appendix—Selected Process Profile

Cluster 1: Pre-Separation Marital Relationship

1. Who suggests separation
2. Level of pre-separation marital conflict

Cluster 2: Custody Choice

3. Agreement: formal vs. informal
4. Agreement: legally binding or not

Cluster 3: Child-Sharing Schedule and Child-Care Costs

5. Initial arrangement
6. Type of child-sharing schedule
7. Parent satisfied with schedule
8. Child satisfied with schedule
9. Satisfaction with process of arranging child custody
10. Schedule effect on child
11. Financial adherence

Cluster 4: Outcome Satisfaction

12. Global satisfaction
13. Custody experience
14. Time to smooth working arrangement
15. Satisfaction index

Cluster 5: Parent–Child Relationship

16. Joint decisions re child
17. Involvement in childrearing: pre-separation
18. Involvement in childrearing: post-separation
19. Involvement in childrearing: change pre-post
20. Satisfaction with childrearing responsibilities
21. Child satisfaction with childrearing arrangement

Cluster 6: Co-Parental Relationship

22. Communication with former spouse

12

Co-Parenting in the
Second Year After Divorce

ELEANOR E. MACCOBY
CHARLENE E. DEPNER
ROBERT H. MNOOKIN

This chapter describes the kind and degree of co-parenting being maintained by a group of divorcing families approximately 18 months after parental separation. The sample was taken from court records of divorce filings in two California counties in 1984–85, and includes nearly 1,000 families who had children under age 16 at the time of filing. Three patterns of de facto residential custody (children living with mother, with father, or having dual residence) are compared. While dual-residence parents maintained higher levels of communication, their levels of conflict did not necessarily differ from those of primary-residence parents. The amount of conflict in co-parenting is shown to be related to the intensity of interparental hostility at an earlier time.

Prior to the 1970s, there was a strong presumption—both in the law and in popular expectations—that custody of minor children would be awarded to the mother when

Eleanor E. Maccoby, Ph.D., is Professor Emeritus of Psychology at Stanford University.
Charlene E. Depner, Ph.D., is Coordinator for Research and Statistics, Statewide Office of Family Court Services, Judicial Council of California.
Robert H. Mnookin, J.D., is Adelbert H. Sweet Professor at Stanford Law School and Director, Stanford Center on Conflict and Negotiation.
This research is supported by Grant HD #19386 from the National Institute of Child Health and Human Development, and by Stanford University's Center for the Study of Families, Children and Youth. The authors wish to thank Sue Dimiceli for her assistance in data analysis. This chapter is reprinted with permission from *The Journal of Marriage and the Family*, Vol. 52, Number 1, Feb. 1990 (pp. 157–170).

parents divorced, unless the mother was shown to be unfit. In the last fifteen years, such presumptions have changed greatly. Most states have erased formal maternal presumptions from their divorce statutes. A few have specified that custody should go to the parent who has been the primary caretaker, a standard that favors mothers in a large majority of cases. In most states, however, the maternal presumption has been replaced by a "best interests of the child" standard (Mnookin, 1975). In addition, laws have increasingly recognized joint custody as a viable arrangement for the children of divorcing families. A number of states have enacted a "friendly parent" provision, so that in cases in which parents are disputing for primary residential custody, preference goes to the parent who is most willing to encourage or allow ample visitation with the other parent (i.e., Cook, 1980c).

An assumption underlying some of these legal changes has been that the best interests of children are served if they continue to have close contact with both parents after the parental separation. This assumption rested in part on two major studies of mother-custody divorced families (Hetherington et al., 1978, 1982; Wallerstein & Kelly, 1980b), both of which indicated that children living with their mothers seemed to do better if they had continuing contact with their fathers. However, in the mother-custody families with high father-child contact, the divorces may well have been less conflictual initially than in families where father-child contact was low, so that the children's better progress might have been due to their having been exposed to less parental conflict, rather than to their continued contact with their fathers. In any case, results based on these fairly restricted groups of families might not generalize to a broader spectrum of divorcing families. Two recent reports based on larger, more representative samples (Furstenberg et al., 1987; Zill, 1988) indicate that the well-being of children who live with their mothers following divorce is *not* related to the amount of continued contact between fathers and children.

Assuming for the moment, however, that there may be benefits, at least for some children at some ages, stemming from continued contact with both parents, a persisting question is whether there are costs associated with this continuing contact that may outweigh the benefits. Possible costs are: (1) continued or even exacerbated conflict between the parents; this would occur if continued contact for the child with both parents required continued contact *between* the parents, thus increasing or maintaining opportunities for parental conflict. It is a consistent finding in the research on families that parental conflict entails substantial risks for the development of children (Rutter, 1971, 1982; Zill, 1978; Emery, 1982; Lowery & Settle, 1985; Crosbie-Barnett, 1988). Parental conflict appears to be particularly dangerous for children when it occurs in combination with other risk factors (Rutter & Quinton, 1977; Emery & O'Leary, 1984); (2) if children spend significant amounts of time in two different households, the children are likely to be exposed to different and perhaps conflicting values and demands; also, schedules may be excessively complex, unless the parents are willing and able to coordinate their plans so as to achieve some consistency across households and make the transitions between households relatively smooth for the children; and (3) if the parents do not communicate cooperatively, there may be increased opportunities for children to play off one parent against the other, the result being a weakening of effective parental supervision. It becomes important to know how well parents can coordinate their parenting efforts when there are areas of conflict between them deep enough to have precipitated divorce.

In intact families, parents do not always agree on such things as discipline, household rules, or standards to be applied, but in most families parents make some effort to present a united front to the children on these matters. When divorced parents are attempting to maintain an arrangement in which both continue to be involved in the children's lives—either through joint custody or visitation—do they separate their spousal conflicts from their functions as parents, and maintain common goals and some degree of mutual support in their parenting functions? In an important study based on a national sample of children aged 12–16, Furstenberg and Nord (1985) found that the most common pattern in those divorced families in which the children had contact with both parents was "parallel" parenting, where the two parents functioned quite independently of one another. However, for the substantial majority of these families, the parental separation had occurred more than ten years previously. Furthermore, in almost all the families, one parent (usually the mother) had primary custody and the child merely visited with the other, often quite infrequently. Several recent studies have begun to provide information about the relationships between divorced parents in families with more recent divorces, or with younger children, or in which the parents have elected to try sharing childrearing more equally. For the most part, these studies utilize relatively small, selected samples, and they are primarily concerned with the effects of post-divorce parental conflict on children's adjustment and competencies (Johnston et al., 1985; Lowery & Settle, 1985; Luepnitz, 1986; Crosbie-Barnett, 1988). There is still relatively little information concerning the details of interparental cooperation—i.e., the logistics of managing visitation and alternation, the division of responsibilities, the frequency and nature of communication, and the amount of mutual undermining vs. mutual back-up—that prevails under different custodial arrangements. Especially interesting to those concerned with the impact of joint custody is the question of how much cooperation is possible in the relatively small number of high-conflict families in which one or both parents did not initially want to share custody, but who adopted a joint arrangement as the only compromise they could reach.

The Stanford Custody Project (Maccoby, Depner, & Mnookin, 1988) offers an opportunity to examine some of these issues. The sample is relatively large, including over a thousand families selected so as to reflect a cross-section of the heterogeneous population of parents who filed for divorce in two California counties during several months in 1984–85. This study is not an "effect" study in the usual sense, since it does not include in-depth assessments of the psychosocial functioning of individual children or parents. Rather, through three rounds of parent interviews, it focuses on the processes whereby divorcing couples arrive at their decisions about custody and visitation for their children, and on post-divorce family functioning. The first interview (Time 1) was conducted with the parents a few months after filing and commonly about six months after the couple separated. The second interview (Time 2) was done a year after the first interview—18 months, in the most usual case, after the couple separated. A third interview is being completed at the time of this writing, approximately three years after the first. The present report focuses on data collected in the second interview, with some predictive information being drawn from the first interview and from court records.

The objectives of the present analysis are as follows:

1. *To compare co-parenting in three custodial arrangements*: where (a) children live with their mothers and visit their fathers, (b) where they live with their fathers and visit their mothers, and (c) where they spend substantial time in each household (dual residence). Such comparisons will show whether parents maintain greater coordination, and moderate their personal conflicts to a greater degree, under a dual residential (as compared to a single primary residential) arrangement.

2. *To determine whether the degree and kind of co-parenting* maintained following divorce *depends on the level of initial conflict* between the divorcing couple. Are highly conflicted couples able to maintain any degree of cooperation? This question is particularly important for those couples who have adopted a residential arrangement (dual residence) which would seem to demand co-parenting.

As noted above, existing studies look upon interparental conflict as an antecedent condition, and analyze psychosocial deficits in either parents or children as consequences of conflict. In our exploration of question 2, we differentiate between the initial levels of hostility and conflict attendant upon the divorce itself, and the subsequent patterns of cooperation or discord in the processes of co-parenting. Thus, we see co-parenting processes as mediators between initial hostility or conflict and the levels of psychosocial functioning which others have examined, and propose to study the links between these processes and possible anteceding conditions.

Method

Sampling and Interviewing Procedure—Court records of all divorce filings in two California counties during the period September 1984 through March 1985 were reviewed. Families having at least one child of this marriage under 16 years of age, and in which the parents had not been separated for more than 13 months, were listed as eligible, yielding 2,000 potentially eligible families. Interviews were obtained at Time 1 with at least one parent in 1,128 of these families. In the large majority of cases, the interviews were lengthy ones conducted by telephone; for a subsample, respondents answered mail questionnaires. The primary reason for non-response was failure to locate families on the eligible list. Only 11% of eligible families who were reached declined to be interviewed. Both parents were interviewed in 43% of the families at Time 1, so that data were obtained from a total of 1,620 individual parents. In the 1,128 families included at Time 1, there were 1,890 children (*see* Maccoby, Depner, & Mnookin, 1988, for more detail concerning the sampling procedures).

At Time 2, 50 families were no longer eligible for the study (primarily because of reconciliation). Interviews were obtained with at least one parent in 959 of the Time 1 families. The Time 2 families included 1,590 children. Once again, the primary reason for failure to reinterview an eligible family that had been included at Time 1 was the inability to locate either parent. The large majority of the interviews were conducted by telephone, although there were a few respondents who elected to come to our office for a face-to-face interview. The interview included both open-ended and fixed-alternative questions (more of the latter) and generally took between one hour and one-and-a-half hours to complete.

Families included in the study represent a wide range of socioeconomic levels. For example, 28% of the parents had high school education or less; 41% had some college, and 30% had completed college or beyond. The range of earnings was very wide, from a number currently unemployed to seven respondents with annual earnings of over $150,000. The mean earnings for mothers in the sample was approximately $16,000 at Time 1, $35,000 for fathers. The modal age of respondents was in the early thirties. At Time 1, the ages of the children ranged from infants (one as yet unborn) to age 18. Although only families having at least one child under 16 were included, some of these families also had older teenagers, and these children were included in questions about individual children. Family size varied from one child to eight. Forty-seven percent of the Time 1 sample had one child, 41% had two, and the remaining families had three or more.

Classifying Families by* de Facto *Residence of Children—At Time 1, most of the families in the sample had not yet obtained final divorces, and even at Time 2, 37% of the divorces had not been finalized. For those families whose divorces were still being processed, physical and legal custody of their children had not yet been specified in a court order. However, it was possible to determine the children's *de facto* residence. Parents were asked to report the amount of time each child spent with each parent during the two-week period immediately preceding the interview. Since all interviewing was done during the school year, this did not include summer vacations. Respondents were then asked whether the last two weeks were typical in terms of the amount of time the child usually spent with each parent, or exceptional for some reason. If not typical, respondents were asked to describe the usual division of the child's time between the two households. Some families said that there was no regular pattern—that the non-custodial parent could take the children at any convenient time and that this varied from week to week. In such cases, the amount of contact with each parent during the two-week period preceding the interview was entered to represent the *de facto* arrangement for this family. In all other cases, the usual pattern was entered. Children were designated as residing with their mothers if they spent fewer than four overnights per two-week period with their fathers. They were designated as residing with their fathers if they spent fewer than four overnights with their mothers. All others—i.e., those who divided their overnights 7/7, 8/6, 9/5, or 10/4 between the two households—were designated as being in dual residence.[1]

The subsample of Time 1 families (n=969) who remained in the sample at Time 2 [hereafter "panel" families] is almost identical to the full Time 1 sample with respect to the proportion of families in each residential category. At both time periods, over two-thirds of the children resided with their mothers and about half of the mother-residence families sent children for overnight visits to the father. About a sixth of the families had dual residence, and in 10% of the families, the children lived with the father (with the majority of these children having overnight visits with the mother). In a small number of families, one or more of the children lived with the mother while one or more lived with the father ("split" custody). However, in the large majority of families having more than one child, the same pattern of residence and visitation prevailed for all the children, and the classification of residential and visitation patterns utilized in the analyses for this chapter represent the patterns for *families* rather than individual children. Although the distributions of *de facto* residence were almost identical at Times 1 and 2, this does not mean that all children remained in the same residence over the year. There was a certain amount of shifting in and out of each of the residential arrangements, but 79% of the families having one of the three major residential arrangements at Time 1 (mother, father, or dual) retained the same arrangement at Time 2.

Subsample of Co-Parenting Families—In the Time 2 interview, we asked a number of questions about co-parenting, i.e., about logistical problems in getting the children back and forth between households, the coordination of rules in the two households, and the backing-up or undermining of each parent's childrearing by the other. Such questions were relevant only for the families in which the children were spending at least minimum amounts of time with each parent. We selected those families in which the children were spending at least four hours a week of face-to-face visitation with the "outside" parent, resulting in the following groups of families who are included in the analyses reported below: 450 families in which the children live with the mother, 71 families in which they live with the father, and 170 dual-residence families, with a total n of 691 families. The analysis of co-parenting which follows excludes not only those families in which the children did not see both parents, but also those relatively rare cases with "split" arrangements in which the children lived with someone other than a parent.

Merging Reports of Two Parents—In one-half of the subsample families (i.e., 346), both parents were interviewed. As might be expected, the two parents did not always agree when reporting on events they both presumably would have knowledge

---

1. Our choice of cutoff points between single-parent primary residence and dual residence was supported by other information from the interviews. Parents were asked whether the children lived primarily with mother, primarily with father, or "with both of you." When children spent more than three, but less than 11, overnights with the other parent, both mothers and fathers tended to answer "with both of us."

about. In such cases, for most of the measures in the study, we have averaged the two parental scores. There are some exceptions to this rule, however. For some questions, we judged that respondents might be motivated to report fewer problems than actually existed. Thus, for example, if one parent reported considerable logistical difficulty with the children being brought back late from visits with the other parent, or inconvenience caused by the former spouse making last-minute changes in visitation arrangements, and the other parent did not report such problems, the score of the parent reporting the higher level of discord was accepted as probably being a more accurate representation of the actual level of problems being experienced by the family. Questions for which this strategy was used to merge the reports of two parents are marked with asterisks in Table 1.

Measures of Co-Parenting—While some questions concerning co-parenting were asked at Time 1, this topic was explored more fully at Time 2. Table 1 shows the questions asked at Time 2 that provided information on co-parenting. We wished to combine these items into one or more composite scales that would reflect the degree and quality of co-parenting being maintained by the families in which children were seeing both parents. The first step was to recode items so that they would have comparable standard deviations. The recoded items were then subject to component analysis (with varimax rotation). Two factors emerged. The first factor has five items (labeled A in Table 1), and the combined score for the five items is called "discord." This scale has a range of 1–10, with a mean of 4.6 and a standard deviation of 2.0. High scores reflect the following cluster of characteristics: the parents often argue, one or both may have threatened to cut off visitation, they have a high incidence of logistical problems in getting the children back and forth between households, and the parents report that their former spouses undermine their parenting efforts and deliberately instigate conflict. The second factor includes three items (labeled B in Table 1). these three items have been combined into a score called "cooperative communication," having a range of 2–10; the mean score on this measure is 5.3 and the standard deviation is 2.0. High scores are received by parents who talk frequently about the children, try to coordinate rules, and do not try to avoid contact with each other. The two factor scores are not completely orthogonal ($r=-.39$) but the correlation is low enough to permit their having somewhat independent relationships with other measures.

When the two scales were plotted against one another, it was evident that most cases were falling into three main clusters. Table 2 shows the cross-classification of cases on the two factor scores. The three major patterns are (1) a disengaged pattern, (2) a cooperative pattern, and (3) a conflicted pattern. Some parents, even when their children are spending time in both households, disengage themselves as completely as possible from the former spouse; they seldom talk to their "ex," do not attempt any coordination in the activities or rules of the two households, and manage the logistics of visitation with little conflict—often because they exchange the children at times and places where the parents will not have to come into contact with each other (i.e., one parent brings the child to school or a day-care center, the other parent picks the

TABLE 1
Questions on Co-Parenting in the Time 2 Interview*

		Factor
In general, do you and (OTHER PARENT) argue these days?**		
Percent reporting "sometimes" or "often"	33.0%	A
Does it ever happen that either parent refuses to let, or threatens not to let, the other parent see the children when he/she would like?**		
Percent "yes"	26.0%	A
Thinking about how you and (OTHER PARENT) reach decisions these days, how would you rate (EX) on his/her desire to avoid emotional outbursts? (Where 1 is someone who is trying to upset people and 10 is somebody who tries hard not to upset people.)		
Mean on 10-point scale	4.7%	A
(After a number of possible logistical problems in getting children back and forth between households have been described and discussed): How big a problem have these kinds of things been for you? (Use a scale from 1 to 10, where 1 means no problem at all and 10 means a very serious problem.)**		
Mean on a 10-point scale	3.6%	A
Your relationship with your children can sometimes be affected by what (OTHER PARENT) says or does. (I'm thinking about whether the other parent backs you up on discipline, what the other parent says about you to the children, and so on.) In your case, would you say that (OTHER PARENT) makes it easier or harder for you to be the kind of parent you want to be? Use a scale from 1 to 10, where 1 means the other parent makes it very difficult for you, and 10 means that (OTHER PARENT) makes it very very easy.**		
Mean on 10-point scale	6.2%	A
How often do you and your (EX, OTHER PARENT) talk with each other about the children?		
Percent of parents who report once a week or more	48.0%	B
Do you and (OTHER PARENT) try to have the same rules about bedtime, TV, and so on in both households, or do you each decide these things for your own household?		
Percent who try to coordinate rules	34.0%	B
Do either of you deliberately try to limit the amount of contact between the two parents?		
Percent reporting that one or both try to limit contact	40.0%	B

*The percentages and means reported here are based on all reports of parents interviewed in the families where children have contact with both parents

**When both parents were interviewed and their answers differed, the score of the parent reporting the higher level of discord was entered as the family score.

TABLE 2
Co-Parenting Patterns, Time 2*

| | | Discord | |
		Low	High
	Low	Disengaged (196)	Conflicted (231)
Cooperative Communication			
	High	Cooperative (172)	Mixed (76)

*This table is based on all families in which children have contact with both parents and in which scores are available on both the Discord and Cooperative Communications factor scales.

child up at the end of the day). Anecdotes reported to us by some of these parents indicate that they may be slow to try to renegotiate their initial arrangement for visitation, even when changes in family circumstances might indicate that changes are desirable.

A second pattern is a cooperative one, in which the parents attempt to isolate their interpersonal conflicts from their functions as parents. They discuss plans for the children or problems encountered with them, attempt coordination between households, and back up each other's parenting.

A third group we have labeled "conflicted"—these parents have low levels of cooperation but do not disengage; their conflicts remain active and spill over into the parenting domain. These parents could be said to be engaged in "parallel" parenting, in that they seldom talk to each other about the children's welfare, schedules, etc., and do not attempt to coordinate the children's environments in the two households. At the same time, there is considerable conflict between the parents: they argue and do not manage the children's transitions between households well; they are likely to make threats concerning visitation and more often than other parents report that each is undermining the other's parenting. This is the group in which the children are most likely to witness quarrels between the parents; among the parents (both mothers and fathers) in this group who report that fights occur between them "sometimes" or "often," approximately half say that the children witness them. A much smaller proportion of children with cooperative parents are witnesses to their fights—27% according to mothers, 12% according to fathers.

A fourth group—the one we have labeled "mixed"—is somewhat puzzling: they do discuss matters related to the children's welfare and do attempt to coordinate schedules; but at the same time they maintain relatively high degrees of interparental conflict. In this group as well as in the "conflicted" group, children are relatively likely to witness parental quarrels when they occur—43% of the mothers and 39% of the fathers in this group say the children witness their fights.

In some of the analyses below, we have utilized the four co-parenting clusters or patterns as our "outcome" variable. For multivariate analyses, however, we have used the two factor scores separately, since they provide continuous distributions rather than categorical classifications.

Results

With respect to the coordination of rules, families vary with respect to the kinds of coordination they attempt: some report discussing such matters as whether and when they will allow a young adolescent girl to wear makeup; how much use of the family car they will allow a teenager old enough to drive; how many hours they will require for doing homework, and what weeknight and weekend curfews will be. However, it may be seen (Table 1) that the majority of parents do not attempt to coordinate rules between the two households.

With respect to logistical problems, parents were first asked about specific issues, such as the children not being ready for pick-up, children being brought back late, or ex-spouses making last-minute changes in arrangements for visitation. In mother-residence and dual-residence families, the latter two problems were reported more often by mothers than by fathers—a fact which may have something to do with the fact that fathers do more of the chauffeuring of the children for visitation than do the mothers. But this is not the whole story: even in the mother- and dual-residence families where both parents share the chores of driving the children back and forth between the two residences, mothers report a higher incidence than fathers of the ex-spouse making last-minute changes in visitation arrangements.

When parents were asked to rate the seriousness of their logistical problems, most reported that the problems were not serious (see Table 1), although there was considerable variation, and their answers covered the full range of the 10-point scale. In a similar vein, the majority of parents rated their ex-spouses above the mid-point of the scale in being supportive of their parenting. However, there was a substantial minority who did report active undermining by the other parent, and ratings on this scale once again covered the full range from one to ten.

Co-Parenting in Each Residential Group—Table 3 shows the frequency of each co-parenting pattern in each of the three primary residential groups at Time 2. The three residential groups are quite similar in the distribution of cases into the four co-parenting patterns. Levels of cooperation appear to be somewhat higher in the dual residence families, but the difference between groups in the distribution of the four patterns does not reach significance ($p=.11$).

When residential groups are compared with respect to their scores on the two factor scores from which the co-parenting groupings were derived, it may be seen (Table 3) that families in which children spend substantial time in both households have higher scores on Cooperative Communication than do families where one parent or the other has primary residential custody. The discord scores, however, do not differ by residential group.

The families in the three primary residential groups differ with respect to certain demographic characteristics. Specifically, families with dual residence have somewhat

TABLE 3
Co-Parenting Patterns in Each Residential Group
(Percent of Families)

| | Children's Residence | | | |
Co-Parenting Pattern	With Mother	With Both	With Father	Significance
	(436)	(170)	(69)	
Cooperative	23%	34%	23%	
Conflicted	36	30	32	chi-square – 10.43
Disengaged	30	23	35	$p<.11$
Mixed	11	13	10	
	100%	100%	100%	

Factor Scores:

Mean:	Cooperative Communication	4.64	5.16	4.78	$F=4.71$**
Mean:	Discord	4.63	4.48	4.67	$F= .41$

**$p<.01$

higher parental income and education, smaller-sized families, and fewer adolescent or very young children (Maccoby, Depner, & Mnookin, 1988). It is possible that the higher levels of cooperation in the dual-residence families are a function of their socioeconomic status or family composition. We have examined these issues by using analysis of variance to predict both the Discord and the Cooperative Communication factor scores, in each case cross-classifying our cases by residential group and a demographic grouping. Dual-residence families remain significantly higher on Cooperative Communication after the number of children, age of youngest child, and parental education and earnings have been partialled out. Residence still does not emerge as a significant differentiator for the Discord scores when the various demographic factors have been taken into account.

Co-Parenting Pattern and Parental Satisfaction—At Time 2, parents were asked to rate themselves (on a 10-point scale) with respect to their degree of satisfaction with the current arrangements for their children's division of time between the two parental households. Not surprisingly, parental satisfaction with the existing residential arrangements at Time 2 was lowest among non-custodial parents. For other parents (i.e., primary-residence and dual-residence parents), satisfaction did not depend on the children's residence, but rather on the co-parenting pattern prevailing between the divorced couple. Both fathers and mothers were most satisfied when they were able to maintain a cooperative pattern (*see* Table 4), and the highest levels of satisfaction were achieved by the cooperative parents whose children were in dual residence.

The high satisfaction of cooperative parents could arise in more than one way. It may be that parents are able to cooperate because they are satisfied with the residential arrangement for their children, or they are satisfied because they are able to cooperate. Perhaps both are true.

The next most satisfactory co-parenting pattern for both mothers and fathers is one of disengagement. The least satisfactory pattern is the conflicted one. For conflicted families, the usual situation is that one or both parents would like to have more time with the children—or would like the other parent to have less—but since the parents talk to one another as seldom as possible, they have not worked out any direct means of resolving conflicts involving the children and resort to indirect warfare in which the children frequently become embroiled.

TABLE 4
**Parents' Time 2 Satisfaction with Residential Arrangements for Children,
in Relation to Co-Parenting Patterns, by Residential Group**

		Co-Parent Pattern			
Children's Residence	*n*	Coop-erative	Con-flicted	Dis-engaged	Mixed
With Mother					
Mother's satisfaction	(379)	7.3	5.5	6.9	6.7
Father's satisfaction	(257)	7.4	4.1	6.7	5.9
With Both					
Mother's satisfaction	(144)	8.6	5.4	6.9	7.3
Father's satisfaction	(132)	8.3	5.9	7.3	6.1
With Father					
Mother's satisfaction	(36)	6.6	3.0	5.2	3.5
Father's satisfaction	(55)	7.5	7.0	7.1	4.5

	F Values	
	Mothers	Fathers
Residence	10.39***	4.79**
Co-Parenting Pattern	13.06***	13.21***
R x C	1.34, N.S.	2.85*

*$p<.05$
**$p<.01$
***$p<.001$

Table 4 reveals a surprising situation for non-custodial parents. Although non-custodial parents in general have low levels of satisfaction with the custodial arrangement, Table 4 shows that in families in which the children are living with their mothers, fathers are as satisfied with the arrangement as are the mothers, provided that the two parents are not involved in a conflicted relationship with each other. In families in which the children are living with their fathers, however, mothers are less satisfied with the arrangement regardless of the co-parenting pattern maintained by the two parents. Even so, mothers' satisfaction is especially low when conflict between the two parents is high.

For parents in each residential arrangement, their satisfaction is closely related (negatively) to the amount of discord between them. In a multiple regression (data not shown), parental scores on the two co-parenting scales (discord and communication) were entered as co-predictors of the parents' satisfaction scores, and the communication score added relatively little to the prediction, although its importance varied with residence and parent. Among mothers in dual-residence families, their satisfaction was somewhat enhanced by frequent communication with the former spouse, but the same was not true for dual-residence fathers. Fathers who had the children living with them most of the time tended to be more satisfied if their level of communication with their former wives was *low*; a number of these fathers appeared to prefer having as little to do as possible with the children's mother, even if the children were seeing her for regular visitation. While the cooperative pattern clearly carries benefits, it also entails effort and stresses which some parents prefer to avoid.

Demographic Correlates of the Co-Parenting Patterns—Does the incidence of the different co-parenting patterns vary with the income or education of the parents, or with the number, age, or sex of the children? A comparison of families having only male children with those having only female children showed no effect of the children's sex on co-parenting patterns. Similarly, neither the level of earnings of either parent, nor the father's education was significantly related to these patterns (although there was a borderline tendency for discord to be higher in families with poorly educated fathers—(less than .10). The mother's education was related, but not in a linear fashion. Mothers with mid-level education were the most likely to be involved in a cooperative co-parenting relationship, and the least likely to be disengaged from interaction with the former spouse (see Table 5).

Family composition was clearly important for co-parenting: the older the youngest child, the more likely the parents were to have disengaged from one another with respect to the parenting functions. Separate analysis of the two co-parenting scales (data not shown) indicated that within each residential category, discord was higher, and cooperation lower, for larger families and those with younger children. (The correlation between family size and age of youngest child is .05, and thus these two predictors are not confounded and multivariate analysis is not required.)

Co-Parenting as a Function of Earlier Conflict—Our first interview was conducted about six months, on the average, following the couples' separation, and many

TABLE 5
Co-Parenting Patterns in Relation to Maternal Education, Children's Age, and Family Size

Co-Parenting Patterns	Mother's Education			Chi-Square
	High School or Less	Some College Technical	College Grad or More	
	(175)	(228)	(140)	
Cooperative	18.9%	32.0%	24.3%	18.0%**
Conflicted	36.5	34.2	30.7	
Disengaged	34.9	21.1	35.7	
Mixed	9.7	12.7	9.3	
	100%	100%	100%	

	Age of Youngest Child			
	Under 6	6–10	11+	
	(323)	(217)	(135)	
Cooperative	28.5%	22.1%	23.7%	25.5%***
Conflicted	38.1	32.3	28.2	
Disengaged	20.1	35.5	40.0	
Mixed	13.3	10.1	8.1	
	100%	100%	100%	

	Family Size			
	One Child	Two Children	3 or More	
	(332)	(274)	(60)	
Cooperative	29.5%	23.0%	15.9%	17.2%**
Conflicted	28.9	36.1	52.2	
Disengaged	30.7	28.1	24.6	
Mixed	10.8	12.8	7.3	
	100%	100%	100%	

**$p<.01$
***$p<.001$

couples were still negotiating the terms of their divorce. At that time, levels of anger and overt conflict were very high in some couples, while other couples were separating with less conflict and even some degree of mutual good will. The interviewers rated each respondent's hostility toward the former spouse, using a ten-point scale. At Time 1, the ratings ranged from 1 to 10 and were normally distributed, with a mean of 5.7 for mothers and 5.3 for fathers. For families in which both parents were interviewed, the hostility ratings were not highly correlated ($r=.17$), and therefore the relationship between Time 1 hostility and Time 2 co-parenting patterns has been analyzed separately for mother-hostility ratings and father-hostility ratings. Respondents were divided into three groups on the Time 1 hostility score: scores of 1–4 are in the low group, 5–6 in the medium group, 7–10 in the high group. Table 6 shows how these groups differ on Time 2 co-parenting patterns.

For both mothers and fathers, the level of Time 1 hostility strongly predicts the co-parenting pattern reported at Time 2. For initially hostile parents, the most common Time 2 picture was that they avoided communicating when possible, but

TABLE 6
Time 1 Hostility as a Predictor of Time 2 Co-Parenting Patterns

Time 2 Co-Parenting Patterns	Mother's Time 1 Hostility			Chi-Square
	Low	Med.	High	
	(123)	(190)	(139)	
Cooperative	34%	27%	15%	
Conflicted	17	31	58	
Disengaged	38	29	21	
Mixed	11	13	6	50.9***
	100%	100%	100%	

	Father's Time 1 Hostility		
	Low	Med.	High
	(119)	(133)	(108)
Cooperative	39%	25%	17%
Conflicted	18	29	57	51.2***
Disengaged	36	29	9
Mixed	7	17	17
	100%	100%	100%

***$p<.001$

were still highly conflicted in that they quarreled relatively often, had trouble working out the logistics of visitation, and undermined one another's parenting. For parents with low levels of Time 1 conflict, on the other hand, the cooperative pattern (high communication, low discord) was the most common one. Chi-square tests reveal that the relationship between initial hostility and the nature of the co-parenting patterns in place a year later is highly significant (chi-square = 50.7 for mothers' Time 1 hostility, 57.4 for fathers').

The question arises as to whether it is the father's or mother's earlier hostility that has the greatest bearing on the couple's ability to sustain cooperative parenting a year later. With the subsample of families in which both parents had standard telephone interviews at Time 1 (a minority of families returned mail questionnaires which did not provide a hostility rating), a multiple regression was done in which the mother's and father's Time 1 hostility scores were entered as joint predictors of the cooperation and discord scores. The two parents had almost exactly equal weight in the prediction of the discord scores (standardized beta for mother hostility, .350; for father, .348). In predicting the scores on cooperative communication, the mother's hostility had somewhat more weight (beta for mothers, .298; for fathers, .187). There is a hint here, then, that mothers' attitudes may have more effect on the amount of communication that occurs between the parents at Time 2 than does that of fathers. But the more important point (and the one more strongly supported by the data) is that the emotional state of both mothers and fathers during the immediate post-separation period has a considerable impact upon the nature of the co-parenting (or lack of it) that develops during the ensuing year.

Further evidence that early conflict is carried over into patterns of co-parenting at Time 2 comes from an analysis of the bargaining positions each parent took up in the initial negotiations over custody and other aspects of the divorce settlement. At Time 1, some parents had already reached an agreement concerning the terms of their divorce, and these parents were asked how difficult it had been to reach this agreement. In Table 7, these families have been divided into those who reported difficulty reaching agreement (having rated themselves 5 or more on a 10-point scale of difficulty) and those who had little or no difficulty (rated 4 or less). Those reporting difficulty reported more discord and less cooperative communication at Time 2 than the families who had reached agreement easily at Time 1. It is interesting that disagreement over child support predicts subsequent discord and lack of cooperative communication at least as strongly as disagreement over custody.

In the smaller group of families who had not yet agreed on the terms of their divorce at Time 1, parents were asked what each parent was asking for. As Table 7 shows, when parents were asking for different legal or residential custody at Time 1, they were more likely to be discordant in their co-parenting at Time 2 than were parents who had not initially differed about what custodial arrangements they wanted.

In the early summer of 1988 (after the completion of Time 3 interviewing, and three-and-a-half to four years after the sample couples had filed for divorce) court records of the sample families were examined. At this time, slightly over 80% of the panel families had final divorces. For these cases, information was available from court records concerning the involvement of the family in legal actions and court-ordered

TABLE 7
Co-Parenting at Time 2 in Relation to Initial Conflict
Over Terms of the Legal Settlement

		Mean	(n)	t	Mean	(n)	t
Couples Who Had Reached Agreement on Divorce Terms at Time 1							
Did they have difficulty reaching agreement on:							
Custody:	Yes (>5)	4.70	(178)	2.31*	5.03	(192)	5.44***
	No (>5)	5.10	(282)		4.06	(289)	
Child Support:	Yes (>5)	4.70	(182)	2.98**	5.00	(187)	4.96***
	No (>5)	5.23	(210)		4.04	(215)	
Couples Who Had Not Reached Agreement at Time 1							
Asking different physical custody?							
	Yes	4.09	(74)	2.00*	5.53	(75)	3.47***
	No	4.71	(95)		4.47	(101)	
Asking different legal custody?							
	Yes	3.73	(55)	3.38***	5.82	(56)	3.78***
	No	4.78	(121)		4.61	(129)	

*$p<.05$
**$p<.01$
***$p<.001$

procedures with respect to (1) custody and/or visitation and (2) financial matters, up to the time the divorces were finalized. In addition, in the Time 3 interviews, the parents were asked to rate their family with respect to the amount of legal battling that had taken place over these two kinds of issues. On the basis of both court record and interview information, families were classified into four groups: those having low, moderate, considerable, or high levels of legal conflict. In arriving at the classification of each family, the following court-record information was taken into account: Was the case contested? Did the family see a mediator? Was there a custody evaluation? In addition, parents' ratings took into account whether there had been any restraining orders, or any court actions with respect to payment of child or spousal support.

As may be seen from Table 8, the nature of the co-parenting relationship being maintained at Time 2 was related to the amount of legal battling that occurred over the 3–4 years since the couple filed for divorce. Cooperative communication was lower, and discord higher, in the couples who carried their disputes into the legal system. It is possible that experiencing difficulty in co-parenting at Time 2 (about a year and three months after filing, in the most common case) was a factor that led some families to contest custodial or visitation arrangements. But it should be noted that disagreements over money were as closely related to difficulties in co-parenting as were disagreements over custody or visitation—a fact which suggests that the parental legal disputes (whatever their nature) are carried over into the co-parental relationship.

Summary and Discussion

At the beginning of the chapter, we cited evidence that, although some children survive parental conflict without overt signs of difficulty, such conflict does increase

TABLE 8
Relation of Amount of Legal Conflict Over Custody
or Money to Co-Parenting Factor Scores

	Mean Factor Scores, Time 2	
Amount of conflict over custody:	Cooperative Communication	Discord
Low (n=196)	5.2	3.6
Moderate (n=172)	4.7	4.6
Considerable (n=65)	4.7	5.2
High (n=114)	4.1	5.7
$F =$	9.07***	37.3***
Amount of conflict over money:		
Low (n=180)	5.2	3.7
Moderate (n=146)	4.9	4.3
Considerable (n=121)	4.5	5.3
High (n=100)	3.9	5.7
$F =$	12.8***	36.8***

***$p<.001$

the risks that children will develop behavioral or psychosocial problems. When parents divorce, it might be expected that children's exposure to parental conflict would diminish, since they are no longer living under the same roof with the two warring parents. However, many children of divorcing parents have been shielded from the parental conflict when both parents were still at home, and have been unaware how poorly their parents were getting along (Wallerstein & Kelly, 1980b). Furthermore, in the post-divorce period, interparental conflict frequently continues. Thus, it is not necessarily the case that children will experience less parental conflict after the divorce than they did before. In some cases, the departing parent simply drops out of a child's life and a new family unit is formed around the custodial parent, the child, and often, the custodial parent's new partner. In such cases, the only conflict between the custodial parent and the departed parent to which the child is exposed stems from attitudes expressed to the child by the custodial parent. At present, however, there are widespread assumptions that it is desirable for the child to have continuing contact with both parents, and both the law and many current custodial agreements embody this principle. Essentially there are three ways in which inter-parental conflict can be handled in situations where children do spend time in both households: (1) the parents can cut off contact between one another entirely, so that the child has two entirely distinct environments that are not bridged by interparental communication; (2) parents can separate their parental functions from the other aspects of the conflict that led to divorce, and maintain a cooperative, communicative relationship with respect to childrearing; or (3) they can continue to fight, with the child frequently becoming embroiled in loyalty conflicts and cross-pressures.

At Time 2, in most cases about 18 months after the parents had separated, we found that approximately one-fourth of the divorced couples whose children spent some time in both households were maintaining a cooperative co-parental relationship; about one-third were engaged in conflict that involved quarreling, difficulties in managing the logistics of visitation, and mutual undermining; nearly one-third of the couples had disengaged, with low levels of both communication and conflict. The remainder of the couples had mixed patterns. Parents were more likely to be disengaged if their children were older than if they had at least one child under the age of six. Also, the amount of conflict was related to family size: parents evidently found it easier to avoid discord if they had only one child, and especially difficult to do so if they had three or more children.

We raised the question at the beginning of the chapter as to whether interparental conflict is mediated by the residential arrangement for the children. That is, do parents who have chosen dual residence (i.e., joint *de facto* residential custody) perforce cooperate more fully, and quarrel less, than divorced couples whose children live primarily with either the father or the mother? Our answer to this question is mixed. Dual-residence parents talked to each other more frequently, and in general maintained a higher level of cooperative communication. However, they did not experience less discord, and the prevalence of the conflicted pattern was as great in the dual-residence families as in the primary-residence ones. Within each residential group, there was great variability in how much cooperation or conflict the divorced couple maintained when both continued to be involved in parenting. These results would appear to indicate that sharing the residential custody of children following divorce does not systematically exacerbate conflict between the parents, nor does it systematically moderate such conflict.

Our finding that the *de facto* residential custody of children has little bearing on the amount of conflict between the divorced parents of children who are continuing to see both parents is consistent with what other recent studies report. Bowman and Ahrons (1985) reported that the quality of co-parental communication did not differ between families with maternal custody and families with joint legal custody (the majority of which also had substantial sharing of physical residence). Luepnitz (1986), comparing 16 families with mother custody, 16 with father, and 11 with joint, found that children's adjustment was not related to whether they resided with mother, father or both. If we make the assumption that children's adjustment is to some degree a function of the quality of co-parenting (or the absence of parental conflict), then this study is consistent with the finding that the residential arrangement is not related to co-parenting.

Although the *de facto* residential arrangement for children did not appear to have much bearing on the amount of discord between parents in the early post-divorce period, the initial level of conflict between the parents did have a substantial impact on the quality of co-parenting maintained by the divorced parents. The ability to cooperate was closely linked to the degree of hostility and conflict that existed close to the time of break-up. If couples could not agree easily on what kind of custodial arrangement they wanted, and/or if their initial level of hostility toward one another was high, they were unlikely to be managing a cooperative arrangement 18 months after their separation. This was true even for those couples who adopted a dual-residence arrangement. Even for these couples, if they were initially highly conflicted, they usually tried to have as little communication with one another as possible. However, their hostility continued, and manifested itself in mutual undermining and/or difficulties in managing visitation.

At Time 2, primary custodians and dual custodians were essentially equal in their satisfaction with the custodial arrangement. It might have been predicted that dual custodians would be *more* satisfied, in that neither fathers nor mothers would have been left with the sole (or major) responsibility for childrearing; each would have time off from parenting. Furthermore, many parents believe that their children benefit from continued contact with both parents, and this should be an additional source of satisfaction for dual custodians. On the other hand, if we assume that the more contact parents have with their children the more satisfied they are, then we would have predicted that dual custodials would be *less* satisfied than primary custodians. Furthermore, there are some possible disadvantages to the dual arrangement, such as logistical complications, the effort of maintaining contact with the former spouse, and the lack of independence in decision making. Our findings suggest that the sources of special satisfaction with dual residence and the factors creating dissatisfaction with this arrangement offset one another.

"Outside" parents, with whom the children only visited, were considerably less satisfied than primary residential parents. These "outside" parents were particularly unhappy if they were involved in a conflicted co-parenting relationship with the former spouse. Non-custodial parents appeared to be more satisfied if they and their "Ex" could either cooperate or disengage completely. It is worth noting that in families in which children spent substantial amounts of time in both households, neither parent is an "outside" parent in terms of parental satisfaction.

Custodial parents report more logistical problems over visitation than "outside" parents. They express more hostility toward their former spouses, and make fewer efforts to coordinate rules in the two households than do non-custodial parents. Evidently, it is not any sense of harmonious resolution of their conflict with the ex-spouse that leads to the relatively high levels of satisfaction among primary custodial parents. Indeed, many primary-custodial parents were resentful over having been left with the responsibility for raising the children on their own. Their satisfaction appears to come from having been able to keep intact their close daily family ties with their children, and from being in control of their own lives and those of the children. In some cases, custodial parents derive bitter satisfaction from having bested their ex-spouses in a struggle over the children. In other cases, they are satisfied with the present arrangement simply because they think it is better for the children than residence with the other parent would be.

The fact that custodial parents (both primary and dual) were more satisfied than non-custodial parents raises some interesting policy issues. If dual residence for children maximizes the satisfaction of the two parents taken jointly, does this constitute an argument in favor of joint physical custodial arrangements? Are there concomitant costs? We did not uncover extra costs for dual residence, at least not in the form of added difficulties in managing the transitions between households, or additional conflict between parents. It was the case, however, that nearly one-third of joint custodians maintained high levels of conflict—as many as did so in the other custodial arrangements. It remains to be seen whether high conflict between joint custodians generates more or fewer psychosocial problems in children and/or parents than similar conflict in families where the children live primarily with one parent and only visit the other. Our Time 3 data will provide information concerning how these patterns work themselves out over the two years following our Time 2 interviews. In addition, we will have a follow-up study of the adolescent children of the divorced families in our sample, and will be able to assess the impact on these children of both the residential arrangements the families have adopted, and the patterns of co-parenting they have maintained.

13

Joint Custody and the Preschool Child

ROSEMARY McKINNON
JUDITH S. WALLERSTEIN

This chapter reports on a longitudinal study of 25 joint custody families, with children aged fourteen months to five years, who sought counseling or other help from the Center for Families in Transition. Varying motivations that lead divorcing parents to undertake and sustain joint custody are discussed, together with the stresses and gratifications of these arrangements for parents and children. The findings indicate that where both parents are motivated primarily by interest in the child, where the parenting is sensitive, and where the child is shielded from interparental conflict, young children do well. Such families were not the majority in this self-selected group. Significant differences emerged in the adjustment of the one-to-three age group as compared with the three-to-five age group.

Parents in divorce face a range of choices in restructuring their relationships with their children and in making arrangements for their continued care. The reasons underlying the choices are complex and involve psychological, social, and economic considerations. In recent years an increasing number of families have decided to embark on joint physical custody of their children. Very little is known about

Rosemary McKinnon, M.S.W., is a Senior Clinician at the Center for the Family in Transition, Corte Madera, California, and in private practice in San Rafael, California.

Judith S. Wallerstein, Ph.D., is the Executive Director of the Center for the Family in Transition, Corte Madera, California, and Senior Lecturer at the University of California at Berkeley School of Social Welfare and School of Law.

This research has been supported by the San Francisco Foundation. Reprinted with permission from *Behavioral Sciences & the Law*, Vol. 4, No. 2, pp. 169–183 (1986). Copyright 1986 John Wiley & Sons, Inc.

the motivations that lead parents to make this choice and how this decision is implemented in the daily routines of the child, or about the gratifications and stresses of this new family arrangement for parents and children. This chapter examines these issues.

Sample and Methodology

Between the years 1981 and 1985, 25 families with children under the age of five applied to the Center for the Family in Transition with questions or concerns about joint physical custody arrangements. All of these families were included in the study and were followed for periods ranging from one to four years. Two-thirds of the children were initially seen at the time of separation and the remaining one-third were seen up to two years later. Only one family had two young children in the sample. Four families had older children in addition to the child in our sample. Twenty of the 25 families had only one child.

For purposes of the study and analysis, the young children were divided into two groups: those under three at the time of separation and those between three and five years of age. Of 26 children, three boys and four girls were under three when they were first seen. The youngest child was aged fourteen months at the time of the marital breakup. Two of these children were younger siblings. Of the nineteen older children, eleven boys and eight girls were aged three to five when first seen.

All of the parents were white and primarily middle class. Three of the fathers were born and raised abroad, two in the Orient, and one in Western Europe. There was a wide range in occupational status of the fathers: 68% were professionals, including two owners of small businesses, one entrepreneur, and one entertainer. One-third (32%) were semiskilled and unskilled workers. All the mothers were employed, over half worked full time. Forty-four percent were professional women; 56% were skilled or semiskilled workers. Parents had been married from three to seventeen years. Fifty-six percent were married from three to six years. Two couples had never been married and their relationships had ended before their children were born. Over half of the separations took place in an atmosphere of intense conflict, some of which involved the child as a central figure. For the most part, the parental conflicts diminished gradually over the period of ongoing contact with the Center. To some extent, this reflected our interventions.

Two-thirds (66%) of the families had made custody arrangements prior to coming to the Center for service. The remainder requested help in making appropriate arrangements. However, they all had some questions and varying concerns about the effects of these arrangements on their children. The service offered to the parents consisted of an initial three- to eight-week comprehensive clinical assessment of both parents and the child, which included data from teachers and other professionals involved with the child, followed by checkup reassessments at six-month intervals or more frequently if necessary. The parents were informed that we would help them to set up or maintain a joint custody arrangement in accordance with their wishes and its suitability to the child, but that we would also inform them at each assessment whether the ongoing arrangement appeared to be helpful or detrimental to their child; and that, if detrimental, we would recommend a temporary or more lasting change to a single residence for the child. Only in one situation did we advise against joint custody at the outset—for a child whose parents were locked in bitter combat directly involving him and who showed signs of being severely stressed. Fees were based on the ability of each parent to pay, and the cost of the assessment of the child was split between the two parents.

Arrangements

Division of Time—In our sample most schedules were variations on a "50/50" theme. The most common was one in which the child spent three days with one parent and four with the other. Other children alternated weeks with each parent or alternated weeknights between their two parents and split the weekend in half. Two families had entirely irregular arrangements from week to week, based on the mothers' erratic schedules as flight attendants, and two families "birdnested," i.e., the parents moved in and out of the family home to join the children on a weekly basis. One family had a two-week/two-week arrangement, and another operated on a two-week/one-week split.

Distance—Following separation, most parents remained within 25 miles, or less than an hour's drive, from each other. None of them lived within walking distance of each other. One set of parents lived a distance of 60 miles apart. In another set, the mother moved to a neighboring county, but was ordered by the court to return to Marin or forfeit joint custody of her child. A third set of parents struggled with the father's extended business travels out of state.

Stability and Duration of Arrangements

It was our expectation that parents would modify their arrangements of the child's schedule in accordance with the needs of the child, as these needs might change over time. We found, however, that schedules, once established, were likely to be inflexible and extremely difficult to change. The schedules were often tied to work and school programs, to the availability of babysitters, and to the social calendars of the formerly married partners, and their respective friends and lovers. Given such inflexibility, it is possible for an arrangement to become frozen, and over time, it may indeed become detrimental to the child.

We fully expected to find joint custody arrangements used on a temporary basis to facilitate the establishment of the postdivorce family and to help children assimilate changes. During four years, however, only three families changed from joint custody to a more customary visitation with the father on weekends. In addition, one mother petitioned the court for sole custody and two other mothers in our sample seriously considered taking this step. This data points to the unexpected duration of joint custody arrangements.

Motivation for Selecting Joint Custody

Although all of the parents in our sample chose joint custody voluntarily and not as a result of a court order or of court-ordered mediation, the reasons behind their choices varied. All acknowledged the value to the child of the continued presence of the opposite parent, but some held to this belief strongly and others were less committed. Still others paid only lip service to this ideal. Though it is generally assumed that the desire to nurture the child in continuing close contact with both parents is the primary motivation for making joint custody arrangements, we found this to be the main driving force only among an estimated one-third of our sample. Some of the motivations underlying the decision for joint custody derived from practical and economic considerations; others had psychological roots in the conscious and unconscious needs of the parents at the time of separation. Often several motivations overlapped. Whatever the initial incentives proved to be, they continued to exercise a major influence on the pattern and duration of the arrangements. It also became clear that these motivations were linked to the quality of the parent–child relationship. We discuss here five different motivational sets.

Joint Custody as a Commitment to the Child

Parents within this group were of several kinds. Some held coparenting as a high value in their lives and wished to continue a close parental relationship with their child after the separation. Others held this as a high value although it had not necessarily been part of the marriage. Still others came to it as part of the divorce, in response to their own experience—as well as that of others in the community— and their desire to do well by their children. One family in our sample went to great lengths to minimize the stress of their separation on their two children, aged two and four, by setting up a "birdnesting" arrangement whereby the children continued to live in the family home, while the parents took turns living with them every other week. They maintained this arrangement over the course of a year, at which point they established separate homes and the children alternated between the two parental locations on a week-in week-out basis. In this situation, a genuine, loving attachment existed between parents and children, and the parents were willing to inconvenience themselves greatly to put their children's needs ahead of their own. This attitude is by no means as common as it is generally assumed to be, by proponents of joint custody.

Joint Custody as a Limited Parental Partnership

In a significant number of families, parents chose coparenting, not necessarily for the reasons normally assumed—i.e., that a child who has the benefit of two parents is "doubly blessed"—but, on the contrary, because each parent had had only a partial commitment to the child as well as to the marriage. In such instances, parents were either unwilling or unable to make care of the child a priority over their working and social lives. In several such situations joint custody was continuous, with the limited parenting style that the child had experienced in the intact family. One example, of several in our sample, is that of a family in which the mother was ambivalent about caring for her child and found full-time paid care for her daughter, from three months of age on, so that she could return to school. When the child was two years old, the mother returned to full-time work, and when the child was four, the parents separated and opted for joint custody. The father continued to care for the child with the help of a series of babysitters and girlfriends, for three days of the week. The mother, however, still spent very little time with the child, and even after work she left her daughter with friends and neighbors so that she might attend night classes and date. The pattern of limited parenting within the marriage continued almost unchanged within the arrangements that followed the divorce.

Joint Custody in Response to the Demands of the Workplace

All of the mothers in the study were working parents. Most worked full time. The shared parenting of the joint custody arrangement allowed the parents the possibility to work and to pursue personal relationships. For example, in two families the mothers worked as flight attendants and the fathers cared for the children in the mothers' absences, making constant accommodations to everchanging flight schedules, much as they had done during their marriages. When these mothers returned from their trips, they resumed full responsibility for the care of their children.

Joint Custody in the Service of Denying the Divorce

Joint custody arrangements are conducive to meeting psychological needs of the adults that have been intensified by the divorce. Thus, since in most divorcing families the decision to divorce is not mutual (Wallerstein & Kelly, 1980b), the parent who opposes the divorce, especially the one who feels humiliated or rejected, may hold onto the marital relationship with the ex-partner via the joint custody of their child. Joint custody lends itself not only to a greater continued emotional involvement, but also to physical contact and frequent communication between ex-spouses. In this way, the pain of rejection can be muted by holding onto the marriage symbolically and by the many real ways in which the partners continue to relate to each other. Joint custody, in this instance, represents a partial continuation of the marriage, which the unhappy partner may or may not recognize as the primary motive.

A second mechanism operating in the choice of joint custody is the largely unconscious identification of one parent with the child who goes back and forth between both homes and bridges the relationship between the former partners. In this way the parent is able to defend against his or her pain of abandonment and to ward off awareness of depression, rejection, and narcissistic injury. Such projective identification with the itinerant child may be a useful temporary mechanism in a gradual disengagement from the marital relationship. The hazard of this identification is that it may also lead to the fantasy that, indeed, no divorce has occurred.

The fantasy of "no divorce" is serious in its implications. The effect is particularly noticeable in those situations where spouses take new partners after the divorce and their ex-spouses react with extreme distress, as though to adultery. One illustration of this circumstance is a family who began with a most amicable parting of the ways based on the wife's wish for increased independence. The couple were at pains to work out the best possible joint custody arrangement for their four-year-old daughter. Several months after the initial separation, the ex-husband became alarmed when his former spouse took up with a lover of whom he heartily disapproved. He hired a private investigator to follow this man, and he formally accused the mother of child abuse on the basis of one spanking incident. The courts were soon involved and joint custody deteriorated.

Joint Custody as Symbolic of the Need to Make Restitution

Over three-quarters of the divorces in this sample were initiated by women. Among these women there was a subgroup who were profoundly concerned about the suffering that they were causing and who felt very guilty about leaving a husband who was dependent on them and, in several instances, cared very much about them. Several of these women consciously proposed joint custody to soften the blow of their departure. Knowing well that most women have sole custody, these women felt that they were extending themselves by inviting a former husband to share parenting. They were aware that the presence of a young child could help to alleviate suffering and even provide some measure of care for the father. One such mother reported spontaneously that she felt that the father needed the child for his own emotional stability. Some women who felt most intensely in this regard had had an extramarital affair before leaving the marriage.

Changing Motivations

When divorce occurs, people find it difficult to predict the changes that the separation of their lives will entail. Therefore, the motivations which lead people to select joint custody at the time of the marital rupture are likely to be modified over time. Some parents find reinforcement in the gratifications of parenting that the joint custody arrangement encourages. Others find that difficulties increase, or that new relationships cause their parenting commitment to diminish. Thus, some come in time to see the child as a blessing, others as a burden.

Additionally, parents have told us that the many transitions that joint custody requires of them can be extremely difficult. The young child, when present, requires the full attention of the parent, so that the alternating presence and absence of the child requires radical shifts in parental attention, attitude, and sometimes in the rearrangement of the household. One joint custody mother attempted to schedule all her work, including night meetings, only when her two children were absent, and to give them her exclusive attention when they were with her, but she confessed at the end of the first year of this arrangement that she found it unrealistic to compartmentalize her life. Joint custody parents are forced also to withstand repeated separations from their children and, in doing so, to face their own loneliness. Some find this very difficult to tolerate, and one mother expressed her extreme distress, saying, "If I can't have [my child] all the time, I don't want him." The impact of these experiences affects the parents' attitudes toward a continued joint custody arrangement and sets the stage for the child's experience.

Some mothers and fathers differed in their attitudes to joint custody. Many fathers found their relationships with their young children to be gratifying well beyond their experiences within the marriage. They enjoyed their role as primary parent when the child was in their care and took pride in their newly honed parenting skills. They were especially pleased to feel as important to their children as were the children's mothers. One father spoke of his relationship with his two-year-old son in the following way: "I really think that it has forced a different type of relationship between myself and my son. When we are together, we're totally together. I plan my entire life essentially around [the times] when I have him and when I don't have him, and it seems to me that we have a closer relationship than we might otherwise have had."

The women were more likely to take the parenting role for granted and to speak with pleasure of the new freedom that the joint custody arrangement permitted. They did not resolve their earlier misgivings about the capacity of the fathers to parent, especially if the father had not participated in his child's care during the marriage, but their anxieties diminished as they saw evidence of the fathers' competence. They became increasingly able to acknowledge openly and fairly, though not without a sense of wonder, that their ex-husbands were capable, reliable parents. A subgroup of women, however, continued to be very worried whenever the children were in their ex-husbands' care; they maintained the joint custody arrangement only with great misgivings about the psychological and physical well-being of their children. One mother expressed her anxieties vividly: "I'm her mother. I want her with me 24 hours a day. I can't tell you how many nights I've sat and cried because she was gone, and she was two, and I ached because she wasn't there, and I was afraid that he wasn't going to brush her teeth and put clean pajamas on her."

Factors That Govern Outcome

Strength of Commitment to Parenting

It is impossible to predict outcome for a child on the basis of the initial decision for joint custody. One important outcome factor will be the satisfaction parents come to feel long after the decision is initiated. Joint custody works best, and is most satisfying to children and their parents, in cases where both parents can sustain a strong commitment to the child. In this collaborative atmosphere, a child is likely to do well. Unfortunately, such cooperation between divorcing partners is rare. A further danger is that when this kind of collaboration exists, the intimacy that it encourages brings with it the risk of sexual jealousy if one parent takes a lover. Developments of this sort undermine cooperation and quickly destroy what may have been an excellent arrangement.

Parental commitment is critical, for the child's prognosis is determined by the parent–child relationship. Joint custody does not necessarily preclude parental neglect, for when the arrangement reflects limited interest in the child by both parents, the child is unlikely to receive adequate care. Children subjected to this kind of paltry care and inattention by both parents are described by teachers and clinicians as "needy" and "overburdened." They frequently do poorly in school and teachers may blame joint custody for these difficulties. One teacher, faced with a neglected child in our sample, felt that this child would be better off in a foster home. Another was worried because a child's shoes were always too big or too small and neither parent would buy the child a new pair. In situations where coparenting was stingy at the outset of the joint custody arrangement, we found the least change over time; children in these situations looked forlorn and needy and were perceived to be at risk.

Doubts about Joint Custody

Many of the women in our sample remained dubious about the custody arrangements they had agreed to accept. Irving, Benjamin, and Trocme (1984b) reported that parents who were most dissatisfied with joint custody were (1) those who came to it via the legal process of divorce, and (2) those who retained the most guilt about the breakup. This coincides with our findings. Several mothers in our sample who came to joint custody as a result of mediation remember resentfully that this arrangement was never their own idea; although the arrangement was, strictly speaking, a "voluntary" one, in actuality, the mother's misgivings had been overridden by a mediator or had given way to the father's insistence.

When maternal misgivings were taken seriously by fathers who, over time, proved themselves in the eyes of their ex-spouses to be valued and trustworthy coparents, the children did well. But, when time did not dispel the doubts of one or the other parent, the children did poorly. For example, one father's passionate enthusiasm for his daughter evaporated when he found a girlfriend, and the child was bereft when her father lost interest in her. The mother felt that her original doubts were borne out.

Parental Disagreement and Overt Animosity

The intensity of enduring hostility between divorced parents varies generally, and it varies greatly among parents who are trying to work with joint custody. Even when violent animosity persists, some parents manage to encapsulate their marital anger and make a separate peace over parental issues so that, around the child, there can be an oasis of communication and cooperation. In such situations, the child tends to do well. On the other hand, the failure to keep the child out of continued hostilities has troubling effects. In one such situation, a father asked for help in achieving joint custody of his five-year-old daughter, but, both parents were so deeply embroiled in struggles over the child, we recommended against joint custody. Three years later, the child remained troubled, primarily because of her parents' failure to curtail their anger while in her presence.

Common Areas of Stress

Marriage, whose core theme is "sharing," fosters collaboration in parenting. Separation and divorce signal a profound parting of the ways, and joint custody, in particular, tends to highlight the differences in parental styles and values. Diet, discipline, and television were divisive issues in several of our joint custody families. Although the children had less difficulty adjusting to disparate rules, the parents sometimes reacted with vigorous resentment. One parent's different practices were sometimes perceived as intrusive attempts to exert control over the life of the other.

Bedtime rituals and rules also become divisive factors in some families. We found that when one parent slept with the child and the other did not, the child began to resist sleeping alone in the house of the latter parent. Furthermore, given the bed's powerful symbolism, it was not unusual for a parent to react strongly to the child having taken his or her "place" in the bed of the recently divorced partner.

In intact families, it is not uncommon for young children occasionally to sleep with their parents, and there is little evidence that this practice makes for marital conflict or troubled children. In sole-custody arrangements, young children also frequently sleep with their parents, though this can become a problem when a parent begins to date and abruptly ejects the child from the parental bed. Rarely, however, does this practice produce the kind of conflict it often generated in our joint custody families. This was especially true for the "oedipal" (three to five) age group of children, who wanted to sleep in both parental beds, making a particular nuisance of themselves when they tried to displace a current lover.

Thus, because of the sexual valence involved and the tendency for every small debate concerning the bedroom to become symbolically overdetermined, both for parents and children, we have found this issue to be particularly inaccessible to rational discussion and resolution.

The Child as a Replacement for the Marital Partner

In some families that we observed, the child not only slept with the parent but appeared to have inherited emotionally the role of the marital partner. These youngsters seemed profoundly troubled psychologically. Such eroticized relationships may become overtly incestuous, as was indeed reported to us to have occurred in some instances.

The eroticized violence of sadomasochistic marriages is particularly difficult to bring to an end, particularly where the wife assumes responsibility, consciously or not, for provoking the anger of the husband. This kind of violence threatens to become part of a child's identification, as in the case where a mother left her violent marriage, but agreed to a joint custody arrangement for her four-year-old daughter. The father's passionate attachment to his child took the form of sleeping with the girl after keeping her up late while he told her frightening ghost stories. Although she was initially a well-adjusted, competent four-year-old, the girl's school began to report that she was bullying other children and scaring them with her stories. By the time she was six years old, this had become a serious problem.

In other families with four- and five-year-old children, though they benefited from their parents' interest and affection, there was also an intensification of oedipal conflicts beyond what might have been expected in intact families. One father, extremely upset over the breakup of his marriage, transferred all his romantic love to his young daughter and took her into his bed. Although this relationship was not overtly sexual, it was highly eroticized. The danger in these situations is from the child's exposure to parental needs, feelings, and expectations, which only another adult should be asked to meet. To the extent that the child does "take the place" of the departed parental partner, that child may suffer emotional injury.

New Romances for a Parent

All of the motivations that sustain joint custody are vulnerable to disruption when new relationships occur. The children often react strongly. For some children in our sample, particularly in the three to five age range, new parental romances provoked symptoms of undisguised anxiety, eneuresis, and tantrums. One four-year-old boy became hysterical when his mother took a lover. If this man so much as brushed against his mother, the boy would scream, "Don't touch her! I saw you! You touched her! Don't let him touch you!" It was six months before he reconciled himself to this new relationship.

Children's Experiences and Adjustments

We had hoped to find that joint custody would protect young children from experiencing the grief and anxiety that have been described for this age group (Hetherington, 1979; Wallerstein & Kelly, 1975, 1980b), but we did not find this to be so. We found, instead, that children in joint custody are indistinguishable in their initial distress and early responses to marital rupture from their counterparts in sole-custody arrangements. The joint custody children were acutely aware of the marital separation and of conflict between their parents. Joint custody did not sustain the illusion of an intact family. Parents who hope thus to spare their children pain will be disillusioned.

Children Aged One to Three Years

There were seven children in the younger group, three boys and four girls, who ranged from one to three years of age at the time they were first seen at the Center. Living arrangements varied widely, even in this small group. Where possible, we have followed these very young children over a period of two or three years, and we have found no correlation between the type of custody arrangement and the child's adjustment.

Those Who Did Well—Overall, of the seven very young children, three did well, as measured by clinical play interviews and parents' and teachers' reports. They were on target developmentally, showed good object relationships and appeared spontaneous and happy at home and at school. These were the children whose parents were highly motivated to maintain their parental commitment and who had managed to isolate the child from their marital disputes. A striking example of this kind of commitment was the oasis created for a child who was fourteen months old at the time of separation. This child was in an arrangement that included daycare and alternate nights with each parent. He showed excellent development during our observations, and this was confirmed by the staff of his daycare center.

In general, both at the separation as well as over the course of time, the younger children appeared less troubled by the divorce and by their changing living arrangements than did the older group. Contentment seemed primarily related to the availability of two loving and sensitive parents who were able and willing to synchronize the child's routines so that the child continued to experience a stable environment in both households. The success of these arrangements required daily communication and willing cooperation between the parents about the details of their child's functioning. Since in these families both parents were working, the arrangements also required excellent daycare.

Those Who Did Less Well—Of the four children who were not doing well, two had shown excellent development at the initial observation but deteriorated over time when their parents became embroiled in open conflict. Of the remaining two children, one had very young parents who had trouble giving her appropriate nurturance and structure. Her teachers reported that she was fearful in school and had trouble with peer relationships. The teachers of the second child likewise reported that she was anxious and withdrawn, and her mother was concerned that the father's chronic drinking impaired his ability to care for his daughter.

Thus, the younger children who did less well reflected continuing interparental conflict as well as parenting that was deficient in some significant regard. The support that these children received from their parents was insufficient to compensate for the major changes that the joint custody arrangement imposed.

Three- to Five-Year-Old Children

The older group (ages three to five when they were first seen) consisted of nineteen children, eleven boys and eight girls, whose arrangements were as follows: ten were in split-week arrangements; five had a week-to-week arrangement; two had irregular schedules; two had "birdnesting" arrangements for the first year of joint custody (one on a week-to-week basis and one on a month-to-month basis); and one child was in a two-week/two-week arrangement. By and large, the adjustment of the children was not correlated, from our observations, with the kinds of arrangements or the amount of change required. Change, itself, appeared to be a primary issue for only two children in our sample.

Children Who Did Well—Only three of the nineteen older children were doing well—in that they were symptom free, developmentally on course, and reported to be well adjusted both at school and at home—when they were seen initially, as well as at the followup contacts six months and one year later. Of these three, Jimmy, a five-year-old, and his younger sister, who was also doing well, were in a "birdnesting" arrangement over the course of the first year. They then switched to a week-to-week joint custody arrangement in which the children, not the parents, did the moving. Jimmy's mother was a social worker who was not only committed to her children, but skillful and sensitive in her responses to them as well. The father's motivation was reinforced by the pleasure he received from his continuing contact with his children. He was able to integrate his new love relationship into his children's lives with thoughtfulness for their feelings. As an example of the result, Jimmy was sad about his parents' separation, saying that he wanted them to live together and not stop loving each other, but his high self-esteem and recognition of his importance to both parents was expressed in the threats that he sometimes made to each of them: "You don't get to be with me if you make me mad."

Mary, another child doing well, suffered medical problems during her first three years which had necessitated tube feeding. Her overall development was delayed a year, in effect putting her in the same developmental category as the younger children. Her parents maintained an irregular schedule revolving around the mother's work as a saleswoman, and each parent took turns at caretaking. Mary received glowing reports from her teachers and appeared secure and happy despite the changes in her environment.

Another child who received excellent reports from her teachers was Betty, who was highly valued by both her parents though they had never married or even lived together since her birth. They maintained a successful shared-custody arrangement which enhanced this child's self-esteem.

Children Who Did Less Well—Of the remaining sixteen children, ten—four girls and six boys—were doing poorly as measured by clinical assessment, as well as by their parents' and teachers' reports, when they were first seen. At followup interviews, these children showed varying degrees of improvement in their relationships at home and at school, but all continued to have serious symptoms. Most of these children endured a range of stresses following the separation of their parents, and it is difficult, therefore, to assess the impact of any single component of their lives.

Six children, four girls and two boys, were reacting to further changes in their families. Most had difficulty integrating new family members into their lives. One five-year-old boy viewed his stepfather as the "enemy" and became eneuretic and encopretic when his mother remarried, even though she maintained a commitment to him, as did his natural father. Other children became acutely anxious and regressed. Several were particularly anxious at night, and one boy developed chronic nightmares following a two-week separation from his mother who had recently acquired a boyfriend. Two mothers had new babies—one a set of twins—so that the older children experienced fluctuation in parental attentiveness, despite the best intentions of their parents. A subgroup of little girls showed much overtly seductive behavior with their fathers and were particularly upset when the parent, who had earlier fully reciprocated his child's affection and admiration, acquired an adult companion and abruptly turned his attention elsewhere.

The remaining four boys were anxious, symptomatic children doing poorly in school. Two boys each had one disorganized parent and, consequently, had more difficulty than usual in making the many shifts that joint custody required of them. One boy, who moved frequently between his parents' homes, panicked on one of these journeys and clung to his car seat, refusing to get out of the car. Later, when asked about the cause of his distress, he said, "Mommy has a home and Daddy has a home, but I have no home." We recommended psychotherapy for two of the boys in this group on the basis of their aggressive and out-of-control behavior both at home and at school.

Those Who Deteriorated—The remaining six children in this older group, four boys and two girls, appeared to be stressed initially, and at the followup interviews they appeared to be deteriorating further. We were profoundly concerned. Four of these children suffered from limited coparenting, a minimal investment in the children. They looked needy and vulnerable and they were having severe, chronic difficulties at home and at school. The other two children were exposed to severely disturbed parents whose marriages had been marked by open violence which the children had witnessed. In one family, the child was also exposed to alcohol and drug abuse by both his parents as well as to their frequent violent meetings throughout the joint custody arrangement. In another family, a four-year-old girl was drawn into the orbit of her father's fantasies of eroticized violence. Although the child appeared to be well adjusted initially, her school reported after a year that she was having difficulty socially. By the time the girl was six, her mother felt that only a change in custody would stabilize her downhill course. For these six children, joint custody failed to offset the neglect in both parental homes, or protect the child from the psychopathology of one or both parents.

Conclusion

The conclusions from this report of 26 children under the age of five years in joint physical custody arrangements are sobering. Although this group is small, there is very little other data about young children in joint custody. What emerges clearly, however, is that there is scant evidence to suggest that joint custody protects the young child against the stress of divorce. At the same time, there is no evidence that these young children would have been better served in single-parent custodial arrangements.

Parents agree to share custody for a variety of reasons, besides a genuine wish for a continued close relationship with their child. Some arrangements are based on practical or economic considerations, and some are governed by distorted or dysfunctional psychological needs, such as the fantasy of preserving the marriage or the wish to make restitution. There is some evidence that among the critical components in the success or failure of the joint custody arrangement are (1) the motivation of the parent in seeking joint custody; (2) the investment of the parents in their child; and (3) the parents' ability to keep interparental conflicts separate from those issues that concern the child. Joint custody frequently reinforces the father–child relationship, and, where this is desirable, the child will benefit. But, when either parent substitutes the child for the lost spouse, the child can become caught up in a skewed relationship that will threaten his or her development.

The sharing of children lightens maternal responsibilities, making it possible for the ex-wife to meet the demands of the workplace; but, for many of the mothers in our sample, especially in those families where the father had not participated in the child's care during the marriage, the high price of this freedom was unrelenting worry about whether the child was being adequately cared for by the father.

For those fortunate children whose parents continued to provide loving, sensitive care, joint custody nurtured the child in both homes. Unfortunately, for a significant subgroup in our sample, joint custody merely extended parental neglect. The children who fared worst were those whose parents each had only a limited investment in their child's well-being, or those who were exposed in one or both homes to severe parental violence or psychopathology.

One of the most surprising findings in this study was that the children below the age of three seemed well able to handle the many transitions of the joint custody arrangement, whereas the three- to five-year-olds seemed to have more difficulty. We have speculated that this phenomenon was related to the greater complexity of the older children's lives, by virtue of the increased demands of nursery school, together with their greater awareness of (and resistance to) the changes in their families. Certainly a range of symptoms emerged when the child was required to adjust to the introduction of new members into the family, or when the family moved many times. Younger children did not react as strongly to these same kinds of changes.

It appears that family structure does not dictate the quality of the relationships among its members, and that children, whether in intact or divorced families, continue to need committed, sensitive parents who can support each other's parenting styles and keep disagreements from interfering with the child's upbringing. None of these findings warrants a presumption of joint custody, although they surely point to its potential for young children under the conditions which we have delineated.

14

Joint Custody Through Mediation: A Longitudinal Assessment of the Children

MURIEL BROTSKY
SUSAN STEINMAN
STEVEN ZEMMELMAN

Forty-eight families attempting to develop joint custody arrange-
ments at the time of divorce were studied to distinguish the charac-
teristics of those parents who successfully maintain joint custody
and those who do not, as well as the characteristics of children who
do well in such arrangements and those who do not.

Description and Findings of the Joint Custody Project

The Joint Custody Project was a combined research and service project for families developing joint physical and legal custody at the time of divorce. The sample consisted of both parents who were motivated to choose joint custody and agreed

Muriel Brotsky, L.C.S.W., is Director of the San Francisco branch of Jewish Family and Children's Services.

Susan Steinman, D.S.W., was Director of the Joint Custody Study Project, Jewish Family and Children's Services.

Steven Zemmelman, M.S.W., is a Clinician at Jewish Family and Children's Services.

The project was sponsored by Jewish Family and Children's Services of San Francisco in collaboration with the Center for the Family in Transition in Corte Madera, California. It was funded by the San Francisco Foundation, the Jewish Community Endowment Fund of the Jewish Community Federation of San Francisco, the Zellerbach Family Fund, the Morris Stulsaft Foundation, and the Benjamin and Mae Swig Foundation. This chapter is reprinted by permission from *Conciliation Courts Review*, Vol. 26, No. 2, pp. 53–58, December 1988.

to it voluntarily, and parents who were in dispute over custody and were court-referred or court-ordered to work out joint custody through the services of the project.

The services to the families consisted of: (1) a six-week education and support group for the parents; (2) up to twelve sessions of child-custody mediation which resulted in a written parenting plan; (3) a child assessment which provided data to individually tailor the parenting agreement; and, (4) follow-up sessions six months and one year after the completion of the initial service.[1] These services were provided free in exchange for participating in the research.

Population Description

Forty-eight families and their 67 children (ages 1–15) participated in the Joint Custody Project. These families resided throughout four counties of the greater San Francisco Bay Area and ranged across a broad demographic spectrum. Psychologically, these families were in the throes of the emotional disequilibrium of the first year of separation. Twenty-two families were referred by the Domestic Relations Courts of three counties because of a custody dispute; the rest were self-referred (4), referred by an attorney (13), or by a community mental health agency (11).

At the completion of the study, 38 families had developed a joint custody agreement and a written Parenting Agreement. Four returned to court and six opted for sole custody.

Research Goals and Methodology

Because of the need for research on disputing families who come to joint custody via court order or court-ordered mediation, the project focused on the decision-making process and its implementation and outcome among initially disputing, as well as motivated, parents. We wanted to distinguish the characteristics of those parents who were successfully maintaining a joint custody arrangement at follow-up from those who were not, and to identify the characteristics of the children who were doing well in joint custody from those who were seriously stressed.

The research approach of the Joint Custody Project was prospective and longitudinal in nature. The assigned clinicians who functioned as mediators collected data throughout the course of the mediation. The joint custody arrangement was then followed as it unfolded and the outcome assessed for both parents and children six months and one year after mediation was completed.

In addition to clinical interviews with each family member, interviews with children's school teachers and day care personnel were conducted. This clinical data was supplemented with data gathered by a research psychologist using standardized psychological measures, as well as a variety of objective and projective measures, for each parent and child—separately and in interaction with one another.

---

1. Zemmelman, Steve E., "A Model Project on Joint Custody for Families Undergoing Divorce." *Social Work*, Vol. 32, No. 1, January–February 1987.

Summary of Outcome of Joint Custody Arrangement for Parents[2]

For purposes of analysis, the families were placed by project staff at the one-year follow-up evaluation into one of three outcome categories, (1) successful, (2) stressed, or (3) failed.

Twelve "successful" parent couples were able to cooperate and negotiate issues around the children and make decisions with a minimum of conflict and distress. They generally felt positive about the arrangement.

Twenty "stressed" families were those who were able to work out an agreement in mediation and were maintaining their agreement legally and technically. They were only able to cooperate and make decisions some of the time and experienced periodic eruptions of conflict which threatened the arrangement. They also experienced a varying amount of frustration and distress with the situation.

Fifteen "failed" families were those who were unable to agree in mediation or sustain an agreement, or whose decision had been made for them by the courts or attorneys. These parents were extremely distressed, dissatisfied with the custody arrangements and each other, and could not share childrearing responsibilities without bitter and overt conflict.

A profile of the parents in these groups was then developed as follows:
The "successful" parents demonstrated:

1. A valuing of the other parent on behalf of the child, and trust in their parental ability;

2. A strong capacity for empathy for the child and, at times, the other parent;

3. Basically good psychological functioning and high self-esteem, despite the expected feelings of depression, anger, and anxiety;

4. A low level of anger and the capacity to suppress or modulate aggression;

5. A tolerance for a wide range of affect and the ability to manage ambivalent feelings;

6. A strong ego capacity including the capacity to self-reflect and engage in rational problem solving.

The "stressed" parents were characterized by:

1. More severe and long-standing psychological problems and greater frequency of drug and alcohol problems;

2. Greater variation in the degree of hostility and conflict and the extent of negative feelings toward the spouse, and less ability to modulate or suppress feeling;

2. Steinman, Susan B.; Zemmelman, Steven E.; Knoblauch, Thomas M. "A Study of Parents Who Sought Joint Custody Following Divorce: Who Reaches Agreement and Sustains Joint Custody and Who Returns to Court." *Journal of the American Academy of Child Psychiatry*, Vol. 24, No. 5, pp. 554–562, 1985.

3. Intense and ambivalent feelings toward former spouse (i.e., guilt, dependence, missing former spouse, anger, etc.) and little ability to recognize and tolerate these;

4. More vulnerable to these feelings being stirred up through contact around the children, and less ability to see the child as separate from themselves;

5. A valuing of the other parent on behalf of the child, but less respect for, and trust in, their parental ability.

The "failed" parents had a different and quite distinct profile:

1. Intense and unremitting anger and hostility and a strong wish to punish the spouse; the child continues to function as a vehicle for the expression of hostility;

2. Projection of blame onto the spouse—for the divorce, the child's problems, and their own problems;

3. Very low self-esteem and rigidity in thinking; history of substance abuse and physical abuse;

4. Deep mistrust and feeling of vulnerability and powerlessness in relation to spouse;

5. Ego capacities might function well in other areas of life, but the capacities to be rational, to problem solve, to reality test, to control anger, and to step back to observe and analyze were easily overwhelmed in relation to former spouse;

6. A view of the spouse as a bad parent who is harmful to the child, and an inability to see the child's experiences and needs as separate from their own.

Patterns of Child Adjustment

For purposes of analysis, at one year after conclusion of service, the children were assigned to one of three adjustment groups: (1) doing well, (2) stressed, or (3) children at risk.

Nineteen children (28%), 14 girls and five boys, were judged to be "doing well." They had mastered the developmental tasks appropriate for their age group and were minimally symptomatic. These children thought well of themselves and expected positive, loving responses from the adults in their lives. They responded initially to their parents' divorce with the feelings, behavioral symptoms, and regressions observed as normal reactions to parental separation and divorce. Joint custody did not spare them the experience of family loss, yet, by and large, their experience did not interfere with their developmental progress or sense of self-esteem and pride in mastery. All of these children were doing well at school or in their daycare setting.

Thirty-three children (50%), 18 girls and 15 boys, were judged to be "stressed." They were functioning at or near their developmental level but were experiencing some significant problems at home or at school, and were moderately symptomatic in some areas. These children were quite distressed about the divorce. They were burdened by the distress their parents were experiencing and by the conflict and hostility between them. The transitions between homes, while manageable, precipitated anger or anxiety, and adjustment to the routine of each home took longer.

Sixteen children (24%), four girls and 12 boys, were found to be seriously at risk of major emotional disturbance. They presented serious symptoms and/or developmental delays or regressions. For these children "at risk" the joint custody family structure could not provide the support necessary, because the parents were typically unable to cooperate. It was found that the problems of these children and the conflict of their parents was often a two-way relationship: the parental hostility and conflict appeared to be one of the major impediments to the happiness and development of these children, and the children's difficulties seemed to fuel the parental conflict.

In general, the younger children seemed to be better able to adjust to the divorce. Of the 19 well-adjusted children, 14 (73%) were four or younger at separation; 12 were under three years old. Three were six or seven. These preschoolers seemed to be less involved and preoccupied with the post-separation problems of their parents and resumed their normal functioning quickly, as long as the parental care they received was good and the home environments well organized.

Of the "stressed" group, only seven (21%) were preschoolers. The "at risk" group had five (27%); however, these children showed very serious developmental problems.

In this study, the girls were doing better than the boys. Of the 19 well-adjusted children at follow-up, 14 were girls and five were boys. Of the 18 children considered "at risk," five were girls and 13 were boys. The "stressed" group, which presented a less clear-cut picture, was more evenly divided (18 girls and 15 boys).

In general, there was a very high correlation between the "successful" parent group and the children doing well. Of the 13 "successful" families, only three of their 14 children (21%) were even showing stress. It was found that well-functioning children could do well when raised in a joint custody family where parents could focus on their needs and concerns while working to resolve the ambivalent feelings from the marriage. The capacity of their parents to continue to nurture and support them, their commitment to the joint custody arrangement because they valued their child's relationship with both parents, and their ability to put aside their anger and shield the child from conflict and to cooperate and problem solve on behalf of their child, all helped these children cope with the divorce.

In direct contrast were the families where the court ordered or influenced a joint physical and legal custody arrangement, but could not create a family structure to nurture and support the children. Where the parents were unremittingly hostile, did not value and support the child's relationship with the other parent, could not make decisions or coordinate childrearing responsibilities, and could not protect the child from their conflict, the children were doing very poorly. In these cases, the joint custody family was dysfunctional.

Follow-Up—Purpose and Method

From January 1986 to June 1986, the Joint Custody Project conducted a mail follow-up study of its families. Its purpose was: (1) to continue to maintain contact with the families so that long-term follow-up research in the future could be a viable possibility, (2) to learn from the parents their assessment of how the custody arrangement was working out, and how their children were adjusting.

A letter was sent to all parents offering them a copy of the paper describing the service project, telling them of the follow-up, and asking for a return card with current addresses and telephone numbers. A four-page questionnaire on the parent and each child was then mailed to all parents who responded. Personal telephone calls, when possible, were additionally used to enlist parental cooperation from those who had not responded. The questionnaires included standardized child adjustment questions and parental hostility and intimacy measurements as developed in conjunction with the Center for the Family in Transition. It also included specific information on the status of their present custody arrangement, important events in their lives during the last 18 months, and their satisfaction with the existing arrangement.

Analysis of the Results

Of the 48 families who completed the study, we received a child questionnaire and at least one parent questionnaire from 40 families (83%) that included 55 children and 56 parents (22 fathers and 34 mothers). These represent the most positively involved parents, since we were unable to get replies from a number of the families who were very dissatisfied with the project, and who were in litigation at the time the project ended. Also, where sole custody was the outcome, we heard primarily from the person who had sole custody, usually the mother.

It is important to note that the following discussion is based on the parents' subjective reports screened through their own needs and desires. The incomplete results and lack of independent clinical evaluation limits the research statement. It does, however, clearly indicate how these parents are viewing their mediated custody arrangement 18 months post-study.

We had a response from 12 "successful" parent couples (92%). Ten had continued physical and legal joint custody, while two had voluntarily arranged for sole physical custody (one to the mother, one to the father) without changing the legal joint custody decree or returning to court. Both parents remained involved with the child.

From the "stressed" parent group, we had a response from 17 (85%). Twelve had continued their mediated physical and legal joint custody arrangement. In three families, the fathers had ceased to participate as joint custody fathers, and two were maintaining the sole physical custody to the mother agreement in effect at the end of the project.

Eleven (73%) families from the "failed" group responded. These represented the most successful of this group. We know that children of two of the unrepresented families had to be placed in treatment centers and the other two had been in litigation when the study ended. If we had received replies from all of these families, the results would be much more negative. Of the families responding, four remained with the physical and legal joint custody order arranged either through mediation or court order. Four families continue with sole physical custody to mother which had been in effect at the completion of the study. Two went back to court to change to sole custody and one kept legal custody the same, but the father was not involved.

The parent questionnaires reported on their subsequent court involvement, changes in their own personal lives, satisfaction with the present arrangement, continued contact with spouse, and the comfort with which they and their children experienced continued contact with both parents. These questionnaires were then analyzed by outcome group, as determined by the Joint Custody Project staff at the end of the study, and by present custody arrangement.

The child questionnaires required the parents to identify difficulties the children might be having in the areas of emotional and behavioral adjustment, school adjustment and performance, social and peer relationships, and severe health problems. These questionnaires were then analyzed along five axes; age at the time of separation, sex, present custody arrangement, sex and custody arrangement together, and the adjustment group to which the children had been assigned by the joint custody staff at the end of the study.

Discussion

The "successful" and "failed" parent groups at outcome clearly maintained their profile in the follow-up. The "successful" group rated consistently high in stability (84%), satisfaction with the arrangement (72%), importance of ex-spouse to children (96%), and shared information (63%). Their joint custody arrangement had not prevented them from remarriage and having new children. The only legal involvement reported were two mothers who had gone back to court to obtain more adequate child support, and were bitter that the parenting agreement had not addressed this issue more adequately. Financial arrangements in joint custody need to be looked at carefully. Male/female incomes are usually unequal and joint custody, if not accompanied by child support, may penalize the woman.

The "failed" group (even the best adjusted of them) had more difficulty maintaining the agreement (46%), and were more dissatisfied with the present arrangement (50%). They had difficulty sharing information (46%), and perhaps most importantly, their children had more discomfort when they moved from parent to parent. The higher percentage of those who returned to court and the low level of remarriage suggest that the psychological difficulties noted in the study continued to play an important role in their subsequent life.

The most interesting findings concerned the middle or "stressed" group—the largest group numerically (50%). They had been able to reach agreement only with considerable professional help and still had unresolved difficulties, and it was not clear if they could maintain the arrangement at the time the study ended. A large proportion of this group would have been in the court system if not for the extensive services offered through the project. However, according to self reports 18 months later, they now looked substantially the same as the parents who had mutually and successfully agreed on joint custody originally. They had maintained their custody arrangement (84%), had made new relationships, and were feeling positive (68%) about the present situation. The other spouse was now considered to be very important (93%). While less information was shared than in the "successful" or mutually agreed upon group, they were more satisfied with the amount of information shared and more comfortable when their children moved from home to home than the successful group. It is possible that having experienced and worked through greater hostility and distrust originally, their expectations became more realistic, and the separation between the parents more complete. This, of course, is speculative at this time and could only be assessed in a future clinical evaluation. It does seem clearly indicated that previously disputing couples can, with professional assistance, come to an agreement, maintain the arrangement, and continue to improve their relationship in the ensuing years. This project provided an intensive service including both group discussion and individual mediation on a time-limited basis, and follow-up seems to show the efficacy of such a model in resolving conflict.

The parental questionnaires, when analyzed by present custody arrangement, seem to endorse many of the claims of joint custody proponents. In our study, it has provided stability (93%), parental satisfaction (68%), valuing of the other spouse (97%), and comfort for the children in relating to both parents (82%). In sole custody, which was arrived at when joint custody could not be established, the degree of satisfaction (53%) with the arrangement may be somewhat higher than it actually is, since non-custodial fathers are poorly represented. The low level of information shared (44%), the satisfaction with the sharing (52%), and the child's degree of comfort (66%) in relating to both parents could suggest that their children are having to function in a less supportive milieu than their joint custody counterparts.

It is now interesting to look at how these parents report their children are doing. When analyzed by outcome groups, the figures show a marked similarity to the report of the parents on how they are finding the arrangement with the "doing well" and "at risk" groups clearly maintaining their profile.

"At risk" children are clearly having more difficulty than the children judged to be "doing well" (54% to 29% when difficulties exist in more than one area). In looking at these figures, it is important to note that the parents of the "doing well" group were found to be the most aware and concerned about their children. They are more apt to notice emotional and social difficulties their children might be experiencing, so that their concerns in this area might be greater than the other parents. These children still have the lowest percentage of multiple problems of any group.

One of the most interesting findings concern the apparent improvement in the "stressed" group of children who overall are reported to have the fewest incidents of adjustment problems. Since these children come primarily from the "stressed" parent groups, this would appear to confirm the inference from the parental questionnaire that a large number of the questionable families have worked out a comfortable, stable joint custody arrangement. Other research studies have found that children who experience difficulty immediately post-divorce seem to overcome the trauma and continue a normal pattern of development if the home situation stabilizes. A question can be raised about the accuracy of parental reports (what is a problem to one parent might not be to another). It will, therefore, be important to have a consistent independent clinical evaluation in the future.

While our original study found that those children who were preschool at the age of separation seem to be doing very much better than the others in many areas, this did not appear to hold up strongly 18 months later as they also reached latency age. Their profile now is quite similar to those children who were latency age at the time of separation. However, since the largest group of preschool children were in the families of the "successful" parent group, they would have been scrutinized more carefully for evidences of emotional problems or a difficult school adjustment than those in the other age groups. There is an indication that their problems are less severe (multiple problems 31%, as opposed to 41% for latency, and 44% for adolescence). Living in two homes did not seem to affect the cognitive functioning of the preschool children as they began their class work. The school adjustment problems noted in the responses were of a behavioral nature, and none of the preschool children were reported to be having difficulty with schoolwork. This group of children who lived in two homes as preschoolers will particularly need further evaluation to help us understand whether this age child can successfully master the more complex demands of joint custody.

The adolescent group were clearly having the most difficulty. Our adolescent figures are not totally representative of post-divorce adjustments since the families who were most interested in joint custody had younger children, and the adolescents in a number of cases came from long-term dysfunctional families who had been in conflict at the time they came into the project.

While our original study seems to show that the boys were showing more signs of stress than the girls, there was, at 18 months, no substantial difference between the sexes as reported by the parents. However, the boys in sole custody did seem to be showing far greater symptomatology than the girls in either category and the boys in joint custody. This is in accordance with previous findings which emphasize the importance of an active father in the development of boys.

When analyzed by present custody arrangement, children in joint custody homes, like their parents, are reported to be doing better in all areas. While this cannot be viewed as a definitive finding on children in joint custody versus those in sole custody, it strongly supports a finding that a stable joint custody arrangement can provide a supportive home which enhances growth. Children do have the capacity to adjust to a variety of living patterns, including living in two homes. It would appear to depend on whether the parents can successfully minimize their conflict, value each other as parents, share important information, and attend to the needs of their children. Assistance at the crucial time of separation would appear to enhance the possibility of joint custody working out.

Summary

This chapter reports on a follow-up questionnaire filled out by 56 parents who participated in a service and research project conducted by Jewish Family and Children's Services, September 1981–November 1984. This project provided 50 families with group and individual services to help them work out a joint custody agreement at the time of separation. Research findings discussed the outcome of the service project—defining for whom the joint custody model seemed to be working, and for whom it didn't, in both parent and child groups.

The parental questionnaire reported on the status of the custody agreement, parental satisfaction with the arrangement and a check list on the adjustment of the children. In general, these parental follow-up reports support the earlier profiles of successful or failed joint custody as developed by staff. However, the largest group of parents and children who were judged to be having moderate difficulties at the time the project ended, seemed to be much more satisfied—and their children showed fewer problems—18 months later. Joint custody appears to be working out well for these families and their children who had needed considerable assistance to work out an agreement. Sex and age no longer seemed as important an indicator of how well the children were doing as these variables had at the time the study ended.

An independent clinical evaluation of these children in the future can continue to provide valuable longitudinal information about how joint custody works—and for whom. It can also provide important information about the child's view of joint custody.

15

Ongoing Post-Divorce Conflict in Families Contesting Custody: Do Joint Custody and Frequent Access Help?

JANET R. JOHNSTON
MARSHA KLINE
JEANNE M. TSCHANN

Most of the chapters in this volume focus on post-divorce parenting where the parents were able to agree upon custody, or at least subdue their conflict, following divorce. Here the authors look at high-conflict parents who continue to expose their children to unresolved hostility. Parental conflict and children's behavioral and social adjustment were measured in one-hundred families entrenched in custody and visitation disputes at two periods: the time of litigation and two-and-one-half years later, at which point 35% of the children were in joint physical custody and 65% were in sole physical custody. More frequent access to both parents was associated with more emotional and behavioral problems in the children, with different effects for boys and girls.

Janet R. Johnston, Ph.D., is Director of Research at the Center for the Family in Transition, Corte Madera, California, and Consulting Associate Professor at the Department of Sociology, Stanford University.

Marsha Kline, Ph.D., and Jeanne M. Tschann, Ph.D., were Research Associates at the Center for the Family in Transition.

This chapter is a condensation of an article, complete with data and methodology, which appeared in the *American Journal of Orthopsychiatry*, Vol. 59, pp. 576–592, October 1989.

The disposition of custody and visitation disputes in the courts poses serious dilemmas for judges, mediators, mental health professionals, and lawmakers. Under what conditions should litigating parents be granted substantial visitation and access rights to the child? Should they be encouraged or even mandated to under-take joint custody with the hope that sharing parental rights, responsibilities, and time with their children will ultimately resolve their disputes; or, is it likely that co-parental arrangements will place the children in an unstable environment and an intolerable position between warring parents? Decision makers must weigh two sets of evidence with contradictory implications for social policy: On the one hand, living in a single-parent home and the absence of the father have been linked to children's cognitive and learning deficits, conduct disorders, and problems in gender identification (Biller, 1981; Hetherington, 1972; Hetherington, Cox, & Cox, 1982; Kalter, Riemar, Brickman, & Woo Chen, 1985; Radin, 1981; Santrock & Warshak, 1979; Wallerstein & Kelly, 1980b). On the other hand, children with more access to both parents, particularly in joint custody situations, may be exposed to ongoing parental hostility (Nelson, in press). Parental conflict and hostility have been consistently linked to behavioral and emotional disturbances, especially for boys (Emery, 1982; Hetherington et al., 1982; Jacobson, 1978b; Johnston, Gonzalez, & Campbell, 1987; Porter & O'Leary, 1980; Shaw & Emery, 1987; Rutter, 1971; Wallerstein & Kelly, 1980b).

The issue of joint custody has been hotly debated in state legislative bodies across the nation during the past decade. About 40 states have passed some kind of joint custody legislation, which is analyzed in Chapter 17 of this volume. The legislation delineates two types of joint custody: Joint *legal* custody usually refers to parents assuming equal responsibility for major decisions about their children, and joint *physical* custody indicates the children are living for substantial amounts of time with each parent.[1] Since our concern in this chapter is with the impact of the actual living arrangements on children, the term *joint custody* will henceforth be used to refer to joint physical custody.

These recent legal changes imply that the weight of opinion favors promoting parental sharing of rights and responsibilities after divorce. However, there are three different kinds of statutes which differ in the extent to which shared parenting is supported, encouraged, or mandated: those in which joint custody is an *option*, those where it is the *preferred* custody arrangement, and those in which it is *presumed* to be in the best interests of the child unless there is evidence to the contrary. Moreover, along with the implementation of joint custody legislation, there are laws and policies which, to varying extents, encourage more frequent visitation of the noncustodial parent. For example, in California, the law expressly states that if sole physical custody is to be awarded, it should be to the parent who provides the child with frequent and continuing access to the other parent.

---

1. However, the manner in which each of these terms is defined and interpreted varies greatly between states and even between local jurisdictions. Moreover, in many cases where a court stipulation provides for joint custody, parents may or may not act upon their legally defined rights.

Prior Research

Joint custody legislation is supported by a sparse body of research evidence, most of which comes from small studies of families who have voluntarily undertaken the arrangement. Exploratory studies by Greif (1979a) and Ahrons (1979b) found that joint custody parents were able to successfully separate and protect their children from their marital hostilities. However, studies of children's adjustment in joint custody have yielded inconclusive or mixed results. Descriptive research has reported increased self-esteem, competence, and diminished sense of loss in joint custody children, but it has also noted that a substantial proportion of the children were visibly distressed and confused (Abarbanel, 1979; Steinman, 1981; McKinnon & Wallerstein, 1986). Some quantitative studies found no differences in symptomatology between joint and sole-custody children (Luepnitz, 1982, 1986; Wolchik, Braver, & Sandler, 1985), whereas in another study, latency-age boys in joint custody showed superior behavioral adjustment and were less distressed by the parental divorce and conflict than were those in sole custody (Shiller, 1986a, 1986b).

In a recent larger study of shared parenting (Kline, Tschann, Johnston, & Wallerstein, 1988), the multi-dimensional nature of physical custody arrangements was considered in terms of its title as defined by the legal decree, and the frequency, continuity, and duration of time spent in each parent's home. The adjustment of 35 children in joint custody was compared with that of 58 children in sole mother-custody situations. The several dimensions of joint custody did not significantly influence the children's behavioral and social adjustment two years post-separation. Instead, differences in the children's adaptation were linked to the child's sex and age, parental psychological functioning, and interparental verbal and physical aggression.

The effects of frequent visitation by the noncustodial parent upon children's adjustment are also equivocal. Two studies found it was associated with better child outcomes (Jacobson, 1978a; Lowenstein & Koopman, 1978); three other studies found no relationship (Hess & Camara, 1979; Hodges, Buchsbaum, & Tierney, 1983; Kurdek & Berg, 1983). One study found that regularity and consistency of visitation were more important than frequency (Isaacs, Montalvo, & Abelsohn, 1986). Longitudinal research indicates that frequent visiting is beneficial only in the absence of sustained parental hostility and where the noncustodial parent is not emotionally disturbed (Hetherington et al., 1982; Wallerstein, 1987; Wallerstein & Kelly, 1980b).

All of the above studies of the effects of custody and visitation have been undertaken with populations that have voluntarily and mutually agreed to the arrangements. However, there is no evidence that encouraging or mandating joint custody and frequent visitation through the legal system either diminishes hostility between those parents who are severely disputing such arrangements, or increases their cooperation in parenting their children. Moreover, there is as yet no evidence, for or against, that joint custody and frequent access when recommended by a court evaluator, or ordered by the court in cases where there are ongoing disputes, is beneficial to the child. The question of whether children in enforced joint custody differ in their psychological and social adjustment from children living under sole-custody awards has not been addressed by researchers.

Only a few studies, to our knowledge, have even tangentially considered this issue. Steinman and colleagues (1985, 1986) have presented the best available data (see Chapter 14). They studied 67 children from 49 families which were attempting to establish joint custody arrangements. Twenty-two of these families were referred by the courts because of a custody dispute; the remainder came voluntarily to work out a joint custody arrangement. When they were reassessed one year later, they were classified into *successful*, *stressed*, and *failed* subgroups. Children in *successful* joint custody families (27%) had high self-esteem and emotional distance from parental conflict. However, in 42% of the sample, parents were classified as *stressed*, and another 31% had failed to sustain joint custody. The two subgroups experiencing difficulties were more likely to have had the joint custody arrangement imposed upon them and to be relitigating. These parents were significantly more hostile, physically abusive, and distrustful towards each other, and had difficulty communicating. Their children were also more likely to be stressed or severely at risk for major emotional disturbance. This was primarily a clinical, descriptive study; standardized measures were not reported and a sole-custody comparison group was not available.

On the other hand, Simring (1984) interviewed 44 fathers with joint custody and concluded that this arrangement was the best alternative when the ex-wife is hostile and likely to sabotage the father's attempts to relate to his children. A large proportion of these fathers reported they were more satisfied and actively involved with their children and believed that the joint custody arrangement gave them equal power and opportunity to function as a father, somewhat independently of the quality of the co-parental relationship. Simring studied only joint legal custody, did not report standardized measures, had no control group of sole-custody fathers, and did not examine the children's adjustment.

Ash and Guyer (1986) interviewed 100 families approximately four years after the divorce decree and concluded that the adjustment of children who had been subject to contested custody evaluations was no different from those whose custody was not contested. Frequency of visitation and type of custody (joint, mother sole and father sole) was not associated with child functioning. Rather, their adjustment was related to the quality of the current interparental relationship. However, their data indicated that children who had been subject to custody/visitation litigation saw their noncustodial parent relatively infrequently at the four-year mark. Most had patterns of access that were similar to those children in noncontested sole custody. Hence, their study does not address the impact of frequent access and joint custody on children of ongoing disputes. Moreover, an attrition rate of 63% of their original sample raises questions about the representativeness of those parents they did interview.

Purpose and Hypothesis

The purpose of the present study was to examine the incidence of joint and sole physical custody awards, the stability of custody and access arrangements, and the relative levels of communication and conflict between parents in litigating families who are unable to settle their differences between one and four years after the legal dispute. First, we hypothesized that children's behavioral and social adjustment would differ according to type of custody arrangement. Age and gender effects were explored, by themselves and in interaction with the patterns of access/visitation. Second, we theorized a chain of events occurring in families who contest custody and proposed a set of hypotheses, which were tested. These were as follows:

The court's recommendation or enforcement of frequent visitation/joint custody was likely to put into effect a time-sharing arrangement that would endure over the follow-up period. We thought it possible that parents who had more frequent contact with each other—coincident upon the child's increased access—would learn to communicate more rationally and resolve their differences over time. To the extent that they were able to do this, we predicted that the child's distress would be ameliorated. Alternatively, the child's more frequent access could prolong and exacerbate parental disputes, over and above levels that might be expected because of their past conflictual relationship. Increased parental discord, in turn, was predicted to intensify the child's sense of being caught and used in the conflict (triangulated) and this would result in children having more emotional, behavioral, and social problems at follow-up.

Method

The sample of 100 families was obtained between 1981 and 1983 from family courts within the San Francisco Bay area. All parents were disputing custody and access arrangements and had failed to settle their differences through attorney negotiations or brief mediation that is mandated by the California courts. They were undertaking, to some degree involuntarily, custody and access arrangements that were recommended by a court mediator or an evaluator, or were ordered by a judge. Hence they represent the more entrenched and ongoing divorce disputes.

The oldest child between the ages of 1 and 12 years at intake was selected from each family for this study. The 100 children (50 boys, 50 girls) were ethnically diverse: 62% White, 23% of mixed racial origin, 8% Hispanic, 4% Asian, 2% Black, and 1% other. Their families were of low/middle socioeconomic status. The children and their parents were assessed at the time of the legal dispute (baseline) and at the follow-up (30 months later) with standardized measures, parent questionnaires and clinical ratings. (For a more complete discussion of the methodology, see Johnston et al., 1989.)

Discussion

This longitudinal study investigated the emotional, behavioral and social adjustment of 100 children whose families were in entrenched disputes over custody and visitation, on the average, four-and-one-half years after the parental separation and two-and-one-half years after the legal dispute. Thirty-five of these children were in joint custody and 65 in sole custody at the follow-up.

While there was no clear evidence that children are better adjusted in either custody type, joint custody is highly related to more frequent access and we found consistent evidence that children who have more frequent access are more emotionally troubled and behaviorally disturbed. In particular, children who share more days each month with both parents are significantly more depressed, withdrawn, and uncommunicative, have more somatic symptoms and tend to be more aggressive, according to the perceptions of their parents. Although noncustodial fathers are more likely to cease contact with their child than those with joint custody, this is not associated with child outcome. However, since the total dropout rate in the present study was small (13%), the effects would have been difficult to observe.

The family relationships which might explain the association between access and behavior problems were explored. Parents who are more actively hostile at the time of the custody dispute are also more conflictual two to three years later, although the intensity of the discord diminishes with time. Increased parental verbal and physical aggression appear to be generated between parents when children have more frequent access arrangements. The higher incidence of parental conflict to which children are exposed is associated with their increased vulnerability to being caught and used in the parental disputes, and in turn, this partially explains the higher incidence of emotional and behavioral problems. It is important to note, however, that the level of parental conflict and its sequelae are not the only factors implicated in children's post-divorce disturbances. In addition, we found that the more often children have contact with both parents in distressed families, the more problematic is their adjustment, regardless of the level of interparental aggression. Children of severe divorce disputes appear to be more symptomatic in response to living in and making transitions between parental homes, even when their parents are not fighting.

Although children's frequent access to both parents also generates more coparental discussion and reasoning, unfortunately we found no evidence that this ameliorates the children's distress. Kline et al. (1988) also reported no connection between interparental communication and support and child adjustment.

The clinical observations of the majority of the children in this study (70%) have been reported elsewhere and are generally consistent with these empirical findings (Johnston, Campbell, & Mayes, 1985; Johnston & Campbell, 1988). Clinically, the children of ongoing divorce disputes were described as highly distressed and symptomatic in response to witnessing parental fights and in making transitions between parental homes. About two-fifths had fairly severe somatic symptoms. At the time of litigation, the children were typically hypervigilant with respect to their parents and emotionally and behaviorally constricted and withdrawn. However, there was considerable individual variation in response to their disputing parents. Whereas some children actively maneuvered between the parents or strategically withdrew from the conflict, others tried to be very fair and equidistant with both sides but were very conflicted in their loyalties. A large number attempted to align with one or both angry parents, and a small minority became diffusely disturbed in response to the conflict. In general, they seemed to feel both very important (by virtue of being the centerpiece of the parental fight) and vulnerable (they feared being rejected or abandoned). They were also burdened by requests for support and nurturance from their distressed parents. Aggression and more overt behavioral problems were likely to be observed at the follow-up (Johnston et al., 1987). A vicious cycle was at times created in that the child's distress and symptomatic behavior fueled the fight over the custody and visitation arrangements.

In this study we found that older children are more enmeshed in parental conflicts. This is also consistent with previous analyses (Johnston & Campbell, 1987), which showed that as children develop the cognitive capacity for self-reflexive thinking and can simultaneously perceive the opposing views of their disputing parents, they become more vulnerable to acute loyalty conflicts. Moreover, their parents, perceiving them to be more mature, tend to expect the children's support and ask them to take sides in the fight. Alliances with one parent accompanied by varying degrees of negativity towards the other parent—the child may refuse to see or visit with the rejected parent—are typical responses of older children to being caught in the middle, especially where parental disputes are chronic.

Some interesting gender differences were found in this study. Girls' emotional and behavioral adjustment is more negatively affected by frequent access to both parents. Our clinical observations of these children suggested possible reasons for this. Girls in highly disputed joint custody/frequent visitation arrangements tend to form close, emotionally dependent relationships with their fathers and display hostility and ambivalence towards their mothers. Some level of sustained rivalry with the mother (as well as loyalty conflicts) appears to be experienced by the daughters, which is manifested in emotional and behavioral difficulties. On the other hand, girls in sole mother custody at this age tend to have close, nonconflictual relationships with their mothers (Hetherington, Cox, & Cox, 1985; Wallerstein, 1984). Our parallel findings for boys indicate that their behavioral adjustment is not affected by high access to both parents, but that they are more likely to be caught and used in the parental disputes. In this sense, they are more vulnerable to parental conflict, as has been reported in other studies (Block, Block, & Morrison, 1981; Hetherington et al., 1982; Porter & O'Leary, 1980; Rutter, 1971; Whitehead, 1979). Their social competence (school performance, involvement with friends, and outside activities) also appears to be disrupted by more frequent movement between parental homes.

It is necessary to caution against overgeneralizing these rather pessimistic findings. Patterns of access and parental conflict, and their correlates, explain one-fifth of the variance of the children's disturbed behavior. There are other factors which contribute to children's adjustment that have not been included in this study. Important criteria to consider when helping divorcing parents make custody and visitation plans or making judgments on their behalf in court include, foremost, the parents' psychological functioning and the quality of the parent-child relationship. Custodial parents who are anxious and depressed, and those who suffer from substantial emotional or personality disturbance, are likely to have disturbed children (Emery, 1982; Guidubaldi & Perry, 1985; Kline et al., 1988; Rutter, 1971; Wallerstein & Kelly, 1980b). Conversely, a supportive empathic relationship with the custodial parent has been found to protect the child against both parental psychopathology and marital conflict (Hess & Camara, 1979; Hetherington et al., 1982; Rutter, 1971). Second, one should evaluate the extent to which the custody arrangements disrupt the child's wider social support system, which includes school, social activities, contacts with friends, and extended kin (Sandler, Wolchik, & Braver, 1985). Finally, the individual temperament of the child must be considered. A wide range of individual coping responses and degrees of resilience has been found in children of distressed family situations (Anthony, 1987; Garmezy, Masten, & Tellegen, 1984; Rutter, 1985). A number of children are able to maintain a distance from parental conflicts and psychopathology and can resume their development, sometimes at a quickened pace. Some emerge as particularly empathic and interpersonally aware children. Others become overburdened by adult responsibilities, constricted by their fears, enmeshed in the parental conflict, and manifest stress symptoms and emotional and behavioral problems. We need to know much more about what makes for these differential outcomes in children in order to help parents make appropriate individualized child care plans after divorce.

This study helps remind us that it is important not to make custody and visitation decisions, or to frame social policy and laws, based on studies from unrepresentative populations. Most of the evidence for the viability of joint custody and frequent, continuing contact between parents is based on studies of families who have volun-tarily undertaken the arrangements. The experiences of divorcing families who have contested custody and visitation in the courts appear to be different in important ways. This study evaluated only the more extreme subgroup of litigating families who were unable to resolve their differences despite the help of court mediators. The findings indicate that recommending or ordering joint custody or frequent visitation in these cases is contraindicated. This study did not address child outcomes for the much larger group of litigating families who are able to successfully mediate with the help of family court services. This population has yet to be studied.

The climate of controversy over joint custody statutes and their implementation is reputed to have nurtured very different attitudes and policies towards shared parenting in the states and local courts throughout the country. Some jurisdictions are ideologically more committed than others to encouraging joint custody and frequent visitation, which directly influences custody and access outcomes through judicial orders and indirectly influences parental bargaining in attorney negotiations and mandatory mediation (Mnookin & Kornhauser, 1979). Especially under these conditions, it is important to continually review these attitudes and policies, not only in the light of new evidence, but from the perspective of the accumulating body of related research findings.

16

Child Custody and Child Support After Divorce

JESSICA PEARSON
NANCY THOENNES

Few studies directly assess the economic characteristics of those divorced parents and children who have sole versus joint custody and the impact that such arrangements have on both parenting and child-support patterns. The literature has suggested, based on sparse initial data, that parent–child and spousal relationship factors are relevant to the payment of support following divorce. Here the authors have researched empirical patterns associated with various types of sole- and joint custody arrangements following divorce and their impact on the financial experiences of women and children. After explaining their research methodology and stating the results, the authors find no evidence that joint custody is harmful to the economic interests of women and children.

Method

This chapter presents a secondary analysis of samples of divorced parents originally interviewed in several prior research projects. These include the Denver Custody Mediation Project (Pearson & Thoennes, 1983), the Divorce Mediation Research Project (Pearson & Thoennes, 1984a, 1984b), the Joint Custody Project (Steinman

Jessica Pearson, Ph.D., and Nancy Thoennes, Ph.D., are both associated with the Center for Policy Research, an independent nonprofit research organization in Denver, Colorado.

This chapter is based in part on an article which appeared in Family Law Quarterly, Volume 22, p. 319 (Fall 1988) and in part on an article in the American Journal of Orthopsychiatry, Volume 60(2), p. 233 (April 1990).

et al., 1985), and the Child Support and Child Custody Project (Pearson & Thoennes, 1985).

The design, methodology, and instrumentation used in these four studies are described in detail in other published sources. Briefly put, the Custody Mediation Project began in 1979 and involved the random assignment of cases of contested child custody in the Denver metropolitan area to an experimental group, which was offered free mediation services to resolve their custody/visitation problems, or to a control group, which was not offered services. Experimental group members who refused mediation services were also tracked and all respondents were interviewed three times over a two-year period of time: once before and twice following the promulgation of final orders. The Custody Mediation Project yielded interview data at three different times for 459 respondents with sole maternal custody, 76 with sole paternal custody, 89 with joint legal custody, and 62 with joint residential custody (Pearson & Thoennes, 1983).

The Divorce Mediation Research Project began in 1981 and involved a survey of individuals utilizing court-based custody/visitation mediation programs of the Los Angeles Conciliation Court, the Family Relations Division of the Connecticut Superior Court, and the Domestic Relations Division of the Hennepin County, Minnesota, Family Court. These individuals were interviewed immediately prior to the start of mediation and at two points—three and fifteen months—following mediation. Comparable interviews were also conducted with a group with similar custody/visitation disputes in Colorado who did not utilize mediation and a group who divorced without formally contesting custody or visitation issues. The Divorce Mediation Research Project yielded interview data at three different times for 276 respondents with sole maternal custody, 168 with sole paternal custody, 168 with joint legal custody, and 39 with joint residential custody. Interview data at two different times were available for an additional 153 Divorce Mediation Research Project respondents. They were distributed across custody categories as follows: 83 with sole maternal custody, 21 with sole paternal custody, 40 with joint legal, and 9 with joint residential custody.

The Joint Custody Project at Jewish Family and Children's Services of San Francisco involved 51 divorcing families who were offered up to twelve mediation-counseling sessions free of charge in exchange for participation in the research project aimed at assessing the longer-term effects of joint custody. We received contact information for these families in order to assist us in our examination of child-support patterns associated with joint custody, and ultimately 27 such interviews were conducted in connection with the Child Support and Child Custody Project.

The Child Custody and Child Support Project was initiated in 1984 to assess the relationship between custody, visitation, and child support and to analyze the conditions that enhance the voluntary payment of child support. To achieve these objectives, court files were reviewed and 426 interviews were conducted with individuals in the Custody Mediation Project, Divorce Mediation Research Project, and Joint Custody Project who were most likely to be receiving rather than paying child support, who could be located, and who agreed to participate. Thus, mothers were interviewed in all cases of maternal custody ($n=211$), joint legal custody/primary maternal residential custody ($n=64$), joint legal/joint residential custody ($n=63$), and split custody ($n=8$). Fathers were interviewed if the custody type was sole paternal ($n=54$) or if the joint custody arrangement called for primary residence with the father (joint legal/primary paternal residential, n=26). Viewed another way, the Child Support and Child Custody Project interviews were conducted with 96 respondents from Los Angeles, 40 from Minneapolis, 47 from Connecticut, and 243 from Colorado. About 20 percent of the interviews were with primary and sole custodial fathers and 80 percent were with sole and primary custodial mothers.

Taken together, the interview data generated in the original Custody Mediation and Divorce Mediation Research Projects and the subsequent Child Support and Child Custody Project yielded detailed information on the respondents' demographic and socioeconomic characteristics, marital and divorce history, spousal cooperation factors, agreement about post-divorce child care and financial arrangements, compliance patterns and attempts to modify court orders, and a host of attitudinal patterns.

Although originally collected and analyzed for different purposes, our data are useful for assessing the implications of various custodial arrangements for several reasons. First, they are the largest and most heterogeneous samples in the literature dealing with custodial dispositions following divorce and contain substantial numbers of families with sole maternal, sole paternal, joint legal, and joint residential arrangements. Secondly, the reanalysis is longitudinal. Thirdly, the Child Support and Child Custody Project reanalysis provides data on the child-support implications of various custody arrangements. Men's and women's rights advocates have urged, respectively, that joint custody is beneficial and harmful to the economic status of women and children following divorce, but these debates have occurred in an empirical vacuum.

Among the limitations of our study is its exclusive focus on legally married and divorced parents; we have not considered the experiences of the never married. Another limitation on the generalizability of our findings is that many respondents were exposed to court-based or court-affiliated mediation programs. Although this is a growing type of intervention, it is not a typical feature of the divorce experience.

Finally, our assessment of child-support payment patterns is potentially biased due to our reliance on payment reports by recipients. The states from which our samples were drawn did not maintain objective court or agency-based records of payments made by non-custodians. Thus, the most reliable source of information about payment was unavailable. We rejected the option of relying on reports by obligors given the pressure to provide socially acceptable answers and the likely difficulties in attempting to locate non-paying obligors. Lacking other practical alternatives, we relied on reports by recipients and court records indicating legal efforts to generate payment, but these data sources and measures are certainly less than ideal.

Results

Demographic, Attitudinal, and Emotional Outcomes

Demographic and Economic Characteristics—Our research confirms the characterization of joint custody families as more highly educated and wealthier than their sole-custody counterparts. In the Divorce Mediation Research Project, Custody Mediation Project, and the subsample studied in the Child Support and Child Custody Project, respondents with residential custody were substantially more apt to have attended or completed a graduate-level training program, and at the time of the separation, these families had the highest household incomes. The lowest household incomes were reported by those awarded sole paternal custody. Thus, average household income at separation stood at $45,900 for joint residential families while those awarded sole maternal custody reported household incomes of $38,680. Joint legal/maternal residential respondents reported household incomes of $35,700 at separation. For those awarded joint legal/paternal residential and sole paternal custody, the figures were $31,800 and $19,940, respectively.

In addition to higher combined incomes, women in joint residential custody arrangements had the highest absolute earnings at the time of separation. Women awarded joint legal/maternal residential and joint residential custody earned an average of $11,500 and $14,500, respectively, at separation. In 1984–85, 70 percent and 76 percent, respectively, were employed on a full-time basis. Among women with sole-custody arrangements, average earnings at the time of separation stood at $9,300, and in 1984–85, 62 percent worked full time and 22 percent worked part time.

One reason why shared legal and residential arrangements after divorce may be more attractive and feasible for the highly educated and wealthier segments of the population is the high economic cost of joint residential custody arrangements. Housing and child-care costs require an additional $12,354 for children aged 8–13 to $15,617 for preschool children (Patterson, 1982). Another reason is that more highly educated and better paid employees generally enjoy greater flexibility in their work schedules and are able to engage in regular child care. Lastly, it is possible that women who work full time in higher earning occupations have strong professional identities and are more amenable to joint custody arrangements because they derive satisfaction from non-parenting roles.

In addition to these economic differences, the custody groups differed in family size and the children's age. While 70 percent of the parents with joint residential custody had only one child, at least half of the respondents in every other custody category had two or more children. And the children who resided with fathers, either in a sole-custody arrangement or a in joint legal/paternal residential custody arrangement, tended to be older than children who resided solely or primarily with mothers or in joint residential custody. The average age of children in paternal versus maternal residential arrangements was 10 versus 8.

Paternal Cooperation Factors—Our analysis supports some of the allegations of both critics and supporters of joint custody. As supporters contend, conflict between divorcing parents does not appear to worsen as a result of the increased demand for interparental cooperation in joint legal or joint residential custody arrangements. Only 5 to 15 percent of parents with non-maternal custody awards reported that cooperation with their ex-spouse had deteriorated, whereas nearly 25 percent of parents with sole maternal custody who had initially reported that cooperation with their ex-spouse was "easy" or "strained" reported that the relationship was "impossible" or something they no longer tried.

Nor do parents who continue to deal with one another in a joint custody arrangement appear to suffer from intensified attachment bonds or a prolonged adjustment process. In the Custody Mediation Project, at the third interview, respondents in each custody group exhibited lower and roughly equivalent scores on the Index of Attachment (Kitson, 1979) as compared with their scores at the first interview. This suggests that, over time, all respondents come to accept the divorce.

As the critics allege, on the other hand, our analysis also shows that parents who are attracted to joint legal and joint residential custody in particular are predisposed to cooperate and do not suffer from the higher levels of family violence observed in sole-custody situations. For example, in the initial interview conducted with respondents prior to the promulgation of a divorce decree, the proportions of parents in each custody category reporting their relationship with their ex-spouse as "friendly" or "strained but able to cooperate" were 37 percent for sole maternal custody, 43 percent for sole paternal custody, 44 percent for joint legal/maternal residential custody, and 67 percent for joint legal and joint residential custody.

Approximately three years later, joint residential custodians continued to report the most cooperation. At that time, the proportions of parents in various custody situations describing their ability to cooperate with an ex-spouse as "impossible" or something they no longer attempted stood at 10 percent for parents with joint residential custody, 15 percent for those with joint legal and paternal residential custody, and 30 percent for those with sole custody or joint legal and maternal residential custody. In a similar vein, sole-custody respondents in the Divorce Mediation Research Project were more likely to report that physical violence had occurred during the marriage. Those reporting the absence of physical violence during the marriage were more likely to opt for shared residential and legal custody arrangements.

Given these pre-existing differences, it is risky to attribute more lasting differences among parents of various custody groups exclusively to the type of custody in effect. In addition, we can offer little evidence on the fate of parents with joint custody who were initially uncooperative.

Initial Custody Preferences—One of the keenest joint custody debates is whether it should be ordered when at least one party is opposed to the arrangement. A related concern, according to some writers, is that women increasingly find themselves pressured to bargain away spousal and child support in order to avoid losing custody (Polikoff, 1985; Bottomley, 1984).

To examine these issues, we asked respondents about the kind of custody arrangement they and their ex-spouse initially wanted. We also asked parents whether they had been pressured into a custody arrangement and the extent to which financial considerations featured in their decisions regarding custody.

We found that parents who were awarded joint custody were most likely to have developed their custody agreement on their own, perhaps with the assistance of their attorneys. Thus, while 41, 52, and 58 percent of those awarded joint legal/maternal, joint legal/paternal, and joint residential custody, respectively, recall favoring some form of joint custody, and 50 to 70 percent report reaching their agreement on their own, with the remainder settling in mediation, sole-custody parents report different patterns. Among these parents, only 4 to 11 percent recall an initial interest in any type of joint custody arrangement and only about 20 percent decided on their custody agreement independently, without the assistance of mediators or the court. Slightly more than half of the sole awards were developed in mediation, and most of the split and almost 20 percent of the sole paternal awards were resolved in court.

Receptivity to joint custody, however, does not mean wholehearted commitment. Many parents with joint custody view it as a compromise arrangement and initially preferred sole custody or another form of joint custody. For example, among Child Support and Child Custody Project respondents in each joint custody category, at least 40 percent wanted sole custody, and among joint residential respondents, another 20 percent wanted joint legal/maternal custody. To contrast, virtually all (90%) of the sole-custody parents reported receiving exactly the award they wanted. These patterns perhaps explain why parents with joint legal or joint residential custody were more apt (40%) than sole-custody parents (15%) to feel that someone had tried to talk them into the arrangement they wound up with. Ex-spouses were the most commonly cited source of pressure but mediators and attorneys were also frequently mentioned.

To assess the incidence of financial trade-offs, or what has been termed "custody blackmail," we asked respondents whether they had ever felt pressured to give their ex-spouse more time with the children in order to gain financial support, or conversely, whether they had settled for less money to minimize their ex-spouse's demands for time with the children. Their responses reveal that such trade-offs do occur but at a relatively modest level. Mothers with joint legal/maternal residential arrangements reported the highest level of financial pressure: 20 percent felt at least somewhat pressured to trade time for money and another seven percent were uncertain about whether they had been influenced by such factors. Mothers with sole or joint residential arrangements were less likely to report pressure with 13 and 14 percent, respectively, responding with uncertainty or conceding that economic pressure might have entered into their decision making. Not surprisingly, fewer than ten percent of fathers with sole or primary joint custody expressed any sense of being pressured by financial considerations.

Taken together, our analysis indicates that joint custodians tend to be predisposed to the arrangement before they formally adopt it and reach such agreements on their own without the assistance of mediators or the courts. Nevertheless, for many, it is a compromise arrangement and falls short of the sole-custody situation they initially preferred. And although some mothers with joint legal/maternal residential arrangements report being pressured by financial considerations in making their custody decisions, this was a negligible problem for fathers or mothers with whole or joint residential arrangements.

Parental Satisfaction, Conflict, and Relitigation—In our samples, we find mixed evidence on satisfaction, conflict, and relitigation among parents with various types of sole- and joint custody arrangements. For example, in the Custody Mediation

Project, joint custody respondents were more likely to report satisfaction with the terms of their divorce settlement one year following its promulgation than their sole-custody counterparts. A review of court files for these cases two years following final orders revealed that while 20 percent of mothers with sole-custody awards had filed at least one citation for child support, only 8 to 10 percent of the respondents with joint legal or joint residential custody had filed such citations.

Among the subsample analyzed in the Child Support and Child Custody Project, however, the patterns were not as straightforward or favorable to the joint custody population. With that set of respondents, a one-year post-order query revealed that the most satisfied parents and the ones least interested in modification were those with sole custody with 88 percent of such mothers and 74 percent of such fathers reporting extreme satisfaction. Joint custody parents reported the greatest inclination to modify and the lowest levels of satisfaction. The percentages of mothers with joint legal and joint residential custody reporting strong satisfaction stood at 39 and 43, respectively.

The responses of the same population to questions concerning satisfaction with actual custody and visitation practices rather than the formal legal agreement, however, yielded a slightly different picture. Joint residential and joint/maternal mothers were no longer substantially less satisfied. Sole fathers and joint/paternal primary respondents continued to be the most apt to report themselves "very" or "fairly" satisfied. However, about 70 percent of the sole maternal, joint residential, and joint/maternal respondents also reported they were "very" or "fairly" satisfied with the actual custody and visitation situation and there were no dramatic differences by custody type.

The discrepancy between evaluations of the legal agreement and the actual practice of joint custody is puzzling. One possible explanation for the harsher assessments of legal agreements by joint custodians is that, for many, it represented a compromise from original sole-custody desires. Their more favorable evaluations of joint custody in actual practice may reflect the fact that the arrangement works and is satisfactory when not compared with a hypothetical, sole-custody ideal.

As to reported levels of disagreement and conflict, we find that visitation was a fairly regular problem for about 30 percent of all parents, although the nature of the problem differed for the custody groups. For sole-custody mothers, the most frequent complaint was canceled or missed visits (50%). For joint residential and joint legal/joint residential cases, the opposite was a problem and a sizable proportion of mothers with joint legal (15%) and joint residential (38%) custody complained that their ex-spouse had the children too much of the time. Disputes occurred over requests for changes in visitation times with 15 percent of custodial mothers, but only five percent of custodial fathers, citing this as a problem. With the exception of the joint legal/paternal parents, about 20 percent of the parents in each category reported that problems arose because children were returned late after visitation. Finally, some mothers with joint residential custody (19%) disliked the arrangement because they had to interact with their ex-spouse, and several fathers with joint legal/maternal residential custody were critical of the award because they felt that the label implied elements of sharing and equality that were missing in actual practice.

Relitigation patterns in our Child Support and Child Custody Project samples also defy simple generalizations. Although the incidence of child-support modification was negligible and barely varied by custody group, attempted custody modification was substantial, and there were clear differences by group, with sole paternal custody (39%) and joint varieties exhibiting the highest levels of change and sole maternal families (10%) exhibiting the lowest incidence of custody modification. Custody modification activity among those with joint custody stood at 14 percent of the joint/maternal, 29 percent of the joint residential, and 33 percent of the joint/paternal cases. These levels were comparable to rates observed for sole-custody cases in some studies (Ilfeld, Ilfeld, & Alexander, 1982) but fell below levels of contest over a two-year period reported by others (Cline & Westman, 1971).

An examination of the nature of the modification requests made by respondents in each custody category adds to the confusion. Although sole maternal custody groups exhibited the lowest levels of change, there was decidedly more attempted movement from sole custody to some form of joint custody than the opposite. Further, when modification did occur in joint custody cases, it tended to involve a move to another form of joint custody rather than an abandonment of joint custody in favor of a sole-custody arrangement. Thus, although the incidence of modification among those with joint custody exceeded levels for sole-custody families, it typically involved a shift to another form of joint custody rather than a rejection of shared parenting.

Access and Childrearing Patterns—Our data indicate that joint legal and residential custodians are decidedly more involved with their children following divorce than sole custodians. For example, sole-custody cases with court orders that specified visitation called for the non-custodian to have access to the child for only about 20 percent of the child's time with the mean number of weekday, weekend, and overnight stays per year standing at 18.6, 29.5, and 43.0, respectively. Substantial proportions of mothers (40%) and fathers (30%) with such arrangements reported that their children never stayed overnight with the other parent or engaged in a weekend visitation; and visitation by the absent parent was often reported to be sporadic and infrequent by sole-custody mothers (54%) or fathers (44%).

Court orders specifying visitation patterns in joint legal custody agreements called for the non-custodian to have access to the child for approximately 28 percent of his/her time with weekday, overnight, and weekend contact averaging 44.6, 54.5, and 87.4 days per year. Interviews with mothers and fathers with joint legal arrangements revealed that overnight and weekend visitation failed to occur in only seven and 20 percent of such cases, respectively. Canceled, missed, or sporadic visitation was reported to be a problem in about 25 percent of such cases.

Where the allocation of the child's time in joint residential cases was specified in court records, the 60 percent/40 percent division was most common. This translated into an average number of weekday, overnight, and weekend stays per year of 188, 49.2, and 136.7, respectively. None of these parents reported the absence of overnight or weekend visits and only 12 percent complained about missed or unpredictable visitation patterns.

These differentials in access persisted when we controlled for residential patterns of the parents and compared respondents living within ten miles of their ex-spouse. It is also relevant to note that ex-spouses in joint custody arrangements tended to be more geographically stable than their sole-custody counterparts, with 81 percent of joint residential and 72 percent of joint legal parents reporting that neither parent had moved as compared with 60 percent of sole-custody parents.

Assessments by mothers and fathers with various types of sole- and joint custody arrangements reveal that the pressures of parenting following divorce are felt more acutely in sole-custody situations, and that there is greater, if not equal, sharing of childrearing tasks in joint custody cases. Typically, 90 percent of sole-custody parents report full responsibility for assisting with homework, driving the children to friends or activities, attending daytime and evening school events, arranging and executing visits with friends, and staying home with sick children. In joint legal arrangements, the primary residential custodian also feels solely responsible in 73–85 percent of the cases, depending on the task. However, in joint residential arrangements, about half the mothers report that these items are shared equally with their ex-spouse and the other half report that the task is always or usually her responsibility. Staying home with sick children is the task lease apt to be shared. Fewer than 35 percent of the joint residential parents and less than 10 percent of respondents in all other custody categories report sharing this job equally.

These task-sharing patterns help to explain why joint residential parents are least apt to report feeling overwhelmed by the amount of time and energy their children require. As we have previously noted, these feelings are reported by 40 percent of sole maternal and 25 to 30 percent of the parents with sole paternal or joint legal agreements, but are reported in only 13 percent of parents with joint residential arrangements. In addition, these differences persist when we control for the fact that joint residential families generally have fewer children than families with other arrangements.

Another difference by custody category is the tendency to criticize the performance of the ex-spouse as a parent. About 50 percent of the sole maternal, 60 to 65 percent of the sole paternal and joint/legal parents, and 90 percent of the joint residential parents report their ex-spouse has a good relationship with the children. Similarly, 30 percent of the sole maternal, 50 percent of the sole paternal and joint legal, and 65 percent of the joint residential parents report being "very" or "somewhat" satisfied with their ex-spouse's parental performance. Thus, although parents in all custody categories are critical of their ex-spouse, this is more apt to characterize sole custodians than their counterparts with shared-parenting arrangements.

Children's Adjustment to Divorce—Perhaps the most controversial and critical issue in the joint custody debate is its impact on children and their adjustment following divorce. To assess this, we used different measures of child adjustment in our Custody Mediation Project and Divorce Mediation Research Project studies, although both involved checklists of child behavior completed by the parent rather than direct observations or interviews with the children.

In the Custody Mediation Project, child adjustment was measured with the Child Behavior Checklist developed by Hodges and Bloom (1984). It consists of 25 items describing behaviors and mental states which yield three clusters dealing with depression, disruptive behavior, and agitation, and a total score utilizing all items.

An analysis of scores for these clusters for boys and girls separately in each custody group reveals that while the children scored comparably at the initial interview prior to the divorce and development of various sole- and joint custody arrangements, there were significant differences between groups at the final interview. At this phase, children in joint residential arrangements had lower scores, indicative of more favorable adjustment than their counterparts in sole-custody arrangements. Average total scores for boys of all ages in maternal, joint legal, and joint residential custody arrangements were 40.2, 39.8, and 37.8, respectively. Average total scores for girls in these categories were 38.7, 38.9, and 36.3, respectively.

The child adjustment measurement we utilized in the Divorce Mediation Research Project was a parental checklist developed by Achenbach and Edelbrock (1980). Unlike the Custody Mediation Project results based upon the Hodges and Bloom scale, the Divorce Mediation Research Project analysis of global scores and subscales from the Achenbach and Edelbrock checklist revealed no significant differences at the initial and final interview. Essentially, children in all custody categories scored similarly on subscales dealing with depression, aggression, delinquency, social withdrawal, and somatic complaints. While there was overall improvement in scores at the final interview compared with the first, children in all groups demonstrated this pattern. Based upon this analysis, we could not discern more favorable adjustment patterns for children in any of the sole- or joint custody arrangements under consideration.

To identify the factors that best help to explain the variance in child adjustment at the final interview observed in the Divorce Mediation Research Project, we conducted a multiple regression using the global Achenbach score and its various subscales as the dependent variables. Our list of possible predictors included custody type as well as a variety of items that have been mentioned in the literature: the general background of the family, divorce/dispute-specific variables, characteristics of the child, the parental relationship, and variables relating to custody and visitation. Using the backward model of regression, variables were entered simultaneously and removed step-by-step until the optimum combination remained to explain the variance in the dependent variable. Using this technique, we were able to explain 10 to 16 percent of the explained variance in each of the Achenbach subscales as well as the global scale.

Five variables appeared in more than half of the resulting regressions and none of these five dealt with specific custody arrangements. In descending order of frequency they were: the parents' degree of interest in reconciling at the initial interview, the level of physical violence in the home during the marriage, custodian's financial stress as reported in the first interview, the parents' level of cooperation at the first interview, and the parents' level of cooperation at the final interview. The pattern was for better adjustment in those families where (1) parents were cooperative, (2) there was no history of violence, and (3) the parents did not experience high levels of financial stress at the initial interview. Despite the mixed messages that may have been sent, we also found better adjustment in homes where reconciliation was considered at the time of the initial interview.

Regular visitation was one of nine variables that were significant in half the regressions aimed at explaining positive adjustment patterns. Along with visitation, favorable adjustment patterns were also associated with fewer changes in the child's life (e.g., moving and changing schools) and more attachment and less conflict between ex-spouses. As in the Custody Mediation Project, girls experienced more favorable adjustment patterns than boys.

These analyses suggest that while regular visitation is predictive of child adjustment in about half the analyses, the more compelling variables are ones dealing with family dynamics, child characteristics, and parent relationships. In and of themselves, formal custody arrangements are not predictive of subsequent adjustment patterns, although visitation and contact with the non-custodial parent remains a compelling factor in the adjustment process.

Child-Support Patterns

In the following analysis, we consider whether child support is more or less apt to be ordered in certain types of custody arrangements, whether there are relationships between custody type and the adequacy of ordered levels of child support, and the relationship between child custody and the regularity and completeness of support payments.

Child-Support Orders—There was a definite relationship between child custody and the existence of a child-support order. Child-support orders were most common in sole maternal custody cases with 93 percent of such fathers ordered to pay support. Child-support orders were also fairly common in joint legal custody cases where the mother retained primary residential responsibilities. For example, in these cases, the incidence of a year-round child-support order stood at 81 percent, and an additional nine percent of cases involved an order calling for support during part of the year.

Child-support orders were much less common in paternal custody situations and arrangements calling for joint legal and joint residential custody. As to joint legal and residential cases, a support order was present only 44 percent of the time, and an additional five percent were ordered to pay support during a portion of the year. Mothers were ordered to pay child support in 37 percent of the cases involving sole paternal custody and in 27 percent of the cases calling for joint legal custody with paternal residential arrangements.

To determine whether the absence of a child-support order in approximately half of the cases calling for shared legal and residential custody represented a hardship for the affected women and children, we compared the characteristics of joint custody families with and without a child-support order and the responses of women to direct queries about their satisfaction with child-support arrangements. Several significant differences emerged. Joint residential cases without an order had significantly fewer children, higher income levels for mothers and lower income levels for fathers, higher ratios between earnings for husbands and wives, and more overnight visitation with the father. Typically, this arrangement involved a family consisting of a single child with an employed mother earning approximately 87 percent of what her husband earned (average parental income at the time of separation was $24,000 for fathers and $17,000 for mothers). Although the differences were not statistically significant, a high portion of such cases (65%) involved at least 180 overnight visits with the father per year. And in the final follow-up interview, such fathers were reported by their ex-spouses to be earning an average of $29,000 per year while mothers earned an average of $18,700.

To contrast, joint residential cases with child-support orders tended to involve larger families with two or more children; at separation, wives earned approximately 41 percent of what their husbands earned and average incomes for husbands and wives stood at $38,000 and $12,000, respectively. A somewhat lower percentage of cases involved overnight visitation in excess of 180 days per year (41%) and income estimates for such fathers made by wives in the final interview stood at $49,000 while the reported earnings for mothers stood at $19,000.

The responses of mothers with and without support orders to a battery of questions concerning possible episodes of "custody blackmail" or pressures to trade money for access revealed that mothers who opted for joint residential custody without child support did so despite considerable pressure from family, friends, and attorneys to avoid this arrangement. Enthusiastic about joint custody from the time of separation onwards, their commitment did not waver, and they remained significantly more satisfied with the joint custody arrangement in actual practice at the final interview. Although there was some differential in the proportion of joint custody mothers with and without child support who reported some pressure to trade time for money (14 percent versus 8 percent), none of the mothers expressing dissatisfaction attributed their feelings to the lack of support. To the extent these women were dissatisfied, they tended to blame their feelings on the amount of visitation the arrangement involved as well as having to see their ex-spouse and continued arguments over visitation.

Joint residential mothers who did not have support orders were significantly more likely than those with orders to rate their relationship with their ex-spouse as "friendly" (39% vs. 8%) and more likely to say they were "very satisfied" with the job their husband was doing as a father (35% vs. 25%). When asked how agreeable they found the absence of child support, 57 percent said they found the arrangement "very agreeable," 30 percent said it was "somewhat agreeable," 13 percent said the arrangement was "not very agreeable," and no one said that the arrangement was "not at all agreeable." Although one woman reported that she offered her ex-husband, whom she described as "alcoholic and violent," the option of not paying support in order to keep him away from her and the children, there was a strong association between frequent overnight visitation and satisfaction with a lack of support. Thus, 84 percent of those who said the lack of support was "very agreeable" also reported at least 180 overnight visits per year. Among those who said the lack of support was only "somewhat" or "not very" agreeable, only 40 percent reported this much overnight visitation.

In this sample, child-support orders were more apt to be omitted in joint residential custody arrangements, but the omission was reportedly not a source of disagreement, disaffection, or hardship. The chief characteristics of joint residential cases without support orders were fewer children, lower paternal earnings, and higher maternal earnings. With only knowledge of the relative earnings of the parents and the number of children in the family, we could correctly classify 74 percent of the joint residential cases according to whether or not child support was ordered. Clearly, there was little mystery about the decision to order support among those opting for joint residential custody although the advantaged economic characteristics of this subsample set it apart from the majority of the divorcing population and makes a greater range of support options, including the absence of child support, practical.

Child-Support Levels—We found no statistically significant differences in order levels by custody type. Modal per monthly support obligations for each child stood at $100 in sole paternal custody cases, $150 in joint legal and joint residential cases, and $200 in sole maternal custody cases. These differences were not statistically significant.

Among those with sole maternal custody, child support represented an average of 20 percent of fathers' estimated gross income at separation. For joint legal/maternal residential cases, the comparable figure was 17 percent. For joint residential cases, the median child-support level was 14 percent of fathers' gross income. Again, these differences were not statistically significant. In the few instances where support was awarded to sole custodial fathers, the median award comprised 16 percent of the mother's gross income.

Still another indicator of the adequacy of child support orders was the percentage of the recipient's gross income that it comprised. A comparison across custody groups revealed that the award was generally no more than five percent of the recipient parents' gross income. This was true of all sole paternal cases, 90 percent of the joint residential cases, and 81 percent of the sole maternal and joint legal/maternal residential cases.

Further indication that custody type was irrelevant to the determination of the level of ordered child support came from a multiple regression analysis aimed at determining the level of support. The variables which helped to predict the level of the award were the obligor's income at the separation, the recipient parent's income at the separation, and the relative earning power of the spouses. The higher the earnings of the obligor, the higher the support order. The income of the recipient parent was also positively correlated with the level of support. However, the higher the recipient's earnings relative to the obligor's earnings, the lower the support order.

Although child-support-order levels did not differ by custody group, there is evidence that across each group, they were inadequate and the source of much dissatisfaction by custodial parents. For example, about 30 percent of mothers with sole custody, joint legal/maternal residential custody, and joint residential custody said the award was "definitely not enough." This was expressed by 17 percent of fathers with sole custody.

Doubtlessly, the reactions of these parents reflected the fact that child-support orders for each group fell at or below minimum poverty income guidelines and well below estimated expenditures on children in all households. For example, the poverty guideline established that the incremental cost of each child in the household, at a minimum subsistence level, was $157 per month (Federal Register, 1986). According to the USDA, average per-child expenditures in households were $446 per month (USDA, 1982). Clearly, child-support orders in every custody group in our sample fell at or below these "reasonable benchmarks."

Despite widespread dissatisfaction with child support-levels, few parents returned to court to modify support. Only 11 sole-custody mothers (5%), two joint legal/maternal residential mothers (3%), and one joint residential mother (2%) reported instigating a return to court to alter child-support arrangements. Moreover, when asked how much additional support they needed to achieve adequacy, parents in all custody categories indicated that they needed an average of $200 to $240 per child per month—amounts which also fell below documented expenditure levels and recommended benchmarks. This suggests that custodial parents themselves may be uninformed about the true economics of childrearing and may set their expectations for support unreasonably low.

Other Financial Provisions—In addition to specifying monthly payment levels, some child-support orders included provisions dealing with educational or medical expenses and the allocation of life insurance benefits. To the extent these provisions were included in orders, there was little systematic difference across custody categories. For example, as to future educational expenses, only five percent of all orders in our sample specified that the obligor would pay educational expenses; another five percent of most custody groups specified that educational expenses would be shared. It is relevant that even among the most cooperative parents with joint residential custody arrangements, only 20 percent had negotiated any provision dealing with methods of meeting the future education needs of their children.

Cost-of-living increases in child-support orders were extremely rare too. They were mentioned in only about five percent of the support orders in the sample and there were no differences in the incidence of these provisions across custody categories. As to life insurance benefits, about 11 percent of the joint residential, 16 percent of the sole paternal, and 30 percent of the sole maternal and joint legal/maternal residential cases stipulated that the obligor would be covered by life insurance and that the children would be designated as the beneficiaries. Finally, about 40 percent of the joint residential, joint legal/maternal residential, and sole maternal custody cases specified that medical expenses would be shared. Fathers were designated the responsible party for providing medical coverage in 14 percent of the sole paternal, 20 percent of the sole maternal, and 26 percent of the joint legal/maternal residential and joint residential custody cases.

Child-Support Payment—According to advocates, joint custody enhances the child's financial standing because it stimulates the voluntary payment of child support. To assess this proposition, we compared payment patterns, as reported by the parent designated to receive the money, across all custody categories. As previously noted, this method of assessment was less than ideal but was the only one available, given the absence of court or agency-maintained objective records of payment.

In our analysis of voluntary payment patterns, we eliminated all cases for which no child-support order was promulgated which included approximately 50 percent of the cases with joint legal and joint residential custody. We also eliminated cases in which there appeared to be a garnishment of wages, payment thorough the court, or some other method of automatic payment. Garnishment occurred in 17 percent of the sole paternal custody cases, 14 percent of the sole maternal custody cases, 10 percent of the joint legal/maternal custody cases, and 10 percent of the joint legal/maternal residential cases. None of the joint legal/joint residential cases involved a wage garnishment. Payment of support through the court was reported by over a third (34%) of the sole-custody mothers, 17 percent of the sole-custody fathers and joint legal/maternal residential mothers, and 14 percent of the joint residential mothers. In the remaining cases, payment was presumed to occur voluntarily and represented uncoerced compliance with court orders.

A comparison across custody groups of full, partial, timely, and late payments during the preceding year revealed some significant differences. Of those with sole maternal custody, almost half (46%) reported receiving all twelve monthly support payments. For joint legal/maternal residential cases and joint residential cases, the figures were 64 and 75 percent, respectively. Conversely, 30 percent of the sole maternal, 17 percent of the joint legal/maternal residential, and none of the joint residential cases reported the total absence of child-support payments in the preceding year. A one-way analysis of variance confirmed that payment patterns were more favorable for those with joint residential custody as compared with those with sole maternal custody.

The analysis of the number of complete payments which arrived on time was less favorable for all custody groups, although mothers with joint residential custody remained significantly better off than their counterparts with sole custody. Thus, although 49 percent of the sole-custody mothers said they received eleven or twelve complete payments during the preceding year, only 35 percent reported that this many arrived on schedule. Similarly, while 67 percent of the joint legal/maternal residential respondents received twelve payments, only 51 percent received them on time. And while 79 percent of the mothers with joint residential custody acknowledged receiving eleven or twelve full payments, only 54 percent said this many payments arrived on time.

We calculated the percentage of the child-support obligation actually met by adding together partial and full payments and dividing by the ordered support figure. Like other measures of compliance, this analysis confirmed the significantly more favorable performance of fathers with joint residential custody as compared with those in sole maternal custody arrangements. On the average, sole-custody mothers reported receiving 63 percent of what they were owed. For joint legal/maternal residential custody and joint residential custody parents, the percentages were 81 and 95 percent, respectively. Phrased somewhat differently, 31 percent of the mothers with sole custody and 20 percent of those with joint legal/maternal residential custody reported receiving no more than half of what they were owed. There were no instances in which fathers with joint residential custody were reported to have met less than half of their support obligation. Thus, when child support was ordered in a case calling for joint residential custody, this obligation was typically met.

Predictors of Child-Support Payment—To assess the relative importance of custody factors in the voluntary payment of child support, we conducted a multiple regression analysis using fourteen variables of an economic, social, and psychological nature that were expected to influence support performance. These variables were entered simultaneously and removed one at a time until the optimal set of predictive variables remained. Ultimately, five variables explained 20 percent of the variance (adjusted r^2) in the amount of the support order that was actually paid. The pattern was for greater compliance in cases where the obligor did not experience job problems (as reported by mothers), where initial anger levels between the spouses were low enough so that fathers did not criticize mothers in front of the children, where cooperation between ex-spouses following the promulgation of final orders was greater, where fathers had higher occupational status, where fathers had no additional children to support, and where the decision to divorce was mutual and not made solely by mothers.

To assess the relative predictive power of visitation, access, and paternal participation factors, we repeated this analysis after adding to the equation the number of weekday, weekend, and overnight visits per year and a composite indicator of the degree to which fathers were involved with children in activities like helping with homework, attending daytime and evening school events, driving children to friends and activities, arranging extracurricular activities, and staying home to care for sick children. Our measures of paternal participation were gleaned from interviews with mothers. After adding the visitation and paternal participation variables, the explained variance rose only from 20 to 22 percent.

To assess the explicit impact of custody type on child-support payment performance, we repeated the analysis and added a variable indicative of the type of custody in effect. The explained variance now stood at 23 percent and the predictive variables (from greater to lesser importance) were as follows: presence of employment problems, number of weekend visits, level of cooperation at the second interview, denigration of mothers by fathers during visitation as measured by the initial interview, type of custody, father's occupation, mutuality of the divorce decision, number of weekday visits, and presence of additional children for the father to support.

This series of regression analyses showed that although custody arrangement and amount of visitation were relevant variables, they were not compelling predictors of child-support payment behavior. The more relevant variables dealt with the financial status and resources of the obligor and parental cooperation. Taken together, variables pertaining to these characteristics of obligors and their ex-spouses explained 20 percent of the variance in payment.

These statistical patterns were fully consistent with the accounts of mothers in all custody categories and non-paying fathers who were interviewed about their payment behavior. The two most common explanations for non-payment offered by mothers were that the obligor was unemployed much or all of the preceding year or that he was angry with his ex-wife and withheld support as a means of getting even with her. The third item mentioned with some frequency was that the ex-spouse did a poor job of managing his finances.

The importance of employment stability was further revealed when we compared the support performance of those fathers who allegedly had job problems in the past year with those who did not. Fathers with no such problems reportedly failed to make all child-support payments in only five percent of all cases. In 81 percent of the cases, all twelve payments were made. Conversely, those with employment problems failed to make all payments in 36 percent of the cases; only 45 percent of such fathers made all twelve payments.

Other Economic Contributions—In addition to child support, absent parents may make a variety of direct expenditures toward the upbringing of their children. To discern whether there were differences in levels of such expenditures by fathers with different custody arrangements, we presented all mothers in the sample with a list of 21 child-care expenditures and asked them to indicate whether their ex-spouse had made a contribution and the regularity of such contributions. The response options to each item were "regularly," "occasionally," "rarely," "never," or that the item was not relevant to their family.

The responses provided by mothers indicated that joint residential custodians in particular and fathers who paid child support regularly, in general, were more faithful in making additional expenditures. Whether or not they were ordered to pay child support, fathers with joint residential custody were more apt to contribute than fathers of children in sole maternal custody on the "in-kind" and "medical" indices. On the "luxuries," "extras," and "household" categories, joint residential fathers were more likely to contribute than their counterparts with sole maternal and joint legal/maternal residential custody. Finally, those who paid regular child support were significantly more likely to make extra contributions than their non-paying counterparts. Thus, the contributions noted above did not represent payments made in lieu of ordered support but rather supplemented the regular payment of support.

To assess the predictors of supplementary child-care payments, we performed a series of multiple regressions using the indices of "luxuries," "extras," "medical," "housing," and "in-kind" contributions as dependent variables. Our independent variables consisted of the same economic and cooperation measures used to predict support performance. Unlike the analysis of support payment, however, where economic and cooperation measures explained the bulk of the variance, these variables explained only a slim proportion of the variance for supplementary contributions. On the other hand, visitation and paternal involvement indices explained a good deal of the variance. With the addition of information on paternal contact with the children to the financial and cooperation measures that predicted support performance, the explained variance in each of the dependent variables increased dramatically. For example, the explained variance in the "luxuries" category rose from 22 to 48 percent. In the "extras" category the increase was from 10 to 33 percent. The "medical" category increased from 10 to 18 percent; the "in-kind" index rose from 6 to 19 percent; and the "household" index increased from 3 to 11 percent.

After all independent variables had been added and the optimum set of predictors had been selected, we found that for each of the indices, the best predictor was a measure of paternal contact based upon weekend or overnight visits or the index of paternal involvement based upon maternal reports of fathers participation in activities like helping with homework, driving the children to friends, attending daytime and evening school events, and staying home to care for sick children. Thus, while visitation and paternal participation played only a modest role in explaining support payments, these variables played a more central role in explaining contributions outside of regular support payments. It is also relevant to note that custody type per se was neither a powerful predictor of payment of ordered child support nor of supplementary child care expenditures. The more critical variables dealt with the amount of time the non-custodian spent with the child and his involvement with the daily life of the child.

Conclusion

Our analysis confirms many of the conclusions about the viability of joint custody arrangements noted in the experimental and anecdotal literature. Overall, joint custody, especially residential custody, is attractive to more affluent parents who are more cooperative in the early stages of their separation and divorce. Over time, parents who opt for joint legal and residential custody remain more cooperative and positive about their ex-spouse as a parent. And although custody in and of itself is not predictive of adjustment with children across custody categories exhibiting compara- ble adjustment patterns, visitation is one of the variables that is predictive of adjust- ment.

Our analysis also reveals a number of unexpected patterns. While parents who opt for joint versus sole custody are initially more receptive to the idea, joint legal and joint residential custody represents compromise arrangements for many. Although relatively few joint residential parents report pressure to trade time for money, or what has been dubbed "custody blackmail," this was a problem for about 20 percent of mothers with joint legal custody. Perhaps because it represents a compromise, mothers with joint legal and residential custody are more critical of their legal custody arrangement as compared with their sole-custody counterparts. However, evaluations of various custody and visitation arrangements in actual practice reveal that mothers with all types of joint and sole custody are equally pleased and displeased.

Our analysis of the child-support implications of joint custody confirms some of the claims made by both supporters and critics. As to the supporters, the results of the Child Support and Child Custody Project revealed no evidence that joint custody was harmful to the economic interests of women and children.

Although a higher proportion of joint residential custody cases lacked a support order, this was reportedly not a source of disagreement, hardship, or dispute, and reflected the more equitable and substantial income statuses of divorcing parents who opted for this form of custody. Among those with a child-support order, the best payment patterns were exhibited by those with joint residential and joint legal arrangements. Patterns for absent fathers with sole maternal custody arrangements were the least favorable, although economic factors appeared to be more compelling in explaining this phenomenon than custody type, with employment stability emerging as the most powerful predictor of child-support payments. Visitation and paternal participation did affect the economic welfare of children. They were the best predictors of financial and in-kind payments, outside of support, by absent parents.

Joint custody, however, does not guarantee that the financial needs of the child will be met. Despite more favorable patterns of payment of child support and financial and in-kind extras associated with joint custody, ordered levels of child support in every custody category were extremely low and fell well below estimated levels of expenditures for children in intact families and even poverty level requirements for maintaining a child in a household. As the critics of joint custody allege, the arrangement does not ensure that children will be adequately provided for following divorce and is not a substitute for policies requiring the use of guidelines that reflect the true costs of raising children to establish and update adequate child-support orders.

These findings have several implications for policy. One deals with the issue of voluntary versus mandatory joint custody. Although our findings clearly favor optional joint custody statutes and court rules, they do not support the routine imposition of joint custody arrangements on divorcing couples. Our sample consisted of those who opted for joint residential custody; we had no reading on the child support, not to mention other socio-psychological and child-adjustment experiences, of those who were ordered into this arrangement over the objections of one or both parents. More critically, respondents with joint residential custody in our sample were decidedly upper-middle class and shared a variety of pre-existing economic and attitudinal characteristics that distinguished them from their divorced counterparts with more conventional sole-custody arrangements. In addition to being more cooperative at the time of separation and divorce, they enjoyed higher levels of maternal and paternal earnings, had fewer children to support following the divorce, and did not experience the employment problems reported for their counterparts with sole custody. No doubt, these differences affected their ultimate child-support payment performance. We have no reason to believe that the imposition of joint custody would induce the general population in our sample with joint custody. Given the economic profile of those who opted for joint custody in our sample, we were also unable to assess whether fathers with joint residential custody would have exhibited more favorable payment patterns had they also experienced employment discontinuities and upsets.

Although our data does not support more aggressive joint custody policies, they do support policies calling for the provision of more widespread and effective information about the joint custody option to divorcing couples. We found that mothers with joint residential custody were generally satisfied with both the custody arrangement and the accompanying financial agreement. Child-support payment among this population was significantly more regular and complete. While these patterns clearly underscore the financial viability of the joint custody arrangement, they are frequently not known or presented to divorcing couples. For example, we found that many mothers with joint residential custody had initially assumed that sole custody would be best, and reported that many people had tried to talk them into and/or out of joint custody (Pearson & Thoennes, 1988). They would have welcomed accurate, detailed, and neutral information about their joint- and sole-custody options.

Moving beyond the issue of custody, our findings revealed the importance of access and paternal participation for the financial welfare of children. Visitation and paternal participation were the key predictors of financial and in-kind payments outside of support by absent parents. We found that extra payments served to supplement child support and were not paid in its stead. According to other researchers, supplementary and in-kind payments are common among both AFDC and non-AFDC fathers (Haskins, 1987) and represent a substantial ingredient in the post-divorce welfare of children. If, as we have found, such payments are maximized by visitation and paternal participation, future policy should seek to enhance access. The Child Support Enforcement Amendments of 1984 contains no mandates on visitation but urges state and local governments to address the issue, and several states have developed mechanisms to remedy visitation violations (Horowitz & Dodson, 1985). Future research is needed to determine whether these remedies are adequate and whether programs can be developed to help to resolve visitation disputes in an amicable fashion.

In addition to custody and visitation factors, our analysis revealed the importance of employment stability in the payment of child support. Of all the factors considered, job stability proved to be the most important in predicting payment. This was consistent with the explanations of non-payment offered by fathers themselves (Haskins, 1987) and argues for interventions aimed at alleviating employment problems. Naturally, in some instances, chronic unemployment or underemployment reflects basic personality characteristics and values that can not easily be altered. However, support arrearages also result from a lack of job skills, seasonal unemployment, or declines in employment opportunities in certain fields. In these instances, demonstration and research programs might identify ways in which the need for training, retraining, financial and job counseling, and job placement could be quickly established and the appropriate action taken before fathers develop non-compliance habits and before mothers resort to attorneys, AFDC, or simply resign themselves to non-support.

Next to employment stability, the relationship between the parents was a key predictor of whether child support was paid. Mothers who were re-interviewed frequently felt that their ex-spouse refused to pay support because of anger and a perception that the support money was going to the wife rather than to the children. Interviews with fathers subject to the child-support enforcement program in North Carolina revealed that unemployment of the father and the belief that the mother does not spend the money on the children were the two justifications for missed child-support payments that fathers believed were defensible (Haskins, 1987). These findings argue for child-support payment methods that are neutral, automatic, and free of any contact with an ex-wife. Future research is needed to determine whether the 1984 legislation has translated into the more extensive use of automatic wage withholding and whether this has improved the payment of child support.

Lastly, and perhaps most importantly, the analysis revealed the woeful inadequacy of ordered levels of child support across all custody categories. Modal, per-child orders in our sample were approximately at the poverty standard and only about one-third of the estimated normal levels of expenditures on children with intact families. These shortfalls appear to be consistent with national estimates (Williams, 1987). In addition to being established at unrealistically low levels, few orders in our sample contained provisions for modification or for the payment of the child's future, higher-education costs. Interviews with mothers regarding their child-support needs revealed unrealistically low estimates and suggested a good deal of ignorance regarding the true costs of raising children. It is relevant to note that although the bulk of federal and state efforts are directed at improved enforcement measures, it has been estimated that the amount of money lost as a result of inadequate orders is five times as great as the amount of money lost as a result of the failure to collect ordered support (Haskins, 1987).

The deficiency in child-support orders results from both inadequate initial child-support orders as well as the absence of systematic updating procedures for orders in effect (Williams, 1987). As a result, policies are needed to insure that initial orders are established in accordance with sound economic evidence on the costs of childrearing as well as effective programs for periodic updating of child support to reflect changed circumstances of the parents and needs of the children, including higher-education costs. It is unclear whether the Child Support Enforcement Amendments of 1984 have adequately addressed these problems. Although the law required that each state develop a child-support guideline by October 1, 1987, it did not specify the type of guideline that must be adopted, require that the guideline may be systematically applied to new orders, or address the issue of systematic updating procedures for child-support orders. While some states have made efforts to facilitate modifications, the procedures remain considerable in most states and serve to deter most parents from trying. Research is needed to assess the results of the 1984 law on state legislation and to determine whether requirements for guidelines need to be strengthened.

IV
The Law of Joint Custody

17

Issues and Trends in the Law of Joint Custody

MAUREEN McKNIGHT

Only a few states have no legislation or case law recognizing joint custody. This chapter identifies statutory trends and analyzes the legal issues surrounding joint custody decisions. A schematic state-by-state comparison of legislative approaches and summaries of joint custody cases is presented in Appendix A of this volume. The discussion here provides a narrative explanation of the emerging legal developments occurring with the increased focus on shared parenting.

Joint custody has swept the country, leaving few family law codes and practices untouched. In 1984, approximately thirty states had some form of joint custody statute.[1] Now over forty states have enacted legislation dealing with shared parenting and most other states have recognized the concept in case law.

No uniform approach to joint custody has emerged in these laws.[2] No national consensus exists on how, if at all, legislative and judicial policies on child custody should be recast.[3] On the other hand, certain specific aspects of shared parenting

---

Maureen McKnight is an attorney with Oregon Legal Services, Portland, Oregon. She is also chair of the Joint Custody Task Force of the Oregon State Bar, Family and Juvenile Law Section.

1. J. Folberg (ed.), *Joint Custody and Shared Parenting*, Appendix A (1984).

2. A Model Joint Custody Statute does exist, drafted by the Child Custody Committee of the American Bar Association's Family Law Section. Approved by the ABA House of Delegates in August 1989 as ABA policy, this version of the Model Act was the product of extensive debate and carries several dissents.

3. Compare, for example, the position of Florida, which mandates shared parental responsibility even over the objection of a parent, unless detriment to the child can be shown, and the caution of Nebraska, which disfavors joint custody. Fla. Stat. Ann. § 61.13 (West 1991). Wilson v. Wilson, 399 N.W.2d 802 (Neb. 1989) (Joint custody is reserved "for only the rarest of cases").

have been widely approved.[4] The chart in Appendix A of this book presents a state-by-state comparison of legislative approaches and summarizes the statutes on joint custody in each jurisdiction. The trends and issues represented by the chart are discussed here.

Little question remains that courts may award joint custody under the general "best interest of the child" test even when no statute provides explicit authority.[5] Moreover, the confusion over the meaning of joint custody has been substantially clarified in recent years. Almost all jurisdictions which have enacted joint custody legislation have now set out definitions of the term. The number avoiding the use of traditional custody terminology has grown. At least six states have now chosen less possessory designations such as "parental responsibility,"[6] "decision-making authority,"[7] and "parenting."[8]

Definitional sections vary considerably in terminology but little in substance. Nearly all states have explicitly or implicitly distinguished shared decision-making authority (typically known as joint legal custody) from shared residential or day-to-day control (known as joint physical custody).[9] The trend favoring shared legal authority over joint physical control persists. Several states expressly limit application of their joint custody laws to the decision-making component.[10] Others nominally allow both joint legal and joint physical awards but give the latter less statutory definition[11] or favor.[12]

No dominant pattern has yet emerged among the various legislative approaches. The most common mode is treatment of joint custody simply as an option, accorded no greater deference than sole custody. Twenty-three states have adopted this approach.[13] Trendsetting California joined this plurality with 1988 legislation that clarifies language which some had argued established a preference for joint custody

---

4. More than one-half the states, for example, have enacted legislation generally ensuring that whatever the custodial arrangement, each parent has equal access to the health and educational records concerning the child.

5. See, e.g., Lowe v. Lowe, 370 S.E.2d 731 (W. Va. 1990) and cases cited in Appendix A to this book under "Approach" for Alabama, Arizona, New York, Rhode Island, South Carolina, and South Dakota.

6. See, e.g., 15 Vt. Stat. Ann., tit. 15 § 665(a) (Supp. 1989).

7. See, e.g., Wash. Rev. Code Ann. § 26.09.187 (Supp. 1991). "The terms 'custody' and 'visitation' are not found in the new [Washington parenting] act. Children are not property." Gaddis and Sooter, "The New Era in Child Custody Resolution," 42 Wash. St. B. News 13 (1988).

8. See, e.g., 40 Ill. Rev. Stat. § 602.1 (1990).

9. See, e.g., Mo. Rev. Stat. §§ 452.375(1), (2) (1991):

> "Joint legal custody" means that the parents share the decision-making rights, responsibilities, and authority relating to the health, education, and welfare of the child, and unless allocated, apportioned or decreed, the parents shall confer with one another in the exercise of decision-making rights, responsibilities, and authority. "Joint physical custody" means an order awarding each of the parents significant periods of time during which a child resides with or is under the care and supervision of each of the parents. Joint custody shall be shared by the parents in such a way as to assure the child of frequent and continuing contact with both parents.

10. See, e.g., Colorado, Massachusetts, New Hampshire, Oregon, and Wisconsin.

11. See, e.g., Minn. Stat. Ann. §§ 518.003, .003(d), defining joint physical custody as the routine daily care, control, and residence of the child being "structured between the parties."

12. See, e.g., Utah Code Ann. § 30-3-10.2(1) (Supp. 1990), which sets out a rebuttable presumption applying only to joint legal custody. Utah statutes disclaim the practice of awarding equal or nearly equal periods of physical custody of and access to the child "as the best interest of the child often requires that a primary physical residence for the child be designated." Utah Code Ann. § 30-3-10.1(4) (Supp. 1988).

13. See, e.g., Indiana, Massachusetts, and West Virginia.

over sole custody.[14] Only two states have created such a preference.[15] Twelve jurisdictions have established presumptions that shared parenting is in the child's best
interest, half limiting application to cases where the parents are in agreement.[16] Six
states require joint custody in some circumstances, all but one conditioning that
mandate on parental agreement.[17]

The propriety of ordering joint custody over parental objection continues to
be hotly debated.[18] Although legislatures have been somewhat cautious in favoring
the award when a parent opposes it over sole custody,[19] the majority of jurisdictions
which have addressed the issue give courts the option to make joint awards despite
a parent's objections. Several of these states have unequivocally set out in statutes
that parental objections and findings of hostility alone are insufficient to defeat
preferences and presumptions for joint awards.[20] Other states have concluded that
parental agreement is "a matter of primary but not determinative importance,"[21] or
although not required, parental concurrence is preferred.[22] Recent Washington
legislation provides perhaps the most comprehensive statutory attention to this
issue. The Washington statute prohibits awarding mutual decision-making authority when both parents oppose it but allows the award over the objection of one
parent when the court determines the objection unreasonable based on specific
criteria, including demonstrated ability to cooperate, geographic proximity, history
of participation in parenting, and the absence of evidence of substance abuse,
domestic violence, and child abuse.[23]

States have increasingly required findings in joint custody cases. The trend had
been, and the rule remains, that findings are most frequently required when joint

---

14. The 1979 version of Section 4600 of the California Civil Code codified a preference for joint
custody in the same sentence, but immediately preceding, the existing preference for sole custody. Some
interpreted this placement to mean that joint custody was preferred over sole custody; others argued that
joint and sole custody were co-equal preferences. *See generally* the discussion in J. Folberg (ed.), *Joint
Custody and Shared Parenting* 160 (1984) and in particular, Chapter 17 of that book, Cook, "California's
Joint Custody Statute." In 1988, the California Legislature resolved the confusion by clarifying that no
preference or presumption for or against joint or sole custody was created by that section. 1988 Cal. Stat.
ch. 1442, § 1; Cal. Civ. Code § 4600(d) (Supp. 1991). The presumption in § 4600.5 that joint custody is
in the child's best interests when the parents agree was left untouched. See Chapter 21 of this volume.
15. *See* Kansas and Louisiana.
16. *See, e.g.*, California, Connecticut, and Mississippi for presumptions limited to parental agreements
and Minnesota, Montana, and New Hampshire for presumptions not so restricted.
17. Maine, Michigan, Oregon, Texas, and Washington require joint awards in some circumstances
but only when the parents are also in agreement. Only in Florida must shared responsibilities be ordered
over parental objection (unless detriment to the child is proven).
18. *See, e.g.*, Mummery, *Whose Custody Is It Anyway? Awarding Joint Custody Over the Objection of One
Parent*, 15 Fordham L. Rev. 625 (1987) for the arguments allowing the award; Elster, *Solomonic Judgments:
Against the Best Interest of the Child*, 54 Univ. Chi. L. Rev. 1, 40 (1987) for the contrary view. It is perhaps
noteworthy that in their first comprehensive legislation on joint custody in 1987, two neighboring states
adopted opposite views: Oregon requires parental agreement but Washington does not. Or. Rev. Stat.
§ 107.169(3) (1990); Wash. Rev. Code Ann. § 26.09.187(2) (Supp. 1989).
19. *See supra* notes 15-16 and accompanying text.
20. *See, e.g.*, Mo. Rev. Stat. § 452.375(4)(1) (Supp. 1991) ("Joint custody to both parents . . . shall
not be denied solely for the reason that one parent opposes a joint custody award"); Mont. Code Ann. §
40-4-224(1) (1987) ("Objection to joint custody by a parent seeking sole custody is not a sufficient basis
for a finding that joint custody is not in the best interest of a child, nor is a finding that the parents are
hostile to each other").
21. Ind. Code Ann. § 31-1-11.5-21(g) (1987).
22. Rolde v. Rolde, 425 N.E.2d 388, 392 (Mass. 1981).
23. Wash. Rev. Code Ann. §§ 26.09.187(2), 26.09.191, 26.09.184(4) (Supp. 1991).

custody is denied,[24] especially if the denial overrides parental agreement.[25] Findings ensure that state policies preferring or encouraging joint custody are not taken lightly. In recent years, several more cautious jurisdictions have required findings when joint custody is granted. Legislation adopted in Utah in 1988, for example, creates a presumption for joint legal custody when the parents agree, but requires a finding that the parents appear capable of implementing the order.[26] Nebraska, which allows but disfavors shared parenting, requires a hearing in open court to support the award and a specific finding that joint custody is in the child's best interest regardless of parental agreement.[27] Several states require findings whenever joint custody is granted or denied.[28]

A much higher percentage of states with joint custody laws requires a parental plan for implementing that arrangement than did six years ago.[29] Moreover, in many jurisdictions where a plan is mandatory, it must contain certain minimum specifications, typically including the child's residence, the amount of support, medical and dental care, schooling, and visitation.[30] Illinois also requires that its joint-parenting agreements and orders address religion, resolution of disputes, and provisions for periodic review.[31]

Washington requires particular thoroughness in development of parenting plans.[32] As a part of the process of identifying and allocating parental responsibilities and time with the child under that state's 1987 Parenting Act, a temporary plan must first be formulated. Each parent may submit separate plans addressing required elements including work schedules and the historical allocation of parenting responsibilities, which the court then considers in addition to any other relevant evidence. Although the court then approves a temporary plan and the same form could be used for the final order, the court may not draw any presumptions from the provisions of the interim plan. The final plan must contain certain clauses dealing with Washington's parenting policies.

Mediation of custody disputes enjoys greater recent statutory recognition. In most states, mediation is discretionary,[33] in some mandatory.[34] The appropriateness of mediating family issues with parents who have a history of domestic violence continues to be argued.[35] At least two states have recently addressed this concern

---

24. *See, e.g.*, Alaska, Connecticut, Idaho, Iowa, Kansas, Nevada, and New Hampshire.
25. *See, e.g.*, Massachusetts and Pennsylvania.
26. Utah Code Ann. § 30-3-10.2(2) (Supp. 1990).
27. Neb. Rev. Stat. § 42-364(3) (1991).
28. *See, e.g.*, California, Michigan, and Montana.
29. One-tenth of those states required plans in 1984. Folberg, *supra* note 1. Now more than one-quarter of the jurisdictions with joint custody laws require plans. *See* Appendix A, *infra*.
30. *See, e.g.*, Ohio and Oklahoma.
31. 40 Ill. Rev. Stat. Ann. 602.1(b) (Supp. 1990). *In re Marriage of Drummond*, 509 N.E.2d 707 (Ill. App. 3d 1987) (Specifications in plan are mandatory).
32. Wash. Rev. Code Ann. §§ 26.09.187-.220 (Supp. 1991).
33. *See, e.g.*, Iowa, Kansas, and Louisiana.
34. *See, e.g.*, California, Maine, and New Mexico.
35. *See, e.g.*, Silberman & Schepard, *Consultants' Comments on the New York State Law Revision Commission Recommendation on the Child Custody Dispute Resolution Process*, 19 Colum. J. L. & Soc. Prob. 399, 408 (1985); Keenan, *Domestic Violence and Custody Litigation: The Need for Statutory Reform*, 13 Hofstra L. Rev. 407 (1985).

specifically in a joint custody context.[36] Oregon, whose 1987 legislation otherwise requires mediation when a joint custody request is made, allows a court to waive the process on a finding of severe emotional distress.[37] In 1988, California law was amended to allow in some circumstances, and require in others, that separate mediation appointments be set for parents with a history of domestic violence.[38]

Advocates for battered women have also pressed for and won other legislative reforms dealing with the statutory treatment of abuse in the joint custody context. These advocates argue that family violence does not end with the separation of the parents and that joint custody may perpetuate abuse by maximizing the parents' access to the child and requiring their contact with each other.[39] A growing number of states have responded to this concern; several have included evidence of spousal abuse[40] as a factor which must be considered when deciding joint custody.[41] Others have gone a step further and legislatively declared that evidence of such conduct must be considered harmful to the child[42] and sufficient to defeat statutory favor for shared parenting,[43] or required findings if joint custody is ordered despite such evidence.[44] Texas flatly prohibits joint managing conservatorships whenever credible evidence of spousal or child abuse is presented.[45]

Colorado law provides a precise legislative articulation of the issues involved: in that jurisdiction, credible evidence of spousal abuse precludes an award of joint custody[46] unless the court finds the parties are able to make shared decisions about their child without physical confrontation and in a place and manner which is not a danger to the abused spouse or child.[47]

Another related item appearing in a growing number of custody statutes and tracked on the legislative chart in Appendix A is the favorable consideration given a parent's promotion of the child's relationship with the other parent. At least fourteen states[48] now have this "friendly parent"[49] inducement. At least ten other states express a similar theme in declaring legislative policies to ensure frequent and continuing contact for the child with both parents, and shared responsibility for

---

36. North Dakota prohibits mediation whenever any custody, support, or visitation issue involves or may involve physical or sexual abuse of any party or child of any party. N.D. Cent. Code § 14-09.1-02 (Supp. 1989).

37. Or. Rev. Stat. § 107.179(3) (1990).

38. Cal. Civ. Code §§ 4607, 4607.2 (West 1991).

39. *See, e.g.,* Keenan, *supra* note 35.

40. These joint custody statutes usually refer to or adopt the definition of domestic violence set out in that state's abuse prevention act. *See, e.g.,* N.H. Rev. Stat. Ann § 458:17II(c) (Supp. 1990), referring to other statutes on interspousal battery.

41. *See, e.g.,* Wis. Stat. Ann. § 767.24(5)(i) (Supp. 1990).

42. *See, e.g.,* N.H. Rev. Stat. Ann. § 458:17II(c) (Supp. 1990).

43. Montana law, for example, presumes that joint custody is in the best interest of a child unless the court finds under specified factors that the award is contrary to the child's best interest. "[A] finding that one parent has physically abused the other parent or the child is a sufficient basis for finding that joint custody is not in the best interest of the child." Mont. Code Ann. § 40-4-224(1) (1989).

44. *See, e.g.,* Colorado and New Hampshire.

45. Tex. Fam. Code Ann. § 14.021(h) (Supp. 1991).

46. Colorado's joint custody definition covers only decision-making authority.

47. Colo. Rev. Stat. § 14-10-124(1)(m) (1987).

48. *See, e.g.,* California, Iowa, and Louisiana.

49. The term "friendly parent" is borrowed from Schulman & Pitt, *Second Thoughts on Joint Custody: Analysis of Legislation and Its Impact for Women and Children,* 12 Golden Gate U.L. Rev. 538, 554 (1982).

childrearing.[50] Both provisions have been criticized for encouraging tactical posturing and for unfairly disadvantaging abused parents attempting to protect themselves and their children.[51]

Although those objections have not deterred an increasing number of state legislatures from proclamations encouraging joint custody, what has developed is a cautious tempering of those policy statements. Vermont, for example, declares its policy of encouraging the child's maximum contact with each parent inapplicable where direct physical harm or significant emotional harm to the child or a parent is likely to result.[52] Oregon's 1987 legislation bears the now standard language about frequent and continuing contact, but limits it to "parents who have shown the ability to act in the best interest of the child."[53] Several other states which have declared public policies on joint custody in the last six years have also qualified with similar limitations the broader statements generally endorsed by earlier lawmakers.[54]

Access to records is another aspect of shared parenting which has received growing but now slightly qualified legislative approval. As of 1990, over one-half the states have enacted provisions giving each parent the same access to records and information concerning the child. Many jurisdictions, however, specifically allow the court to deny access when not in the best interests of the child or if access may cause detriment to the other parent, as in situations of domestic violence.[55] Similarly, some legislation allows good-cause exceptions for the increasingly common requirement that each parent keep the other advised of addresses and telephone numbers.[56]

Joint custody awards have unquestionably complicated the determination of child-support obligations. States have consistently responded by setting out disclaimers and guidelines in either custody or support statutes. Typical provisions declare that joint custody awards do not abolish,[57] limit,[58] or affect[59] the court's authority to order support. Also common are statutes providing that joint custody orders do not constitute reason to depart from statutory support guidelines[60] or grounds for modification of support orders.[61]

Orders of joint physical custody, rather than joint legal custody, pose the greater complication since they require financial resources sufficient to provide two households for the child. Several states provide that when each parent has physical custody a requisite period of time,[62] the support obligations of each are offset, such that the

---

50. *See, e.g.,* Nevada and Montana.
51. *See* Schulman & Pitt, *supra* note 49.
52. Vt. Stat. Ann., tit. 15 § 650 (Supp. 1989).
53. Or. Rev. Stat. § 107.149 (1989).
54. *See,* e.g., Pennsylvania, Texas, and Iowa, the latter restricting amending its policy by amendment. *See* Pa. Cons. Stat. § 5301, appen. 23 (1988); Vt. Fam. Code § 14.021(a) (Supp. 1989); Iowa Code § 598.41(1) (Supp. 1988).
55. *See, e.g.,* Vt. Stat. Ann. tit. 15, § 670 (Supp. 1989).
56. *See, e.g.,* Pa. Cons. Stat. § 5309, appen. 23 (1990); Or. Rev. Stat. § 107.164 (1989).
57. *See, e.g.,* Fla. Stat. Ann. § 61.13(5) (West. 1991); Mo. Rev. Stat. § 452.375(9) (Supp. 1991).
58. *See, e.g.,* Utah Code Ann. § 30-3-10.3(4) (Supp. 1988).
59. *See, e.g.,* Wis. Stat. Ann. § 767.25(7) (Supp. 1990).
60. *See, e.g.,* Minn. Stat. Ann. § 518.17(6) (Supp. 1991).
61. *See, e.g.,* La. Civ. Code Ann. art. 146A(a)(c) (Supp. 1990).
62. Colorado sets a 25% figure, as does Oregon. Colo. Rev. Stat. § 14-10-115(8) (1987); Or. Admin. R. 137-50-255(i) (1988). Vermont has set the period at 30%. Vt. Stat. Ann. tit. 15, § 657(a) (Supp. 1990), as does California effective March 1, 1991 (Cal. Rules of art. No. 1274(b)(6)).

obligor with the greater income (and therefore the greater obligation) pays only the proportionate difference to the other parent each month.[63] Other jurisdictions have likewise adopted an annualized approach for meeting the child's needs by providing that when necessary to ensure that a parent can maintain adequate housing for the child, that parent may continue to receive some child support from the other parent, even during periods when the child is with the payor.[64] At least one court has cautioned that the needs of the children must justify a support obligation to the parent with the lower income, refusing to otherwise have child-support payments equalize income between parents who share a child's physical care.[65]

A related issue posed by joint custody arrangements, but not charted in the Appendix, concerns claims of tax-dependency exemptions. The federal 1984 Tax Reform Act set out the general rule for post-1984 decrees that the parent having custody of the child for the greater portion of the year is entitled to the exemption.[66] Although parents in joint (or sole-) custody cases may privately arrange to share this tax advantage because of shared custodial responsibilities,[67] courts are split nationally on whether a court may determine the issue by ordering a parent to waive the exemption otherwise claimable under federal law.[68] Contractual provision for this exemption has therefore assumed much greater significance than in the past. Unless parents negotiate and agree upon a resolution, dependency qualification could be decided by the application of federal tax law.

Problems have also appeared for parents sharing custody when one part of the divided family attempts to qualify for public assistance.[69] The federally supported Aid to Families with Dependent Children program (known as AFDC or ADC) provides monthly cash subsistence benefits and medical coverage for qualified needy children.[70] A parent's continued absence from the home is one type of deprivation qualifying low-income families for aid,[71] but where the children have significant contact with or periodically reside with this "absent" parent, the children and their caretaker parent may be denied needed assistance. Many states have therefore required[72] or allowed[73] courts making joint custody awards to designate a primary

---

63. The Colorado and Vermont statutes and California rule are cited in the preceding note.

64. *See, e.g.*, Louisiana and Michigan.

65. Hortis v. Hortis, 367 N.W.2d 633 (Minn. Ct. App. 1985).

66. 26 U.S.C. § 152(e)(1) (1988). Several exceptions to this rule exist, the primary one being a release of the claim by the "custodial parent" (the parent having custody for a greater portion of the year); 26 U.S.C. § 152(e)(2);, and the multiple support arrangement, 26 U.S.C. § 152(c). Subsequent changes to the Tax Code have not altered these sections. *See also* Treas. Reg. § 1.152-4(b) (as amended in 1979) (Physical custody controls the right to the exemption). Joint "legal" custody is irrelevant to the determination.

67. The simplest arrangement for parents with comparable responsibility for the child is to alternate the claim yearly. When one parent has considerably more time than the other with the child, the "custodial" parent might release the claim every third year or according to some other schedule which recognizes the second parent's substantial, though not equal, custody.

68. *See, e.g.*, Cross v. Cross, 363 S.E.2d 449 (W. Va. 1987); Fleck v. Flec, 427 N.W.2d 355 (N.D. 1988) (Holds that state courts may order the custodial parent to waive the exemption); Lorenz v. Lorenz, 419 N.W.2d 770 (Mich. App. 1988) (Holds that the federal Tax Code divests state court of that jurisdiction).

69. Chapter 19 of this book provides an in-depth discussion of the effect of joint custody on eligibility for public assistance.

70. 42 U.S.C. §§ 601 *et seq.*

71. 42 U.S.C. § 606(a).

72. *See, e.g.*, Texas, Utah, and Washington.

73. *See, e.g.*, California and Wisconsin.

caretaker or primary residence specifically for the purpose of determining welfare eligibility.[74] In 1988, Utah took the unique step of requiring that the court inform both parties that an order for joint custody may preclude eligibility for public assistance and that if welfare is needed for the support of the child anytime after entry of a joint custody order, the order may be terminated.[75]

The standards for modification have continued to occupy both the legislatures and the courts. Even though more joint custody laws have been enacted and applied, no consistent body of law regarding modification to or from joint custody, or changes in the terms of a joint custody order, has yet developed on a national level. Some trends perceptible six years ago remain evident. The majority of states considering the question have determined that a change in circumstance need not be demonstrated to modify a sole-custody order to a joint one.[76] In these jurisdictions the agreement of the parties or a showing of the child's best interest is all that is needed. States remain split on the issue of whether enactment of new custody laws justifies the modification to joint custody.[77]

Most states appear reluctant to require strict showings when just the terms of the joint custody order are modified.[78] In Wisconsin and Ohio, for example, parents with joint legal custody may generally alter the terms concerning the child's physical placement on a showing of best interest alone.[79] States using this more liberal standard for changing terms often require findings when a parent objects to the modification.[80]

The direction of American law is clearest on the issue of standards for terminating joint custody orders. Jurisdictions requiring a change of circumstance outnumber by a two-to-one margin those allowing merely a best interest showing.[81] Recent legislatures have declared the "inability or unwillingness to cooperate"[82] and "substantial and unexcused violations of joint awards"[83] to constitute sufficient grounds for termination. Likewise, in 1988 Utah did permit the end of joint custody by one parent's filing, and serving by certified mail, a motion to terminate.[84]

The most frequently appealed basis to modify or terminate joint custody continues to be a parent's desire to move. Courts have been reluctant to allow modification of an otherwise workable joint legal custody arrangement for the sole reason that one parent's residence will change.[85] However, when the relocation results in a substantial

---

74. Many other states require or allow the designation of a primary residence for general purposes. *See, e.g.*, Florida and Oregon.
75. Utah Code Ann. § 30-3-10.2(5) (Supp. 1990).
76. *See, e.g.*, California, Hawaii, Louisiana, Oklahoma, and Pennsylvania. Montana, New Mexico and Washington do require a change in circumstances.
77. In Iowa, Missouri, and Ohio, for example, the enactment of joint custody legislation itself appears to constitute grounds for modification. In Texas and Washington, this is not a basis to modify sole-custody awards.
78. *See, e.g.*, Colorado, Nevada, Massachusetts; Ohio Rev. Code Ann. §§ 3109.041(2)(a)&(b) (Supp. 1990).
79. Wis. Stat. Ann. § 767.325 (Supp. 1990).
80. *See, e.g.*, California, Illinois, Louisiana, Nevada, and Wisconsin.
81. Compare Iowa, Washington, Maine, Missouri, Montana, New Mexico, Oregon, Texas, and Utah *with* Kentucky, Louisiana, Massachusetts, and Oklahoma.
82. Or. Rev. Stat. § 107.169(5) (1989).
83. Tex. Fam. Code Ann. § 14.081(d)(1)(B) (Supp. 1991).
84. Utah Code Ann. § 30-3-10.4(2) (Supp. 1990).
85. *See, e.g.*, Powell v. Powell, 336 N.W.2d 166 (S.D. 1983) (A move out of state by a mother with joint legal custody does not constitute a substantial change in circumstance justifying a modification of joint legal or primary physical custody when the distance was only two-and-one-half hours by car).

distance between the parents,[86] or evinces the insensitivity and uncooperativeness which prevents shared decision making,[87] custody awards have been terminated. Adjustment of the custody order is even more likely to occur upon one parent's move when physical placement of the child had been substantially shared.[88]

Wisconsin has enacted particularly detailed statutes dealing with modifications in joint custody orders occasioned by a change in residence. When the parents have joint legal custody but not substantially equal periods of physical placement, a presumption supports continuation of the "primary" physical placement but not of the shared decision making. When the parents have joint legal custody and comparable periods of time with the child, no presumption applies at all; the test is one of the child's best interests.[89] Wisconsin, like an increasing number of jurisdictions, generally requires a parent to notify the other of any planned change of residence or removal of the child from the state for a period exceeding a defined minimum.[90]

The enforceability of custody rights under shared-parenting decrees has been an area of legitimate concern. Joint custody orders which did not designate a residential parent, delineate specific periods of physical control of the child, or restrict out-of-state moves left many parents with custodial rights on paper but no enforcement remedy in reality. The concern has lessened somewhat because of the now common mandate that periods of physical care be specified in plans and orders,[91] or described in enough detail that a parent be able to utilize laws for relief of child-snatching and kidnapping.[92] Moreover, family law practitioners are seeking amendments to criminal statutes to specifically include shared-parenting violations as punishable custodial interference.[93]

As was the situation six years ago, joint custody statutes differ significantly on a national level. Even on an individual state level, refinement in the law of joint custody is evident; one need only compare the 1981 and 1987 versions of the California and Iowa statutes, for example, to track the progression of legislative experimentation. Initial enthusiasm has been replaced by a more thoughtful, cautious interest over the last six years. Further reform is inevitable; further debate, imperative.

---

86. *See, e.g.*, Matter of Ehlen, 303 N.W.2d 808 (S.D. 1981) (Although not every out-of-state move is a substantial and material change, relocation of 1500 miles is "such a great distance away so as to render impractical the joint custody arrangement").

87. *See, e.g.*, Wittke and Wittke, 738 P.2d 206 (Or. App. 1987) (A move from Oregon to Utah by a joint legal custodian, and the attendant conflict, makes improbable shared authority and easy mutual decision making; "essence of joint custody no longer exists" and joint award is terminated).

88. *See, e.g.*, Stewart v. Stewart, 525 So. 2d 218 (La. App. 1988) (Joint custody was modified to sole custody for a mother who was moving out of state, even where sole custody impaired the father's involvement in the child's life and where both parents were found fit). Under Louisiana law, joint custody means the parents shall share physical custody to the extent possible. La. Civ. Code Ann. art. 146(D) (Supp. 1989). *See also* Rosson v. Rosson, 224 Cal. Rptr. 250 (Cal. App. 1 Dist. 1986) (Joint custody with approximately equal physical time was modified to joint custody with primary physical custody given to the father when the mother plans career-based relocation; mother is an excellent parent and her career advancement is a valid goal, but stability and the desires of the children require their remaining in a familiar community with the father, also an excellent parent).

89. Wis. Stat. Ann. § 767.327 (Supp. 1990).

90. *See, e.g.*, California and Oregon.

91. *See, e.g.*, Florida and Michigan.

92. *See, e.g.*, California and Wisconsin.

93. *See, e.g.*, Or. Rev. Stat. §§ 163.245, 163.257 (1989).

18

Reconciling the Primary Caretaker Preference, the Joint Custody Preference, and the Case-by-Case Rule

ROBERT F. COCHRAN, JR.

Custody preferences have been adopted by courts in an attempt to bring order and predictability to the difficult process of deciding custody. The two most recent preferences, that for joint custody and another for the "primary caretaker," appear to be in conflict as mutually exclusive. In this chapter, Robert Cochran, Jr., attempts to reconcile the primary-caretaker preference and the preference for joint custody, granting physical custody to the parents jointly and legal custody to the primary caretaker. This amalgamated preference would be afforded an "intermediate" weight, allowing the preferred approach to be overcome by the establishment of an alternative custody arrangement which is better for the child.

The law of child custody at parental separation is probably one of the most unsettled areas of the law in the United States today. During the 1970s, a substantial majority

Robert F. Cochran, Jr., J.D., is an Associate Professor at Pepperdine University School of Law, Malibu, California.

Portions of this chapter are based on the author's more extensively footnoted article, *The Search for Guidance in Determining the Best Interests of the Child at Divorce: Reconciling the Primary Caretaker and Joint Custody Preferences*, 20 U. Rich. L. Rev. 1-65 (1985). The author would like to thank Walter J. Wadlington, Charles H. Whitebread II, and Buddy O. H. Herring for their review and criticism of early drafts, and Melinda C. McCauley, Beth A. Scagline, and Susan I. Strong for their assistance in research.

of states adopted a case-by-case best-interests-of-the-child rule.[1] In recent years, however, many states have rejected the case-by-case best-interests-of-the-child rule and have adopted a preferred custody arrangement that goes into effect unless one of the parents can show that it is not in the child's best interests. In some states, when one parent has been the child's primary caretaker, that parent is the preferred custodian.[2] Other states, through legislative action, have adopted a preference for placing the child in joint custody.[3] Each of these preferences creates significant problems for parents and children.

The Case-by-Case Rule and the Need for a More Determinate Standard

The Development of the Case-by-Case Best-Interests-of-the-Child Rule

By the middle of this century, almost all states had developed a presumption that the child of "tender years" is best cared for by the mother.[4] But during the 1960s and 1970s, the maternal preference was rejected[5] on the grounds that it did not serve the best interests of the child[6] and that it unfairly discriminated against men.[7] In its decision rejecting the maternal preference, the New York Family Court stated, "Studies of maternal deprivation have shown that the essential experience for the child is that of mothering—the warmth, consistency and continuity of the relationship rather than the sex of the individual who is performing the mothering function."[8] Studies also showed the importance of the father to the psychological development of both boys and girls.[9]

---

1. *See* cases and statutes cited in Freed & Foster, *Divorce in the Fifty States: An Overview*, 14 Fam. L.Q. 229, 263-66 (1981).

2. *See In re* Weatherly v. Weatherly, 330 N.W.2d 890, 892 (Minn. 1983); Berndt v. Berndt, 292 N.W.2d 1, 2 (Minn. 1980); In re Marriage of Van Dyke, 48 Or. App. 965, 618 P.2d 465, 467 (1980); In re Marriage of Derby, 31 Or. App. 803, 571 P.2d 562, 564 (1977); Garska v. McCoy, 278 S.E.2d 357, 362 (W. Va. 1981); *see also infra* text accompanying notes 146-71; In re Maxwell, 8 Ohio App. 3d 302, 456 N.E.2d 1218, 1222 (1982); Commonwealth ex rel. Jordan v. Jordan, 302 Pa. Super. 421, 448 A.2d 1113, 1115 (1982).

3. *See* Fla. Stat. Ann. § 61.13 (West Supp. 1988); Idaho Code § 32-717B (1983); Iowa Code Ann. § 598.41 (West Cum. Supp. 1988); Kan. Stat. Ann. § 6-1610 (Supp. 1987); La. Civ. Code Ann. pt. 146(c) (West Supp. 1989); Mont. Code Ann. § 40-4-224 (1987); N.H. Rev. Stat. Ann. § 458.17 (Supp. 1988); N.M. Stat. Ann. § 40-4-91 (Supp. 1986); Okla. Stat. Ann. tit. 10, § 21.1 (West Supp. 1989).

4. *See* cases cited in Roth, *The Tender Years Presumption in Child Custody Disputes*, 15 J. Fam. L. 423, 432-34 n.38 (1976-77). The preference for the mother in child-custody cases is sometimes called the tender years doctrine. Courts have held that a child grew out of the "tender years" category at ages ranging from four to fourteen.

5. *See, e.g.*, State ex rel. Watts v. Watts, 77 Misc. 2d 178, 181, 350 N.Y.S.2d 285, 287 (1973); Marcus v. Marcus, 24 Ill. App. 3d 401, 320 N.E.2d 581 (1974); In re Marriage of Bowen, 219 N.W.2d 683, 688 (Iowa 1974); Carey v. Carey, 211 N.W.2d 342 (Iowa 1973); Knight v. Knight, 196 Neb. 63, 241 N.W.2d

6. *See* Foster & Freed, *Life With Father: 1978*, 11 Fam. L.Q. 321, 334 (1978); Podell, Peck, & First, *Custody—To Which Parent?*, 56 Marq. L. Rev. 51, 52-56 (1972); Roth, *supra* note 4, at 448-57; Comment, *Measuring the Child's Best Interests—A Study of Incomplete Considerations*, 44 Den. L.J. 132, 138-42 (1967).

7. *See* Watts, 77 Misc. 2d at 183, 350 N.Y.S.2d at 290-91; Ex parte Devine, 398 So. 2d 686, 695-96 (Ala. 1981). *See also* Foster & Freed, *supra* note 6, at 333-34; Podell, Peck, & First, *supra* note 6, at 54-56; Roth, *supra* note 4, at 442-48.

8. Watts, 77 Misc. 2d at 182, 350 N.Y.S.2d at 290; *see also* Roth, *supra* note 4 at 449.

9. *See* Roth, *supra* note 4, at 45-51 nn.104-05 and sources cited therein.

Decisions and statutes rejecting the maternal preference called on judges to determine custody based on the best interests of the individual child without a preference for either parent.[10] Typically, a statute or court decision listed numerous factors that the trial judge was to consider in awarding custody.

Increased Uncertainty and Decreased Bargaining Power of the Mother/Primary Caretaker Under the Case-by-Case Rule

The case-by-case best-interests rule affects the bargaining positions of the parents in a way that is detrimental to mothers and children when it is compared with either the maternal preference or the primary-caretaker preference. Generally, the mother is preferred under the primary-caretaker rule, as well as the maternal-preference rule, since the mother, even in two professional families, is generally the child's primary caretaker.[11] Under the primary-caretaker preference, primary caretakers can approach custody and child-support negotiations knowing that the law gives them an advantage as to custody. Settlement of disputes over child support is based primarily on the factors that the judge must consider under the state's child-support statute: the needs of the child and the financial resources of the parties. If spousal support or property division are also at issue, those matters can be negotiated based on a consideration of the factors the judge is to consider.

When primary caretakers cannot be confident that they will win a custody fight, there is a great danger that another factor will enter into the settlement decision: the primary caretakers' fear that they will lose custody. The other parent can threaten a custody fight, whether he or she wants custody or not, in order to obtain concessions from the primary caretaker on financial issues.[12] The danger that the other parent will threaten a custody fight in order to gain support concessions is especially unfair because the stronger the ties of the primary caretakers to the children, the more subject they are to the threat of child-custody litigation.

Increased Uncertainty, Increased Parental Conflict, and Increased Litigation Under the Case-by-Case Rule

In addition to the financial hardships that result from unfair settlements, children are likely to be subject to more parental conflict and more litigation under the uncertainties of the case-by-case best-interests rule than would occur under a more determinate standard. If the secondary caretaker uses the threat of custody litigation under the case-by-case rule as a bargaining tool against a parent with deep ties to the child, resentment and parental conflict certainly will follow. If the secondary caretaker

---

10. *See supra* note 5.

11. In spite of changing perceptions of the roles of the sexes, women, including those who are highly career-oriented, have continued to be the primary caretakers of children. *See* Heckman, Bryson, & Bryson, *Problems of Professional Couples: A Content Analysis*, 39 J. Marriage & Fam. 323, 327-29 (1977).

12. In a study conducted in California by Lenore Weitzman, one-third of the mothers of divorced families reported that their husbands had used the threat of a custody dispute in financial negotiations. L. Weitzman, *The Divorce Revolution: The Unexpected Social and Economic Consequences for Women and Children in America*, 310 (1985), cited in Polikoff, *Custody and Visitation: Their Relationship to Establishing and Enforcing Support*, 19 Clearinghouse Rev. 274, 275-76 (1985).

honestly wants to get custody of the children, he or she is more likely to pursue custody under the case-by-case rule, and increased parental conflict and litigation are also likely to result.

Settlement takes place in light of what the parties expect to happen if there is litigation. Under the case-by-case best-interests rule it is more difficult for parents to determine what custody arrangement will be ordered if there is litigation. Parents do not know which of the numerous criteria that a judge might consider will be most influential. Uncertainty breeds conflict and litigation. Parental conflict is emotionally destructive to children,[13] especially when the conflict occurs after parents separate.[14] Not only do children suffer from the conflict, but increasing amounts of interparental hostility cause increasing levels of psychological difficulty.[15] If the amount of custody litigation increases under the case-by-case rule, a child will not only be more likely to suffer the detriment of increased parental conflict, but is also more likely to be required to participate in the litigation. The child's role in the trial may have a long-lasting detrimental effect and also affect the child's relationship with one or both parents.[16]

Our Inability to Determine the Best Interests of the Child in Cases in Which the Case-by-Case Rule Makes a Difference in Placement

One of the major sources of disagreement between those who advocate the case-by-case rule and those who oppose it is the question of whether a judge actually can determine what placement will be in the best interests of the child in a significant number of cases. Advocates of the case-by-case rule believe that, if there is sufficient factual investigation, the court generally can determine the custody placement that will be in the best interests of the individual child.[17]

The difficulty in determining the best interests of a child is described by Chief Judge Hood of the District of Columbia Court of Appeals in *Coles v. Coles*.[18] The trial in *Coles* was "reported in over 2,000 pages of transcript,"[19] and "[a]ll phases of the backgrounds and lives of the parties were fully explored."[20] Judge Hood states:

> [The best interests of the child] principle is easily stated but its application in a particular case presents one of the heaviest burdens that can be placed on a trial judge. Out of a maze of conflicting testimony, usually including what one court called "a tolerable amount of perjury," the judge must make a decision which will inevitably affect materially the future life of an innocent child. In making his decision the judge can

---

13. *See* Hetherington, *Family Interaction and the Social, Emotional, and Cognitive Development of Children After Divorce*, The Family: Setting Priorities 71 (V. Vaughn & T. Brazelton eds. 1979); Jacobson, *The Impact of Marital Separation/Divorce on Children: II. Interparent Hostility and Child Adjustment*, 2 J. Divorce 3 (1978); *see also* Emery, *Interparental Conflict and the Children of Discord and Divorce*, 92 Psychological Bull. 310 (1982) and sources cited therein.
14. *See* Hetherington, *supra* note 13, at 74.
15. Jacobson, *supra* note 13, at 17.
16. For a further analysis of the costs to society and children created by additional litigation under the case-by-case rule, *see* Elster, *Solomonic Judgments: Against the Best Interest of the Child*, 54 U. Chi. L. Rev. 1, 22-26 (1987).
17. *See* Foster & Freed, *supra* note 6, at 332.
18. 204 A.2d 330 (D.C. 1964).
19. *Id.* at 330.
20. *Id.*

obtain little help from precedents or general principles. Each case stands alone. After attempting to appraise and compare the personalities and capabilities of the two parents, the judge must endeavor to look into the future and decide that the child's best interests will be served if committed to the custody of the father or mother. . . . When the judge makes his decision, he has no assurance that his decision is the right one. He can only hope that he is right. He realizes that another equally able and conscientious judge might have arrived at a different decision on the same evidence.[21]

Opponents of the case-by-case rule argue that there are very few cases in which a judge can determine the placement that will be in the best interests of the child.[22] The judge in a custody case generally is presented with much highly unreliable evidence. This often includes conflicting testimony of the two parents as to events that only they have witnessed, the parents' self-serving statements as to their intentions, and the testimony of the child who may have been influenced by parental persuasion, bribery, or coercion.

The custody determination must be made at a time when reliable evaluation of the parents by the judge or mental health professionals is difficult, if not impossible. It is an abnormally stressful time for parents and children, and "the behavior of children and adults toward each other may bear little resemblance to the past or the future."[23] The fact that parents are being evaluated during the divorce period for child-custody purposes is likely to cause them to behave differently than they would under normal circumstances, further complicating the evaluation.

Even if a judge could determine the effect that each potential custody choice would have on a child, the judge must then place some value on the effect of each possible living situation on the child.[24] Mnookin states:

Deciding what is best for a child poses a question no less ultimate than the purposes and values of life itself. Should the judge be primarily concerned with the child's happiness? Or with the child's spiritual and religious training? Should the judge be concerned with the economic "productivity" of the child when he grows up? Are the primary values of life in warm, interpersonal relationships, or in discipline and self-sacrifice? Is stability and security for a child more desirable than intellectual stimulation? These questions could be elaborated endlessly. And yet, where is the judge to look for the set of values that should inform the choice of what is best for the child? Normally, the custody statutes do not themselves give content or relative weights to the pertinent values. And if the judge looks to society at large, he finds neither a clear consensus as to the best child rearing strategies nor an appropriate hierarchy of ultimate values.[25]

Some have suggested the use of mental health professionals in child-custody choices,[26] but they can be of only limited help. They are confronted with the same

---

21. Id. at 331-32.
22. Mnookin, Child-Custody Adjudication: Judicial Functions in the Face of Indeterminacy, 39 Law & Contemp. Probs. 226, 282 (1975).
23. Chambers, Rethinking the Substantive Rules for Custody Disputes in Divorce, 83 Mich. L. Rev. 477, 484 (1985).
24. See Mnookin, supra note 22, at 260.
25. Id. at 260-61 (footnotes omitted).
26. See sources cited in Chambers, supra note 23, at 483-84 n.20.

difficulty that judges face regarding unreliable information at the time of divorce. There is little consensus among mental health professionals with respect to aspects of psychological development that are basic to the custody choice,[27] and many of the factors that mental health professionals agree that children need give little or no help in deciding the typical custody case.[28] The financial cost of what mental health professionals consider to be an adequate evaluation prevent courts and most parents from obtaining such evaluations,[29] and evaluations prepared by experts hired by the parties are typically so biased as to be of little value to courts.[30] Also, of course, mental health professionals have no special expertise as to the ultimate purposes and values of life.

The case-by-case rule only makes a difference in custody placement in those close cases in which it is least likely that a judge can determine which custody decision will be better for the child. These are the very cases that should not be the subject of child-custody litigation. They are so close that the judge is unable to determine that one alternative is better than the other. The judge must make a custody choice based on arbitrary, or worse, unfair criteria[31] after everyone has suffered through the trauma of the custody case. The case-by-case rule is unable to benefit the child in the close case, the very case in which it would yield a different result than under a custody preference.

The Developing Preferences in Child-Custody Cases

Two alternatives to the case-by-case rule have received substantial support in recent years: the "primary caretaker" and "joint custody" preferences.

The Primary Caretaker Preference

Under the primary caretaker preference, when one parent is able to establish that he or she is the child's primary caretaker, a preference arises in favor of granting custody to that parent. Primary-caretaker status has emerged as the most important factor in child-custody cases in several states.[32] A party establishes his or her status as primary

---

27. Mnookin identifies five competing theories of human behavior, each with different implications for child-custody choice. *See* Mnookin, *supra* note 22, at 258 n.161.

28. *See* Okpaku, *Psychology: Impediment or Aid in Child Custody Cases?*, 29 Rutgers L. Rev. 1117 (1976).

29. *See, e.g.*, Chambers, *supra* note 23, at 482 n.15. Chambers cited R. Gardner, *Family Evaluations in Child Custody Litigation* (1982), in which psychiatrist Richard Gardner gives his views as to what is necessary for a good custody evaluation. Gardner generally charges more than two thousand dollars for an evaluation.

30. *See* R. Neely, *The Divorce Decision: The Legal and Human Consequences of Ending a Marriage* 74 (1984).

31. As Justice Neely of the West Virginia Supreme Court of appeals said in J.B. v. A.B., 242 S.E.2d 248, 254 (W. Va. 1978):

> In any hearing concerning child custody, does not the party who emotes most easily in public, the party who is most articulate, and the party who makes the most attractive physical appearance have the greater chance of persuading the trial court in a close case? Yet none of these qualities is particularly germane to the issue of which parent will make a better custodian. Furthermore, does not a hearing raise the specter of the richer party retaining more numerous and better qualified experts to offer evidence of the richer parent's own superior parental competence?

32. See explanatory citations in 20 U. Rich. L. Rev. 1-65 (1985), n. 40.

caretaker through evidence of his or her caretaking role. Duties indicative of a parent's status as primary caretaker are:

1. preparing and planning of meals;

2. bathing, grooming, and dressing;

3. purchasing, cleaning, and care of clothes;

4. medical care, including nursing and trips to physicians;

5. arranging for social interaction among peers after school, i.e., transporting to friends' houses or, for example, to girl or boy scout meetings;

6. arranging alternative care, i.e., babysitting, daycare, etc.;

7. putting the child to bed at night, attending to the child in the middle of the night, waking the child in the morning;

8. disciplining, i.e., teaching general manners and toilet training;

9. educating, i.e., religious, cultural, social, etc.; and,

10. teaching elementary skills, i.e., reading, writing, and arithmetic.[33]

If neither parent can demonstrate that he or she is the primary caretaker, no preference arises.[34]

A primary-caretaker preference reduces some of the dangers that exist under the case-by-case rule. If there is a primary caretaker, the parents will know that that parent will get custody unless the other parent can overcome the preference. The dangers of the non-primary caretaker threatening a custody fight in order to gain a bargaining advantage and of parental conflict and litigation are reduced.

The parent who has been the child's primary caretaker generally will have several advantages as custodian. The primary caretaker will be the parent who has met the child's food, clothing, and medical care needs in the past[35] and therefore will be most familiar with those needs. The primary caretaker will be the parent who has disciplined and taught the child[36] and who can provide consistency in those areas. The primary caretaker will be the parent who has spent the most time caring for the child in the past and generally will have developed what one court has called "a high tolerance for a close, grating, aesthetically unpleasant, and frequently oppressive" relationship with children.[37] The primary caretaker will be likely to continue to spend substantial time caring for the child in the future.[38]

---

33. Garska v. McCoy, 278 S.E.2d 357 (W. Va. 1981).
34. *Id.*
35. *See* Garska, 278 S.E.2d at 363.
36. *See id.*
37. J.B. v. A.B., 242 S.E.2d 248, 252 (W. Va. 1978).
38. As Ramsay Klaff has said concerning the mother who has been primary caretaker:

> [T]here is no better means by which a judge can measure a parent's capacity or willingness to provide primary care than his or her past performance. In the typical case, the mother's

Some courts and advocates of the primary-caretaker presumption argue that the child benefits from the continued primary care of the primary caretaker. The Minnesota Supreme Court states: "Continuity of care with the primary caretaker is not only central and crucial to the best interest of the child, but is perhaps the single predictor of a child's well-being about which there is agreement. . . ."[39] Though most agree that it is more important to maintain the bond to the primary caretaker than the bond to the secondary caretaker, there is no firm empirical evidence to support this position.[40] A child needs to remain in the care of a "psychological parent," someone who has regularly cared for the child's needs and is emotionally involved with the child,[41] but it appears that for most children, both parents are psychological parents.[42]

The primary-caretaker preference is generally an easy rule to apply. It is likely to discourage litigation, because parents will know that generally, if there is litigation, the primary caretaker will receive custody. The primary caretaker preference does not give the secondary caretaker as great an opportunity to gain an unfair bargaining advantage by threatening a custody fight as does the case-by-case rule.[43]

The primary caretaker preference is superior to the maternal preference in two respects. First, it is sex neutral.[44] A father who has been the primary caretaker of his children would be entitled to the primary caretaker preference. The primary caretaker preference does not discriminate against men, nor does it perpetuate the stereotype of women as the proper caretakers of children.[45]

Second, the primary caretaker preference serves the interests of children better than the maternal preference because it more accurately identifies the trait of the custodial parent that is important to the child. One value of the maternal preference

---

willingness and capacity to provide primary care has been demonstrated, while the father's is either speculative or clearly inferior.
Klaff, *The Tender Years Doctrine: A Defense*, 70 Calif. L. Rev. 335, 348 n. 16 (1982), (footnote omitted); *see also* Commonwealth ex rel. Jordan v. Jordan, 302 Pa. Super. 421, 448 A.2d 1113 (1981).

39. Pikula v. Pikula, 374 N.W. 2d 705, at 712 (Minn. 1985).

40. David Chambers reports that he shared early drafts of his article on custody disputes with a substantial number of persons with training in psychology or psychiatry. Nearly all acknowledge the absence of a firm empirical foundation for the conclusion that preserving the bond of children to primary caretakers is more critical than preserving the bond to secondary caretakers and yet nearly all believe that there is something special in that relationship worthy of weight in making decisions about placement. Chambers, *supra* note 23, at 537 (footnotes omitted).

41. The need of the child to be cared for by a psychological parent is discussed in J. Bowlby, *Attachment and Loss* (1969); J. Bowlby, *Loss: Sadness and Depression* (1980); J. Bowlby, *Separation: Anxiety and Anger* (1973); J. Goldstein, A. Freud, & A. Solnit, *Beyond the Best Interests of the Child* 17-20; Klaff, *supra* note 11, at 344-46 and sources cited therein; and sources cited in Mnookin, *supra* note 22, at 265 n.183. For reviews and criticism of the psychological parent theory literature, *see* Chambers, *supra* note 23, at 528-38; Waters & Noyes, *Psychological Parenting vs. Attachment Theory: The Child's Best Interests and the Risks in Doing the Right Things for the Wrong Reasons*, 12 N.Y.U. Rev. L. & Soc. Change 505 (1983-84).

42. *See* Lamb, *Father-Infant and Mother-Infant Interaction in the First Year of Life*, 48 Child Dev. 167, 177 (1977) [hereinafter *First Year*]; Lamb, *The Development of Mother-Infant and Father-Infant Attachments in the Second Year of Life*, 13 Developmental Psychology 637 (1977) [hereinafter *Second Year*].

43. *See* Klaff, *supra* note 38, at 346.

44. The Minnesota Supreme Court has said: "[T]he primary parent rule is gender neutral. Either parent may be the primary parent; the rule does not incorporate notions of biological gender determinism or sex stereotyping." *Pikula*, 374 N.W.2d at 712 n.2 (Minn. 1985).

45. *See* Polikoff, *Why Mothers Are Losing: A Brief Analysis of Criteria Used in Child Custody Determinations*, 7 Women's Rts. L. Rep. 235, 243 (1982).

was that it generally gave a preference to the parent who was the child's primary caretaker and therefore the parent who had the most experience caring for the child. As the Missouri Court of Appeals suggested, the maternal preference was "predicated on the *acts* of motherhood—not the *fact* of motherhood."[46] Under the maternal preference, however, there is a danger that some courts, parents, and lawyers will give undue weight to the fact of maternity rather than to the caretaking role.

The major problem with the primary-caretaker preference is that when one parent is given sole custody, the child may not maintain a sufficiently close relationship with the other parent. Maintaining a close relationship with both parents is generally important to the child when his parents divorce. When one parent is given sole custody, the other parent typically is given the right to visit with the child, but periods of visitation may be too short to enable the parent to develop a close relationship with the child.

The Joint Custody Preference

The term "joint custody" refers to parents sharing one or both of two distinct groups of rights and responsibilities relative to children: physical custody and legal custody. The California joint custody statute gives typical definitions of "joint physical custody" and "joint legal custody":

> "Joint physical custody" means that each of the parents shall have significant periods of physical custody. Joint physical custody shall be shared by the parents in such a way so as to assure a child of frequent and continuing contact with both parents.
>
> * * *
>
> "Joint legal custody" means that both parents shall share the right and the responsibility to make the decisions relating to the health, education, and welfare of the child.[47]

Beginning in the late 1970s, several mental health professionals and legal commentators supported the granting of joint custody, some advocating that joint custody be ordered when parents are able to agree to it,[48] some advocating that joint custody be awarded with or without parental approval when the trial court finds that the parents can work together for the benefit of the child,[49] and others advocating a

---

46. Garrett v. Garrett, 464 S.W.2d 740, 742 (Mo. Ct. App. 1971) (emphasis added).

47. Cal. Civ. Code §§ 4600.5(d)(3), (5) (West Supp. 1985); *see also* Beck v. Beck, 86 N.J. 480, 486-87, 432 A.2d 63, 65-66 (1981).

48. *See, e.g.*, Cochran & Vitz, *Child Protective Divorce Laws: A Response to the Effects of Parental Separation on Children*, 17 Fam. L.Q. 327, 353-54 (1983) (where parents request it); Scott & Derdeyn, *Rethinking Joint Custody*, 45 Ohio St. L.J. 4555, 487 (1984) (Cooperation and respect between parents is important for successful joint custody arrangement).

49. *See, e.g.*, Folberg & Graham, *Joint Custody of Children Following Divorce*, 12 U.C.D. L. Rev. 523 (1979). The authors advocate that courts "decree joint custody when (1) both parents are fit; (2) both parents wish to continue their active involvement in raising the child; (3) both parents are capable of making reasoned decisions together in the best interests of the child; and (4) joint custody would disrupt the parent-child relationship less than other custody alternatives." *Id.* at 579.

preference for joint custody in all cases.[50] Several states have adopted a preference for joint custody.[51]

The strongest argument advanced in favor of joint custody is that children benefit from the additional time with the less-seen parent.[52] Studies show that children of divorce who do not have substantial contact with both parents suffer reduced I.Q. and cognitive performance,[53] sex role identification problems,[54] and long-term depression.[55] They are more aggressive than children who have regular contact with their noncustodial parent.[56] A few recent studies find that children in families in which there is high conflict may suffer harm from increased contact with the less-seen parent,[57] and that there is no correlation between the child's psychological health and contact with the less-seen parent.[58] The studies are discussed in the following section.

Children under a traditional sole-custody arrangement generally desire significantly more time with the noncustodial parent than is provided by traditional visitation. Following their extensive five-year study of sixty divorced families, Judith Wallerstein and Joan Kelly stated:

> [C]hildren expressed the wish for increased contact with the fathers with a startling and moving intensity. . . .
> . . . Complaints about insufficiency of parental visits were heard not just from those youngsters who rarely saw the absent parent, but from many who were being visited

---

50. *See* Blond, *In the Child's Best Interests—A Better Way: The Case for Presumptive Joint Custody in Missouri,* 52 UMKC L. Rev. 567 (1984); Miller, *Joint Custody,* 13 Fam. L.Q. 345, 411 (1979) [hereinafter Miller]; Schepard, *Taking Children Seriously: Promoting Cooperative Custody After Divorce,* 64 Tex. L. Rev. 687 (1985); Robinson, *Joint Custody: An Idea Whose Time Has Come,* 21 J. Fam. L. 641, 676-84 (1982-83); Trombetta, *Joint Custody: Recent Research and Overloaded Courtrooms Inspire New Solutions to Custody Disputes,* 19 J. Fam. L. 213, 230-33 (1980) ("Presuming joint custody as a first stage in resolving a custody dispute eliminates the necessity of proving which parent should 'have' the children; there is no battle because there is no contest and no prize to win." *Id.* at 231). *See generally* Roman & Haddad, The *Disposable Parent: The Case for Joint Custody* 5-6 (1978) [hereinafter Roman & Haddad]; *Contra* Scott & Derdeyn, *supra* note 48, at 496 ("[L]egal policy that encourages the formation of joint custody arrangements between hostile parents does not promote the welfare of children"); Singer & Reynolds, *supra* note 40.

51. *See, e.g.*, Idaho Code § 32-717B (1983); Iowa Code Ann. § 598.41 (West Supp. 1988); Kan. Stat. Ann. § 60-1610(4)(A) (Supp. 1987); La. Civ. Code Ann. art 146 (West Supp. 1989); Mont. Code Ann. § 40-4-224 (1987); N.H. Rev. Stat. Ann. § 458.17 (Supp. 1988); N.M. Stat. Ann. § 40-4-91 (Supp. 1986); Okla. Stat. Ann. tit. 10, § 21.1 (West Supp. 1989).

52. *See* Cochran & Vitz, *supra* note 48, at 353; Miller, *supra* note 48, at 362; Robinson, *supra* note 50, at 649-50; Trombetta, *supra* note 50, at 218-19. Some studies have found that children benefit from additional contact with the less-seen parent, others have found no correlation. For a discussion of both groups of studies, *see infra* text accompanying notes 75-79.

53. Miller, *supra* note 50, at 358; Robinson, *supra* note 63, at 649; Trombetta, *supra* note 63, at 219.

54. Miller, *supra* note 50, at 358; Robinson, *supra* note 50, at 649; Trombetta, *supra* note 51, at 219.

55. Wallerstein & Kelly, *Surviving the Breakup: How Children and Parents Cope with Divorce* 132 (1980) [hereinafter Wallerstein & Kelly], at 211, 215.

56. *See* Miller, *supra* note 50, at 358-59. Additionally, children who do not have regular contact with the noncustodial parent often have problems arising from fantasies about that parent. Trombetta, *supra* note 50, at 218; *see* Miller, *supra* note 50 at 364. "No matter what type of parents the child has, sooner or later he must see them in accurate perspective and eliminate whatever fantasies he may have had about them." *Id.* (quoting Watson, *The Children of Armageddon: Problems of Custody Following Divorce,* 21 Syracuse L. Rev. 55, 58 (1969)).

57. *See* Johnston, Kline, & Tschann, *Ongoing Post-Divorce Conflict in Families Contesting Custody: Do Joint Custody and Frequent Access Help?,* Chapter 15, this volume.

58. *See* Kline, Tschann, Johnston, & Wallerstein, *Children's Adjustment in Joint and Sole Physical Custody Families.* Paper presented at the 65th Annual Meeting of the American Orthopsychiatric Association, San Francisco, March 1988 [hereinafter Kline study].

rather frequently as well. . . . The intense longing for greater contact persisted undiminished over many years. . . .[59]

Part of the reason for the lack of noncustodial parental contact is that noncustodial parents often do not exercise the visitation rights to which they are entitled.[60] Failure to exercise visitation rights has been attributed in part to the unattractiveness of the superficial, artificial relationships that can be developed during visitation[61] and to the feelings of powerlessness that fathers feel because of their lack of decision-making responsibility regarding major aspects of their children's lives.[62]

Advocates suggest that joint physical custody will enable the less-seen parent to develop a significant relationship with the children by providing more time with the children, during which they can share the important, regular, day-to-day activities.[63] The opportunity for additional time with the children under a joint physical custody arrangement will give a psychological boost to the parent that will encourage him or her to spend extra time with the children.[64]

Fathers may fail to exercise available visitation rights because they are deprived of decision-making responsibility regarding major aspects of their children's lives. Some joint custody advocates assert that joint legal custody will cure this problem by giving fathers equal power over such decisions.[65]

A major problem with both joint legal and physical custody is that they may lead to substantial conflict between the parents. Marriages often end in hostility, and parents who were unable to make decisions together during a marriage often find it difficult to do so when the marriage ends. Parental contact that occurs when the child is transferred from one parent to the other or when parents discuss decisions concerning the child can create occasions for parental conflict. Parental cooperation is least likely when one or both parents are unwilling to agree to share joint custody and it is ordered by a court.[66] The problem of parental conflict when joint custody is imposed on one or both parents is discussed further in the following section.

---

59. Wallerstein & Kelly, *supra* note 55, at 134.
60. Wallerstein & Kelly, *supra* note 55, at 134-38.
61. Miller, *supra* note 52, at 356.
62. *See* Wallerstein & Kelly, *supra* note 55, at 310.
63. Sharing day-to-day activities can give the child and noncustodial parent the daily intimate contact that living together provides, thus fostering more "'natural' relations within the divorced family." Miller, *supra* note 50, at 363; *see* Greif, *Fathers, Children, and Joint Custody*, 49(2) Am. J. Orthopsychiatry 311, 315-16 (1979). Frequent association and involvement "with both parents is usually beneficial for the child." Miller, *supra* note 50, at 362.
64. Comment, *Joint Custody: An Alternative for Divorced Parents*, 26 UCLA L. Rev. 1084 (1979). "A continuing, broad-based relationship with the child, an inherent component of joint custody, would considerably diminish the psychological effects of single custody on the non-custodian." *Id.* (footnote omitted); *see* Greif, *supra* note 63, at 316 (Fathers with greater child absence evidence considerable depression, as well as a sense of loss); Miller, *supra* note 50, at 365 (Joint custody has an ego-boosting function, giving the noncustodial parent "a sense of self worth and dignity").
65. *See* Robinson, *supra* note 50, at 670-71.
66. *See* Scott & Derdeyn, *supra* note 48, at 494-95. One study found that children of parents who were unable, after negotiation and mediation, to reach agreement concerning custody, suffer greater psychological harm from increased contact with the less-seen parent. Johnston, *supra* note 57.

A Proposal: Reconciling the Primary Caretaker and Joint Custody Preferences for the Sake of the Child

The primary caretaker preference and the joint custody preference each has strengths and weaknesses. The primary-caretaker preference clearly identifies the physical custodian and decision maker and thereby reduces potential conflict, but it does not meet the child's need for a deep relationship with the other parent. The joint custody preference generally enables the child to continue a close relationship with the parent who would otherwise lose custody, but at some point, increased contact with the less-seen parent may become counterproductive and joint legal custody will lead to conflict as parents who have been unable to work together in the past attempt to reach decisions about the child's future.

I propose that the differences between the primary caretaker and joint custody preferences be reconciled in a single preference that is based on the importance to the child's psychological well-being of regular contact with both parents and of avoiding conflict between the parents. I propose that when parents are unable to agree concerning custody of a child and one parent can establish that he or she is the child's primary caretaker,[67] the following custody arrangement be preferred:

1. *Physical Custody*: The parents shall have joint physical custody, the child to spend most of his time with the parent who has been his primary caretaker and to spend substantial, regular periods of time with the other parent;[68] and

2. *Legal Custody*: The primary caretaker shall have legal custody, that is, he or she shall have the authority to make decisions as to the child's life that do not affect the physical-custody relationship.

The preference could be overcome by clear and convincing evidence, presented by either parent, establishing that another custody arrangement would be better for the child.

A Preference for Joint Physical Custody, the Primary Caretaker to Be Primary Custodian

When parents are unable to reach agreement in a child-custody dispute and one parent can establish that he or she is the child's primary caretaker, there should be a preference for joint physical custody. The primary caretaker should be primary custodian, and the other parent should have substantial, regular time with the child.

---

67. Within almost all homes, one parent—the mother—serves as primary caretaker. If the father is the primary caretaker, he would receive the benefit of the preference. In those cases in which parents have shared the child-care responsibilities equally, custody would be determined in the best interests of the child without the benefit of an established preference. *See* Garska v. McCoy, 278 S.E.2d 357, 363 (W. Va. 1981).

68. I have chosen not to designate how the child's time should be divided with more particularity than that he would spend "most of his time" with the primary physical custodian, and "substantial, regular periods" with the secondary physical custodian. This is designed to give parents and courts flexibility, much as the traditional term "reasonable visitation" and the modern joint physical custody terms "significant periods of physical custody" and "frequent and continuing contact" give parents and courts flexibility. The

As under the primary caretaker preference, the proposed preference identifies the parent with whom children are to have their primary residence, and the likelihood that there will be litigation or threatened litigation over who will be primary custodian is reduced. The proposed preference for joint physical custody is superior to the primary caretaker preference because, as under the joint custody preference, children generally will be able to "grow up knowing and interacting with each parent in an everyday situation."[69] Joint physical custody not only gives the less-seen parent the legal right to more time with the child, but that parent will be more likely to exercise the right to spend time with the child—the parent can have sufficient time with the child so that he or she can maintain a meaningful relationship, rather than the superficial relationship that is likely under traditional visitation.

It might appear that the proposal advanced here is little more than a primary caretaker preference coupled with a proposal that children be given greater visitation rights with the noncustodial parent.[70] In some cases, parents with "visitation rights" visit with their children "for substantial, regular periods of time"[71] and maintain a close relationship with them.[72] However, the label "joint physical custody" is an important aspect of the proposal advanced here. It signals courts, attorneys, parents, and the public that a custodial relationship is being established that is significantly different from the traditional custodial parent/visiting parent relationship, much like the shift in terminology from "divorce" to "marital dissolution" emphasized the break with the fault concept in many states that adopted no-fault divorce.

Hopefully, the new label will signal the less-seen parents that they are being given a different responsibility and a different status than under a traditional visitation order. As noted previously, children often fail to receive sufficient time with noncustodial parents because the noncustodial parents fail to exercise the visitation that they do have. Very little stigma is attached to noncustodial parents' failure to exercise visitation rights, but parents are stigmatized and punished for abandoning children over whom they have custody.[73] Mental health professionals also believe that the ego-boosting function of the status of joint custodian will give the parents a sense of self- worth and dignity and reduce the depression that often leads non- custodial parents to fail to exercise visitation.

---

preference is designed to encourage somewhat more contact with the less-seen parent than occurred under traditional visitation, but not as much contact as might occur under statutes that create a preference for joint physical custody without designating one parent as the preferred primary physical custodian. If pressed, I would say that generally, an average of one day per week with the secondary custodian is not a substantial period of time and that two days per week is a substantial period of time.

69. Woolley, *Shared Custody*, 1 Fam. Advoc. 6 (1978).

70. I proposed increased rights of visitation in an earlier article. *See* Cochran & Vitz, *supra* note 48, at 355.

71. David Chambers has said that "some children in single custody spend more time 'visiting' with the noncustodial parent than some other children in joint custody spend 'living' with one of their parents." Chambers, *supra* note 23, at 550 n.277.

72. *See* Wallerstein & Kelly, *supra* note 55, at 215.

73. I am not suggesting that sanctions be imposed on secondary physical custodians who fail to care for their children during the time they are scheduled to care for them, but such a proposal may have merit. I am merely illustrating the importance of the distinction between the labels "visiting" parent and "custodial" parent.

The "joint physical custody" label may also be of benefit to children. Joint physical custody may signal to children that both parents want to be involved in caring for them and this may help children to adjust to the divorce.[74]

The physical custody proposal advanced herein is based on the assumption that children benefit from more time with the less-seen parent than they are likely to have under traditional sole-custody rules, but that too much contact with the less-seen parent can be counterproductive. Studies of the effects of the amount of time spent with the less-seen parent on children support this assumption. Studies conducted in the mid-seventies generally found that children with increased amounts of contact with the less-seen parent did better.[75] A recent study, conducted in California by Marsha Kline and others, found no relationship between the amount of time spent with the less-seen parent and the children's psychological health.[76] The differences between the mid-seventies studies and the Kline study can be explained based on differences in the amount of contact that the groups of children had with the less-seen parents. The children in the mid-seventies studies, on the average, saw the less-seen parent substantially less than the children in the recent study.[77] This is not surprising. Two weekends per month was the prevailing visitation pattern in the mid-seventies. Since that time, several factors have encouraged parents, mediators, and judges, especially in California, to give children more time with the less-seen parent: the findings of the mid-seventies studies that children who do best following divorce are those who have the most contact with the less-seen parent were widely reported.[78] Many books and articles extolled the virtues of joint custody; and statutes passed in California in 1980 actively encouraged joint custody in several ways.

It may be that children benefit from more contact with the less-seen parent than is provided by traditional visitation, but that the benefits of increased access to the less-seen parent are subject to diminishing marginal returns. Children benefit from additional amounts of contact, but each increment of additional contact is

---

74. *See* Kline, *supra* note 58.

75. *See* Jacobson, *The Impact of Marital Separation/Divorce on Children: I. Parent-Child Separation and Child Adjustment*, 1 J. Divorce 341, 356 (1978). Wallerstein & Kelly, *supra* note 55, at 219; Lowenstein & Koopman, *A Comparison of the Self-Esteem Between Boys Living with Single-Parent Mothers and Single-Parent Fathers*, 2 J. of Divorce 195, 204-05 (1978); Kundek & Berg, *Correlates of Children's Adjustment to Their Parents' Divorce*, in New Directions for Child Development, Children and Divorce, 19, 47-60, 58 (1983) ("[T]he amount of time non-custodial parents spent in direct exclusive contact with the children did show a significant relationship to the children's divorce adjustment"). *But see* Hess & Camara, *Post-Divorce Family Relationships as Mediating Factors in the Consequences of Divorce for Children*, 35 J. of Soc. Issues 79, 92-94 (1979) (The quality of the relationship with the father is important, but more related to length than to frequency of visits).

76. Kline, *supra* note 58. *See also* Hodges, Buchsbaum, & Tierney, *Parent-Child Relationships and Adjustment in Pre-School Children in Divorced and Intact Families*, 7 J. of Divorce 43 (1983).

77. In one of the mid-seventies studies, the Wallerstein & Kelly study, noncustodial parents generally were given twice-monthly overnight or weekend visitation, Wallerstein & Kelly, *supra* note 55, at 132, and many failed to exercise the visitation rights that they did have, *id.* at 136. In another of the mid-seventies studies, the Jacobson study, noncustodial parents saw the child an average of 20.12 hours during the two-week period after separation. Jacobson, *supra* note 75, at 351. These stand in stark contrast to the recent Kline study, in which the less-seen parent saw the children an average of 16.62 days per month initially and 10.41 days per month at a two-year follow-up. Kline, *supra* note 58.

78. *See, e.g.*, Wallerstein & Kelly, *California's Children of Divorce*, Psychology Today 67, 76 (Jan. 1980).

somewhat less beneficial than the prior increment of additional contact. At some point, additional increases in increments of visitation are no longer beneficial.[79] The physical custody preference advocated herein will encourage parents to agree to greater access than they would have agreed to under traditional custody and visitation rules, but it will not push parents as hard toward increased access as would a preference for joint physical custody that does not identify the preferred primary physical custodian.

One problem with joint physical custody is the danger of increased conflict between the parents. Such conflict may occur when the children are transferred or when parents make arrangements to transfer the children.[80] As noted previously, when children are exposed to parental conflict, they suffer emotional difficulties, especially when the conflict occurs after parents separate. When parents are extremely hostile and unable to cooperate, increased contact with the less-seen parent may be detrimental to children.[81] When parents have a history of conflict and are unable to reach agreement concerning custody, judges should be alert to the possibility that joint physical custody will not be in the best interest of the child and that the child's contact with the less-seen parent should be limited.[82]

It may be that some of the conflict created by the additional contact with the less-seen parent can be avoided if judges establish a clear, somewhat rigid transfer schedule. Constance Ahrons, following a study of joint custody families, reports that:

> In some families [the times the children were to be transferred] were flexible and divorced parents were able to negotiate changes with relative ease; in other families the time that the nonresidential parent spent with the children was fixed and maintained on a rigid schedule because attempts at changes had resulted in conflict. . . . Some of

---

79. This is not to suggest that there is some ideal amount of contact with the less-seen parent that will be the same for each child. The ideal amount of contact with the less-seen parent probably varies substantially from child to child. Parents are in the best position to determine the amount of contact that is best for their children, though in many cases they will not initially agree. The amount of contact that they ultimately give the child will be a function, to some extent, of the incentives created by legal rules. The law should provide parents with the incentive to give children somewhat more contact than was given under traditional visitation, but it should not push parents too far in the direction of increased contact.

80. Under traditional visitation, parental conflict often occurs when parents transfer children. *See* Wallerstein & Kelly, *supra* note 55, at 125; *see also* Goldstein, *supra* note 41, at 37-38.

81. *See* Johnston, *supra* note 57 (In a study of families in which the parents were unable to reach agreement concerning custody after negotiation and mediation, children who had greater access to the less-seen parent suffered greater emotional difficulty). *See also* Steinman, Zemmelman, & Knoblauch, *A Study of Parents Who Sought Joint Custody Following Divorce: Who Reaches Agreement and Sustains Joint Custody and Who Returns to Court*, 24 J. Am. Acad. Child Psychiatry 554, 558 (1985) (There were no successful court-imposed joint custody arrangements one year later).

82. The proposed preference for joint physical custody can be overcome by a showing of clear and convincing evidence that another arrangement would be better for the child.

In light of studies that indicate that increased contact is detrimental if parents are unable to reach agreement, it is tempting to suggest that there should be no preference for joint physical custody unless parents agree to it. Such a rule, however, would encourage parents who want no joint physical custody to merely refuse to seriously negotiate the issue. Courts must consider the impact that such a rule will have on those "bargaining in the shadow of the law." *See* Mnookin & Kornhauser, *Bargaining in the Shadow of the Law: The Case of Divorce*, 88 Yale L.J. 950, 977-80 (1979). There should be a story of an inability to cooperate, before the inability, by itself, should overcome the preference for joint physical custody.

the families . . . had learned . . . that negotiating the arrangements created conflict for the parents and distress for the children; so they established patterns and adhered to them, except in cases of emergencies.[83]

Once a schedule is established, if transfer continues to be an occasion for parental conflict, many parents can pick up and drop off children at some designated place and need not even have contact with one another.[84]

The proposal here advanced that courts prefer the primary caretaker as primary physical custodian is superior to a joint custody preference that does not designate a preference for one parent as primary physical custodian. Uncertainty under such a rule creates the same dangers as the uncertainty of the case-by-case best-interests rule. The problems of whether physical custody will be split equally and, if not, who will be primary custodian, are a likely source of conflict between the parents under a rule that fails to designate a preferred, primary physical custodian. If no parent is identified as the preferred primary custodian, the other parent may use the threat of seeking to be the primary custodian as a means to obtain concessions from the primary caretaker on child support and other matters.[85]

My goal in establishing a physical custody preference has been to establish a preference for the custody arrangement that generally will be in the best interests of the child. This preference will give children the best combination of security, contact with both parents, and freedom from parental conflict. The proposal has the added benefit of being a fair compromise of the interests of the primary caretaker and the other parent. It is similar to the agreements of most couples that are able to reach agreement in mediation.[86] The interest of the primary caretaker in being primary custodian is protected, as is the interest of the other parent in maintaining a significant relationship with his child. Since such a preference strikes a good balance between the interests of both parents and generally will be for the good of the child, it is likely to remain more stable than if one parent receives substantially less than he or she desires.

---

83. Ahrons, *Joint Custody Arrangement in the Post-Divorce Family*, 3 J. Divorce 189, 194 (1980) (a study of 41 parents who voluntarily established joint custody). As Judge Nanette Dembitz of the New York Family Court has said in the context of court resolution of visitation disputes, "[a] clear demarcation of rights and obligations . . . sometimes quiets the custodial parent's anger." Dembitz, *Beyond Any Discipline's Competence*, 83 Yale L.J. 1304, 1310 (1974).

84. Greif reports that a number of the fathers with joint custody interviewed in her study

> reported angry, hostile relationships with their ex-wives. Some families use the school, rather than the parents' homes, as the drop-off point for the child, so that months can go by without the parents having to see or talk with one another, thus avoiding tense flare-ups in front of the child.

Greif, *Fathers, Children, and Joint Custody*, 49(2) Am. J. Orthopsychiatry 311, 318 (1979).

85. This type of pressure is especially likely under a case-by-case best-interests rule. Though the fear of sharing joint physical custody would not be as troublesome to the primary caretaker as her fear that she would lose custody under the case-by-case rule, there still would be the opportunity for unfair advantage. See Schulman & Pitt, *Second Thoughts on Joint Child Custody: Analysis of Legislation and Its Implications for Women and Children*, 12 Golden Gate 539, 554 (1982).

86. See Pearson & Thoennes, *Divorce Mediation: Strengths and Weaknesses Over Time, Alternative Means of Family Dispute Resolution*, 51, 61 (H. Davidson, L. Ray, & R. Horowitz, eds. 1982).

A Preference for the Primary Caretaker as Legal Custodian

When a parent in a child-custody dispute establishes that he or she is the child's primary caretaker, that parent should also be the preferred legal custodian. This proposal is superior to a preference for joint legal custody because a preference for joint legal custody may cause substantial parental conflict and additional litigation.

Proponents of joint legal custody argue that, under sole custody, designating one parent with power greater than the other encourages power struggles and that joint legal custody will reduce such conflict.[87] On the contrary, joint legal custody is likely to lead to serious parental conflict as parents struggle for control.[88] Child psychiatrist Andre Derdeyn and law professor Elizabeth Scott state:

> A common theme in marriages that fail is a struggle for control. Even if competition was not a central marital issue, spouses in a deteriorating relationship may become intensely competitive in an effort to protect themselves from distress caused by the partner and to blame the spouse for the failing relationship.[89]

Joint legal custody provides many opportunities for such conflict as parents share equal power to determine those facets of the child's life beyond his immediate daily requirements.[90] This parental conflict should be avoided by giving one parent decision-making authority.

When parents that have joint legal custody are unable to resolve their disputes, they will, at times, bring those disputes to court. Some disputes may be resolved through mediation,[91] if available, but others will not. The areas of responsibility that traditionally belong to the legal custodian are inappropriate for judicial determination, and should be left to the ultimate discretion of one of the parents. Legal custody involves authority over issues beyond the child's day-to-day needs,

---

87. *See* Beck v. Beck, 86 N.J. 480, 486, 432 A.2d 63, 65 (1981) (The best interests of the child are disserved by many aspects of sole custody, in which one parent "wins" and the other "loses"); Miller, *supra* note 50, at 366 (Argues that joint custody may produce less post-divorce litigation than sole custody); Robinson, *supra* note 50, at 645-46 (States that the child should not be the prize in a contest between parents); Schepard, *supra* note 50, at 716-19.

88. In Chapman v. Chapman, 352 N.W.2d 437 (Minn. App. 1984), the trial court granted joint legal custody in the hope that it would encourage the parents to cooperate. The court of appeals stated:

> Instead of granting joint custody because the parties *can* cooperate and amicably settle disputes about the children, the judge granted joint custody because they *cannot*. Although ideally the parents should make major decisions concerning their children jointly, joint legal custody should not be used as a "legal baseball bat" to coerce cooperation, as advocated by the father's attorney.

Id. at 441 (emphasis in original); *see also* Smith v. Smith, 673 P.2d 282, 283 (Alaska 1983); Andersen v. Andersen, 125 N.H. 686, 484 A.2d 1180, 1183 (1984).

89. Scott & Derdeyn, *supra* note 48, at 493.

90. *See, e.g.,* Broome County Dept. of Social Service v. Dennis, 97 A.D.2d 908, 470 N.Y.S.2d 741 (1983); In re Marriage of Drummond, 156 Ill. App. 3d 672, 109 Ill. Dec. 46, 509 N.E.2d 707, 713 (Ill. App. 4 Dist. 1987).

91. Andrew Schepard suggests that a joint legal custody preference, coupled with mandatory mediation of disputes, would encourage parental cooperation. Schepard, *supra* note 50, at 718, 756-69 n.131.

including the child's health care,[92] education,[93] and religious upbringing.[94] Dis-agreement over such issues should not cause inaction, delay, or judicial intervention.

The issues traditionally decided by the legal custodian often have no clearly correct answer. Judges have no special ability to determine which of two schools, which of two doctors, or which of two religions is best for a child.[95] Courts should not have to determine the religious upbringing of a child, thereby raising troublesome "establishment of religion" issues.[96] As one court stated:

> Courts are not so constituted as to be able to regulate the details of a child's upbringing. It exhausts the imagination to speculate on the difficulties to which they would subject themselves were they to enter the home or the school or the playground and undertake to exercise on all occasions the authority which one party or the other would be bound to ascribe to them.[97]

Some "legal custodian" issues must be decided quickly. When parents with joint legal custody cannot agree and the school year is approaching,[98] the child needs an operation,[99] or a settlement offer is made in a child's personal injury suit,[100] the delay for a court hearing is not in the child's interest.

When parents do not agree to share joint legal custody, one parent should be given such responsibility. Ideally, the legal custodian will involve the other parent in important decisions, but there should be one person with the child's interests at heart who has the ultimate decision-making authority.[101] If there has been a primary caretaker and the

---

92. *See* Lerner v. Superior Court, 38 Cal. 2d 676, 681, 242 P.2d 321, 323 (1952); People ex rel. Sisson v. Sisson, 271 N.Y. 285, 287-88, 2 N.E.2d 660, 661 (1936).

93. *See* Lerner, 38 Cal. 2d at 681, 242 P.2d at 323; Schumm v. Schumm, 122 N.J. Super. 146, 150, 299 A.2d 423, 426 (N.J. Super. Ct. Ch. Div. 1973); Rosenthal v. Rosenthal, 26 N.J. Super. 400, 402, 98 A.2d 338, 338 (N.J. Super. Ct. App. Div. 1953); Sisson, 271 N.Y. at 287-88, 2 N.E.2d at 661.

94. *See* Donahue v. Donahue, 142 N.J. Eq. 701, 61 A.2d 243, 244-45 (1948); Boerger v. Boerger, 26 N.J. Super. 90, 105, 97 A.2d 419, 427 (N.J. Super. Ct. Ch. Div. 1953); Ex parte Kananack, 272 A.D. 783, 784, 69 N.Y.S.2d 889, 891 (1947).

95. *See, e.g.,* Strosnider v. Strosnider, 101 N.M. 639, 686 P.2d 981 (Ct. App. 1984); Broome County Department of Social Services v. Dennis, 97 A.D. 2d 908, 909, 470 N.Y.S. 2d 741,743 (1983).

96. *See* Munoz v. Munoz, 79 Wash. 2d 810, 812-14, 489 P.2d 1133, 1135 (1971); *see also* Angel v. Angel, 2 Ohio Op. 2d 136, 137-38, 140 N.E.2d 86, 87-88 (C.P. 1956). For a helpful discussion of several issues that arise when parents of differing religious beliefs separate, *see* Note, *The Religious Upbringing of Children After Divorce,* 56 Notre Dame Law. 160 (1980).

97. Jenks v. Jenks, 385 S.W.2d 370, 377 (Mo. Ct. App. 1964).

98. *See, e.g.,* In re Marriage of Heinel & Kessel, 55 Or. App. 275, 637 P.2d 1313 (1981); (Joint custodial father unilaterally removed child from school near mother's home and transferred him to another school).

99. *See* Levy & Chambers, *The Folly of Joint Custody,* Fam. Advoc. 8 (Spring, 1981) (A hospital refused to perform an operation on a child in danger of appendix rupture because one parent refused consent; the hospital obtained a court order permitting the surgery).

100. Burge v. City & County of San Francisco, 41 Cal. 2d 608, 618, 262 P.2d 6, 13 (1953) (en banc) (Although the parents were given joint custody of their minor child, the court held that the mother who had been awarded physical custody had the authority to compromise the minor's claim for personal injuries).

101. The Maryland Court of Appeals has suggested that judges exercise great caution before awarding joint legal custody. The court says:

> Even in the absence of bitterness or inability to communicate, if the evidence discloses the parents do not share parenting values, and each insists on adhering to irreconcilable theories of childrearing, joint legal custody is not appropriate. The parents need not agree on every aspect

primary caretaker is made primary physical custodian, that person should be given legal custody. The child's primary physical custodian generally is going to have to make most of the logistical arrangements for health care or education and will be in the best position to make the most reasonable decisions.[102] Given the primary caretaker's history of contact with the child, he or she is also most likely to know the child's needs.

Advocates of joint legal custody maintain that it will encourage the parent who otherwise would not have legal custody to spend time with the children.[103] Holly Robinson argues that when one parent is given legal custody:

> [b]oth the custodial parent and the child are fully aware of the custodial parent's virtually exclusive right to control the major aspects of the child's life. Given this custodial parental power and corresponding noncustodial parental powerlessness, the maintenance of a close and meaningful relationship between the child and the noncustodial parent is extremely difficult, if not virtually impossible, to achieve and maintain.[104]

Empirical studies, however, show that many fathers that do not have legal custody spend substantial time with their children, maintain a significant relationship with them, and have a positive impact on them.[105]

The status of joint legal custodian may give some parents "a sense of self worth and dignity"[106] that will lead them to spend time with their children, but joint physical custody is a better way to provide the needed sense of self-worth. Day-to-day interaction with a child provides an important influence on the development of a child's character and emotional stability. Regular interaction is a much more important source of satisfaction to a parent than the right to make decisions for the child. In a study of forty divorced fathers, Judith Brown Greif found that "[a]ttending to the emotional needs of a child was consistently ranked by [divorced fathers] as the most important of the paternal roles."[107]

The Weight of a Custody Preference

The weight given to the primary caretaker and joint custody preferences varies substantially (see Appendix A). The choice of what weight to give a child-custody

---

of parenting, but their views should not be so widely divergent or so inflexibly maintained as to forecast the probability of continuing disagreement on important matters.

Taylor v. Taylor, 306 Md. 290, 508 A.2d 964, 971-72 (Md. Ct. App. 1986). For a discussion of the *Taylor* case and a criticism of joint custody, *see* Singer & Reynolds, *supra* note 40.

102. The frustration of parents who retain primary responsibility for caring for children and are forced to share joint legal custody is expressed by Valerie Pitt and Joanne Schulman, *supra* note 85, at 570.

103. *See* Greif, *supra* note 63, at 319 "[A]rrangements such as custody and visitation are crucial to the post-divorce adjustment of fathers, and, ultimately, of their children"); Miller, *supra* note 50, at 365 (Joint legal custody "gives the non-physical-custodial parent a sense of self worth and dignity. Members of the legal and mental health professions place considerable importance on this symbolic, ego-boosting function of joint legal custody"); Robinson, *supra* note 50, at 650.

104. Robinson, *supra* note 50, at 670-71 (footnote omitted).

105. *See* Wallerstein & Kelly, *supra* note 55, at 215. The one-third of the children studied by Wallerstein & Kelly that did very well were generally those that had a close relationship with the noncustodial, visiting parent. *Id.* at 209, 218-19.

106. *See supra* note 103.

107. Greif, *supra* note 63, at 314.

preference is difficult because there are advantages and disadvantages to both strong and weak preferences. Under those preferences that place the heaviest burdens on the party opposing the preference, i.e., showing the unfitness of the primary caretaker or that joint custody would be detrimental to the child, the party opposing the preference is least likely to overcome the preference and therefore is least likely to litigate custody. The danger of parental conflict and the use of threats of child-custody litigation in bargaining will be greatly reduced. The party favored by the preference can be more confident that if there is litigation, the court will order the preferred custody arrangement and that party will be less subject to threats of litigation.[108]

A strong preference, however, is more likely to cause placements that will not be in the interests of the child. A strong preference will discourage parents from opposing the preferred custody arrangement in some cases in which a different custody arrangement would be in the interests of the child. The strong custody preferences not only place heavy burdens on the parent opposing them, but a parent may overcome the burden only by establishing a negative, such as the unfitness of the primary caretaker or the detrimental nature of the joint custody. The strong preferences do not permit the party opposing the preference to win based on the positive aspects of the custody arrangement that he or she is proposing.[109] A court should be able to reject a preferred custody arrangement if a parent can establish clearly that another custody arrangement will benefit the child, even if he or she cannot establish the unfitness of the other parent or the detrimental nature of the preferred custody arrangement.

Those preferences that place a weak burden on the party opposing the preference, i.e., showing that the preferred arrangement is not in the best interests of the child will benefit the child if the situation is such that a judge can determine that a custody placement other than the preferred one would be better for the child. Such weak preferences, however, are not as likely to discourage litigation as is a stronger preference.[110] In cases in which another custody arrangement would not be better than the preferred arrangement, as well as in the substantial number of cases in which a judge cannot determine that another custody placement would be better than the preferred custody arrangement, children will suffer the traumas of litigation and increased parental conflict without any benefit.

The choice between the benefits of predictability under a strong preference and the benefits of the individual determinations under a weak preference would be more difficult if courts had the ability to determine the best interests of the child in a larger percentage of cases. As noted previously, however, there is a broad range of cases in which courts, either because of an inability to predict the future life of a child or an

---

108. In Garska v. McCoy, 278 S.E.2d 357, 360-63 (W. Va. 1981), the West Virginia Supreme Court of Appeals emphasized the importance of creating a difficult burden for the parent opposing the primary caretaker presumption, but explained that the presumption can be overcome by a showing of the unfitness of the primary caretaker. The presumption may lose its effect when the child indicates a justified desire to be placed in the custody of the parent that is not the primary caretaker and the trial court feels that he is old enough to formulate such an opinion. *See Garska,* 278 S.E.2d at 363.

109. *Cf.* Chambers, *supra* note 23, at 562. Klaff advocates a maternal presumption that can be rebutted by a showing that "the child's immediate developmental needs would be better served by paternal custody." *See The Tender Years Doctrine: A Defense,* 70 Calif. L. Rev. 335, 349 (1982).

110. *Cf.* Chambers, *supra* note 23, at 563.

inability to determine which of two lifestyles would be best for a child, are unable to determine the best interests of a child.

In light of the inability of courts to determine the best interests of the child in many cases, a child-custody preference should have an intermediate weight, requiring the parent opposing the preference to establish by clear and convincing evidence that some alternative to the preferred custody arrangement would be better for the child.[111] Such a standard strikes the best balance between avoiding litigation and conflict and allowing courts to reach individualized decisions. In those cases in which courts can not clearly determine that a custody arrangement other than the preferred one would be better for the child, litigation is unlikely. A parent who does not have evidence that an alternative custodial arrangement is justified will be discouraged from litigation, and he or she will not be able to mount an effective threat of litigation in custody negotiations. A "clear and convincing" standard will result in more litigation than an "unfitness" or "detrimental to the child" standard, but in those cases in which a party can establish by clear and convincing evidence that the alternative is better for the child, the risks of danger from litigation and parental conflict are outweighed by the benefit to the child of the better custody placement.

Age Limitations and the Proposed Custody Preference

The joint physical custody/primary caretaker-as-legal-custodian preference advocated herein should apply to minor children of all ages because the underlying policy justifications for the proposed preference, protection of the child's relationship with both parents and protection of the child from parental conflict, apply whatever the age of the child.

The maternal preference was based on a belief that very young children, children of "tender years," need the care of their mother.[112] The maternal preference, therefore, applied only to children of "tender years."[113]

Courts that have recognized a primary caretaker preference also have limited it to custody disputes involving children of tender years.[114] These courts have offered two justifications for the primary caretaker preference, and each has different implications for the question of whether the preference should be limited to disputes involving young children. One justification is that young children have a special need

---

111. David Chambers advocates a preference for the primary caretaker that could only be overcome by "clear and convincing" evidence that granting custody to the other parent would be better for the child. *See* Chambers, *supra* note 23, at 563.

112. *See, e.g.*, Commonwealth v. Addicks, 5 Binn. 520, 521 (Pa. 1813) ("Considering their tender age [ten and seven], they stand in need of that kind of assistance, which can be afforded, by none so well as a mother").

113. The age at which courts held that a child had grown beyond "tender years" varied from four to fourteen years.

114. *See* Pikula v. Pikula, 374 N.W.2d 705, 712 (Minn. 1985); Derby v. Derby, 31 Or. App. 803, 807, 571 P.2d 562, 564 (1977); Garska v. McCoy, 278 S.E.2d 357, 363 (W. Va. 1981); *see also* Commonwealth ex rel. Jordan v. Jordan, 302 Pa. Super. 421, 425, 448 A.2d 1113, 1115 (1982).

Chambers advocates a primary caretaker preference in disputes over "children up to about five years of age." *See* Chambers, *supra* note 23, at 564.

for the care of the primary caretaker.[115] This justification for the primary-caretaker preference loses its force as children become older and can care for themselves.

A second justification for the primary-caretaker preference is the need for a reliable rule that will reduce the possibility of unfair threats of custody litigation during negotiation and also reduce parental conflict and litigation. This justification supports a custody preference with no age limitation because the problems arising from uncertainty of outcome may arise whatever the age of the child.

In *Garska v. McCoy*,[116] the leading primary-caretaker preference case, the West Virginia Supreme Court of Appeals justifies the primary-caretaker preference entirely on the basis of the need for a reliable rule that will discourage unfair bargaining and encourage settlement. Both are worthwhile goals; yet both are unrelated to the age of the child. As children get older, the primary caretaker's ties to them are likely to continue to be strong. If the primary-caretaker preference expires, the primary caretaker will be subject to the danger of custody litigation threats. Parental conflict and litigation do not become less of a danger as a child gets older.[117]

The statutes that have established preferences for joint custody have not established age limitations. The primary justification for joint custody is the child's need for regular, substantial contact with both parents, and minor children of all ages need such contact.[118]

The proposal advocated here that there be a preference for joint physical custody, the primary caretaker to be primary physical custodian, and a preference for the primary caretaker as legal custodian, should not be limited to cases involving children of a particular age. Though the need of children for the continued care of the primary caretaker may be greatest at a young age, the other justifications for the proposed preference, i.e., the child's need for substantial contact with both parents, the need to reduce parental conflict and litigation, and the danger that the threat of a custody fight will be used in negotiations, apply to child-custody cases involving children of all ages.

Applying the proposed preference to older children does not mean that their desires regarding custody will be given no weight. When an older child desires that some aspect of custody differ from the proposed preference, the child's desire should be a factor the judge considers in determining whether there is clear and convincing evidence that a custody arrangement other than the preferred one is in the interests of the child.

---

115. *See* Pikula, 374 N.W.2d at 711; Derby, 31 Or. app. at 807, 571 P.2d at 564 ("[T]he close and successful emotional relationship between the primary parent and the children coupled with the age of the children [nine and five] dictate the continuance of that relationship").

116. 278 S.E.2d 357 (W. Va. 1981).

117. In Garska, the West Virginia Supreme Court of Appeals held that children cease to be of "tender years" when the trial court feels that they are old enough to formulate an opinion concerning their custody and they indicate "a justified desire to live with the parent who is not the primary caretaker." *Id.* at 363.

118. Wallerstein and Kelly studied children ranging in ages from 1 to 22. *See* Wallerstein & Kelly, *supra* note 55, at 329. They found that "[t]he intense longing for greater contact persisted undiminished over many years," *id.* at 134, and that "boys and girls of various ages who had been doing poorly at the initial assessment were able to improve significantly with increased visiting by the father," *id.* at 219.

Conclusion

The studies of children of divorce show two things clearly. First, children suffer emotional harm when they are exposed to conflict between their parents; second, children generally suffer when they fail to maintain a substantial relationship with both parents. The interest of the child in avoiding exposure to parental conflict justifies a relatively strong preference for an established type of custody arrangement so that parental conflict and litigation over custody will be discouraged. The interest of the child in maintaining contact with both parents justifies a preference for some form of joint physical custody so that both parents will have the right to substantial contact with the child and so that both parents will have the status, and hopefully will assume the responsibility, of a custodian.

Though my primary concern is with the interests of the child at divorce, the importance to the child of limiting parental conflict justifies a preference for a custody arrangement that, to the extent possible, protects the interests of each of the parents. I believe that the proposed preference protects those interests. The proposed preference protects the interests of the primary caretaker by preferring that he or she be the primary physical custodian and the legal custodian. The proposed preference protects the interests of the child's secondary caretaker by giving him or her the right to maintain a substantial relationship with the child and by giving him or her the status of joint physical custodian. In cases in which this preferred custody arrangement is not in the best interests of children, the proposed rule protects their interests by giving either parent the opportunity to show that another custody arrangement clearly would be better for the child.

19

The Effect of Joint Custody and Similar Arrangements on AFDC Eligibility

SHERRY LEIWANT

*The increase in both formal and informal joint custody arrange-
ments has raised serious problems for the applicants and recipients
of Aid to Families with Dependent Children (AFDC). With federal
and state program requirements such as "continued absence" and
"living in the home" both vaguely defined and outdated, those
divorced families opting for equal or near-equal custody arrangements are often precluded from receiving AFDC. The federal
program's mandate of "continued absence" is in direct conflict with
the goal of providing children with frequent and continuous contact
with both parents. Long-term remedies to this problem include the
adoption of explicit state policies that favor joint custody and the
reform of federal regulations that now promote parental dropout.
In the meantime, Leiwant suggests careful framing of custody
awards to clearly define parental responsibilities.*

The increase of joint custody awards in divorce proceedings and the rise in informal
joint custody arrangements between parents raise problems for applicants for, or
recipients of, Aid to Families with Dependent Children ("AFDC"). The AFDC
program is the largest federal cash-assistance program for children serving approximately 3.7 million families. It is not available to all poor families with children,

Sherry Leiwant is a senior attorney with the Center on Social Welfare Policy and Law, New York, New
York.

however. Rather, AFDC is only available to families in which the children, in addition to meeting certain financial eligibility criteria, are also deprived of parental support because of one of the following factors: the death, incapacity, absence from the home, or, in some states, unemployment of a parent.[1] By far the greatest number of AFDC families qualify for assistance by virtue of the absence from the home of one of the parents. In addition to the requirement that there be deprivation in order for a family to receive AFDC, there is also a requirement that an AFDC child live with a relative specified by the statute in his or her own home in order to receive benefits.[2]

Both the "continued absence" and the "living in the home" requirements raise issues with respect to AFDC eligibility when there is a joint custody arrangement following divorce or separation. Questions arise as to whether a child cared for by both parents pursuant to a joint custody arrangement or decree really suffers from parental deprivation, where that child's home is for AFDC purposes, and who is the child's primary caretaker. The resolution of those issues can have an enormous effect on the survival of the family unit. AFDC benefits necessary to meet basic need may be denied to a parent (usually the mother)—even though that parent has assumed the larger share of custodial responsibilities—if the child has significant contact and/or temporarily resides with the absent parent. Medical benefits through the Medicaid program, which may be essential to some families even if cash assistance is not, may be unavailable if the family is disqualified from AFDC.[3] Without AFDC and medical assistance, the parent's ability to care for the child is imperiled. It is important, therefore, for those who represent families in custody or benefit matters, and for those who make decisions about the custody of children, to bear in mind the implications of custody arrangements on families' eligibility for public benefits, particularly AFDC.

In this chapter, we look at the implications of joint custody for AFDC eligibility, first by analyzing the federal policy and case law governing the definitions of "continued absence" and "living in the home" in the AFDC program. We then turn to a discussion of the case law and significant administrative decisions on AFDC eligibility in joint custody situations. Finally, we have included some state policies on joint custody and AFDC eligibility which we believe have been helpful in the states that have implemented them in clarifying the issues in this area.

We believe that our analysis supports the conclusion that joint custody should not automatically preclude AFDC eligibility because of the consistent position of the federal agency and most courts that "continued absence" and "living in the home" should be determined on a case-by-case basis by documenting the actual involvement of the absent parent with the child, not by looking at the language in a divorce decree or separation order or agreement. On the other hand, there are certainly cases where

---

1. 42 U.S.C. § 606(a). Coverage of the unemployed under AFDC is currently optional with the states. However, effective October 1, 1990, all states must cover children deprived of parental support due to the unemployment of a parent for at least six months. Pub. L. No. 100-485 401.

2. 42 U.S.C. § 606(a).

3. In many states, families who do not receive AFDC are not Medicaid eligible. Even in states that cover those who do not receive AFDC ("medically needy"), there is still a requirement that the family be "categorically eligible" for one of the federal assistance programs, so that disqualification from AFDC because of the lack of absence may disqualify the family from Medicaid as well.

joint custody arrangements may affect AFDC eligibility. We conclude by discussing considerations that should be taken into account with respect to AFDC eligibility when joint custody or other similar arrangements are considered for a child.

Federal Policy Governing the Determination of "Continued Absence" and "Living in the Home" in the AFDC Program

The AFDC program is commonly referred to as a program of "cooperative federalism." That means that it is a program governed by a federal statute and regulations which are administered by the states. States need not participate in the program, but if they do (all do), they submit a state plan reflecting federal requirements to the federal agency, receive federal matching payments for their AFDC costs, and promise to administer the program in accordance with their state plan. The Supreme Court has repeatedly held that states must follow federal rules with respect to eligibility criteria in the AFDC program and has specifically held that they must do so with respect to the definition of "continued absence."[4]

Federal policy governing the definition of "continued absence" and "living in the home" can be found from examining the federal statute, the federal regulations, and federal agency interpretations of the statute and regulations.[5] It is necessary to understand the purpose of the "absence" and "living in the home" requirements generally in the AFDC program as well as the way the federal agency and the courts have interpreted them" in order to understand the implications of those requirements in joint custody cases.

The "Continued Absence" Requirement

The Federal Statute—The Social Security Act[6] ("the Act") defines a "dependent child" for purposes of AFDC eligibility as a needy, age-qualified child "who has been deprived of parental support or care by reason of the death, *continued absence from the home,* or physical or mental incapacity of a parent . . ."[7] The statute does not define or amplify the meaning of the phrase "continued absence from the home." In addition, this phrase is discussed only briefly in the legislative history. The Senate Finance Committee, in its deliberations on this provision of the Act, defined a dependent child as a child, one of whose parents is "continuously away from the home."[8]

---

4. King v. Smith, 392 U.S. 309 (1968); Carleson v. Remillard, 406 U.S. 598 (1972).
5. The federal agency responsible for administering the AFDC program was originally the Social Security Board. When the programs under the Social Security Act were brought under the jurisdiction of a cabinet-level agency, that agency was the Department of Health, Education and Welfare ("HEW"). In 1979, the programs within HEW were rearranged and the federal agency became the Department of Health and Human Services ("HHS").
6. 42 U.S.C. §§ 601 *et seq.*
7. 42 U.S.C. § 606(a) (emphasis added).
8. S. Rep. No. 628, 74th Cong., 1st Sess. 36 (1935).

Considerations surrounding establishment of the AFDC program over fifty years ago reflect a significantly different social reality from the present, and arrangements, such as joint physical custody of a child following divorce or separation and the effect of such custody on AFDC eligibility, were not considered at the time of enactment of this legislation. However, a broad interpretation of the phrase "continued absence from the home" is supported by the plain meaning of the statutory language which connotes that a parent may be absent for any reason, by the beneficent purpose of this social legislation introduced in 1935,[9] and by federal agency interpretations of continued absence, which recognized from the beginning of the AFDC program that a child's AFDC eligibility may be preserved even though a continuing relationship exists between the child and absent parent.[10]

Federal Regulations—By a regulation first adopted in 1971,[11] the term "continued absence" has been defined as follows:

Continued absence of the parent from the home constitutes the reason for deprivation of parental support or care when

1) the parent is out of the home,

2) the nature of the absence is such as either to interrupt or to terminate the parent's functioning as a provider of maintenance, physical care, or guidance for the child, and,

3) the known or indefinite duration of the absence precludes counting on the parent's performance of the function of planning for the present support or care of the child.

If these conditions exist, the parent may be absent for any reason, and may have left only recently or sometime previously; . . .[12]

All three criteria of the regulation must be fulfilled for the parent to be considered absent from the home. Presuming that criterion one is fulfilled and the absent parent is not in the home, the remaining issue is whether the parent is "continually absent" based upon the character of the parent's continuing relationship with the child. It is important to note that criterion two of the regulation will be satisfied if the parent's ability to provide for maintenance (i.e., support), physical care, *or* guidance is disrupted by the character of the absence. For example, this means that a child is eligible for AFDC benefits when the absent parent provides child-support payments and occasionally visits the child but does not provide guidance to the child. Similarly, criterion three of the regulation will be satisfied if

---

9. *See, e.g.*, H.R. 4120, 74th Cong., 1st Sess. (1935), § 203 of the proposed "Economic Security Act."

10. This last point is developed further in the next subsection of this chapter.

11. 36 Fed. Reg. 3868 (Feb. 27, 1971).

12. 45 C.F.R. § 233.90(c)(1)(iii) (1982) (The regulation proceeds to discuss special rules concerning the absence of a parent because of military service or incarceration).

the parent's ability to plan for the present support or care of the child is disrupted by the character of the absence.[13]

Federal Agency Interpretations of the Statute and Regulations—The initial interpretations of the statute were incorporated by the federal agency into the *Handbook of Public Assistance Administration*.[14] As a relatively contemporaneous interpretation of a statute by an agency charged with its enforcement, the interpretation is entitled to significant weight in divining Congressional intent.[15] While many of the provisions regarding absence contained in the *Handbook* were incorporated into the codified regulations, one of the provisions which was not explicitly incorporated deserves note. Entitled "Recognition of the Absent Parent's Role," the provision provides, in part:

> Recognition would be given to the fact that the absent parent is often an important influence in the life of the child. Agency policy and practice, therefore, should provide that decisions affecting the return of the parent to the home, and the maintenance of a relationship between the absent parent and other members of the family be clearly left to the individuals involved. It is consistent with the purpose of the program that policy and practice in no way restrict parents in adopting plans that they consider to be in the interest of themselves and their children, or interfere with continuing relationship of the absent parent with his children, whether the parent is temporarily or permanently out of the home.[16]

More recently, the federal agency has issued interpretations of the continued-absence regulation which bear on the effect of joint custody arrangements in the AFDC absence requirement.[17] In 1976, HEW issued a Policy Interpretation Question (PIQ) on the "Definition of Deprivation and Continued Absence."[18] The Idaho Department of Health and Welfare had interpreted the federal regulation regarding continued absence to require a total cessation of the absent parent's functioning as provider of maintenance, physical care, or guidance. The federal agency explicitly stated that this state interpretation was not consistent with the

---

13. This interpretation was most recently discussed in a memo from Linda S. McMahon to Donald Sutcliffe, Regional Commissioner of Region X in Seattle dated July 9, 1982. That letter can be obtained from the National Clearinghouse for Legal Services, Inc., 407 S. Dearborn, Suite 400, Chicago, IL 60605 by citing Clearinghouse Number CH #36,045D.

14. The *Handbook of Public Assistance Administration* [hereinafter *Handbook*] was a compilation of federal interpretations of the statute published as a guide for the administration of the AFDC program. The *Handbook* has been superseded by the Code of Federal Regulations, but to extent that regulations do not contradict it, it is still used as interpretative.

15. *See, e.g.*, General Electric Co. v. Gilbert, 429 U.S. 125, 141-42 (1976), quoting Skidmore v. Swift & Co., 323 U.S. 134, 140 (1944).

16. *Handbook*, pt. iv, 3422.5(4) (Nov. 4, 1946). Available from the National Clearinghouse for Legal Services, Inc., 407 S. Dearborn, Suite 400, Chicago, IL 60605, CH #36,045A.

17. The federal agency issues policy statement formally through Policy Interpretation Questions (PIQs), Action Transmittals (ATs) and Information Memoranda (IMs) as well as informally through letters to the states. For a discussion of the official and binding status of PIQs, see SSA Action Transmittal 78-28 (OFA, July 11, 1978). Available from National Clearinghouse for Legal Services, CH #36,045B.

18. PIQ 76-182 (Nov. 8, 1976). Available from National Clearinghouse for Legal Services, CH #30,320.

law or federal regulation. Only an interruption in the absent parent's role is necessary to support a finding of absence.

The PIQ also elaborates on the terms of the federal regulation. "Physical care" is defined as "actual day-to-day care in the home such as feeding, dressing, supervising, etc." The PIQ holds that telephone communications and correspondence from an absent parent do not suffice as guidance within the terms of the regulation. The PIQ concludes that "[a] parent who is continuously absent does not, in most instances provide continuous care or guidance on a day-to-day basis."

The absence regulation again was interpreted by the federal agency in a letter dated April 26, 1978.[19] The state of New Jersey argued that when an "absent" parent frequently visits in the home or has frequent contact with the child on a regular basis, then the child is not deprived of support or care by the parent's continued absence from the home. The federal agency explicitly stated that this approach improperly constricts the definition of "continued absence" as set forth in the federal regulation and "is at odds with the underlying spirit and purpose of the AFDC program."[20]

The letter incorporates the idea previously discussed in the *Handbook*; that is, a continuing relationship between the child and absent parent by itself cannot be a basis for not finding absence. "Continued parental involvement is to be encouraged by the AFDC program: premising a finding of ineligibility on the fact of visitation standing alone has the opposite effect."[21]

The third policy statement is an internal agency memorandum prepared in 1982 in response to an inquiry from a Regional Commissioner of the Social Security Administration regarding the extent to which absent parents can maintain contact with their families and still be considered absent for AFDC eligibility purposes.[22] The memorandum states, in part:

> The provision [45 C.F.R. § 233.90(c)(1)(iii)] does not require a total cessation of the parent's contact with his/her children for a finding of 'continued absence.' It is recognized that the absent parent may be an important influence in the life of the child and some contacts between the parent and child are consistent with the purpose of the AFDC program as specified in § 401 of the Act 'to help maintain and strengthen family life.'[23]

The memorandum also reiterates that the parental role encompasses maintenance, physical care, and guidance for the child, and that when one of these elements is missing, continued absence generally will be found to exist provided the parent does not reside in the home. Finally, the memorandum makes clear that a

19. Letter from Florence Aitchision, Acting Assistant Regional Commissioner of Office of Family Assistance, Region II, HEW, to G. Thomas Riti, Director, Div. of Public Welfare, New Jersey Dept. of Human Services. Available from National Clearinghouse for Legal Services, CH #36,045C.

20. *Id.* at 2.

21. *Id.* at 5.

22. Memorandum from Linda S. McMahon, Associate Commissioner for Family Assistance, Office of Family Assistance, Dept. of HEW, to Donald C. Sutcliffe, Regional Commissioner, Social Security Admin., Region X, dated July 9, 1982. Available from National Clearinghouse for Legal Services CH #36,045D.

23. *Id.* at 1.

finding of absence is not dependent upon legal status itself (i.e., when there is a decree of joint custody in a divorce proceeding). Thus, a state agency cannot treat families differently depending upon whether the separation is due to divorce or is not legally formalized. Rather, the determination of absence is dependent upon the "facts of each case."

Case Law and Administrative Decisions on Continued Absence—The recent case law on "continued absence" indicates that if a court or administrative agency is aware of the federal policy statements with respect to the definition of "continued absence," and if specific facts are alleged to support the contention that the father is out of the home and is not a constant presence in the child's life, absence will be found even if the father visits and has some involvement with his child.

In *Pellman v. Heim*,[24] the mother sought judicial review from an adverse administrative decision which upheld a termination of her AFDC benefits. The parents were divorced in 1969; the father maintained a regular pattern of visitation with the daughter, who resided in the mother's home. Based on this pattern of visitation, the state welfare department held that the daughter was not deprived of parental support or care. The three-judge panel of the New Mexico Court of Appeals held that an AFDC recipient who is divorced or separated from the absent parent meets the continued absence requirement unless the state welfare department shows that the absent parent has reestablished residence in the home. The court reinstated the mother's benefits and observed that:

> the purpose of AFDC assistance is to strengthen family life and to promote family solidarity. The director's decision would require [the daughter's] father to live away from her present place of abode and not visit her as often. By his decision the director frustrated, rather than furthered, the policies and purposes of the AFDC program.[25]

The development of the law on continued absence in the state of New Jersey is particularly informative. In 1978, the New Jersey Appellate Division upheld the termination of AFDC benefits based primarily on evidence of visitation in *Shannon v. Department of Human Services*.[26] However, in the case of *Simone v. Division of Public Welfare*,[27] AFDC benefits were reinstated for the mother even though the parents lived in the same multi-family residence and the facts indicated frequent visitation between father and children. In *Simone*, the letter discussed above from HHS to the New Jersey Department of Public Welfare, in which HHS stated that denying AFDC benefits based only on a finding of frequent visitation was inconsistent with federal interpretations, was presented to the court. The court in *Simone* relied heavily on the HHS letter in finding in favor of the mother.

In two more recent decisions on continued absence, the New Jersey Appellate Division held directly that a state policy that denied AFDC benefits based on the

---

24. 87 N.M. 410, 534 P.2d 1122 (N.M. Ct. of App. 1975).
25. *Id.* at 411-12; 534 P.2d at 1123-24.
26. 157 N.J. Super. 251, 384 A.2d 899 (App. Div. 1978).
27. 191 N.J. Super. 228, 465 A.2d 1226 (App. Div. 1983).

father's frequent visitation of his child violated federal policy. In *Matter of Souder*,[28] the court held that the father was absent even though he paid child support consistently, visited the child every day, lived two blocks from the child, and had a continuing relationship with the child's mother. The court held that this evidence in the record was insufficient to show there was no absence. The court stated, "There was no evidence, let alone sufficient credible evidence, that the father provided maintenance, physical care and guidance for the child and could be counted on in planning for the present support or care of that child."[29] In *Burris v. Department of Human Services*,[30] the court similarly held that the virtual day-to-day involvement and concern of the absent parent did not negate a finding of absence for AFDC purposes.

Other courts have also held that visitation does not negate absence. In *Brooks v. Dumpson*,[31] the court held that the fact that a parent resided in the same multi-residential building and visited frequently did not negate absence since there could still be interruption of the parent's ability to function as a provider of care and maintenance. In *Snyder v. Commonwealth Department of Public Welfare*,[32] the mother wished to receive benefits under another program but could not if she was AFDC eligible; she therefore claimed that she was *not* eligible for AFDC benefits because the father was too involved with his child to be absent for AFDC purposes. The court held that frequent visitation and support did not preclude a finding of absence of the parent for AFDC-eligibility purposes.

There have also been unfavorable decisions on the absence/visitation issue in addition to the *Shannon* case cited above. In *Fettrow v. Department of Public Welfare*,[33] the Pennsylvania court upheld the denial of a mother's AFDC benefits based on her admission during the application process that "her husband had been back and forth between her house and his parent's house and had spent some nights with her." The husband also informed the caseworker that he was only "sort of separated" from his spouse.[34] In *Hughes v. Adult and Family Services Division*,[35] the Oregon court upheld the termination of the mother's AFDC benefits based on her admission that the father regularly visited the children every day for a two-month period and visited the children at least every other day during the three months prior to the administrative hearing, that he stored personal items at the mother's home, and that he provided transportation for the mother and children when needed.

Finally, in *Freeman v. Lukhard*,[36] the parents separated but did not obtain a divorce; the mother and three children resided with the maternal parents. The mother received AFDC benefits for herself and her oldest child; however, the two younger children were

---

28. 497 A.2d 1258 (N.J. Super. Ct., App. Div., 1984).
29. 497 A.2d at 1265.
30. 476 A.2d 285 (N.J. Super. Ct., App. Div., 1984).
31. 366 N.Y.S.2d 18, 47 A.D.2d 826 (N.Y. App. Div. 1975).
32. 492 A.2d 124 (Pa. Commonwealth Court, 1985).
33. 47 Pa. C. 220, 407 A.2d 487 (Pa. Commw. Ct. 1979).
34. *Id.* 407 A.2d at 488.
35. 648 P.2d 1324 (Or. Ct. App. 1982). It should be noted that the Oregon absence policy was the subject of the policy memo cited at footnote 21 and that the federal agency spoke disapprovingly of Oregon's denial of AFDC based on a father's pattern of visitation.
36. 465 F. Supp. 1269 (E.D. Va. 1979). Available from the National Clearinghouse for Legal Services, CH #25,053.

denied AFDC benefits because the father visited the younger children daily, discussed their care with the mother, and provided the younger children with milk and diapers. The mother challenged the Virginia state regulations which presumed parental absence when caused by divorce, desertion, incarceration, deportation, or lack of paternity, but in any other situation, required the applicant or recipient to establish that the absent parent does not provide maintenance, physical care, or guidance. The district court upheld the denial of benefits to the two younger children and found the classification based on reasons for absence did not contravene the Social Security Act.

The unfavorable decisions on the absence issue that have been reported generally base their findings on testimony of the lives of the family. There is also no indication in the negative decisions that federal policy on continued absence was presented to the court. As indicated above, the New Jersey courts, while willing to uphold the agency determination of no absence based on frequent visitation in the *Shannon* case, came out clearly against any policy that precluded absence based on visitation once it was presented with federal policy material.

The "Living in the Home" Requirement

Although the question of whether one parent is continually absent from the home when both parents are deeply involved in the child's life is a serious problem in joint custody situations, equally troubling for courts, administrators, and caseworkers trying to determine eligibility for AFDC is the related problem of whether a child whose parents have joint custody is "living in the home" of the parent who is applying for AFDC benefits and whether that parent is, in fact, the child's primary caretaker. Although this issue appears to be less of a problem when the child clearly spends more time in a month or year with one of the parents, it is a serious problem when the split in custody is more even.

Federal Statute—The federal AFDC statute requires that the dependent child, in order to receive aid, live with a specified relative (*e.g.*, father, mother, grandfather, grandmother, aunt, uncle, brother, sister, etc.) "in a place of residence maintained by one or more of such relatives as his or her own home."[37] The "living in the home" and "specified relative" requirements in the AFDC program reflect one of the program's major purposes. Passed during the Depression, Congress sought to ensure that families could keep their children despite poverty and the death, absence, or incapacity of one or both parents, and that the children could be raised in a home with a relative rather than being placed in institutional care. Explaining the need for a federal program for dependent children, the Senate Finance Committee stated in 1935,

> Through cash grants adjusted to the needs of the family, it is possible to keep the young children with their mother in their own home, thus preventing the necessity of placing the children in institutions. This is recognized by everyone to be the least expensive

---

37. 42 U.S.C. §§ 606(a), (c); 45 C.F.R. § 233.90(c)(v)(B).

and altogether the most desirable method for meeting the needs of these families that has yet been devised.[38]

The Senate Report further explains the "living in the home" requirement as confining the dependent-child requirement to children "living with a near relative in a residence (house, room, or other place of abode) maintained by such relative as his own home."[39]

Contemporaneous agency interpretations also indicate that the purpose of the "living in the home requirement" was to ensure that aid was being provided for the purpose it was intended; that is, so that children would grow up in a home with their family. The *Handbook* in 1946 discussed the purpose of the AFDC program: "To live in a family in which he belongs is the foundation of a child's security. The public has an interest and an obligation in sustaining the contribution which parents and immediate family members make to the development of a child."[40]

The purpose of this requirement, therefore, is to ensure that AFDC is provided for children to be raised in a family, homelike setting. As long as the parent applying for AFDC for the child maintains such a home and the child can be said to live there, AFDC should not be denied even if the child is absent from the home sometimes to visit with the absent parent.

Federal Regulation and Agency Interpretations—The federal regulation interpreting the "living in the home" requirement clearly envisions and specifically allows for continuation of benefits to the caretaker relative despite temporary absence of the child from the home. The regulation provides:

> A home is the family setting maintained or in the process of being established, as evidenced by assumption and continuation of responsibility for day to day care of the child by the relative with whom the child is living. A home exists so long as the relative exercises responsibility for the care and control of the child, even though either the child or the relative is temporarily absent from the customary family setting.[41]

Examples of temporary absence are given that include probation or protective services under a court's supervision or legal custody held by a state agency.[42]

The federal agency has stated explicitly in response to a question from the state of Massachusetts on the issue of voluntary commitment that if a child is temporarily absent due to, for example, hospitalization, visits with relatives or friends, or attendance at an overnight school, the child is still living in the home, as long as the caretaker continues to exercise care and control of the child.[43]

---

38. Senate Report No. 628, 74th Cong., 1st Sess. 16 (May 13, 1935).
39. *Id.* at 36.
40. Part IV, § 3401 (Oct. 23, 1946).
41. 45 C.F.R. § 233.90(c)(v)(B).
42. *Id.*
43. Letter from Joseph Mirabella, Regional Administrator for Family Assistance, Dept. of Health and Human Services to H. Reed Witherby, Asst. Attorney General, State of Massachusetts, Apr. 25, 1986. Available from the National Clearinghouse for Legal Services, CH #44,474.

Case Law on *"Living in the Home"*—The courts have also recognized that this regulation applies if the child is temporarily out of the home for other reasons but maintains his home with the caretaker relative and returns there consistently. In *McCarthy v. Commissioner*,[44] two boys for whom AFDC benefits were being paid to the mother were voluntarily committed to the Massachusetts Department of Public Welfare which placed them in residential schools, contracting for 52 weeks of care for them. The Department then tried to terminate AFDC benefits paid on behalf of those children, claiming that the children no longer lived with their mother. The court ruled that AFDC benefits could not be terminated, finding that the boys returned home often and were encouraged to do so by their schools, that the mother maintained a separate bedroom for them although she could have rented a smaller apartment for less money, and that the mother spent money on food, transportation, and telephone calls for the boys. Accordingly, the court ruled that the mother maintained a home for the children that was their home.

Moreover, the court ruled that the mother and the school shared physical custody of the children and that the mother was called about decisions involving their day-to-day supervision. The court, therefore, refused to find that the mother did not have custody of the children and ruled that she was entitled to receive AFDC on their behalf. The court found that their conclusion was supported not only by the governing federal regulations but also by "the principal Congressional goals for this form of assistance, namely, 'enabling each state to furnish financial assistance to needy dependent children and the parents or relatives with whom they are living to help maintain and strengthen family life . . .'"

In *Rist v. Missouri State Division of Family Services*,[45] AFDC was denied a mother who had enrolled her child outside the school district in which she lived so that the child could attend what the mother believed to be a better school. An older, married daughter resided in that school district and the child spent most week nights with her sister although she returned to her mother's home on weekends and when school was not in session. The court held that denial of benefits violated federal AFDC law since the mother still maintained full care and control of the child and, under federal standards, temporary absence from the child's normal family home setting could not be a reason for denying benefits.

Agency statements and court cases recognizing that AFDC benefits should continue to the caretaker relative where the caretaker maintains control of the child and the child's absence is "temporary" are useful in the joint custody context. These cases are particularly useful where the child resides with one caretaker who receives AFDC benefits on his or her behalf for most of the year but spends shorter periods of time with the absent parent, for example, residing with the mother during the school year and with the father at school vacations. The cases are also useful where the child spends the majority of time with the AFDC caretaker, *e.g.*, the week with the mother and the weekends with the father or one overnight with the absent parent during the week. If the parent with primary custody can show she maintains the home for the

44. 392 N.E.2d 159 (Mass. Ct. of App. 1979).
45. 595 S.W.2d 783 (Mo. App. 1980).

child and the absence is temporary, there should be no problem with the "living in the home" requirement.[46] On the other hand, as discussed below, where custody is more evenly divided, the living in the home requirement can present a problem.

Case Law and Administrative Decisions Regarding Joint Custody and AFDC Eligibility

Courts and administrative agencies grappling with the question of AFDC eligibility when parents have a formal or informal joint custody arrangement have most commonly addressed both the issue of where is the child's home and who is his primary caretaker, as well as whether the child is deprived because of the absence of the other parent. Almost all courts and hearing officers that have dealt with this issue have been willing to hold, consistent with federal policy statements, that the underlying facts must be examined closely and that a joint custody decree will not, in and of itself, preclude AFDC eligibility. In cases where eligibility has been established, courts and administrative judges have relied on federal policy and case law holding that the temporary absence of the child from the home does not preclude a finding that the child lives in that home and that visitation by itself will not preclude a finding of absence. These principles have made it somewhat easier to make a case that joint custody should not preclude AFDC eligibility.

Three decisions from state courts in Minnesota, Maine, and Vermont have dealt directly with families in which there was a formal joint custody arrangement. The courts in all three cases followed the directive of the federal policy material to evaluate the fact situations underlying the decree rather than taking the joint custody arrangement as dispositive of "no absence." In the Minnesota case, this resulted in a finding that despite the joint custody language in the decree, the mother really had primary custody of the children and the father was in fact absent. In the Vermont and Maine cases, however, two similar situations that were in fact joint custody arrangements with a 50/50 split in physical custody yielded different results with respect to AFDC eligibility.

In *Sorenson v. State of Minnesota Department of Public Welfare*,[47] the state court refused to find that a court order of joint custody was dispositive that the former husband was not "continually absent" from the family home. The mother of the children sought judicial review from an adverse final administrative decision whereby the Commissioner of Public Welfare reversed the findings of the Welfare Appeals Referee and terminated the family's AFDC benefits. The mother and her former

---

46. In fact, a good argument can be made in such situations where the primary home is with the AFDC caretaker, that there should be no interruption of benefits even if the child spends some extended time with the absent parent, as long as that time is really temporary and time limited and the child will be returning to the AFDC home. *See* Davison v. Department of Health and Welfare, 660 P.2d 54 (Supreme Court of Idaho, 1982) in which the Idaho Supreme Court refused a request from an absent father who had his child for June and July to prorate AFDC benefits for that month between himself and his ex-wife who had custody of the child the rest of the year and thus received AFDC benefits on their behalf. The court found no authority for prorating benefits going to the home where the child normally resided.

47. File No. 768475 (County of Hennepin, 4th Judicial Dist., July 17, 1980). Available from the National Clearinghouse for Legal Services, CH #36045E.

husband shared joint custody of their two children pursuant to court order. The Welfare Appeal Referee found that the former husband actually had custody of the children approximately five or six days per month and that the former husband did not provide any support to the children. No evidence was adduced at the administrative hearing as to whether the former husband gave any guidance to the children or made any decisions regarding their lives. After reviewing this evidence, the court reinstated the appellant's AFDC benefits and stated, in part:

> The decisive question is whether the children are actually receiving maintenance, care, and guidance from both parents. From the record before the Court, the Court must conclude, as did the Referee who heard the matter, that [the former husband] is not in fact providing his children with financial maintenance, physical care and guidance.[48]

Harder issues are raised when the facts behind the joint custody award demonstrate evenly divided custody. In *Munro-Dorsey v. Department of Social Services,*[49] the highest court in the state of Vermont held that absence could be found where the parents had separated and the child spent alternating weeks with each parent. The Supreme Court of Vermont upheld the determination of the Human Services Board reversing the denial of AFDC to the family. The Board had found that although the child spent equal amounts of time with each parent, her "primary home" was with her mother who provided most of her food, clothing, and financial support. The Board was influenced by the fact that the child had a separate room at her mother's but not at her father's, where she slept in the living room, that she kept most of her belongings at her mother's and packed a suitcase to go to her father's, and that her mother often provided food for the child even when the child was with her father. The Board then concluded that the father was absent from the child's primary home and that this absence interrupted his provision of support and care of the child. The Board therefore found the child and her mother AFDC eligible. The Vermont Supreme Court held that the record supported the decision of the Board and upheld the finding of absence and reinstatement of AFDC benefits.

On the other hand, the Supreme Judicial Court of Maine was unwilling to reinstate AFDC benefits in a joint custody arrangement not significantly different from the one held to support eligibility in *Munro-Dorsey*. In *Francis v. Commissioner of Department of Human Services,*[50] the parents were divorced with joint custody specified in the divorce decree. As provided in the custody order, the children spent the first fourteen days of each month with their father and the remainder of the month with their mother. The children's clothes and belongings remained at their mother's and they packed a suitcase to go to their father's. The father paid child support of $350.00 per month. The Commissioner of Welfare denied AFDC benefits to the mother concluding that, under the facts shown at the hearing, care and control of the children as well as physical custody were shared almost equally by the parents. In light

---

48. *Id.* at 2 (citations omitted).
49. 481 A.2d 1055 (Supreme Court of Vermont, 1984).
50. 513 A.2d 859 (Supreme Judicial Court of Maine, 1986).

of this, the Commissioner found both that the children did not continuously reside in the home of the mother and that the father was not absent within the meaning of the federal regulations because there was no interruption in his provision of support and care for the children.

The Maine court upheld this finding as supported by the record. The court refused to find that the children's home was with the mother because they spent so much of the month living in their father's home. The court stated that AFDC is a monthly system of benefits and, accordingly, in order to receive benefits, the child must live with a specified relative in the relative's home throughout the month. In response to plaintiff's argument that this position was contrary to federal requirements because it required that the child be "continuously" in the home all month in order to qualify for benefits, the court responded that temporary absences from the home do not preclude AFDC eligibility. In fact, the court quoted the Commissioner of Welfare's statement that when a child's time with one parent significantly exceeds the time spent with the other parent, then it is a fair question as to whether the time with the second parent is really only visitation rather than care or control. In those cases, questions of who is actually making decisions and who has predominant supervision of the child would govern whether there is absence. However, the court found that in a case where the children do not spend more than 17 days with the mother, the absence of the child could not really be characterized as temporary. The court thus upheld the Welfare Department's conclusion that the children did not continuously reside in the home of the mother since physical possession as well as care and control were shared equally by the two parents in any given month and that, therefore, "both parents provide homes for the children, each for approximately two weeks at a time, rather than one parent merely providing accommodations for visits."[51] It went on to uphold the finding that the father was not continually absent since he lived across the street from the mother's house and cared for the children fourteen days in each month. The administrative finding that the children were not AFDC eligible was thus upheld.

The contrary results in these two rather similar cases demonstrate the problem of establishing AFDC eligibility in a case where custody is evenly or roughly evenly divided between father and mother. The key question, however, in both cases, appeared to be whether the home of the caretaker applying for aid could be viewed as the child's home for AFDC purposes. Once the "primary home" conclusion was reached in *Munro v. Dorsey*, the court had no problem upholding the finding that the father was absent from the home and his absence interrupted his ability to provide support or care for the children. Conversely, the Maine court's inability to find that the child's home was with the mother for AFDC purposes was fatal to their request for benefits.

It should also be noted that these decisions indicate that courts do tend to view the question of whether a child in a joint custody arrangement is AFDC eligible as a factual rather than a legal question. This means that the decisions of the agency in these matters will often be sustained if the facts can be seen as supporting that decision. As can be seen here, the facts in an evenly divided custody situation are such that

---

51. 513 A.2d at 862.

they can actually support contrary findings, but a court reviewing the agency's decision on a substantial evidence review will be inclined to support what the agency has done.

Decision making at the administrative level where the facts are presented is thus extremely important. There have been numerous administrative decisions in which AFDC eligibility has been found despite a joint custody arrangement and these are discussed below.

In three fair-hearing decisions in Ohio, Washington, and New Hampshire, the hearing officers reversed denial of AFDC benefits where the denial or termination of benefits was based solely on the existence of a formal joint custody arrangement. These administrative officers ruled that joint custody did not automatically preclude a finding of absence for AFDC purposes and the cases had to be decided by examining the facts on a case-by-case basis. In the Ohio case,[52] the parents had the children in alternating months and in the New Hampshire case[53] the children were with the parents on alternate weeks. In the Washington case,[54] the joint custody order specified that the father would have the children on weekdays and the mother would have them on weekends. The hearing officer reinstated benefits, ruling that a joint custody decree could not form the basis for a finding that there was no continued absence of the father from the home.

In three hearing decisions in Massachusetts, Minnesota, and Oregon, the hearing examiners looked closely at evidence concerning the quality of care given by the parents in determining that the parents applying for benefits provided the home for the child for AFDC purposes and that the other parent was absent from it. In the Massachusetts case, the mother and father were given joint custody following a divorce. The hearing officer found the mother to be the caretaker for AFDC purposes with the father absent even though the children resided with the mother only on weekends and one night a week and spent vacations with her. The administrative law judge reasoned that the children were in school most of the time when they were with their father so that the mother was the primary caregiver.[55]

In re Clinton,[56] the mother and father alternated physical custody of the son two weeks at a time with the father taking the boy on the first Friday night of the month until two weeks later. The child's possessions remained at the mother's and the mother provided the child with medication and clothing while he stayed with the father. The father's mother cared for the child most of the time during the two weeks the child lived with the father. The hearing officer ruled that the mother was the caretaker relative since she provided the majority of the care for the child and that the father did not have sufficient involvement with the child to negate absence for AFDC eligibility.

---

52. Appeal No. 506856, Ohio Department of Human Services (Nov. 27, 1985).
53. Department of Health and Welfare, State of New Hampshire, June 15, 1984. Available from National Clearinghouse for Legal Services, CH #36,045L.
54. *In re JM*, State of Washington, Department of Social and Health Services, Dkt. No. 0482A-463 (June 8, 1982). Available from National Clearinghouse for Legal Services, CH #36,045F.
55. Fair Hearing Decision No. 131058. Available from National Clearinghouse for Legal Services, CH #44,475.
56. State of Oregon, Dept. of Human Resources, Adult and Family Services Div., Case No. 2-2003-BE2066-6 (Apr. 8, 1988). Available from National Clearinghouse for Legal Services, CH #44,476.

In the Minnesota case, *In re Mary M.*,[57] denial of AFDC benefits to a mother where the father visited daily and babysat regularly was reversed. The hearing officer found that the mother was the sole financial support of the child and:

> In terms of physical care or guidance the mother is the sole provider. The absent father does not feed, clothe or bathe the child. He performs no household duties and makes no decisions regarding the child's physical or emotional well being. The mere physical presence of the father in the home of the child on a frequent basis is insufficient to establish him as a provider or preclude him from being considered continually absent . . .

An approach that seems to underlie some of the joint custody decisions, that a child suffers deprivation when there is a divorce regardless of whether he spends time with both parents, was articulated in two California and one New Hampshire decision. In two California decisions, the hearing officers ruled that even where there is a joint custody arrangement or decree, there is an ongoing disassociation of the family, and even if the child spends time with both parents, the child is deprived of parental support and care and should receive AFDC on that basis. In both cases, the mother was awarded benefits. *In the Matter of SF*,[58] the mother had custody of the child from Monday through Thursday and the father had the child Thursday through Monday morning. The hearing officer found that one parent was continuously absent from the home where the child was living at all times and that the mother took more care of the child. In the other case,[59] the child lived with the father from the first through the fifteenth of each month and then lived with the mother. The hearing officer in that case also ruled that there was continual absence for the child wherever he was, and that the facts indicated that the mother should get the benefits.

A similar result was obtained in New Hampshire[60] where the state welfare department terminated the mother's AFDC grant because, the state welfare department alleged, the divorced parents had joint custody and the children spent approximately forty percent of their time with the father so that the father could not be considered continuously absent. The hearing officer reversed this decision, finding that the facts at the hearing showed that the children spent 206 days a year with the mother, residing with the father at various times during a month, that the children attended school in the mother's community, that the mother provided for the children's medical and dental care, and that the mother considered herself as "having ultimate daily responsibility for the children."[61]

---

57. State of Minnesota, Dept. of Public Welfare, Dkt. No. 6387 (Feb. 26, 1981). Available from National Clearinghouse for Legal Services, CH #36,045J.

58. California Dept. of Social Services, State Hearing No. 83131081 (Aug. 8, 1983). Available from National Clearinghouse for Legal Services, CH #36,045G.

59. California Fair Hearing Decision, Hearing No. 82238107 (Dec. 6, 1982). Available from National Clearinghouse for Legal Services, CH #36,045K.

60. New Hampshire Fair Hearings Decision, Portsmouth Div. office (Feb. 23, 1984). Available from National Clearinghouse for Legal Services, CH #36,045H.

61. As of October 1, 1981, a waiting period of thirty days to establish absence due to separation, divorce, or desertion was required in five states: Kentucky, New Hampshire, Oregon, Vermont, and

In light of this, the hearing officer designated the mother's residence as the children's home because the children resided with the mother for the majority of time. He then went on to find that New Hampshire's requirement that "continued absence" be the continued absence of the parent "from the home" for at least thirty days was fulfilled because the father was continuously absent from the mother's home for more than thirty days. The hearing officer then found that the father's role as a parent had been interrupted even though he spent a good deal of time with the children. He based this finding on the fact that the father's parental functions of care and guidance were interrupted every time the children returned to the mother's home.

Despite the tendency of courts and hearing officers to try to continue benefits despite a joint custody decree or arrangement where the facts can be construed to support such a decision, there have been hearing decisions in which denial of AFDC benefits was upheld due to the nature of the custody arrangement.[62] In Minnesota, for example, a hearing officer upheld denial of benefits finding there was no continued absence where the mother was awarded joint custody of the two minor children. The father visited the children daily for four to six hours at the mother's home. In essence, the father served as a babysitter for the children during the mother's work hours. Although the mother established that she prepared the children for school, assisted the children with their homework, prepared their food, and arranged for their medical care, the administrative decision upheld the termination of benefits. The hearing officer cited the great amount of time during which the father cared for the children and found that no deprivation existed.

Model State Policies on Joint Custody

Because joint custody arrangements do raise issues with respect to the "living in the home" and "absence" requirements of the AFDC program, it is extremely useful for states to have clear policies with respect to joint custody and AFDC eligibility. Clear policies can make it easier for family law practitioners and family courts to make arrangements for the children with some certainty of the effect those arrangements will have on potential eligibility for public benefits. They also make decision making more consistent, since, as we have seen, reasonable courts and administrators can differ over whether a given joint custody fact pattern gives rise to AFDC eligibility.

Several states have policies in their welfare manuals or regulations which are explicit with respect to the "absence" and "living in the home" requirements when there is joint custody. In Pennsylvania, a previous state policy precluded AFDC eligibility if the parents each had the children 50% of the time. Under a policy, which

---

Washington. Three states required a thirty-day period to establish absence for any reason: Ohio, South Carolina, and Texas (except Ohio required a seven-day waiting period if the absence was due to divorce, separation, or desertion). Massachusetts imposed a twenty-day waiting period to establish absence for any reason. The remaining states did not use a period of time to define absence.
    62. Minnesota Fair Hearing Decision, No. 6240, Hennepin County, Jan. 8, 1981. Available from National Clearinghouse for Legal Services, #36,045.

became effective September 1, 1988, in a joint or shared-custody situation, the parent applying for assistance is designated the caretaker relative and the other parent is automatically considered the absent parent. The caretaker is expected to comply with all AFDC eligibility requirements including assigning support and cooperating in obtaining support. She is designated the caretaker and receives AFDC on behalf of the child.[63]

In 1987, Wisconsin statutes were amended, effective in 1988, to include a section on joint custody as a preferred mode of resolving custody disputes. Under the new statute, the courts are instructed that, "In making an order of joint legal custody and periods of physical placement, the court may specify one parent as the primary caretaker of the child for the purpose of determining eligibility for aid . . ."[64] At the time this statute was passed, Wisconsin's AFDC manual was amended to provide specifically for determinations in joint custody cases. Under the Wisconsin policy, if the court has designated a "primary caretaker" in the award, that is the person who should be considered the caretaker for AFDC purposes. If the court decree is silent on this, the caseworker asks the parents to designate a primary caretaker and, if they respond within the thirty day processing period, she uses their response. If the parents do not respond within 30 days, the caseworker has a checklist of questions she is to use in determining the AFDC caretaker.[65] Those questions are:

1. If the parents reside in different school districts, which school does the child attend?

2. Who helps the child with homework and other school related tasks?

3. If there are tuition costs for the child's school, who pays?

4. If the child is enrolled in day care, who arranges for and pays those costs?

5. Who is responsible for taking the child to and from school and/or day care?

6. Which parent is listed as the school or day care contact for emergencies?

7. Who arranges medical and dental care for the child? Who selects the doctor and maintains the child's medical records?

8. Who initiates decisions regarding the child's future?

9. Who responds to medical or law enforcement emergencies involving the child?

10. Who spends money on food or clothing for the child when the child visits the absent parent?

11. Who disciplines the child?

12. Who plays with the child and arranges for entertainment?

---

63. Commonwealth of Pennsylvania, *Income Maintenance Bulletin*, No. 153-88-1 (Aug. 15, 1988). Available from National Clearinghouse for Legal Services, CH #44,477.

64. 1987 Wisconsin Act 355, effective May 3, 1988, § 767.24(6)(c).

65. These questions are taken verbatim from Jim Johnson's 1984 article on joint custody: *The Effect of Joint Custody or Similar Arrangements on AFDC Eligibility*, 18 Clearinghouse Review.

13. Are more of the child's toys, clothing, etc. kept at one of the parent's homes than at the other?[66]

(Ed. note: California has almost identical language as Wisconsin's to resolve problems regarding qualifications for AFDC. The California legislation, and specifically CC § 4600.5(h), is discussed in Chapter 20, which follows.)

In Alaska, in response to litigation on Alaska's policy of denying AFDC benefits in cases where the absent father visited extensively with his child, the Alaska Department of Health and Social Services agreed to a policy of finding absence automatically where (1) the absent parent has an address separate from the caretaker and child and (2) the absent parent spends less than 49% of the month with the child. The policy also provides that an award of joint or shared custody does not negate absence and that if the parents agree on who is the primary caretaker, no further development is necessary.[67]

All these state policies focus on the designation of the AFDC applicant as the primary caretaker with whom the child resides. Once that is established, absence is assumed as long as the absent parent resides separately. This seems to reflect recognition that divorce or separation ensure that the other parent is not present on a day-to-day basis in the child's home and that this will satisfy federal absence requirements even if the child spends substantial time with the absent parent.

AFDC Considerations in Joint Custody Awards

Several principles emerge from examining the case law in this area. First, the fact of a joint custody award is unlikely to, standing alone, preclude AFDC eligibility. The federal eligibility criteria set with respect to "absence" and "living in the home" requirements clearly direct a case-by-case evaluation, looking at all the facts. Fact finders and judicial decision makers have seemed to accept this directive and most decisions pro or con repeat it, proceeding to rely on the facts of the particular family situation in making a decision on benefit qualifications.

Second, where one of the parents clearly has the child more of the time, overnight, weekend, or summertime visits should not preclude a finding that the child resides in the home. Similarly, in such situations, the argument that the other parent's involvement with the child does not negate absence can be supported by federal policy on visitation and case law on continued absence.

Clearly, the more difficult issues are presented in cases where the facts show equal or nearly equal sharing of custody. Although many courts and hearing officers are willing to find AFDC eligibility in such situations, a serious analysis of the facts must be undertaken in those cases. Most usually, the court or hearing officer will first look at the facts to determine whether the AFDC applicant is the primary caretaker and

---

66. Wisconsin Income Maintenance Manual, No. 87-02. Available from National Clearinghouse for Legal Services, CH #44,478.

67. Sorenson v. Munson, Case No. 3AN-86-14231 (Superior Court for the State of Alaska, Third Judicial District, Feb. 22, 1988). Available from National Clearinghouse for Legal Services, CH #41,769.

her home is the home in which the child lives. Decision makers consider the amount of time actually spent with each parent as well as such underlying indicators as: where the child keeps most of his/her things, whether he/she packs a suitcase to go to the other parent's house, whether the child has his/her own room at one home but not the other, what the nature of the contact between parent and child is when the child is in the home of that particular parent (*e.g.*, is a babysitter used), and whether the primary parent continues to provide some care and direction even when the child is with the other parent. The checklist incorporated in the Wisconsin joint custody policy discussed above is a good one for thinking of evidentiary considerations that might be useful in establishing the AFDC applicant's home as the child's home.

Once it is established that the relative applying for benefits maintains the child's home, the question of whether the other parent is "absent" for AFDC purposes arises. Here again, particular facts must be established. Most critical is that the other parent lives separately from the AFDC family. Once that is established, unless a state has a clear policy like those discussed above which assume absence in a joint custody situation, it will be necessary to show some interruption of day-to-day support and care of the child in order for the child to be AFDC qualified on the basis of the parent's absence. Such interruption can be shown by lack of involvement during the time the child is with the AFDC-caretaker parent and by some of the same factors that went into establishing the primary home. Generally, the facts which indicate that the AFDC caretaker's involvement is primary and the absent parent's contact is more like visitation are useful.

If AFDC eligibility is or may be an issue for one of the parents in a situation where joint custody seems indicated, it is important that the lawyer representing the parent take this into account in determining how to frame the custody award. A few suggestions follow.

1. *Language in the award or decree.* As indicated, the fact that a decree or award states that the parents will have "joint custody" should not be dispositive of AFDC eligibility. Nevertheless, there may be information or statements made in a divorce decree or custody agreement or order which indicate more specific facts about the arrangements for the child and this can certainly be used either as sword or as shield in an AFDC-eligibility determination. Therefore, first, it is probably a good idea to avoid the use of the term "joint custody" in the decree unless there is a reason, such as the state's preference for such awards, to use the term. Second, if possible, it is probably a good idea to specify the primary caretaker as the parent most likely to need assistance. Third, if possible, characterizing the other parent's time with the child as visitation is also likely to be helpful.

2. *Language on parental responsibilities.* Where joint custody is preferred by the courts, parties, or because of a statutory preference for such an arrangement, and there is a problem with designating a primary caretaker, it would be useful to include some language indicating heavier parental responsibilities for the parent more likely to need public assistance.

3. *Documentation of anecdotal information showing greater parental role.* Arrangements which include keeping the child's belongings at the home of the parent who is more likely to be applying for aid, taking primary responsibility for child-care arrangements, etc. should be documented by the client at the beginning of the separation and the client should be advised that it may be helpful to be able to document her greater role in caring for the child should she ever need public assistance.

4. *Testimony at hearings.* Attorneys representing clients involved in divorce proceedings should consider what impact testimony taken in the course of the proceeding will have on eligibility for public benefits. Conversely, if the client is going to a hearing on a benefits determination, the attorney should consider what impact her testimony might have on the divorce proceeding.

5. *Clear state policies.* In states which do not have clear policies on what the impact of a joint custody award is on AFDC eligibility, consideration should be given to the policies adopted by Wisconsin, Pennsylvania, and Alaska. Those policies make the implications of custody decisions for benefits clear to all those who need to consider them and ensure more consistent decision making throughout the state.

20

California Joint Custody Retrospective

HUGH McISAAC

Hugh McIsaac, Director of Family Court Services in Los Angeles, has been involved in the California joint custody legislation from its beginning. Here he examines California's joint custody statute. After presenting the legislative background, McIsaac outlines the major concepts addressed in the original California statute, in addition to those highlighted in 1988 amendments. McIsaac next presents several important case decisions which have affected the implementation of joint custody laws in California and identifies future trends. Concluding remarks include comments about the response of various special-interest groups to joint custody legislation, and suggestions directed at both parents and courts for successful implementation of joint custody. This chapter is particularly instructive to those in states with legislation influenced by the California law, as well as those in states considering joint custody amendments.

California's joint custody legislation, once again, has focused attention upon the concept of joint custody and its impact upon children and families. Some confusion exists around 1988 amendments to California's joint custody legislation, just as confusion existed around the original legislation. The purpose of this chapter is to examine California's joint custody statute, and the recent amendments, in order to

Hugh McIsaac, M.S.W., is the Director of Family Court Services, Los Angeles County Superior Court, Past President of the Association of Family and Conciliation Courts, and Editor of Conciliation Courts Review.

understand the forces shaping the legislative landscape in one of life's most hostile arenas—a child-custody dispute.

In August 1988, Governor Deukmejian signed Senate Bill 1306[1] into law. This bill, which became effective in 1989, clarifies California's law indicating no preference for joint or sole custody and requires parents to select, or courts to order, a "parenting plan in the best interest of the child." This legislation, along with some of the studies by Judith Wallerstein, Janet Johnston, and others, reported elsewhere in this volume, has raised new questions about joint custody. Some of the media, in its rush for controversy as opposed to careful analysis and understanding, have pushed these studies far beyond what the authors intended. Neither these studies nor the passage of SB 1306 challenge the viability of joint custody, rather they require us to examine the implementation of joint custody on a case-by-case basis.

Background

A brief review of the history of joint custody legislation in California will help put recent amendments in context. In 1980, California became the fifth state to legislatively adopt a joint custody option, but California's "frequent and continuing . . ." language became the model for most other statutes. The history of this legislation provides important clues to its proper interpretation. California's law stated it was "presumed to be in the best interest [of the child] if the parents agree [to joint custody] . . . ," creating a presumption for parental agreement, not a presumption or a preference for joint custody absent agreement. The statute allowed wide discretion between joint and sole custody when the parents did not agree, reaffirming the standard for decision as "the best interest of the children."

This 1980 law was essentially conservative, describing and defining events already occurring in private arrangements between parents. The legislation grew out of a dialectic conflict between the Smith Bill SB 477, sponsored by the Senate Subcommittee on the Administration of Justice, and the Imbrecht Bill AB 1480, pushed by fathers' groups who wanted a preference or presumption for joint custody.[2] The Smith Bill for the most part prevailed, establishing in California Civil Code Section 4600 an option for joint custody, but requiring the judge to consider, "which parent is more likely to allow the child or children frequent and continuing contact with the noncustodial parent" as a factor. This provision was included in the legislation, as a compromise between SB 477 and AB 1480, to ameliorate the supporters of a preference.[3] This was later dubbed the "friendly parent" provision by feminist critics of joint custody legislation.[4]

---

1. SB 1306, Cal. Leg., Reg. Sess. (1988), now Cal. Civil Code § 4600(d).
2. Steven Belzer & Hon. Billy G. Mills, "Joint Custody as a Parenting Alternative," *Pepperdine Law Review*, 9:853, 1982.
3. James Cook, "Joint Custody, Sole Custody: A New Statute Reflects a New Perspective," *Conciliation Courts Review*, 18(1), 1980.
4. Final Report of the California State Senate Task Force on Family Equity, June 1, 1987.

The Revised California Legislation

Two attempts were made to amend California Civil Code Section 4600 to declare a clear preference or presumption for joint custody. In 1982, Assemblyman Kapiloff carried Bill AB 1706, sponsored by fathers' groups. In 1983, Assemblyman Imbrecht introduced AB 2202. Opposition to these bills centered around the issue of preferences and presumptions, and the negative, unintended consequences these preferences and presumptions have for families where such an arrangement is not preferred. The real debate was not about the issue of joint custody, but the extent to which the legislation should promote it in the absence of parental agreement.

Opponents pointed out that macro preferences break down in micro application to individual families and place extraordinary burdens on those families where such arrangements are not preferred. Preferences also establish bargaining valences which can be traded off, such as "I will not press my claim for joint custody, if you give me a break on support." AB 2202 was amended into a compromise bill establishing an order of consideration, but no preference. This bill was vetoed by Governor Brown in September, 1982. This legislation and the attendant arguments, however, were instrumental in identifying the need to clarify California's statute through SB 1306.

A component missing from the early debate and opposition to joint custody was the concerns of some feminists. In fact, the women's movement was strangely silent during much of the early debate on joint custody.

With the publication in 1985 of the *Divorce Revolution*[5] the silence changed to a roar. The opposition had found an articulate spokesperson in Lenore Weitzman, who advocated a "primary caretaker" standard. (See Chapter 18 of this volume which attempts to reconcile the primary-caretaker preference with the preference for joint custody.) This standard was in the original version of SB 1306, before the Assembly Judiciary Committee approved the greatly amended version, which restated current law holding no preference for or against joint custody.

Two claims were advanced by these critics: (1) joint custody eroded the traditional role of women as caretakers of children, and (2) fathers were not as interested in taking care of children as they were in reducing support. The feminist opposition to joint custody centered primarily around the latter concern.

Ironically, the war over joint custody legislation now mirrored the war over individual children. Fathers and mothers were elevating parental rights over the needs of their children. Too often, the needs of the children were not being represented.

Frequent and Continuing Contact; Shared Rights and Responsibilities

The original preamble to California Civil Code Section 4600 as it was enacted in 1980 reads as follows: "(a) The legislature finds and declares that it is the public policy of this state to assure minor children frequent and continuing contact with

---

5. Lenore Weitzman, *The Divorce Revolution: The Unexpected Social and Economic Consequences for Women and Children in America*, New York: Macmillan, 1985.

both parents after the parents have separated or dissolved their marriage, and to encourage parents to share the rights and responsibilities of child rearing in order to effect this policy."[6]

This preamble to California's original joint custody legislation set the theme for parental involvement of both parents in the life of their child or children. This sentence was first enunciated in SB 477. In the final version of the statute, as amended by AB 1480, it was moved to the initial statement as part of the compromise between the competing interests.[7] This sentence found its way into most of the statutes passed in other jurisdictions in legislation developed after the California law. Most recently, the initial version of SB 1306 attempted to remove this language, and in subsequent amendments move it to the section dealing only with joint custody.[8]

The children's preference is addressed in the California statute:

> In any proceeding where there is at issue the custody of a minor child, the court may, during the pendency of the proceeding or at any time thereafter, make such order for the custody of the child during minority as may seem necessary and proper. If a child is or sufficient age and capacity to reason so as to form an intelligent preference as to custody, the court shall consider and give due weight to the wishes of the child in making an award of custody or modification thereof. . . .[9]

This section was carried over from prior law, and allows the court to consider wishes of children of "sufficient age and capacity to reason." Generally, California courts have given reduced weight to children's wishes when the child is under twelve years of age; between the ages of 12 and 14, the wishes of the child are given substantial weight; and for children over the age of 14, the wishes of the child are usually controlling.[10]

Determination of Custody; Parenting Plan

The following language from the original 1980 legislation has been the source of considerable misunderstanding and controversy:

> (b) Custody should be awarded in the following order of preference according to the best interests of the child pursuant to Section 4608:
>
> (1) To both parents jointly pursuant to Section 4600.5 or to either parent. In making an order for custody to either parent, the court shall consider, among other factors, which parent is more likely to allow the child or children frequent and continuing contact with the noncustodial parent, and shall not prefer a parent as custodian because of that parent's sex.

---

6. Cal. Civil Code § 4600 (West 1990).
7. James Cook, "California's Joint Custody Law," in J. Folberg, *Joint Custody and Shared Parenting,* Washington, Bureau of National Affairs, 1984.
8. Final Report, *Senate Task Force on Family Equity,* Calif. State Senate, 1987.
9. Cal. Civil Code § 4600 (a) (West 1990).
10. Hon. Frances Rothschild & Ovie Miller, "Custody," in *1989 Family Law Symposium,* Los Angeles, CA.: Family Law Section, Los Angeles County Bar Association, 1989, pp. 5003–33.

Joint custody and sole custody are co-equal under the above language, and neither is given preference over the other. The major criteria for making the decision is the best interest of the child. However, among other factors, the judge must still consider which parent is most likely to allow the other parent frequent and continuing contact. This provision continues to be opposed, without success, by many groups representing women. They contend this provision has been used by fathers to force mothers to enter into joint custody agreements out of the fear that not doing so might be construed as "not willing to allow the other parent frequent and continuing contact," which in turn might result in the award of sole custody to the father. The court, in its discretion, may require the parents to submit to the court a plan for the implementation of the custody order.

Also included in (b)(1) is a paragraph giving courts permission to request parties in agreement to submit a parenting plan even though they agree. The purpose of this provision was to provide the court with information to evaluate the effectiveness of the plan in light of the child's best interest. The State of Washington has taken this concept one step further and as of January 1, 1989, requires all parents to file a parenting plan prior to the granting of the final decree.[11] The California Legislature in 1989 considered similar legislation to eliminate the inflammatory and possessory words "custody" and "visitation," but the legislation was not passed.[12]

Custody When Neither Parent Is to Be Decreed Custodian of the Child

The statute lists the following order of preference when neither parent is to be decreed custodian of the child: "(2) If to neither parent, to the person or persons in whose home the child has been living in a wholesome and stable environment; (3) to any other person or persons deemed by the court to be suitable and able to provide adequate and proper care and guidance for the child." Before custody is awarded to anyone other than a parent without the consent of the parents, the court must make a finding that an award of custody to either of the parents would be detrimental to the child and the award to the nonparent is required to serve the best interests of the child.

No Preference for or Presumption Against Joint Custody

After much contention between mothers' and fathers' groups, the following section was added in 1989 to California's joint custody statute:

(d) This section establishes neither a preference nor a presumption for or against joint legal custody, joint physical custody, or sole custody, but allows the court and the family the widest discretion to choose a parenting plan which is in the best interest of the child or children.[13]

---

11. Washington Stats. 1988.
12. AB 1612, 1989, Bates, died pursuant to Art. IV, Sec. 10(a) of the California Constitution.
13. This writer drafted the final version of SB 1306 as a compromise measure. The original version of SB 1306 would have extensively revised current law and the initial proposal contained a primary-caretaker presumption.

This paragraph clarifies the intent of the original law which stated no preference for or against joint custody.[14] Yet, several appellate court decisions had interpreted the law as establishing a joint custody preference and much confusion existed over whether or not California had a preference statute. The language in this amendment gives families and courts the "widest discretion" to choose a parenting plan in the best interest of the children. The language of the statute emphasizes the family's responsibility to decide and uses the concept of a parenting plan instead of custody, focusing on the child's needs rather than the elevation of the parents' possessory interest.

4600.5 Joint Custody; agreement or application by parents; statement of reasons for granting or denial; definitions; orders of joint legal or joint physical custody; contents; modification or termination; parental access to records; notice to other parent of change of residence.

Joint Custody Is in the "Best Interest of the Child" When Parents Are in Agreement

(a) There shall be a presumption, affecting the burden of proof, that joint custody is in the best interests of a minor child, subject to Section 4608, *where the parents have agreed* [emphasis added] to an award of joint custody or so agree in open court at a hearing for the purpose of determining the custody of a minor child of the marriage.

The presumption is for agreement, not joint custody. Misreading this paragraph as a presumption for joint custody has probably been the major source of confusion with regard to California's law. Importantly, what this paragraph does is reinforce the right of parents to make decisions about their children without court intrusion, so long as they are not harmful to their children and are subject to the same abuse and neglect standards applied to mothers and fathers who live together. In effect, the state acknowledges that parents know their children best, and only in extreme circumstances should it assume the fundamental responsibility of deciding how and with whom a child should live.

Investigation to Determine Appropriateness of Joint Custody

(b) Upon application of either parent, joint custody may be awarded in the discretion of the court in other cases, subject to section 4608.[15] For the purpose of assisting the

---

14. For an excellent discussion of the legislative intent and history of California's joint custody statute, see Hon. Billy G. Mills & Steven P. Belzer, *Pepperdine Law Review*, 9:853, 1982. Belzer was counsel to the California Senate Subcommittee on Administration of Justice and was the primary drafter of California's statute. Judge Mills was a member of the committee and Supervising Judge of the Los Angeles County Superior Court, Family Law Department.

15. Added by stats. 1982, c. 359, p. 2; amended by stats. 1984, c. 1679, p. 3. Calif. Civil Code reads:

In making a determination of the best interest of the child in any proceeding under this title, the court shall, among other factors it finds relevant, consider all of the following:

(a) The health, safety and welfare of the child.
(b) Any history of abuse against the child. . . .
(c) The nature and amount of contact with both parents.

court in making a determination whether an award of joint custody is appropriate under this subdivision, the court may direct that an investigation be conducted pursuant to section 4602.

The court has wide discretionary powers in making decisions deemed to be in the best interest of the child. Section 4608 was added in 1982 as a guide to the court in considering factors for making such decisions. Considerable attention has been paid to this section, and currently the Judicial Council's Family Law Advisory Committee[16] is considering revising this section to better reflect best-interest considerations.

Statement of Reasons for Denial/Granting of Joint Custody

(c) Whenever a request for joint custody is granted or denied, the court, upon the request of any party, shall state in its decision the reasons for granting or denying the request. A statement that joint custody is, or is not, in the best interests of the child shall not be sufficient to meet the requirements of this subdivision.

This section was amended to require the court to state reasons for its decision "upon the request" of either party. This amendment's aim was to require the trier-of-fact to identify specific conditions or behaviors used to reach the decision. The record then might serve as a basis for an appeal if the decision was questioned. This section originally was proposed as a compromise between SB 477 sponsors who wanted to preserve wide discretion for the courts, and AB 1408 advocates who wanted a preference for joint custody. When SB 477 supporters prevailed, this section was added to deal with the concerns of the AB 1408 sponsors who felt the courts would ignore the joint custody option.

Definition of Terms

(d) For the purposes of this part:

   (1) "Joint custody" means joint physical and joint legal custody.

   (2) "Sole physical custody" means that a child shall reside with and under the supervision of one parent, subject to the power of the court to order visitation.

   (3) "Joint physical custody" means that each of the parents shall have significant periods of physical custody. Joint physical custody shall be shared by the parents in such a way so as to assure a child of frequent and continuing contact with both parents.

---

16. The Judicial Council's Family Law Committee of the State of California was convened in 1987 by Chief Justice Malcolm Lucas to advise the Judicial Council regarding family law issues, and to assist the Council in its rule-making responsibilities.

(4) "Sole legal custody" means that one parent shall have the right and the responsibility to make decisions relating to the health, education, and welfare of a child.

(5) "Joint legal custody" means that both parents shall share the right and the responsibility to make decisions relating to the health, education, and welfare of a child.

This section was added in 1984 to better define terms and assist the court in developing joint custody orders. Considerable confusion on the part of parents and the courts existed about elements involved in joint custody. The definitions clearly distinguish between making decisions about childrearing (joint legal), where a child will live (joint physical), and the amount of time spent with each parent. Joint physical custody, for example, does not have to be a fifty-fifty split between parents. In fact, most plans involve the child spending more time with one parent, and in only 9% to 14% of cases do children spend equal time with their parents.[17,18]

Situations Requiring Consent of Both Parents; Situations Where Parent May Act Alone

(e) In making an order of joint legal custody, the court shall specify the circumstances under which the consent of both parents is required to be obtained in order to exercise legal control of the child and the consequences of the failure to obtain mutual consent. In all other circumstances, either parent acting alone may exercise legal control of the child. An order of joint legal custody shall not be construed to permit any action that is inconsistent with the physical custody order unless the action is expressly authorized by the court.

This section was added to require courts to define in their orders those situations needing the consent of both parents. It also specified when either parent could make decisions where an order was silent. To do otherwise would leave decision making related to the child in limbo. Current mediation practice in developing parenting plans often involves drafting a "meet and confer" requirement. Such plans spell out how and when the parents shall meet to make intermediate and long range childrearing decisions. Short-term decisions not affecting the care and control by the other parent may be made without consultation by the parent having temporary physical custody.

Rights and Remedies Regarding Physical Control of Children

(f) In making an order of joint physical custody, the court shall specify the rights of each parent to physical control of the child in sufficient detail to enable a parent deprived of that control to implement laws for relief of child snatching and kidnapping.

---

17. Robert Mnookin, presentation at the Association of Family and Conciliation Conference, Long Beach, California, May 1988.
18. Hugh McIsaac, "Court-Connected Mediation," *Conciliation Courts Review*, 21(2), 1983.

This section was added to the original statute to deal with the child-stealing issue. Penal Code section 278[19] also was changed, making the removal of a child from the other parent's care and control subject to the same criminal sanctions as child stealing. This section was added in 1983, and amended in 1984 at the request of fathers' groups when legislation strengthening child-support collection procedures and mandatory payroll withholding of delinquent child support was being considered.

Award of Joint Legal Custody Absent Joint Physical Custody

(g) In making an order for custody with respect to both parents, the court may award joint legal custody without awarding joint physical custody.

This section was added in subsequent amendments to the original legislation. Some fathers' groups have opposed this provision, viewing "joint legal custody" as a placebo. In reality, any award of time is joint physical custody even though the ratio of time spent with one parent versus the other is considerably less, as long as this parental contact is considered parenting and not merely "visiting" the child.

Primary Caretaker Specification; Eligibility for Public Assistance

(h) In making an order of joint physical custody or joint legal custody, the court may specify one parent as the primary caretaker of the child and one home as the primary home of the child, for the purposes of determining the eligibility for public assistance. CC § 4600.5(h)

This provision was added in by legislation in 1983 to resolve problems in qualifying for public assistance. Public welfare agencies were denying assistance to all joint custody families because the award did not specify a primary caretaker.

Modification/Termination of Custody Order

(i) Any order for joint custody may be modified or terminated upon the petition of one or both parents or on the court's own motion if it is shown that the best interests of the child require modification or termination of the order. The court shall state in its decision the reasons for modification or termination of the joint custody order if either parent opposes the modification or termination order.

These provisions were contained in the original legislation. The purpose was to allow courts to modify or terminate joint custody agreements that were not working.

---

19. Calif. Penal Code § 278.5(a) reads:

> Every person who has a right to physical custody of or visitation with child pursuant to an order, judgment or decree takes, detains, conceals, or retains the child with the intent to deprive another person of his or her rights to physical custody or visitation shall be punished by imprisonment in the state prison for 16 months, or two or three years, a fine of not more than ten thousand dollars ($10,000). . . .

To my knowledge, courts have rarely, if ever, terminated a joint custody agreement on the court's own motion. Courts will change the residential arrangements within joint custody based upon an assessment of the child's best interests. A court order changing the child's primary residence is not considered a custody modification requiring proof of changed circumstances.[20]

Interstate Issues; Jurisdictional Requirements

(j) Any order for the custody of a minor child of a marriage entered by a court in this state or any other state may, subject to the jurisdictional requirements set forth in Section 5152 and 5163, be modified at any time to an order of joint custody in accordance with this section.

This provision appeared in the original legislation and was incorporated to handle interstate issues. This section links the joint custody provisions with the Uniform Child Custody Jurisdiction Act.

Assistance of Conciliation Courts; Parenting Plans

(k) In counties having a conciliation court, the court or the parties may, at any time pursuant to local rules of court, consult with the conciliation court for the purposes of assisting the parties to formulate a plan for implementation of the custody order or to resolve any controversy which has arisen in the implementation of a plan for custody.

At the time this legislation was passed, twelve of the fifty-eight counties in California had a Conciliation Court. One year later, the state legislature added section 4607 to the Civil Code, requiring counties to establish a mediation process and mandating its use in any disputed child-custody case before a custody hearing could be held.[21] The addition of a third option to post-divorce parenting required another forum promoting joint decision making and problem solving through mediation of these disputes. Currently, 20% of all families with children are in dispute and using the county mediation services to develop their custody plans. Of those using mediation, it was reported in 1987 that 68% to 70% were reaching agreement with the help of a mediator.[22] The rest either develop plans by themselves or in consultation with their attorneys. Less than two percent of filings involve a formal custody trial.

Access to Records and Information

(l) Notwithstanding any other provision of law, access to records and information pertaining to a minor child, including, but not limited to, medical, dental, and school

---

20. *Marriage of Birnbaum*, 211 Cal. App. 3d 1508, 260 Cal. Rpts. (1989).
21. Hugh McIsaac, "Mandatory Conciliation of Custody and Visitation Matters: California's Bold Stroke," *Conciliation Courts Review*, 19(2), 1981.
22. *Report of the Advisory Panel on the Child Oriented Divorce Act of 1987: California's Mandatory Divorce Mediation Program*, Senate Office of Research, April 1987.

records, shall not be denied to a parent because that parent is not the child's custodial parent.

This provision was contained in the original legislation and allowed either parent access to his or her child(ren)'s school, medical, and dental records.

Notification to Parent; Change of Child's Residence for More than 30 Days

(m) In making an order for custody, if the court does not deem it inappropriate, the court may specify that a parent shall notify the other parent if he or she plans to change residence of the child for more than 30 days, unless there is prior written agreement to the removal. The notice shall be given prior to the contemplated move, by mail, return receipt requested, postage prepaid, to the last known address of the parent to be notified. A copy of the notice shall also be sent to that parent's counsel of record. To the extent feasible, the notice shall be provided within a minimum of 45 days prior to the proposed change of residence so as to allow time for mediation of a new agreement concerning custody. This subdivision shall not be deemed to affect orders made prior to January 1, 1989.

This last provision was added in 1988 at the recommendation of the Advisory Panel on the Child Oriented Act of 1987. It requires parents to inform each other of moves changing the child's residence for more than thirty days. The provision also encourages mediation of any dispute(s) arising from changes in residence.

Case Law in California

Legislation is only one-half of the equation in exploring joint custody in California. Several important case decisions have had an effect upon the implementation of the law.

Even before the legislation officially became law, *In re Marriage of Neal*[23] held that the mother who had primary physical custody also had primary legal custody. It highlighted the flaw of the original statute, created by a failure to define distinctions between joint legal and physical custody. Another decision that year, *In re Marriage of Carney*,[24] has been used to require a "substantial change of circumstance" before the court will hear requests for modification of a custody order. This case requires the court to consider which parent will provide the child with ethical emotional and intellectual guidance:

The source of this guidance is the adult's own experience of life; its motive power is parental love and concern for the child's well being; and its teachings deal with such

---

23. *In re Marriage of Neal*, 92 Cal. App. 3d 834, 155 Cal. Rptr. (1979).
24. *In re Marriage of Carney*, 24 Cal. 3d 725 (1979).

fundamental matters as the child's feelings about himself, his relationships with others, his system of values, his standards of conduct, and his goals and priorities in life.

The California appellate court held in *Loudin v. Olpin*[25] that the policy statement contained in the law does not raise the right of a child to require a noncustodial parent to maintain close and continuing contact or to have any contact at all. The appellate court held in *In re Marriage of Wood*[26] that awarding joint custody when the parents could not agree was not an abuse of judicial discretion. However, a party is entitled to a statement of decision regarding the court's modifying a sole-custody order.

Other important California decisions affect the joint custody statute. *In re Marriage of Rosson*[27] establishes helpful guidelines for modifying joint custody arrangements when one of the parents in a joint custody arrangement moves from the community. In effect, *Rosson* requires the party moving from the community to show why it is in the child's best interest to accompany the moving parent. *In re Marriage of Levin*[28] requires the court to consider joint custody as an option. *Burchard v. Garay*[29] prohibits the court from considering disparity of income as a factor in making a custody award. *Marriage of Birnbaum* clarified that a court had broad discretion to modify the residential arrangements between disagreeing joint custodial parents based upon the court's assessment of best interests and without requiring a change of circumstances.[30]

Future Directions

Because "joint custody" is a relatively new concept, little or no reliable data is available to establish its benefit or detriment to children. The language, institutional supports, and processes are just being defined through laws such as those formulated in the states of Washington, Florida, Maine, and Vermont where the concept of custody is being replaced by new language such as "sharing of rights and responsibilities," "care and control," and "parenting plans."

Conclusion

How is joint custody working in California? For many families and children, the arrangement appears to be working superbly. For example, at the 1988 California Association of Family and Conciliation Conference held in Long Beach, California, three families reported that while joint custody was "hard," its benefits—namely, continued ties between the children and both parents, were worth the effort. Other benefits were additional financial support by both parents beyond age eighteen when

---

25. *Loudin v. Olpin*, 118 Cal. App. 3d 565, 173 Cal. Rptr. 477 (1981).
26. *In re Marriage of Wood*, 141 Cal. App. 3d 671, 190 Cal. Rptr. 469 (1983).
27. *In re Marriage of Rosson*, 178 Cal. App. 3d 1094, 224 Cal. Rptr. 250 (1986).
28. Op. Cit.
29. *Burchard v. Garay*, 42 Cal. App. 3d 531, 229 Cal. Rptr. 800 (1986).
30. *Marriage of Birnbaum*, 211 Cal. App. 3d 1508, 260 Cal. Repts. (1989).

most support awards end and involvement of both parents in childrearing. Liabilities reported included some disruption in continuity, and a lack of clarity for step-parents. Yet both the parents and the additional adults felt the custody arrangements, for the most part, were better than sole custody. The children were all doing well at school and may have even developed superior social skills, having to deal with many different personalities in their two families.

The economic benefits of joint custody reported by these families also are supported by two studies, one completed by the AFCC research unit in Denver under a United States Government Health and Human Services grant,[31] and the other, a Canadian Government study conducted at four sites in Canada.[32] Both studies' findings indicated fathers having joint custody were significantly more in compliance with support orders than fathers whose former wives had sole custody of their children.

The new studies reported by Wallerstein indicate "joint custody" had no effect on children's adjustment as reported by parents.[33] The most important variables affecting the adjustment of children were the absence of conflict between the parents and the absence of pathology in either of the parents—not a surprising finding.

The fascinating aspect of this legislation has been the confluence of various special-interest groups prosecuting their own concerns: fathers who felt disenfranchised, mothers who felt a loss of power and purpose, mothers who felt a need to share responsibility, courts afraid of being overburdened, and researchers and courts concerned about the need for both parents to be involved and about the effects of a new, emerging family form. The only groups not represented were children themselves and perhaps fathers and mothers who had essentially opted out of parenting completely. Out of this confluence has emerged a new law, reflecting a dramatic and significant change from the past, and a paradigm shift in the family and in the nature of the resolution of conflict in the courts. This chapter is still being written. From the trenches, this system seems to be working, and where both parents have been involved and have cooperated, children are faring remarkably well. In this crucible of change called California, another innovation has borne fruit and multiplied along with silicon chips and hoola hoops. Whether this society is a better place to live remains to be seen.

The answer is joint custody works marvelously for many children and families and has proven a disaster for others. Clearly, both the families and the courts need wide discretion to choose parenting plans best suited to the individual needs and capacities of each family and child. We need more research into what plans work best for what children. What is needed is clearheaded thinking, not rhetoric, and an elevation of parental rights over children's needs.

---

31. J. Pearson & N. Thoennes, *Final Report of the Divorce Mediation Research Project: (90-CW-634)*, submitted to the Children's Bureau, Administration for Children, Youth and Families, U.S. Dept. of Health and Human Services, 1984.

32. C.J. Richardson, *Court-Based Divorce Mediation in Four Canadian Cities: An Overview of Research Results*, Report prepared for the Department of Justice, February, 1988.

33. J. Wallerstein, "Children of Divorce: Report of a Ten-Year Follow-up of Early Latency Children," *American Journal of Orthopsychiatry*, 57:199-211, 1987.

21

Cooperative Parenting After Divorce: A Canadian Legal Perspective

JULIEN D. PAYNE
BRENDA EDWARDS

This chapter presents an overview of Canadian divorce and custody law. Although not included in Canada's first national comprehensive divorce statute in 1968, joint custody was incorporated into the 1985 Divorce Act. Since that time there has been an effort to clarify legal terms such as "custody" and "access," and to identify various forms of joint custody. Although receiving mixed reviews, the current judicial position towards joint custody is favorable where there is hope of cooperation between the parents. Prime considerations in issuing a joint custody order include: the success of shared parenting in the past and the "best interests of the child." The authors provide a Canadian perspective on the "pros and cons" of joint custody in chart form and conclude the chapter by presenting suggestions for the reform of joint custody laws and how to successfully implement individualized joint custody plans.

When Canada established a central Divorce Registry with the passage of its first national comprehensive divorce statute in 1968,[1] no provision was made for the inclusion of data on "joint custody." Any anticipated incidence of joint custody

Julien D. Payne is a Professor of Law at the University of Ottawa, Ontario, Canada.
Brenda Edwards is a Research Associate at the University of Ottawa, Ontario, Canada.

1. Divorce Act, S.C. 1967-1968, c.24, subsequently R.S.C. 1970, c.D-8.

applications and orders was perceived as statistically insignificant. How times have changed! According to data provided by Statistics Canada on June 3, 1988,

> The data collection procedures for divorces granted under the *Divorce Act, 1985* now permit the identification of the "joint custody" of children, under which a former husband and wife can continue to share responsibility for making major decisions affecting their children, regardless of which parent the children live with. Among the 6,105 children involved in the 3,550 divorces granted in 1986 under the new Act in which there was a custody order, the wife was awarded custody of 75% of the children, 12% were awarded to the husband, 11% were involved in a joint custody arrangement and 2% were awarded to a person other than the husband or wife.[2]

Although joint custody is now included among contemporary buzz words in Canada, court orders for joint custody are a relatively modern legal phenomenon.

Qualified legal acceptance of joint custody in Canada does not imply that its parameters are precise or that a monolithic definition has been formulated. Far from it! Lawyers and judges, like people in other walks of life, continue to debate what is meant by "joint custody" and whether it constitutes panacea or anathema. Empirical studies in Canada, like those in the United States, are inconclusive, but there is no corresponding lack of firm convictions in the assessment of joint custody by professional and public-interest groups. The 1970s controversy that centered upon the dichotomy between the inevitability of a "single psychological parent" on marital breakdown[3] and the notion that "both parents are forever"[4] continues to plague professional and public-interest groups in Canada. Perhaps, the wrong question is being posed. To adapt John F. Kennedy's approach: "Ask not what the children can do for Mom or Dad. Ask what Mom *and* Dad can do for the children." Although parents who are experiencing the emotional trauma of marital breakdown cannot be faulted for their inability to discern the long-term interests of all members of the fragmented family, it is much more difficult to justify the polarization of opinions between diverse professional and public-interest groups. Political agendas and power games are not, of course, a monopoly of either sex or any particular profession but they do little, or nothing, to advance the cause of children and members of their extended family networks on marital breakdown or divorce. Unsubstantiated declarations of faith must not become validated by repetition or by shouting them from the rooftops. There are no universal truths about parenting after marital breakdown that can be prepackaged. We are not selling soap; we are dealing with people. All affected family members, including the grandparents, are entitled to be heard when their interests are at stake. Joint custody is, therefore, neither panacea nor anathema in the abstract. Parenting crises that are triggered by marital breakdown will not be resolved by the legal jargon of "custody," "access," or "joint custody," nor by legal presumptions in favor of joint custody or in favor of the primary caretaker during the subsistence of

---

2. The Daily, Statistics Canada, June 3, 1988.
3. *See* J. Goldstein, A. Freud, & A. Solnit, *Beyond the Best Interests of the Child*, New York: The Free Press, 1973.
4. *See* J. Wallerstein & J. Kelly, *Surviving the Breakup*, New York: Basic Books Inc., 1980.

the marriage. Neither do the solutions lie with William Shakespeare's suggestion that we kill all the lawyers. Some progress might be made, however, if we abandoned the ill-conceived legal terminology of "custody" and "access" and stepped up our pursuit of non-adversarial processes that can avoid protracted litigation or unfair bargaining "in the shadow of the law."

By way of elaboration of the above opinions, the authors will examine the following matters: (1) legal definitions of "custody" and "access", (2) forms of joint custody, (3) joint custody dispositions under Canadian federal divorce legislation, and (4) the supposed pros and cons of joint custody—emphasizing Canadian authorities. Thereafter, the authors will present their own conclusions concerning cooperative parenting after marital breakdown.

Legal Definitions of "Custody" and "Access"

Subsection 2(1) of the *Divorce Act, 1985*[5] provides that "custody" includes care, upbringing, and any other incident of custody. This subsection provides no definition of "access" in the English language but the French version provides as follows: "'Accès' comporte le droit de visite." Subsection 16(5) of the *Divorce Act, 1985* qualifies this definition of "access" by entitling a spouse who is granted access privileges to make inquiries and receive information concerning the health, education, or welfare of the child. This right exists in the absence of a court order to the contrary. It does not extend to any person other than a spouse who has been granted access privileges. Subsection 16(5) presumably entitles a spouse with access privileges to direct relevant inquiries to the custodial parent or to a third party, such as the child's doctor or school principal. Subsection 16(5) does not expressly require the custodial parent to consult with the noncustodial spouse who has access privileges before decisions are taken that affect the child's health, education, and welfare.[6] However, the courts have interpreted similar legislation enacted at a provincial level to be a recognition of the right of the noncustodial parent to be consulted prior to important decisions being taken affecting the child. In *Abbott v. Taylor*,[7] wherein the application was made pursuant to the *Family Maintenance Act*,[8] the Manitoba Court of Appeal held that although the legislation stopped short of mandatory joint responsibility for decision making, it did anticipate consultation by the custodial parent whose responsibility for major decisions was characterized as the "ultimate" responsibility rather than the "prime" responsibility.

The term "custody" is imprecise and has in the past been used in both a wide and a narrow sense. In *Hewar v. Bryant*,[9] Sachs, L.J., of the Court of Appeal in England, observed that in its wide sense, custody is virtually equivalent to guardianship, whereas

---

5. S.C. 1986, c.4.
6. *See* Anson v. Anson (1987), 10 B.C.L.R. (2d) 357 (Co. Ct.); *compare* Dipper v. Dipper, *infra* note 13.
7. (1986), 2 R.F.L. (3d) 163, at 169, 172 (Man. C.A.).
8. S.M. 1982-83-84, c.54, s.14.1(4).
9. [1970] 1 Q.B. 357, at 372-73, [1969] 3 All E.R. 578 (Eng. C.A.).

in its narrow sense, custody refers to the power to exercise physical control over the child. In the context of Canadian divorce proceedings, the case law tends to support the conclusion that, in the absence of directions to the contrary, an order granting "sole custody" to one parent signifies that the custodial parent shall exercise all the powers of the legal guardian of the child. The noncustodial parent with access privileges is thus deprived of the rights and responsibilities that previously vested in that parent as a joint custodian of the child. In *Kruger v. Kruger*, Thorson, J.A. stated:

> In my view, to award one parent the exclusive custody of a child is to clothe that parent, for whatever period he or she is awarded the custody, with full parental control over, and ultimate parental responsibility for, the care, upbringing and education of the child, generally to the exclusion of the right of the other parent to interfere in the decisions that are made in exercising that control or in carrying out that responsibility.[10]

Accordingly, although a parent who has been granted access privileges may have some limited powers to make decisions where an emergency necessitates action and the custodial parent is unavailable, these limited powers fall short of any basic right to actively participate in decisions affecting the child's welfare and development.[11] To paraphrase the observations of Spencer, J. in *Pierce v. Pierce*,[12] the parent who is granted custody has the sole right to determine the child's education and physical, intellectual, spiritual, and moral upbringing. The role of the noncustodial parent with access privileges is that of a very interested observer, giving love and support to the child in the background and standing by in case the custodial parent dies.

The stance taken by Canadian judges stands in sharp contrast to that endorsed by the English Court of Appeal in *Dipper v. Dipper*,[13] wherein it was concluded that the custodial parent has no preemptive rights over the noncustodial parent, that full consultation is required, and that any parental disagreement as to the education or religious upbringing of the child, and any other major matter affecting the child's welfare, must be decided by the court.

The provisions of the *Divorce Act, 1985*, and particularly the definitions of "custody" and "access" in subsection 2(1) of the *Act*, apparently preclude Canadian courts from reverting to a narrow definition of custody. The word "includes" in the definition of custody necessarily implies that the term embraces a wider range of powers than those specifically designated in subsection 2(1).[14] The opinions expressed in *Kruger v. Kruger, supra*, have thus been statutorily endorsed by the *Divorce Act, 1985*. Consequently, in the absence of a successful application to vary an unqualified sole-custody disposition with respect to all or any of the incidents of

---

10. (1979), 25 O.R. (2d) 673, 11 R.F.L. (2d) 52, at 78, 104 D.L.R. (3d) 481 (C.A.).
11. See Anson, *supra* note 6, at 368; McCutcheon v. McCutcheon (1982), 29 R.F.L. (2d) 11, at 12 (N.B.Q.B.); Glasgow v. Glasgow (No. 2) (1982), 51 N.S.R. (2d) 13, 102 A.P.R. 13, at 24-25 (Fam. Ct.); Gubody v. Gubody, [1955] O.W.N. 548, [1955] 4 D.L.R. 693 (S.C.); Gunn v. Gunn (1975), 10 Nfld. & P.E.I.R. 159, 24 R.F.L. 182, at 185-86 (P.E.I.S.C.).
12. [1977] 5 W.W.R. 572, at 575 (B.C.S.C.).
13. [1981] Fam. 31, at 45-46 (Ormrod, L.J.) and 48 (Cumming-Bruce, L.J.), [1980] 3 W.L.R. 626, [1980] 2 All E.R. 722 (Eng. C.A.). *Compare* Clarke v. Clarke (1987), 12 B.C.L.R. (2d) 290, 7 R.F.L. (3d) 176 (S.C.).
14. See Anson, *supra* note 6, at 365; *see also* Clarke, *supra* note 13.

custody, the noncustodial spouse with access privileges is a passive bystander who is excluded from the decision-making process in matters relating to the child's welfare, growth, and development. This remains true notwithstanding that subsection 16(10) of the *Divorce Act, 1985* provides that the court shall promote "maximum contact" between the child and the noncustodial parent to the extent that this is consistent with the best interests of the child. It is open to the court, however, to preserve a potentially meaningful role for both parents by way of an order for joint custody.

Forms of Joint Custody

In a limited number of cases, the courts have rejected the traditional approach of granting custody to one parent and access rights to the other. Instead, they have granted "joint custody" to both parents. Such dispositions have taken a variety of forms. Some courts have granted "legal custody" to one parent and "care and control" or "physical custody" to the other;[15] others have granted legal custody to both parents with care and control to one and generous access to the other;[16] still others have ordered care and control to be divided between the parents during different periods of the year.[17] Although orders for joint custody vary in character, it is generally accepted that joint custody gives to each parent something less than exclusive authority over a child's upbringing, which is the essence of an order for sole custody.

Joint custody recognizes that marital breakdown ends the husband–wife relationship but need not, and should not, end the parent–child relationship; it gives to each parent a degree of responsibility for a child's upbringing and development. It may or may not include arrangements for sharing physical custody or care and control. The flexibility inherent in the concept of joint custody allows arrangements to be tailored to the parents' and child's physical, emotional, geographic, and economic limitations.

The terms used by the courts in relation to joint custody are as elusive and uncertain as those used with respect to traditional "sole custody" dispositions. References to "legal custody" and "care and control" are frequently found and generate the same confusion and uncertainty in the context of joint custody as arises with respect to "sole custody" dispositions.[18] By way of further complication, the concept of joint custody has evolved its own terminology. Thus, the term "split custody" is used to refer

---

15. *See, e.g., In re W. (An Infant)*, [1964] Ch. 202, [1963] 3 W.L.R. 789, [1963] 3 All E.R. 459 (Eng. C.A.); *Donald* v. *Donald* (1980), 3 Sask. R. 202 (Q.B.); *compare* Dipper, *supra* note 13, wherein Ormrod, L.J. held that split orders are not desirable.

16. *See, e.g., Jussa* v. *Jussa* (1973), 10 R.F.L. 263 (Eng. H.C. Fam. Div.); *Reil* v. *Reil* (1985), 36 Alta. L.R. (2d) 416 (Q.B.); *Hachett* v. *Hachett* (1985), 43 R.F.L. (2d) 5 (B.C.S.C.); *Swanson* v. *Swanson* (1983), 34 R.F.L. (2d) 155 (B.C.S.C.); *Farkasch* v. *Farkasch*, [1972] 1 W.W.R. 429, 4 R.F.L. 339, 22 D.L.R. (3d) 345 (Man. Q.B.); *Pettigrew* v. *Pettigrew*, [1972] 5 W.W.R. 242, 7 R.F.L. 330, 27 D.L.R. (3d) 500 (Man. Q.B.); *Miller* v. *Miller* (1975), 17 R.F.L. 92 (Man. C.A.); *Babyak* v. *Babyak* (1981), 7 Man. R. (2d) 98 (Q.B.); *Vosper* v. *Vosper* (1981), 7 Man. R. (2d) 92 (Q.B.); *Klachefsky* v. *Brown* (1988), 12 R.F.L. (3d) 280 (Man. C.A.), var'g. (1987), 9 R.F.L. (3d) 428 (Man. Q.B.); *Boody* v. *Boody* (1983), 32 R.F.L. (2d) 396 (Ont. Dist. Ct.); *Daurie* v. *Daurie*, unreported, Oct. 10, 1985 (Ont. Dist. Ct.); *MacRae* v. *MacRae* (1974), 6 Nfld. & P.E.I.R. 1, 15 R.F.L. 270 (P.E.I.S.C.).

17. *See, e.g., Parker* v. *Parker* (1976), 20 R.F.L. 232 (Man. C.A.); *Wagneur* v. *Wagneur* (1975), 17 R.F.L. 150 (Que. S.C.); *Fauvreau* v. *Ethier*, [1976] C.S. 48; *Benoit* v. *Bissaillon*, [1976] C.S. 1651 (Que.); *Droit de la famille - 13*, [1983] C.S. 42 (Que.); *Buchko* v. *Buchko* (1973), 11 R.F.L. (2d) 252 (Sask. Q.B.).

18. *See supra* text subheading "Legal Definitions of 'Custody' and 'Access.'"

to orders granting legal custody to one parent and care and control to the other.[19] And where one parent is granted custody for part of the week, month, or year, and the other parent is granted custody for the remainder of the time, such a disposition is said to involve "alternate" or "divided" custody. Unfortunately, these new "labels" aggravate rather than alleviate the confusion. For example, where an order for "alternate" or "divided" custody is granted, the court does not normally define the specific rights and obligations of each parent. Consequently, it is often impossible to determine the respective rights and responsibilities of the parents. Is a parent, who is for the time being the noncustodial parent, excluded from the decision-making process respecting the upbringing of the child in the custody and control of the other parent, or is it implicit that both parents must cooperate in joint decision making, regardless of which parent has physical custody and control of the child?

The confusion generated by the term "joint custody" is aptly summarized in the following observations of one Canadian judge: "Some suggestion has been made that I grant joint custody of the children to both parents. Unfortunately I have not been able to understand what the term 'joint custody' means, that it may be that the effect of my order is to grant just that."[20]

Joint Custody Dispositions Under Canadian Federal Divorce Legislation

It was not until 1968 that Canada enacted its first comprehensive and nationwide divorce statute[21] to regulate the grounds for, and bars to, divorce and the corollary issues of spousal and child support and custody of, and access to, children on and after divorce. The 1950s and early and mid-1960s in Canada were conformist years. There was no ground swell of public opinion in favor of sexual equality. The traditional nuclear family, with its homemaking mother, bread-winning father, and two children was revered as the ideal family structure. The wife and mother was perceived as the nurturing parent. Consequently, "custody" placements on marital breakdown or divorce were, for the most part, a foregone conclusion. The children stayed with the mother. Rarely did the departing father leave home with a child under each arm. Judicial and public attitudes, including those of mothers and fathers directly involved in marital breakdown, reflected the view that the children of separated or divorced parents belonged with their mother. While the courts in parenting disputes paid lip service to the notion of determining custody dispositions on the basis of "the best interests of the child," the courts were in reality largely guided by presumptions of fact that were accorded the status of rules of law. The three presumptions, or, more accurately stated, assumptions, most frequently invoked by the courts were: (1)

---

19. Unfortunately, the term "split custody" has also been used to signify orders granting the custody of one or more children to one parent and the remaining siblings to the other.

20. Gibbs v. Gibbs, unreported, Sept. 18, 1976 (Ont. S.C.) (Misener, L.J.S.C.), wherein custody was awarded to the mother with "generous right of access to and temporary custody" of the children to the father.

21. Divorce Act, S.C. 1967-68, c.24, subsequently R.S.C. 1970, c.D-8.

children of tender years should usually remain with their mother, (2) courts should, whenever possible, avoid the separation of siblings, and (3) preservation of the status quo is desirable. The courts consistently applied these presumptions throughout the 1950s, 1960s, and early 1970s with the result that in both contested and uncontested divorce proceedings in Canada, mothers received the custody of their children in 85.6% of all cases.[22] Even as late as 1988, statistical data indicates that mothers continue to assume the primary responsibility for the parenting of children after divorce in 75% of all cases.[23] In light of such empirical data, which encompass the *Divorce Act* of 1968[24] and the *Divorce Act, 1985,*[25] popular assumptions that public attitudes towards sexual stereotyping and parenting roles after divorce have undergone radical change must be viewed with caution.

It is open to debate whether the empirical data demonstrate that traditional mores die hard or whether they reflect a normal pattern whereby legal opinion lags behind contemporary public opinion. Whatever the case, there are indications that changes have occurred in judicial attitudes toward joint custody dispositions during the last decade. Until the mid-1970s, no serious challenge was launched by professionals or public-interest groups against orders for sole custody in favor of mothers. For all intents and purposes, they were regarded as the only practicable disposition on divorce. With a 500% increase in the divorce rate between 1967 and 1987, and an ever-increasing incidence in the number of married and divorced women entering or reentering the Canadian labor force, sole-custody dispositions in favor of mothers became no longer perceived as axiomatic. For a brief period of time in the mid-1970s, some courts evinced a preference for joint custody dispositions. Towards the end of the 1970s, however, joint custody orders fell out of favor. In the mid-1980s, joint custody dispositions appear to have regained a limited degree of judicial acceptance. In the short space of ten years, therefore, judicial opinions have fluctuated on the issue of joint custody. Consequently, the future is far from certain. The legislative foundations for the future are currently established by the *Divorce Act, 1985.*[26] It is accordingly appropriate to examine its provisions in some detail, with occasional cross-reference to its predecessor, the *Divorce Act* of 1968.[27]

Subsection 16(4) of the *Divorce Act, 1985*[28] expressly provides as follows: "16.(4) *Joint custody or access.* The court may make an order under this section granting custody of, or access to, any or all children of the marriage to any one or more persons." Although this subsection clearly envisages interim and permanent orders for joint custody as between the spouses, and even third parties, it falls short of endorsing any presumption in favor of joint custody. In the context of the former *Divorce Act,*[29] appellate decisions in the provinces of Nova Scotia and Ontario have asserted a judicial

---

22. *See* Statistics Canada, *Divorce: Law and the Family in Canada* (D. C. McKie, B. Prentice, & P. Reed), Feb. 1983, at p. 207.
23. *See supra* note 2 and accompanying text.
24. *Supra* note 21.
25. *Supra* note 5.
26. *Id.*
27. *Supra* note 21.
28. *Supra* note 5.
29. *Supra* note 21.

aversion to joint custody orders unless both spouses are willing and able to cooperate in discharging their parenting privileges and responsibilities.[30] These appellate rulings may, however, be nothing more than common-sense observations that joint custody should not be imposed by a court order where the parents are too polarized to make it work. They should not be perceived as generalized clinical theories that preclude some form of shared-parenting arrangement.[31] An order for joint custody, which includes equally divided time between two loving and committed parents, may be in the best interests of the children, in spite of the reservations of the parents flowing from occasional disagreements.[32] A total absence of conflict is not a condition precedent to an order for joint custody and the possible prejudicial effect of an order for sole custody resulting in the noncustodial parent losing interest and affection for the children should not be ignored.[33] In *Teigeler v. Santiago*,[34] the Ontario Court of Appeal affirmed without reasons a judgment of Poulin, Surr. Ct. J., wherein an established pattern of alternating monthly custody arrangements was confirmed by an order for joint custody, notwithstanding that each parent sought an order for sole custody. This judgment clearly rejects any notion that all forms of joint- or shared-custody dispositions are conditioned solely on the preferences of the parents. Alternating custody should not be imposed by judicial decree, however, where neither party has sought such an order and no evidence or submissions have been made as to its appropriateness.[35]

In *Gaudin v. Gaudin*,[36] an order was made for alternating custody on an annual basis for a trial period of two years by reason of the inability of the parents to deal with access to the child in a flexible, calm, and reasonable manner. Physical access privileges to the noncustodial parent were denied but the custodial parent was directed to provide monthly written reports to the noncustodial parent concerning the child's welfare and progress and to pay for the child telephoning the noncustodial parent on a weekly basis. This disposition again constitutes a departure from the usual practice whereby any form of joint- or shared-custody order is denied to warring spouses. An order for alternating sole custody may, however, sever the "Gordian knot" where other forms of joint custody are unacceptable, with regard to the best interests of the child or to the distances between the two respective homes. Such an order may be consistent with the philosophy of subsection 16(10) of the *Divorce Act, 1985*, which extols the virtues of "maximum contact" between the child and the noncustodial parent, but is

---

30. Zwicker v. Morine (1980), 38 N.S.R. (2d) 236, 69 A.P.R. 236, 16 R.F.L. (2d) 293 (C.A.); Gordon v. Keyes (1985), 67 N.S.R. (2d) 216, 155 A.P.R. 216, 45 R.F.L. (2d) 177 (C.A.), leave to appeal to S.C.C. refused 69 N.S.R. (2d) 358n, 163 A.P.R. 358n (S.C.C.); Baker v. Baker (1978), 3 R.F.L. (2d) 193 (Ont. S.C.), aff'd. 23 O.R. (2d) 391, 8 R.F.L. (2d) 236, 95 D.L.R. (3d) 529 (C.A.); Kruger v. Kruger (1979), 25 O.R. (2d) 673, 11 R.F.L. (2d) 52, 104 D.L.R. (3d 481 (C.A.). *But see infra* notes 43-44 and accompanying text.

31. *See* Re J. and C.; Catholic Children's Aid Society of Metropolitan Toronto v. S. and S. (1985), 48 R.F.L. (2d) 371, at 381 (Ont. Prov. Ct.) (Nasmith, Prov. J.), rev'd. (1988), 10 R.F.L. (3d) 343 (Ont. Dist. Ct.); *see also* Abbott v. Taylor (1986), 2 R.F.L. (3d) 163, at 170-71 (Man. C.A.).

32. Parsons v. Parsons (1985), 48 R.F.L. (2d) 83, at 92-93 (Nfld. Unif. Fam. Ct.) (Cameron, J.).

33. *See* Banks v. Banks, unreported, Dec. 19, 1986 (Ont. Unif. Fam. Ct.). *See also* Nurmi v. Nurmi (1988), 18 R.F.L. (3d) 97 (Ont. Unif. Fam. Ct.).

34. Unreported, Jan. 24, 1984 (Ont. C.A.).

35. Goslin v. Goslin (1986), 4 R.F.L. (3d) 223 (Ont. C.A.) (Issue remitted to trial judge with direction to hear evidence and submissions).

36. (1986), 76 N.B.R. (2d) 143, 192 A.P.R. 143 (Q.B.).

likely to provoke widely different professional opinions on its merits from the child's perspective.

Custody on a rotating six-months basis has been found impractical for an interim, as distinct from a permanent, order.[37] Alternating care and control during the week may, however, be both feasible and desirable so that the interim order is minimally disruptive of the social environment in which the child is comfortable and secure.[38] In *Abbott v. Taylor*,[39] Twaddle, J.A. of the Manitoba Court of Appeal, observed that "the mere expression by one or both parents of an unwillingness to share custody should not preclude an order for joint custody if the court considers such unwillingness to be a manifestation of temporary personal hostility engendered by the trauma of a recent separation." Where parental conflicts may be resolved through counseling, the court may urge the parties to seek the aid of a conciliator or mediator, or to consult such medical and psychiatric expertise as is appropriate.[40] It is doubtful whether the court has any jurisdiction to compel the parties to have recourse to such services or to condition a custody or access disposition on mandatory recourse to such services.[41] In appropriate circumstances, however, the court could order an independent assessment of the family in an attempt to determine the needs of the child and the capacity of the respective parents to fulfill those needs.[42]

Whether the traditional judicial aversion to joint custody is subject to constitutional challenge under section 7 or subsection 15(1) of the *Canadian Charter of Rights and Freedoms*[43] is a matter that must await final determination by the Supreme Court of Canada. In *Gordon v. Keys*,[44] the Appellate Division of the Supreme Court of Nova Scotia held that joint custody is not mandated by the *Canadian Charter of Rights and Freedoms* and the principle that the welfare or best interests of the child is the primary

---

37. Robinson v. Robinson (1985), 49 R.F.L. (2d) 43 (Ont. C.A.).
38. Friesen v. Petkau (1985), 8 R.F.L. (3d) 158 (Man. Q.B.).
39. (1986), 2 R.F.L. (3d) 161, at 171 (Man. C.A.).
40. Cormier v. Cormier (1984), 49 A.R. 232 (Q.B.); Loewen v. Loewen (1982), 29 R.F.L. (2d) 25, at 27-28 (B.C.S.C.); Wood v. Wood (1981), 12 Man. R. (2d) 265, at 270-71 (Q.B.); Clasen v. Clasen (1984), 42 R.F.L. (2d) 376 (Man. Q.B.); Harris v. Lyons (1987), 8 R.F.L. (3d) 59 (N.B.Q.B.); *compare* McDonald v. McDonald (1987), 10 B.C.L.R. (2d) 257, 6 R.F.L. (3d) 17 (S.C.); *see also* Demchuk v. Demchuk (1987), 73 A.R. 161 (Q.B.); Lake v. Lake (1988), 11 R.F.L. (3d) 234 (N.S.C.A.); Chisholm (Bower) v. Bower (1987), 11 R.F.L. (3d) 293 (N.S. Fam. Ct.); Banks, *supra* note 33; Menage v. Hedges (1987), 8 R.F.L. (3d) 225 (Ont. Unif. Fam. Ct.).
41. *Compare* Demchuk, *supra* note 40; Banks, *supra* note 33; Hedges, *supra* note 40.
42. Clasen, *supra* note 40; Riewe v. Riewe (1985), 35 Man. R. (2d) 33 (Q.B.); Northwest Child and Family Services Agency v. A.L. (1986), 46 Man. R. (2d) 199 (Q.B.) (Right to cross-examine expert considered); Cashin v. Cashin (1985), 48 R.F.L. (2d) 104 (N.S.S.C.); Annis v. Annis, unreported, June 16, 1987 (N.S.S.C.); Cillis v. Cillis (1980), 20 R.F.L. (2d) 208 (Ont. S.C.), aff'd. 33 R.F.L. (2d) 76 (Ont. Div. Ct.); Booth v. Booth (1983), 33 R.F.L. (2d) 330 (Ont. S.C.); Chapman v. Chapman (1985), 49 R.F.L. (2d) 47 (Ont. Dist. Ct.); de Araujo v. de Araujo (1986), 11 C.P.C. (2d) 272 (Ont. S.C.) (fees); Testani v. Mion, [1982] R.P. 335 (Que. C.S.).
43. Section 17 and subsection 15(1) of the *Canadian Charter of Rights and Freedoms* in the *Constitution Act, 1982*, Part I, provide as follows:

7. Everyone has the right to life, liberty and security of the person and the right not to be deprived thereof except in accordance with the principles of fundamental justice.
* * *
15(1) Every individual is equal before and under the law and has the right to the equal protection and equal benefit of the law without discrimination and, in particular, without discrimination based on race, national or ethnic origin, colour, religion, sex, age or mental or physical handicap.

44. (1985), 67 N.S.R. (2d) 216, 155 A.P.R. 216, 45 R.F.L. (2d) 177 (C.A.), leave to appeal to S.C.C. refused 69 N.S.R. (2d) 358n, 163 A.P.R. 358n (S.C.C.).

consideration in matters of custody has not been altered, abridged, or otherwise changed by the *Charter.*

Pursuant to subsection 16(4) of the *Divorce Act, 1985,* the court may grant joint or shared custody to the spouses *inter se* or to one or both of the spouses and any other person or persons, such as a close family relative.[45] Third party orders, whether for sole or joint custody, have been rare under the *Divorce Act* of 1968[46] and will presumably continue to be rare under the *Divorce Act, 1985.*[47] It should be borne in mind, however, that an order granting custody to a third party may be so conditioned as to preserve certain rights to the biological parent(s). The diverse aspects or incidents of custody may be shared or divided between several persons.[48] The major impact of subsection 16(4), *supra,* is nevertheless more likely to be found in an increasing number of orders whereby members of the extended family, and particularly grandparents, will be granted access privileges with respect to children on the dissolution of the parents' marriage.

Subsections 16(10) and 17(9) of the *Divorce Act, 1985* provide that the court in making or varying a custody or access order "shall give effect to the principle that a child of the marriage should have as much contact with each spouse as is consistent with the best interests of the child and, for that purpose, shall take into consideration the willingness of the person for whom custody is sought to facilitate such contact." The use of the word "contact" suggests that subsections 16(10) and 17(9) were not intended to endorse a preference for joint or shared-custody dispositions but were intended to promote maximum access privileges as between the child and the non-custodial spouse.[49] In that respect, these subsections legislatively ratify past and present judicial practices whereby the courts usually grant liberal or generous access privileges to the noncustodial parent. Subsections 16(10) and 17(9) may have an impact, however, on the judicial determination of which spouse should be granted the sole custody of a child of the marriage. If one spouse is prepared to encourage maximum contact between the child and the other spouse, whereas the other spouse is opposed to allowing generous access privileges, and both spouses are equally competent parents, the court may conclude that sole custody should be granted to the spouse who will encourage maximum contact, provided always that this is consistent with the best interests of the child.[50] Such judicial preference for the so-called "friendly parent"

---

45. *Compare* Catholic Children's Aid Society of Metropolitan Toronto v. K.H.; J.H. and H.H. v. K.H. (1987), 6 R.F.L. (3d) 1 (Ont. Prov. Ct.), wherein a joint custody order was granted to the foster parents and the maternal grandparents in proceedings under the *Children's Law Reform Amendment Act,* S.O. 1982, c.20; *see also* Bzdel v. Bzdel (1987), 57 Sask. R. 81, 8 R.F.L. (3d) 1 (Sask. C.A.).

46. *Supra* note 21.

47. *Supra* note 5.

48. *But see* T.V.F. v. G.C., [1987] 2 S.C.R. 244, *sub nom.* Vignaux-Fines and Fines v. Chardon (1987), 9 R.F.L. (3d) 263 (application under Quebec Civil Code). *See also* Marie Pratte, *La garde conjointe des enfants de familles desunies* (1988), 19 R.G.D. 525.

49. *See* Adams v. Adams (1987), 78 N.S.R. (2d) 437, 193 A.P.R. 437, 6 R.F.L. (3d) 299 (S.C.); *compare* Kamimura v. Squibb (Carruthers) (1988), 13 R.F.L. (3d) 31 (B.C.S.C.); *compare* Demchuk, *supra* note 40; Gaudin, *supra* note 36; Banks, *supra* note 33; text, *supra,* at subheading "Legal Definitions of 'Custody' and 'Access.'"

50. *See* Jensen v. Jensen (1984), 30 Man. R. (2d) 137, at 142 (Q.B.), aff'd. (1984), 30 Man. R. (2d) 136 (C.A.); *see also* Tremblay v. Tremblay (1987), 54 Alta. L.R. (2d) 283, 10 R.F.L. (3d) 166 (Q.B.); Gagne v. Gagne (1986), 42 Man. R. 231 (Q.B.); Smith v. Smith (1987), 7 R.F.L. (3d) 206 (N.S. Fam. Ct.); Wainwright v. Wainwright (1987), 10 R.F.L. (3d) 387 (N.S.S.C.).

may indirectly affect the incidence of consensual joint custody dispositions in nego-tiated settlements of the parenting and economic consequences of divorce. Lawyers, courts, and mediators must, therefore, exercise caution and guard against abuse of the "friendly parent" criterion in circumstances where it is likely to be invoked for ulterior motives, perhaps related to preferential property and support rights and obligations on divorce.

The following observations would appear to summarize the current judicial position on joint custody in Canada. Although some courts have held it acceptable to order joint custody notwithstanding the objections of either or both parents where there is hope that the parents can and will cooperate, they are in a minority.[51] The overwhelming preponderance of judicial opinion in Canada asserts that joint custody should not be ordered where the parents are unwilling to cooperate in decision making that affects the growth and development of their children or where there is substantial interspousal hostility.[52] Different considerations now seem to apply where there has been a preexisting pattern of joint custody prior to adjudication. If a court is satisfied that shared-parenting arrangements have worked in the past and are in the best interests of the children, a subsequent application to change the arrangements may be denied.[53] Parents who have agreed to an order for joint custody either through mediation or in minutes of settlement must make every effort to make it work.[54] This is not to say that the courts will subsequently change a joint custody order to sole custody where the parents cannot cooperate[55] and the court feels that it is in the best interests of a child to return to its original home and friends and the full-time attention of one parent,[56] especially where the child is exhibiting behavioral problems[57] and the child needs a more stable environment.[58]

---

51. *See, e.g.,* Charlton v. Charlton (1980), 19 B.C.L.R. 42, 15 R.F.L. (2d) 220 (S.C.); Fontaine v. Fontaine (1981), 18 R.F.L. (2d) 235 (Man. C.A.); Taylor, *supra* note 31; Parsons, *supra* note 32; Charmasson v. Charmasson (1982), 27 R.F.L. (2d) 241 (Ont. Co. Ct.); Santiago, *supra* note 34; Boody v. Boody (1983), 32 R.F.L. (2d) 396 (Ont. Dist. Ct.); Banks, *supra* note 33; McCabe v. McCabe & Daley (1980), 11 R.F.L. (2d) 260 (P.E.I.S.C.).

52. Hintze v. Hintze (1985), 42 R.F.L. (2d) 380 (Alta. Q.B.); Morozoff v. Morozoff (1988), 85 A.R. 126, 58 Alta. L.R. (2d) 421 (Q.B.); Ladner v. Ladner (1980), 20 R.F.L. (2d) 243 (B.C.S.C.); Nicolette v. Nicolette, unreported, Dec. 21, 1984 (B.C.S.C.); Nichols v. Nichols (1985), 47 R.F.L. (2d 436 (B.C.S.C.); Anson, *supra* note 6; Clarke, *supra* note 13; Jensen, *supra* note 50; Riewe v. Riewe (1985), 35 Man. R. (2d) 33 (Q.B.); Donnelly v. Donnelly (1977), 16 N.B.R. (2d) 547, 30 R.F.L. 318 (Q.B.); Winsor v. Winsor (1985), 54 Nfld. & P.E.I.R. 81, 160 A.P.R. 81 (Nfld. S.C.); Mathews v. Mathews, unreported, Dec. 23, 1986 (Nfld. S.C.); Martin v. Martin, unreported, June 3, 1987 (Nfld. Unif. Fam. Ct.); Morine, *supra* note 30; Gilbert v. Gilbert (1980), 39 N.S.R. 92d, 241, 71 A.P.R. 241, 18 R.F.L. (2d) 240 (S.C.); Carruthers v. Carruthers (1983), 55 N.S.R. (2d) 88, 114 A.P.R. 88, 30 R.F.L. (2d) 215 (S.C.); Keyes, *supra* note 30; Adams, *supra* note 49; P.F. v. A.M. (1987), 9 R.F.L. (3d) 410 (N.S. Fam. Ct.); Baker, *supra* note 30; Kruger, *supra* note 30; Goslin, *supra* note 35; Irwin v. Irwin (1986), 3 R.F.L. (3d) 403 (Ont. S.C.); Hedges, *supra* note 40; Cowan v. Cowan (1987), 9 R.F.L. (3d) 401 (Ont. S.C.); McCabe v. Ramsey (1981), 31 Nfld. & P.E.I.R. 481, 19 R.F.L. (2d) 70 (P.E.I.S.C.); Dussault v. Ladouceur (1988), 14 R.F.L. (3d) 185 (Que. S.C.); Stewart v. Green (1983), 26 Sask. R. 80 (Q.B.).

53. Miller v. Miller (1975), 17 R.F.L. 92 (Man. C.A.); Parker v. Parker (1976), 20 R.F.L. 232 (Man. C.A.); Leland v. Nykoliation, unreported, Feb. 11, 1986 (Man. Q.B.); Richard v. Richard (1981), 35 N.B.R. (2d) 383 (C.A.); Santiago, *supra* note 34.

54. Faunt v. Faunt (1988), 12 R.F.L. (3d) 331 (Alta. C.A.); MacKay v. MacKay, unreported, Dec. 14, 1982 (Ont. S.C.); Derosier v. Derosier (1988), 12 R.F.L. (3d) 235 (Ont. Dist. Ct.).

55. Nichols, *supra* note 52; Collison v. Collison (1983), 23 Man. R. (2d) 256 (Q.B.); Silver v. Silver (1979), 35 N.S.R. (2d) 88 (S.C.); Yeates v. Yeates (1982), 52 N.S.R. (2d) 662, 106 A.P.R. 662 (S.C.).

56. Norton v. Korpesho (1981, 7 Man. R. (2d) 39 (Q.B.).

57. Collison, *supra* note 55.

58. Nichols, *supra* note 52; Silver, *supra* note 55.

The Supposed Pros and Cons of Joint Custody

Lawyers, judges, mediators, psychiatrists, psychologists, social workers, feminists, male rights activists, and co-parents have all showed no hesitation in asserting their convictions about joint custody. Notwithstanding the confusion inherent in the term "joint custody" and notwithstanding the inevitable absence of conclusive empirical data, there has been no reluctance to generalize from the particular or to express unsubstantiated opinions. The contradictory stances are amply demonstrated in the following chart:

Is It Good for the Parents?

PROS	CONS
"Joint custody orders would assist recently divorced parents to find stability for their future relationship with their children. They would help them to understand that a divorce is not the dissolution of a family but merely its reorganization."[59]	"Divorce dissolves the family as well as the marriage, a reality that may not be ignored."[60] "If the parents cannot agree even to the initial award of joint custody, it is unrealistic to assume that the parents will be able to agree on the myriad of questions that arise during the growth of a child from cradle to emancipation."[61]
"To require that every conceivable issue in a child's upbringing must be viewed in the same way by the parents and that there must be agreement upon all issues before joint custody is awarded is to relegate it to rare circumstances indeed and to sacrifice the best interests of the child to the need of a parent for control."[62]	"A joint custody order may be helpful, and not harmful, only where the parents agree to cooperate and are capable of cooperating. Paradoxically, such an order would thus be unobjectionable only where the parents are the kind for whom no controlling order is necessary at all!"[63]
"Joint custody seems to serve the best interest of not only the child, who does not feel threatened by loss of either parent, but of both parents as well. It allows each adult to have the benefits of ample time with his/her child as well as critically important time alone to pursue a career, education, a social life . . ."[64]	"[A]ctual or potential custody applications can be used by one parent to pressurize the other and force concessions in an ongoing battle, rather than out of genuine concern for the child. If there should be a stronger move towards joint legal custody or its equivalent, we must try to prevent custody applications being used by parents or their legal advisors as just another card to be played in an adversarial game."[65]

---

59. Baker v. Baker (1978), 3 R.F.L. (2d) 193, at 197 (Ont. S.C.) (Boland, J.).
60. Braiman v. Braiman (1978), 407 N.W.S.2d 449, at 452 (N.Y.C.A.) (Breitel, C.J.).
61. Lampton v. Lampton, 9 Fam. L. Rptr. 2583, at 2584 (Colo. C.A., 1983) (Sternberg, J.). *Compare* dissenting judgment of Van Cise, J. who regarded the issue in dispute as purely semantic.
62. Parsons v. Parsons (1986), 48 R.F.L. (2d) 83, at 92-93 (Nfld. Unif. Fam. Ct.) (Cameron, J.).
63. Zwicker v. Morine (1980), 16 R.F.L. (2d) 293, at 302 (N.S.C.A.) (MacKeigan, C.J.).
64. J. Greif & S. Simring, *Remarriage and Joint Custody* (1982), 20:1 Conciliation Cts. Rev., at 9.
65. L. Parkinson, *Child Custody Orders: A Legal Lottery?* (1988), Family Law 26, at 28.

PROS	CONS
"One of the most positive attributes of joint custody is its potential for avoiding problems of non-support arising out of bitterness over the custodial decision."[66]	"Approximately two-thirds of fathers do not pay ordered support . . . Under a joint custody regime support payments decrease, on the average 12%."[67]
	"[H]usbands will threaten custody fights as a means of intimidating wives into accepting less child support and alimony than is sufficient to allow the mother to live and raise the children appropriately as a single parent. Because most women are unwilling to risk losing custody, such techniques are generally successful."[68]
"[T]he data—both quantitative and qualitative—do not in any way, suggest that women (or men for that matter) felt compelled to accept this kind of order (75 percent of women and 89 percent of men surveyed would choose joint custody again) . . . After living with such arrangements for a time, most cited advantages rather than disadvantages of joint legal and physical custody."[69]	"Although there is no statistical data on this subject, there is evidence from many lawyers and marriage counselors that after a few years of joint custody, many parents want to return to exclusive custody."[70]
"Though court ordered joint custody may be more likely to fail than when parents agree, court ordered joint custody is not necessarily more prone to failure than an order for sole custody following a divisive court contest. The potential benefit to the child is greater because a court ordered joint custody decree may help parents discover their potential for shared parenting and require them to do more for their children rather than less."[71]	"Two major studies to date have examined relitigation data. In one study, voluntarily chosen joint custody resulted in 16% relitigation, while court imposed joint custody and sole custody resulted in relitigation rates of 33% and 32%, respectively."[72] "A study of voluntary and court imposed joint custody arrangements revealed that one year after their commencement, '27% of the families were in the successful group, 42% of the

66. J. Folberg & M. Graham, *Joint Custody of Children Following Divorce*, 12 U.C. Davis L. Rev. 523 (1979), cited in J. Ryan, *Joint Custody in Canada: Time for a Second Look*, 49 R.F.L. (2d) 119, at 139.

67. Amicus Curiae Brief of the Women's Legal Defense Fund: Taylor v. Taylor, as quoted in Bill C-47 [Canada: Divorce and Corollary Relief]: *Joint Custody, Child Support Maintenance Enforcement and Related Issues*, a submission to the Standing Committee on Justice and Legal Affairs on behalf of the National Association of Women and the Law, presented by Louise Lamb and Mona Brown, Sept. 1985. *See generally* "Against Women's Interests: An Issue Paper on Joint Custody and Mediation" prepared for the National Action Committee on the Status of Women by M.L. Fassel and D. Majury, cited in A. Delorey, *Court Imposed Joint Custody: A Reversion to Patriarchal Power* (1989), 3:1 Canadian Journal of Women and the Law (forthcoming).

68. R. Neely, Chief Justice of the West Virginia Superior Court of Appeals in "The Primary Caretaker Parent Rule: Child Custody and the Dynamics of Greed," Trial, Aug. 1985, at 19.

69. Court Based Mediation in Four Canadian Cities: An Overview of Research Results, A Report prepared by C.J. Richardson for the Department of Justice Canada, Feb. 1988 (Minister of Supply and Services Canada, 1988), at 35.

70. R. Joyal-Poupart, "Joint Custody," in *Family Law in Canada: New Directions* (Ottawa: Canadian Advisory Council on the Status of Women, 1985), at 119.

71. H. Folberg & M. Graham, *supra* note 66, at 579, cited in J.P. Ryan, *supra* note 66, at 145.

72. N. Polikoff, *Amicus Curiae Brief, supra* note 67, at 18.

PROS	CONS
	families were in the stressed group . . . , and 31% had failed to agree or sustain the joint custody agreement . . . None of the successful families had involved the court in the determination of their agreement, and only one family in the stressed group arrived at joint custody through litigation and court investigation. However, in almost one-half (46.6%) of the failed cases, the judge, court mediator or attorneys determined the agreement with varying degrees of parental protest . . .'"[73]
"Courts must be responsive to the winds of change, in today's society, the breakdown of the traditional family is increasingly common, and new ways of defining post-divorce family structures are desperately needed. It is apparent that the traditional award of custody to the mother and access to the father is the cause of many of the problems and most of the tensions between parents and children and between the parents themselves. Our courts see many cases in which the father has been deprived of access. Gradually he loses interest or he finds he cannot afford to continue his court battles, and as a result the child is deprived of the love, influence and financial support of its father. Joint custody would seem to be the ideal solution to present challenges and past experiences."[74]	"[J]udges engaged in the resolution of custody litigation must take a realistic and practical approach to joint custody, and limit that form of an order to the exceptional circumstances which are rarely, if ever, present in cases of disputed custody."[75]

"Some advocates have suggested that . . . support is not paid precisely because visitation is obstructed or otherwise wrongfully denied. Data does not support this argument . . . From the mother's perspective there are frequent reports of complaints about the father's failure to visit his children . . . [M]others appear to respond much more cooperatively after visitation complaints are filed than fathers do after support delinquency complaints are filed."[76] |
| "The law should be made more flexible, making custody less an all-or-nothing proposition, a judicial determination that one parent will assume primary responsibility for raising and caring for a child should not necessarily exclude the other from the legal right to participate as a parent in many other significant areas of the child's life . . ."[77] | "I do not see how one parent separated from the child by a distance, with no opportunity to supervise or assist that child's day-to-day care could ever hope to hold joint custodial authority over the child with the person who holds that responsibility on a day-to-day basis."[78] |

73. S. Steinman et al., A Study of Parents Who Sought Joint Custody Following Divorce: Who Reaches Agreement and Sustains Joint Custody and Who Returns to Court?, as reproduced in vol. II appen. to NAWL Brief on Bill C-47, id.

74. Baker, supra note 68, at 196-97.

75. Baker v. Baker (1979), 8 R.F.L. (2d) 236, at 246, 95 D.L.R. (3d) 529, at 534 (Ont. C.A.) (Lacourciere, J.A.).

76. N. Polikoff, Custody and Visitation: Thier Relationship to Establishing and Enforcing Support, referring to studies by J. Greif and Lenore Weitzman and to data gathered in Travis County, Texas in vol. II appen. to NAWL Brief, supra note 67.

77. Kruger v. Kruger (1979), 25 O.R. (2d) 673, 11 R.F.L. (2d) 52 at 69, 104 D.L.R. (3d) 481 (C.A.) (Wilson, J.A. in dissenting judgment, quoting with approval from the Report on Family Law, Law Reform Commission of Canada, 1976).

78. Hackett v. Hackett (1985), 43 R.F.L. (2d) 5, at 10-11 (B.C.S.C.) (Sheppard, L.J.S.C.).

PROS	CONS
"Some women legitimately refuse joint physical custody because they have lived with men who have emotionally or physically abused their children. And some seek relief from physical spousal abuse or harassment. Others who refuse, however, are angry and rejected women who seek revenge and a reinstatement of self-esteem by using their children to punish a spouse who has terminated the marriage. There are also women whose identities are so bound up in their role as full time mother that they cannot envision sharing the parental role with the father without undue anxiety and fear for their own well-being. Further, there are emotionally disturbed women who, due to their own pathology, vigorously fight a father's desire to be involved in the children's lives. Some additional women have been advised by friends or parents not to allow the father anything more than traditional every-other-weekend visitation. In these various instances, there may be no legitimate reasons based on the father's capacity to parent for refusing to consider joint custody. Yet the children of such women would be denied more generous access to their father despite the real possibility that increased contact could be more psychologically beneficial."[79]	"Joint custody arrangements give the parent who does not live with the children (almost always the father) authority and control over decisions affecting the children and thereby authority and control over the mother. Meanwhile, the residential parent (the mother) continues to be responsible for the day-to-day care of the children."[80] "Joint custody legislation has serious ramifications for battered women. Battery does not end with divorce or separation; violence often increases when an abusive husband realizes he is losing control over his victim. Thus joint custody, which forces a continued relationship between the parents, may present an ever present life-threatening situation for the abused wife."[81] "Armed with the knowledge that they can always fight for joint physical custody, fathers are in a better position to negotiate lower support payments, and mothers are more inclined to accept lower maintenance orders, knowing that their unwillingness to cooperate may result in an unwanted joint custody order."[82]

Is It in the Best Interests of the Children?

"Children are part of a family; they have two parents and have a right to be influenced in their upbringing by each of the two parents. They have a right to the affection of each of the two and while divorce may dissolve the marriage it does not dissolve the parenthood."[83]	"[T]he drawbacks of an inappropriate joint custody arrangement are (i) the child may be caught in the middle of parental disagreements; (ii) if the arrangement includes shared physical care, the child can become anxious about his schedule, and feel burdened by maintaining a presence in two homes; and

---

79. J. Kelly, *Further Observations on Joint Custody*, 16 U.C. Davis L. Rev. 762-70 (1983), cited in H. Irving & M. Benjamin, *Shared Parenting in Canada: Questions, Answers and Implications* (1986-1987), 1 Can. Fam. L.Q. 79, at 99.

80. M. Fassel & D. Majury, "Against Women's Interests: An Issue Paper on Joint Custody and Mediation," prepared for the National Action Committee on the Status of Women, Apr. 1987, *supra* note 67, at 1.

81. Memo from the House of Ruth to the Maryland House Judiciary Committee, Mar. 3, 1983, reproduced in vol. II Appendices, *supra* note 67.

82. L. Lamb, *Involuntary Joint Custody: What Mothers Lose if Fathers' Rights Groups Win* (Jan./Feb. 1987) Horizons, at 31.

83. Csicsiri v. Csicsiri (1975), 17 R.F.L. 31, at 32 (Alta. S.C.) (Cullen, J.).

PROS	CONS
"Co-parenting says to the child that which-ever parent has moved out of the home will not move out of the child's life, and co-par-enting assures the child that he is not respon-sible for the break-up of marriage, as so many children imagine."[84]	(iii) if the arrangement is limited to joint legal custody, and the parent with whom the child does not reside in fact spend little time with the child, the parent who provides day-to-day care will be left with all the responsibility but not of the corresponding authority."[88]
"The requirement of the child for a stable environment must be weighed against the child's need for the care and guidance of both parents."[85]	"I am convinced that a young child, say under twelve or so, requires the security, stability and confidence engendered by being continuously with one loving parent."[89]
"Children need stability and stability comes in a variety of forms. I do not assume that stability equals one primary parent and one primary home. Stability can also mean a rela-tionship of constancy and permanence with two parents in two separate homes."[86]	
"The practice of giving sole custody to one parent has the effect of breaking the bond between the child and the noncustodial par-ent. The emotional consequence is equal to a loss as great as the death of the parent with the additional stress of knowing that the lost one is alive and potentially available."[87]	"The Oedipal child—that is the child of two and one half to five, who has plunged into the world of romance with strong love feelings toward the opposite sex parent and strong rivalrous feelings toward the one of the same sex— . . . cannot possibly have understanding or compassion for both parents. He or she needs reassurance that both parents are equally important and cared for but it may be best for that age child to live principally in one home for continuity and stability."[90]
"The advisability of dividing or alternating the custody of the child has been seriously considered. While there are certain disadvan-tages in such a decision, there are also import-ant advantages and benefits. It gives the child the experience of two separate homes. The child is entitled to the love, advice and train-ing of both her father and her mother. Fre-quent associations, contact and friendly rela-tions with both of her parents will protect her welfare, if one of her parents should die."[91]	"Joint custody is a terrible compromise for warring parents. When recommended in such situations, what may actually result is a no-cus-tody arrangement that merely is called joint custody. Neither parent has power nor con-trol, and the children find themselves in a no-man's land exposed to their parents' cross-fire and available to both as weapons. The likelihood of children developing a psycho-logical problems in such a situation is practi-cally 100 percent."[92]

84. M. Galper, Co-Parenting, Philadelphia: Running Press, 1978, at 88.

85. Abbott v. Taylor (1986), 2 R.F.L. (3d) 163, at 171 (Man. C.A.) (Twaddle, J.A.).

86. M. Galper, supra note 84, at 71.

87. E. Rosen, Joint Custody: In the Best Interests of the Child and Parents (1978), 1 R.F.L. (2d) 116, at 122-23.

88. A. Fineberg, Joint Custody of Infants: Breakthrough or Fad? (1979), 2 Can. J. Fam. L. 417.

89. Gerow v. Gerow (1978), 25 N.S.R. (2d) 229, 36 A.P.R. 229, at 230 (C.A.) (MacKeigan, C.J.).

90. R. Schreiber, Sharing Children of Divorce — Duration and Development (1983), 21:1 Conciliation Cts. Rev. 53, at 58.

91. Mullen v. Mullen (1948), 49 S.E.2d 349, at 355 (Sup. Ct. of App. Va.) (Spratley, J.).

92. R. Gardner, Joint Custody Is Not For Everyone, 5 Fam. Advocate, at 9.

PROS	CONS
"Two homes, i.e.: the home of father and mother (not necessarily resulting from remarriage) better meets the child's needs than one home."[93]	"A frequent shifting of the child from home to home exposes it to changes of discipline and habits and may invite lax discipline and disobedience. Stability in the human factors affecting a child's emotional life and development is essential . . ."[95]
"Children can be more fully exposed to the uniqueness of each parent: divided loyalties are no longer a problem when it is O.K. to love both parents freely and openly."[94]	"If the choice, as it may often be in separation and divorce proceedings, is between two psychological parents and if each parent is equally suitable in terms of the child's most immediate predictable developmental needs, the least detrimental standard would dictate a quick, final, and unconditional disposition to either of the competing parents. . . . A judicially supervised drawing of lots between two equally acceptable psychological parents might be the most rational and least offensive process for resolving the hard choice."[96]
	"Practical experience in the matrimonial jurisdiction leads to the conclusions that any separation of the responsibility for the child's upbringing and the authority to control it would in most cases end unsatisfactorily and in some cases disastrously."[97]
	"[T]he decree was open to the objection that it divided the control of the child, which is to be avoided, whenever possible, as an evil fruitful in the destruction of discipline, in the creation of distrust and the production of mental distress in the child."[98]

Conclusions

Parenting is not an abstract notion. The rearing of children, whether during the subsistence of a marriage or on its breakdown, encompasses a wide variety of cooperative relationships. Divorce is intended to sever the marital bond—not child–parent bonds. The twin legal concepts of "custody" and "access," which are used by lawyers and the courts to define parenting privileges and responsibilities on

93. M. Elkin, *Editorial: Reflections on Joint Custody and Family Law* (1978), 16 Conciliation Cts. Rev. iii, at v.
94. V. Eder, *Shared Custody: An Idea Whose Time Has Come* (1978), 15 Conciliation Cts. Rev. 23, at 24.
95. *Annotation: Child Custody*, 22 A.L.R.2d 695.
96. J. Goldstein, A. Freud, & A. Solnit, *Beyond the Best Interests of the Child*, New York: The Free Press, 1973, at pp. 63, 153.
97. Travincek v. Travincek (1966), 7 F.L.R. 440, at 444 (S.C. Vic.) (Barber, J.).
98. McCann v. McCann (1934), 173 A. 7, at 9 (Md. C.A.) (Parke, J.).

marital breakdown or divorce, tend to reinforce individual rights rather than the interests of the family as a whole. The integrity of the fragmented family is thus threatened.

The decision of the Manitoba Court of Appeal in *Abbott v. Taylor*[99] lends credence to the notion that the time is ripe to jettison the use of such ambiguous terms as "custody," "joint custody," and "access." Parenting roles and the feasibility of shared parenting after marital breakdown do not require the use of legal jargon, which itself fuels disputes and the prospect of future protracted litigation. Surely, it is not unreasonable to expect courts and lawyers to define precisely the responsibilities or privileges of each parent on marital breakdown in language that the parents and children can understand. Mediators with a behavioral science background encounter no difficulty in avoiding the use of the legal terms "custody" and "access." Their natural inclination is to think in terms of parenting rights, whether from the perspective of the parents involved or from the child's perspective. Lawyers, however, are reluctant to abandon the legal concepts of "custody" and "access" that have been hallowed over the years in legislative enactments and judicial pronouncements. In *Abbott v. Taylor, supra*, the Associate Chief Justice of the Family Division of the Court of Queen's Bench for Manitoba expressly refrained from using the words "custody" and "access" in a court order granted pursuant to the *Family Maintenance Act*[100] on the ground that the best interests of the child favored this course of action. When this approach was challenged on appeal, Twaddle, J.A., speaking for the three Justices of the Manitoba Court of Appeal, stated:

> The effect of the amendments of 1983 taken together is to emphasize the contribution which each parent can make to the development of his or her child even after cohabitation of the parents has ceased. The court must give effect to the legislative intent by crafting its orders to maximize the opportunities which both parents have to make such a contribution . . .
>
> The language of custody orders has ordinarily followed the language of the statute. Custody has, however, several aspects. If effect can be given to the statutory intention by the use of language more easily understood by the parties to the proceedings and the child whose custody is in issue, there can be no objection to it provided all the responsibilities of custody are conferred on the parents between them. I do not prescribe this choice of language, but approve of it when required in the best interests of the child.
>
> In the case at bar the learned Associate Chief Justice chose to use ordinary language in expressing the responsibilities which each parent should exercise with respect to the child. In principle, for the reasons I have just given, this course is acceptable . . .[101]

It is submitted that the use of ordinary language instead of the legal concepts of custody and access in determining parenting rights on marital breakdown should not merely be "acceptable"; it should be encouraged. The responsibility for drafting

---

99. (1986), 2 R.F.L. (3d) 163 (Man. C.A.).
100. *Supra* note 8.
101. *Supra* note 99, at 170-71.

comprehensive and readily comprehensible terms respecting parenting rights on marital breakdown must be assumed by the legal profession in the drafting of domestic contracts or minutes of settlement seeking to resolve parenting crises occasioned by marital breakdown. Abandonment of present legal terminology would not merely constitute a linguistic change; it would provide the basis for a functional approach that could accommodate the notion that "parents are forever," notwithstanding the breakdown or dissolution of the parents' marriage. Singularly few parents who divorce are incapable of making some positive contribution to the growth and development of their children of the broken marriage. There are those who are mesmerized by legal terminology and who advocate the implementation in Canada of a statutory presumption of joint custody on marital breakdown or divorce. It is submitted that such advocates need to refocus their approach. Such a legal presumption, which of necessity must be provisional and not conclusive, begs the question of the circumstances wherein the presumption of joint custody would be rebutted. Such a presumption opens the door to terminological confusion and to rebuttal evidence that emphasizes misconduct and unfitness to parent. This produces a negative perspective. What is needed is a positive perspective that is premised on past family history and prospective parenting plans that can accommodate the diverse contributions that each parent can make towards the upbringing of their children. Some three years ago, one of the authors (J.D.P.) made the following written submission to the Standing Committee on Justice and Legal Affairs, which was appointed to review Bill C-47, 1985, the *Divorce Bill* introduced by the Liberal government that died on the order paper when an election was called:

Parenting

It is submitted that Bill C-47 should have eliminated the legal labels of "custody" and "access" and should have been drafted in terms of parenting rights and responsibilities. The term custody, and more recently the term joint custody, have been the subject of diverse interpretations in Canadian courts and are obstacles rather than aids to the resolution of parenting disputes on marriage breakdown. Arguments as to whether joint custody is good or bad are futile. What the courts should be required to do is determine the best parenting arrangements that are feasible on the occasion of marriage breakdown. It is ironic that maintenance claims in divorce proceedings require the filing of a mandatory detailed financial statement, whereas no requirement is imposed with respect to spousal plans for the parenting of children after divorce. Although the current divorce petition includes materials relating to children of the marriage, the typical petition simply stipulates the names and ages of the children and the "custody and access" arrangements sought by the respective parties to the divorce proceeding. We hardly serve our children well when we insist on detailed financial statements to determine economic issues but require no detailed submissions respecting the personality, character and attributes of the children and the ability of each of the parents to contribute to their future upbringing. There seems no reason whatsoever why divorcing parents should not be required to submit a detailed plan concerning their prospective parenting privileges and responsibilities after marriage breakdown.

We see no reason to change this opinion. We would, however, add an important rider. Parenting plans must take account of the contribution to a child's growth and development that can be made by members of the extended families, including reconstituted families.

It is obvious that we must look beyond legal solutions. The focus must be on prevention, not punitive sanctions. There is no doubt that Canadian law has come a long way during the past decade in shifting the focus away from the adversarial legal process as a means of resolving the parenting crises of marital breakdown. For example, in 1982, the voluntary mediation of parenting disputes was legislatively endorsed in Ontario by section 31 of the *Children's Law Reform Amendment Act.*[102] In addition, section 30 of the *Act* empowered the courts to order a mandatory independent assessment in custody and access disputes, even if neither parent consented. The federal *Divorce Act, 1985*[103] now imposes a duty on lawyers to advise their clients of the advisability of resolving custody, access and support disputes by negotiation or mediation. These legislative provisions clearly acknowledge the inherent limitations of the adversarial legal process. That is not to say that the arsenal of legal weapons can be consigned to oblivion. The law and the courts still have a limited role to play, but it cannot be at the forefront of endeavors to promote more constructive solutions to the parenting crises of marital breakdown. Practicing lawyers and judges are increasingly recognizing the important role that mediators can play in the resolution of parenting disputes. The strength of mediation lies not only in the substantive dispositions that may be thereby achieved but also in its emphasis on the process of marital breakdown as a multi-faceted problem wherein the interests of all members of the fragmented family must be addressed in order to promote cooperative parenting after divorce. To return from where we started, namely linguistic considerations, even the hallowed legal criterion of the "best interests of the child" is a misplaced concept. In the words of Meyer Elkin, a pioneer in the field of court-connected conciliation services:

> We cannot serve the best interest of the child without serving the best interests of the parental relationship. The two cannot be separated. The kind of relationship the parents maintain during the divorce and after the divorce will have a significant impact on the children involved—for better or for worse. . . .
>
> Effective parenting cannot be proclaimed by court edict alone nor can desirable human behavior be legislated. But, effective parenting can be encouraged and realized with expert educational-counseling help. . . .
>
> Family law courts should allow divorcing couples more self-determination. It is their lives that are involved. It is their future. They should therefore be encouraged and allowed to play a greater part in the decision-making process, particularly in matters like custody and visitation. Rather than fostering increased dependency on the court, these couples should be encouraged to accept more responsibility for decisions affecting their lives and their children. If the anger is too great, if the communication between the parties is broken down, the impulse of the court should be to refer the couples to a court-connected marriage and family counselor before proceeding with the adversary process. Let us not underestimate the ability of divorcing persons to help themselves in their crisis. Let us not rob them of the opportunity to grow with the crisis. More self-determination, when appropriate, increases the chances for this to happen. . . .

---

102. S.O. 1982, c.20.
103. S.C. 1986, c. 4, § 9(2).

> A custody proceeding that focuses solely on what is in the best interest of the child is too restrictive an approach. More realistically we should also strive for what is in the best interest of the family. . . .[104]

In short, what is required in any process established to address the parenting consequences of marital breakdown is an appraisal of all realistic options that may accommodate the interests of all affected family members, including the members of any extended or reconstituted families. The pursuit of this goal must be unfettered by technical legal concepts, definitions, or procedures that impede a comprehensive evaluation of practical alternatives. It was within this framework that the Law Reform Commission of Canada[105] recommended that, whenever children are involved in divorce proceedings, the law should require an "assessment conference" involving the parents, children, and, where appropriate, members of the extended family. This conference should be informal in character and might take place before a court-appointed conciliator or in a community-based service. The purposes of the conference would be as follows:

1. to ascertain whether appropriate arrangements have been made for continued parenting of the children and, if not, to determine whether such arrangements can be worked out by agreement;

2. to acquaint all family members with the available resources in the community or the court that can assist in negotiating reasonable arrangements for continued parenting;

3. to ascertain the need for mandatory negotiation in the absence of an agreement being reached concerning continued parenting;

4. to ascertain the wishes of the children as well as those of the parents and members of the extended family;

5. to ascertain whether the children require independent legal representation;

6. to ascertain whether a mandatory independent psychiatric or psychological assessment is required; and

7. to ascertain whether a formal investigative report by a public authority, such as the Official Guardian, is required.

Whether you agree or disagree with these recommendations, or would prefer a less intrusive "informational or orientation process," there is an apparent need for the implementation of constructive legal and social policies and processes to promote cooperative parenting after marital breakdown so that neither parent is precluded from making a continued contribution to the welfare and development of the children. The notion that parents are forever must be reinforced.

---

104. M. Elkin, *Custody and Visitation: A Time for Change* (1976), 14:2 Conciliation Cts. Rev. at ii-v.
105. Report on Family Law, Information Canada, Ottawa, 1976, at 64-65.

Appendix A

Joint Custody Statutes and Judicial Interpretations

(as of January 1, 1991)

State/Citation	Approach	Terminology	Parental Agreement
ALABAMA Code of Ala. §§ 30-3-1, 30-3-2 (1983).	No mention in statutes. Implicitly precluded by statutory language authorizing award to "either" parent, but case law acknowledges that concept of joint custody is "recognized" in Alabama, *Simmons v. Simmons*, 422 So. 2d 799 (Ala. Civ. App. 1982) and joint custody awards are not a "palpable" abuse of discretion. *Hudson v. Hudson*, 414 So. 2d 196 (Ala. Civ. App. 1982).	None in statutes. Concepts of "joint legal custody" and "joint physical custody" implicitly accepted in case law. *See, e.g., Couch v. Couch*, 521 So. 2d 987 (Ala. 1988).	
ALASKA Alaska Stat. §§ 25.20.060, 25.20.070, 25.20.080, 25.20.090 (Supp. 1990), 25.20.100 (1983), 25.20.110 (Supp. 1990), 25.20.130 (1983).	Option.	*Shared Custody:* An award of shared custody shall assure that the child has frequent, continuing contact with each parent to the maximum extent possible.	Not required.
ARIZONA Ariz. Rev. Stat. Ann. § 25-332 (Supp. 1990).	Option. Shall not be the preferred custodial agreement, but may be granted if both parents agree, submit a written agreement to the court, and the court finds such an order is in the best interest of the child.		Required.

Plan	Findings	Modification	Other
		Change of circumstance needed to modify joint custody. *Means v. Means*, 512 So. 2d 1386 (Ala. Civ. App. 1987).	
Optional, but legislative policy encourages parents to develop own child-care plans outside of the court setting.	Required when parent or child's guardian *ad litem* requests shared custody and request is denied.	Change of circumstance required for custody modifications in general. Findings required when any modification ordered despite parental objection.	(1) Qualified legislative policy for frequent and continuing contact with each parent and encouragement of shared responsibility for childrearing. (2) Mediation is discretionary with court. (3) Equal access to each parent during pendency of proceedings unless detrimental to child. (4) Noncustodial parent has same access as custodian to child's records. (5) In making custody awards, court shall consider parents' past compliance with support orders or other agreements relating to children.
Required.	In considering an award of joint custody, the court shall make a finding that (1) Neither parent, as a condition of granting or withholding his agreement, was influenced by duress or coercion with respect to any factors before the court. (2) The parents can sustain an ongoing commitment to the child. (3) The joint custody agreement is logistically possible.	One year after joint custody order is entered, a parent may petition the court for a sole-custody order based on the failure of the other parent to sustain an ongoing commitment to the child.	(1) Has "friendly parent"* factor listed among those for consideration in custody decisions. (2) Noncustodial parent is entitled to reasonable visitation rights to ensure child's frequent and continuing contact with that parent unless detrimental to child.

*The term "friendly parent" is borrowed from Schulman & Pitt, "Second Thoughts on Joint Custody: Analysis of Legislation and Its Impact for Women and Children," 12 Golden Gate U. L. Rev. 538, 554 (1982).

State/Citation	Approach	Terminology	Parental Agreement
ARKANSAS Ark. Code of 1987 Ann. § 9-13-101 (1991).	No mention in statutes; "best interests" is custody standard. Case law states that although joint or "equally divided" custody is not generally favored, it may be ordered where circumstances warrant it. *Williams v. Williams,* 12 Ark. App. 89, 671 S.W. 2d 201 (1984).		
CALIFORNIA West's Ann. §§ 4600, 4600.5, 4607, 4608, 4727 (Supp. 1991).	**Presumption** that joint custody is in child's best interest when parents agree. CC § 4600.5. **Option** upon the application of either parent. The statute "establishes neither a preference nor a presumption for or against joint legal custody, joint physical custody, or sole custody, but allows the court and the family the widest discretion to choose a parenting plan that is in the best interests of the child or children." CC § 4600(1)(d).	*Joint Custody:* Joint physical and joint legal custody. *Joint Physical Custody:* Significant periods with each parent to assure frequent and continuing contact with both. *Joint Legal Custody:* Both parents share decision making regarding child's health, education, and welfare.	Not required.

Plan	Findings	Modification	Other
		Case law requires change of circumstance for modification of custody awards in general. *See, e.g., Feight v. Feight,* 253 Ark. 590, 490 S.W.2d 140 (1973).	
Court may require parents to submit plan.	Required on request of party in denial or grant of joint custody. Statement that joint physical custody is/is not in child's best interests is not sufficient. Required in modification or termination of joint custody if either parent opposes.	Findings required if either parent opposes. No changed circumstances need be shown to revise residential arrangement (physical custody) where joint legal custody remains unchanged. Court need only consider child's best interest. *Marriage of Birnbaum,* 211 Cal. App.3d 1508, 260 Cal. Rpts. 210 (1989).	(1) Public policy for frequent and continuing contact with both parents and encouragement of shared childraising responsibilities. (2) Joint legal custody may be awarded without joint physical custody. (3) Joint legal custody award must specify decision making that is mutual and that which is sole, and consequences for failure to obtain mutual consent. (4) Joint physical custody award must specify physical control in enough detail to allow enforcement of child-snatching laws. (5) Court may specify one home or parent as primary for purposes of welfare eligibility. (6) Noncustodial parent has same access to child's records. (7) Court may require parents to provide 45 days advance written notice of intent to change child's residence for period exceeding 30 days. (8) Mediation required; separate appointments possible in domestic violence situations. (9) Where both parents have custody more than 30% of the year, the court, in determining support, may take into consideration expenses incurred and savings resulting from shared physical custody. (10) In counties with conciliation courts, the parties may consult with the conciliation court for assistance in formulating a plan for the implementation of custody orders or to resolve controversies over implementation of custody orders.

State/Citation	Approach	Terminology	Parental Agreement
COLORADO Colo. Rev. Stat. §§ 14-123.5, 14-10-124, 14-10-131.5 (1987).	**Option** but legislative policy encourages frequent and continuing contact with each parent and shared responsibilities regarding childraising. Joint custody not in child's best interest when one parent has abused or neglected child and other parent (or child's guardian *ad litem*) objects to joint custody. Joint custody not in child's best interest when one parent has abused the other unless the court finds that the parties are able to share decision making without physical confrontation and danger to abused parent or child. *In re Marriage of Lester*, 791 P.2d 1244 (Colo. App. 1990) rejects argument that in enacting § 14-10-124 that General Assembly intended to state a preference or mandate for joint custody.	*Joint Custody*: Award of legal custody to both parents providing that all major decisions regarding health, education, and welfare shall be made jointly.	Required "except in the most exceptional cases." *In re Marriage of Lampton*, 704 P.2d 847 (Colo. 1985).
CONNECTICUT Conn. Gen. Stat. Ann. §§ 46b-56 and 46b-56a (1986).	**Presumption** that joint custody is in child's best interest when parents agree.	*Joint Custody*: Legal custody to both parents, with decision making joint and physical custody shared to assure continuing contact with both parties.	Not required.
DELAWARE 13 Del. Code Ann. §§ 722, 727, 729 (Supp. 1990).	**Option**, but "the recently enacted custody legislation strongly favors and encourages joint custody." *Dawn B. v. Eric B.*, CN90-7645 (Del. Fam. Ct. Nov. 1, 1990) (Available on WESTLAW, 1990 WL 255830).	*Joint Custody*: Not defined.	Not required.
DISTRICT OF COLUMBIA 5 D.C. Code §§ 16-911, 16-914 (1981, Supp. 1990).	No mention in statutes. Best interest of child is custody standard.		

Plan	Findings	Modification	Other
Required. The court shall formulate plan if the parties fail to submit one or the judge fails to approve it. The parties shall agree on the final plan.		Does not need change of circumstances when modifying from joint to sole custody or modifying any term of joint custody order, but need specified showing or parties' agreement to modify within two years.	(1) One parent may have longer physical custody than the other. (2) Factors for consideration in joint custody decision are listed in statute. (3) Mediation is discretionary with the court. (4) Has friendly parent factor for consideration in custody decisions. (5) Joint custody does not eliminate or by itself constitute change in duty to pay support. Court may order payment of support even when payor has child. (6) Change of circumstance not needed when modifying existing joint custody order. (7) Noncustodial parent has same access as custodian to child's records.
Not required.	Required when court fails to order joint custody despite parental agreement.	Case law requires change of circumstance for modification of custody decrees in general. *See, e.g.*, *Hall v. Hall*, 186 Conn. 118, 439 A.2d 447 (1982).	(1) Joint legal custody may be awarded without joint physical custody if parents have agreed only to former. (2) Discretionary mediation when one parent seeks joint custody. (3) Noncustodial parent has same access as custodian to child's records unless good cause shown.
Not required.		Custody modifications in general subject to best interest standard, with favor for present custodian absent certain factors.	(1) All custody orders must include a contact schedule. (2) Court may grant a temporary custody order to give parents an opportunity to show willingness to comply with the custodial arrangement ordered. (3) Noncustodial parent has same access to records and information about the child.

State/Citation	Approach	Terminology	Parental Agreement
FLORIDA West's Fla. Stat. Ann. § 61.13 (Supp. 1991).	**Mandated** shared responsibility unless finding of detriment to the child. Legislative policy to assure frequent and continuing contact with each parent and to encourage shared decision making.	*Shared Parental Responsibility*: Court may award one party ultimate responsibility over specific aspects of child's life or divide responsibilities.	Not required.
GEORGIA Ga. Code Ann. §§ 19-9-1, 19-9-3, 19-9-5, 19-9-6 (Supp. 1990).	**Option.** Court must ratify any agreement between the parents unless it is not in the best interests of the child.	*Joint Legal Custody*: Both parents have equal rights and responsibilities for major decisions relating to the child, but the court may give one parent sole power to make certain decisions. *Joint Physical Custody*: Custody shared by parents in such a way as to assure the child with substantially equal time and contact with both parents.	Not required.
HAWAII Haw. Rev. Stat. § 571-46.1 (1985).	**Option** upon application of either parent.	*Joint Custody*: Legal custody to both parents with physical custody shared to assure frequent and continuing contact with both parents.	Not required.
IDAHO Idaho Code § 32-717B (1983).	**Presumption** that joint custody is in the child's best interest absent preponderance of evidence to the contrary.	*Joint Custody*: Custody to both parents with physical custody shared to assure frequent and continuing contact with both parents. *Joint Legal Custody*: Parents required to share decision making. *Joint Physical Custody*: Significant periods of time with each parent to assure frequent and continuing contact with each parent; does not require equal or alternating time; court determines actual amount.	Not required.

Plan	Findings	Modification	Other
Optional.		Need change of circumstance to modify custody awards in general.	(1) Legislative policy for frequent and continuing contact and shared responsibility for childraising. (2) Factors for consideration in joint custody decision are listed in statute; friendly parent factor included. (3) Joint custody award does not preclude child-support order. (4) Abuse of parent may justify award of sole parental responsibility. (5) Court may designate a primary residence. (6) Noncustodial parent has same access as custodian to child's records.
		Need change in material condition to modify custody awards in general.	(1) Noncustodial parent has right to be notified of change in address of custodial parent. (2) Joint legal custody may be awarded without joint physical custody.
Optional.	Not required.	Joint custody may be modified or terminated on best-interest showing alone.	Joint legal custody may be awarded without joint physical custody.
Optional.	Required when court declines to order joint custody.	Change of circumstance needed to modify custody awards in general. *See, e.g., Poesy v. Bunney,* 98 Idaho 258, 561 P.2d 400 (1977).	(1) Court may order joint legal, joint physical, or both. (2) Noncustodial parent has same access as custodian to child's records.

State/Citation	Approach	Terminology	Parental Agreement
ILLINOIS Ill. Ann. Stat. Ch. 40, ¶¶ 602, 602.1, 610 (Supp. 1990).	**Option**—statutory preference for arrangements maximizing involvement of both parents is specifically *disclaimed* as presumption favoring joint custody. **Mandatory** for court to terminate joint custody when parties agree to termination.	*Joint Custody*: Custody determined pursuant to Joint Parenting Agreement or Joint Parenting Order. Joint custody does not have to mean equal parenting time.	Not required.
INDIANA Ind. Code Ann. §§ 31-1-11.5-21 (Burns, 1987), 31-1-11.5-22 (Burns Supp. 1990).	**Option**.	*Joint Legal Custody*: Parents share authority and responsibility for decision making. Award of joint legal custody does not require equal division of physical custody.	Not required; parental agreement is matter of primary but not determinative importance.
IOWA Iowa Code §§ 598.1 (1981 & Supp. 1991), 598.21 (1981 & Supp. 1991), 598.41 (Supp. 1991).	**Option** with strong legislative policy favoring maximum continuing contact with each parent and disfavoring parent who denies without just cause the child's opportunity for this contact.	*Joint Custody* or *Joint Legal Custody*: Both parents have rights and responsibilities, neither superior to the other. *Physical Care*: Right and responsibility to maintain child's principal home and to provide routine care; may be awarded to one joint custodial parent.	Not required.
KANSAS Kan. Stat. Ann. §§ 60-1610(a)(2), (4) (A) (Supp. 1990); 23-602 (1988).	**Preference**, yet in *In re A.F.*, 13 Kan. App. 2d 232, 767 P.2d 846 (1989), Court stated that "transferring a child back and forth every few days or alternating custody is, as a matter of law against the best interests of a child and an abuse of discretion."	*Shared* or *Joint Custody*: Equal rights to make decision in the child's best interest.	Not required.

Plan	Findings	Modification	Other
Required. If parents do not produce a Joint Parenting Agreement, the court shall order a plan addressing same required elements, or order sole custody. Required elements include dispute-resolution procedure and periodic review.	Required when court modifies or terminates joint custody over objection of a parent.	Change of circumstance needed to modify joint custody unless both parents agree to termination of award.	(1) Mediation is discretionary with the court. (2) Factors for consideration in joint custody decision are listed in statute. (3) Parents' Plan or court determines child's physical residence. (4) Noncustodial parent has same access as custodian to child's records.
Optional.	Finding of "best interest" required if court orders joint legal custody.	Change of circumstance needed to modify custody awards in general. Same standard should apply in modifying joint custody to sole custody and sole custody from one parent to another. *Meneou v. Meneou*, 503 N.E.2d 902 (Ind. Ct. App. 1987).	Factors for consideration in joint custody decisions are listed in statute.
Optional.	When court denies joint custody requested by one parent, court must cite clear and convincing evidence to support the denial.	Need change of circumstance to modify from joint custody decree to sole, at least where joint decree gave joint legal custody with physical care to one parent. *In re Marriage of Leyda*, 355 N.W.2d 862 (Iowa 1984). Enactment of joint custody legislation is a substantial change for modification.	(1) Mediation is discretionary with court; child's participation possible. (2) Factors for consideration in joint custody decision opposed by one parent are listed in statute; friendly parent factor is included. (3) Legislative policy for maximum continuing physical and emotional contact with both parents except when harmful to child, and shared childraising. (4) Noncustodial parent has the same access as custodian to child's records.
Optional.	Required when court does not order joint custody.	Material change of circumstances needed to modify any custody order.	(1) Child's residency shall be divided equally or established with primary residence arrangement. (2) Mediation available. (3) Friendly parent a factor in list for consideration in general custody decisions.

State/Citation	Approach	Terminology	Parental Agreement
KENTUCKY Ky. Rev. Stat. §§ 403.270(3), 403.340 (1990).	**Option.**	*Joint Custody:* Not defined.	Not required.
LOUISIANA La. Civ. Code Ann. Art. 131, 134 (West Supp. 1991).	**Presumption** rebuttable by parental agreement on sole custody, move by joint custodian out of state, or by other showing (based on consideration of statutory factors) that joint custody is not in child's best interest. **Preference** over sole custody.	*Joint Custody:* Parents share physical custody to the extent feasible and "natural co-tutorship" in accordance with plan; parents obligated to exchange information and unless otherwise ordered, to confer in decision making.	Not required.
MAINE Me. Rev. Stat. Ann. Tit. 19 § 752 (Supp. 1990).	**Mandatory** when parents agree; unless there is substantial evidence it should not be ordered. **Option** otherwise.	*Shared Parental Rights and Responsibilities:* Most or all aspects of child's welfare remain joint responsibility of both parents; each retains equal rights and must confer and make joint decisions. *Allocated parental rights and responsibilities:* a particular parent controls a specific aspect of the child's welfare.	Not required.
MARYLAND Ann. Code of Maryland, Family Law, §§ 5-203, 9-104 (Supp. 1990).	**Option.**	*Joint Custody:* Not defined in statute but discussed and authorized in case law, *Taylor v. Taylor,* 306 Md. 290, 508 A.2d 964 (1986). *Joint Legal Custody:* Both parents have an equal voice in decision making. *Joint Physical Custody:* Obligation to provide a home and day-to-day decisions; may, but need not be, 50/50 basis.	Not required.

Plan	Findings	Modification	Other
Optional.	Not required.	Change of circumstances needed to modify any custody order. When parties disagree about continuation of joint custody, modification should be made anew [under best interest determination] as if there had been no prior custody determination. *Benassi v. Havens*, 710 S.W.2d 867 (Ky. Ct. App. (1986).	
Required. Must address: allocation of time (for physical custody); legal authority; privileges and responsibilities of parents. May address: domicile; access and communication; support.	Required when joint custody is modified or terminated over objection of a parent.	Best interests standard determines modification or termination of joint custody order, and modification of sole-custody order to joint.	(1) Mediation discretionary with court. (2) Friendly parent factor listed among factors for consideration in joint custody decision. (3) Noncustodial parent has the same access as the custodian to the child's records. (4) Joint custody does not eliminate or by itself constitute change in duty to pay support. Court may order payment of support even when payor has child.
Optional.	Required when court denies award of shared parental rights and responsibilities despite agreement of the parties.	Case law clarifies ambiguous statute by requiring change of circumstance. *See, e.g., Philbrick v. Cummings*, 534 A.2d 1307 (Me. 1987). Actual or intended relocation of parent with shared parental rights and responsibilities constitutes a change of circumstance.	(1) Mediation mandatory. (2) Friendly parent factor listed, among others, for consideration in custody decisions. (3) Noncustodial parent has same access as custodian to child's records.
Optional.	Not required.	Case law indicates that change in custody in general requires change in circumstances and is governed by the best interests of the child. *See, e.g., Levitt v. Levitt*, 79 Md. 394, 556 A.2d 1162 (1989).	Noncustodian has same access as custodian to child's records.

State/Citation	Approach	Terminology	Parental Agreement
MASSACHU-SETTS Mass. Gen. Laws Ann. Ch. 208, §§ 28, 31 (Supp. 1991).	**Option.** Parents have shared legal custody during pendency of suit absent emergency, abuse, neglect, or order finding parental inability to cooperate. No presumption in favor of or against shared legal or physical custody at time of the trial on the merits.	*Shared Legal Custody:* Continued mutual responsibility and involvement by both parents in decisions regarding the child's welfare. *Shared Physical Custody:* Periods of residing with and begin under the supervision of each parent, assuring child of frequent and continued contact with both parents.	Not required but preferred. *Rolde v. Rolde,* 12 Mass. App. 398, 425 N.E.2d 388 (1981).
MICHIGAN Mich. Stat. Ann. §§ 25.312(6a) (1984), 25.312(7) (Supp. 1990).	**Mandatory** if parents agree, absent clear and convincing evidence joint custody is not in child's best interest. **Option** otherwise.	*Joint Custody:* Order specifying that child reside alternately for specific periods with each parent and/or the parents share decision making about child's welfare.	Not required.
MINNESOTA Minn. Stat. §§ 518.003, 518.17, 518.18 (Supp. 1991).	**Presumption** that joint custody is in child's best interest if one or both parents request joint custody. **Option** otherwise.	*Joint Legal Custody:* Both parents have equal rights and responsibilities regarding decision making. *Joint Physical Custody:* Child's routine daily care, control, and residence is structured between the parties.	Not required.

Plan	Findings	Modification	Other
Required if issue of custody is contested and either party seeks shared legal or physical custody.	Required when shared legal custody is not ordered during pendency of suit because of parental inability to cooperate. Required when court makes custody award that differs from parents' agreement. Required when court awards shared custody in spite of issuance of restraining order against parent pursuant to laws intended to prevent abuse.	Material and substantial change in circumstances required for modification of any custody order.	(1) Noncustodial parent has the same access as the custodian to the child's records, absent restraining orders. (2) Statute enumerates factors for determining if shared legal custody is in the best interests of the child.
	Required when joint custody request is granted or denied. Required when dispute regarding residency exists; court must state basis for residency award.	Generally need change of circumstance or good cause to modify, and need clear and convincing evidence of best interest to modify any custodial environment.	(1) Parents to be advised of joint custody in custody disputes. (2) Factors, including friendly parent factor, for consideration in joint custody decision are listed in statute. (3) Court may specify periods of child's residence or specify sharing to assure continuing contact. (4) Joint custody does not eliminate or by itself change duty to pay support; court may order support to continue even when payor has the child.
Optional.	Not required. Required as to joint custody factors if joint custody is awarded over the objection of a party. Minn. Stat. Ann. § 518.17a seems to require detail findings relating to best interest in all custody cases. *See also Klecker v. Klecker,* C9-90-1309 (Minn. App. Nov. 6, 1990) (Available on WEST-LAW, 1990 WLL 167817).	Change of circumstance required for custody modifications in general. But standards for modification of a joint custody arrangement do not apply to the modification of a joint physical custody arrangement where neither parent is primary physical custodian. Instead, best interest standard alone applies. *Klecker v. Klecker,* 454 N.W.2d 264 (Minn. App. 1990).	(1) Factors, including ability of parents to cooperate in rearing child, for consideration in joint custody decisions listed in statute. (2) Order must address custody (sole or joint) and physical custody or residence. (3) Joint custody not basis for departure from statutory support guidelines. (4) Noncustodial parent has same access as custodian to child's records. (5) Exchange of information regarding child's school attendance, accident, or illness required.

State/Citation	Approach	Terminology	Parental Agreement
MISSISSIPPI Miss. Code Ann. § 93-5-24 (Supp. 1990).	**Presumption** that joint custody is in child's best interest when parents agree. **Option** otherwise.	*Joint Custody:* Joint physical and joint legal custody. *Joint Legal Custody:* Parents share decision making regarding child's welfare and must exchange information and confer regarding decisions. *Joint Physical Custody:* Each parent has child significant periods of time, shared to assure frequent and continuing contact.	Not required.
MISSOURI Mo. Rev. Stat. §§ 452.375, 452.410 (Supp. 1991).	**Option.**	*Joint Legal Custody:* Parents share decision making and unless otherwise decreed, confer regarding decisions. *Joint Physical Custody:* Each parent has significant periods of time, shared to assure frequent and continuing contact with each parent.	Not required. Joint custody may not be denied for the sole reason one parent opposes the award.
MONTANA Mont. Code Ann. §§ 40-4-219, 40-4-222, 40-4-223, 40-4-224, 40-4-225 (1989).	**Presumption** that joint custody is in child's best interests when either or both parents request joint custody, unless found not in the child's best interest. **Option** otherwise.	*Joint Custody:* Order awarding custody to both parents and providing physical custody and residency be allotted to assure frequent and continuing contact with both parents. Allotment of time shall be as equal as possible but determined by individual practicalities.	Not required. Neither an objection by one parent nor a finding of hostility between the parents is sufficient to find that joint custody is not in the child's best interest.
NEBRASKA Neb. Rev. Stat., § 42-364 (Supp. 1989).	No mention in statutes. Case law states that joint custody is not favored and is reserved for only the rarest of cases. *Wilson v. Wilson,* 224 Neb. 589, 399 N.W.2d 802 (1987).	*Shared* or *Joint Custody.* Parents have equal rights to make decisions.	Yes (implicitly).

Plan	Findings	Modification	Other
Optional.	Not required.	Need change in circumstance to modify or terminate joint custody.	(1) Court may order joint legal or joint physical or joint legal and physical custody. (2) Noncustodial parent has same access as custodian to child's records. (3) Award of joint custody obligates parents to exchange information on child, and unless otherwise allocated, confer with each other in the exercise of decision making.
Required.	Not required.	Change of circumstance needed to modify custody awards in general, except no showing needed to modify to joint custody any decree entered prior to joint custody enactment.	(1) Court may award joint legal or joint physical, or joint legal and physical custody. (2) Factors listed for consideration in custody determinations include friendly parent. (3) Joint custody does not preclude award of child support. (4) Noncustodial parent has same access as custodian to child's records. (5) Obligation to exchange information regarding child.
Required.	Required when joint custody is granted or denied. Finding that one parent has physically abused the other parent or the child is a sufficient basis for finding that joint custody is not in the child's best interest.	Change of circumstance needed to terminate a joint custody-order but case law establishes distinction between this standard for termination and a best-interest standard for modifying terms of joint custody order which will continue. *Bergner v. Owens*, 222 Mont. 305, 722 P.2d 1141 (1986); *Gahm v. Henson*, 222 Mont. 300, 722 P.2d 1138 (Mont. 1986); *Keil v. Ferguson*, 805 P.2d 1334 (Mont. 1990).	(1) Legislative policy for frequent and continuing contact with both parents and encouragement of shared childraising. (2) Noncustodial parent has same access as custodian to child's records. (3) Friendly parent among factors listed for consideration in custody decisions.
Optional.	A hearing in open court is required and a specific finding that joint custody is in the best interest of the child, regardless of parental agreement or consent.	Change of circumstance required for modification of custody decrees in general. See, e.g., *Tautfest v. Tautfest*, 215 Neb. 233, 338 N.W.2d 49 (1983).	

State/Citation	Approach	Terminology	Parental Agreement
NEVADA Nev. Rev. Stat. Ann. §§ 125.480, 125.490 (1986), 125.510, 125A.350 (Supp. 1989).	**Presumption** that joint custody is in the child's best interest when parents agree to the award.	*Joint Custody, Joint Legal Custody, Joint Physical Custody:* Not defined.	Not required.
NEW HAMPSHIRE N.H. Rev. Stat. Ann. § 458:17 (Supp. 1990).	**Presumption** that joint legal custody is in the child's best interest when the parents have agreed or when either parent requests joint legal custody.	*Joint Legal Custody:* All parental rights with the exception of physical custody.	Not required.
NEW JERSEY N.J. Stat. Ann. §§ 9:2-4 (Supp. 1991??). [This statute was amended on 5/21/90 by 1990 N.J. Laws Ch. 26 § 2. The amendments were not yet in the pocket parts at the time of publication.]	**Option.** Court shall order any custody arrangement agreed to by the parents unless contrary to the child's best interests.	*Joint Custody:* Comprised of legal or physical custody. *Legal Custody* and *Physical Custody:* Not defined.	Not required.

Plan	Findings	Modification	Other
Optional unless court requires one be submitted.	Required when court declines to order joint custody despite the request of either parent. Required when either parent opposes court's modification or termination of joint custody.	Joint custody award modifiable or terminable on showing of best interest. Findings required when either parent opposes modification or termination.	(1) Legislative policy for frequent associations and continuing relationship with both parents and for encouraging shared childrearing. (2) Court may award joint legal custody without joint physical custody where parents have agreed on former. (3) Noncustodial parent has same access to child's records. (4) Consent/permission from court is required if child's residence is to be moved outside of state.
Optional.	Required when court declines to order joint legal custody. Required when joint legal custody is ordered despite evidence that abuse to parent has occurred.	Nothing in joint custody statutes shall be construed to alter standard for modifying decrees regarding physical custody. Case law holds that a change in circumstances affecting the welfare of the child is required before a change in custody will be ordered. *Webb v. Knudson*, 582 A.2d 282 (N.H. 1990).	(1) Appointment of guardian *ad litem* for the child may be made when one parent has requested joint legal custody. (2) When considering joint custody award, court shall consider as harmful to child evidence of abuse toward parent.
			Prior to 1990 amendment, joint custody was allowed by case law. *Beck v. Beck*, 86 N.J. 480, 432 A.2d 63 (1981) judicially endorsed joint custody and gave parents equal charge of child's welfare if in the best interests of the child, even over the objection of one parent.

State/Citation	Approach	Terminology	Parental Agreement
NEW MEXICO N.M. Stat. Ann. § 40-4-9.1 (1989).	**Presumption** in initial custody determination that joint custody is in child's best interest.	*Joint Custody:* Award of responsibility to make major decisions to two parents, not implying equal division of child's time or of financial responsibility for child. Each parent to have significant, well-defined periods of responsibility for the child and to consult regarding decisions.	Not required.
NEW YORK N.Y. Dom. Rel. Law §§ 236, 240 (McKinney Supp. 1991).	Not mentioned in statutes. Parents free to reach any custody agreement, subject to supervisory authority of the court. Authorized by case law. *Robinson v. Robinson,* 111 App. Div. 2d 316, 489 N.Y.S.2d 301 (1985), *appeal dismissed,* 66 N.Y. 2d 613, 189 N.E.2d 258.	Case law discusses shared decision making and physical custody as separate concepts. *See, e.g., Odette R. v. Douglas R.,* 91 Misc. 2d 792, 399 N.Y.S. 2d 93 (1977).	Apparently not required, but case law states that imposition over parental objection should be rare. *Braiman v. Braiman,* 61 App. Div. 2d 995, 378 N.E.2d 1019 (1978). *See also Trapp v. Trapp,* 136 App. Div. 2d 178, 526 N.Y.S. 2d 95 (1988).
NORTH CAROLINA N.C. Gen. Stat. §§ 50-13.1 (Supp. 1990), 50-13.2(b) (1987), 50-13.7 (1989).	**Option,** shall be considered on the request of either parent.	No definitions in statute.	Not required.
NORTH DAKOTA N.D. Cent. Code §§ 14-09-04, 14-09-0-6.1 (1981), 14-09-05, 14-09-06.2 (Supp. 1989).	Not mentioned in statutes. Implicitly precluded by language authorizing custody to [singular] "person, agency, organization, or institution."	"Alternating" custody allowed by case law, where each parent had child for six consecutive months. *Lapp v. Lapp,* 293 N.W.2d. 121 (N.D. 1980).	

Plan	Findings	Modification	Other
Required. Must include division of child's time and care. Court may accept parties' plan, agreed plan, or devise own.	Required whenever joint custody is granted or denied. Statement that joint custody is not in child's best interest is not sufficient.	Need substantial change of circumstance to modify to joint custody or to terminate joint custody.	(1) Mediation required when feasible. (2) Factors for consideration in joint custody decisions are listed in statute; includes friendly parent factor. (3) Court may specify circumstances when mutual consent is required for decision making and consequences of failure to obtain that consent. (4) Noncustodial parent has same access as custodian to child's records. (5) Detailed guidelines applying to major changes in child's life are set out in statutes.
		Change of circumstance needed to modify custody awards in general; request of party not enough by itself to terminate joint custody. *Jones v. Jones*, 65 N.Y.2d 649, 481 N.E.2d 241, 491 N.Y.S.2d 609 (1985).	
Optional.	Required for any custody order.	Need change of circumstance to modify custody awards in general.	Noncustodial parent has same access as custodian to child's records.
		Case law requires change of circumstance to modify any custody award. *See, e.g., Voth v. Voth*, 305 N.W.2d 656 (N.D. 1981) and *Reede v. Steen*, 461 N.W.2d 438 (N.D. 1990).	

State/Citation	Approach	Terminology	Parental Agreement
OHIO Ohio Rev. Code Ann. §§ 3109.04, 3109.041 (Anderson Supp. 1990).	**Mandatory** where parties jointly request shared parenting and file plan, if plan is in the best interests of the child. **Option** where one party requests shared parenting and plan is in the child's best interests.	*Shared Parenting*: Parents share, in the manner set forth in the plan, all or some aspects of the legal and physical care of their children. In shared parenting, parents have "custody of child" or "care, custody and control" of child.	Not required.
OKLAHOMA 43 Okla. Stat. Ann. § 109 (1990).	**Option.**	*Joint Custody*: Sharing by parents in all or some of the aspects of physical and legal care, and control of the child.	Not required by statute, but case law states that a cardinal criterion for a joint custody award is the agreement of the parties. It is error for a court to order joint custody *sua sponte* when neither parent has requested it. *Anderson v. Anderson*, 791 P.2d 116 (Okla. Ct. App. 1990).

Plan	Findings	Modification	Other
Required and must address all factors relevant to care of the child, including physical living arrangements, child support, medical and dental care, and visitation.	Required unless court orders shared parenting pursuant to plan jointly filed by both parents. Also required if shared parenting is ordered despite evidence that domestic violence or child abuse has occurred.	Court shall not modify prior decree allocating parental rights and responsibilities without change in circumstances. However: Terms of shared parenting plan may be modified by agreement of parents, or by court, if modification is in the best interests of the child. Court may terminate a jointly agreed-to shared parenting plan at the request of one or both parents if court determines that shared parenting is not in the best interests of the child. The court may terminate a shared parenting plan on its own motion if final plan was not jointly agreed to and if it is not in the child's best interests. Modification of decrees issued prior to shared parenting legislation are modifiable to shared parenting on best-interest standard.	(1) Factors for consideration in joint custody decision are listed in statute. Friendly parent factor is included. (2) A guardian *ad litem* may be appointed to represent the child. (3) Parties to custody decree issued before effective date of new legislation may move for shared parenting.
Required from parent(s) requesting joint custody. Must address at least physical living arrangements, child support, medical and dental care, schooling, and visitation.		Terms of joint custody award modifiable by agreement of the parties, or by the court at the request of one or both parents; with showing of best interest. Joint custody award terminable on showing of best interest.	Court may appoint an arbitrator to resolve disputes between joint custodians. Refusal to consent to arbitration may result in termination of joint custody.

State/Citation	Approach	Terminology	Parental Agreement
OREGON Or. Rev. Stat. §§ 107.105(1)(a), 107.149-.179 (1990).	**Mandatory** when parents agree. Not an option otherwise.	*Joint Custody:* Arrangement by which parents share rights and responsibilities for major decisions concerning the child, including, but not limited to, residence, education, heath care, and religious training. An order providing for joint custody may specify one home as the primary residence of the child and designate one parent to have sole power to make decisions about specific matters while both parents retain equal rights and responsibilities for other decisions.	Required and court may not overrule parents' agreement.
PENNSYLVANIA 23 Pa. Cons. Stat. Ann. §§ 5301–5310 (Purdon Supp. 1990).	Option.	*Shared Custody:* Shared legal custody (decision making) or shared physical custody (actual physical control) or both, in such a way as to assure child of frequent and continuing contact with, and physical access to, both parents.	Not required.
RHODE ISLAND Gen. Laws of R.I. § 15-5-16 (1988).	No mention in statutes but apparently allowed in practice. *See, e.g., Duke v. Duke,* 510 A.2d 430 (R.I. 1986), *cert. denied,* 479 U.S. 864 (1986). *Duke* holds that an award of sole custody was not abuse of discretion where parents were unable to maintain an amicable relationship. In *Marocco v. Marocco,* 571 A.2d 572 (R.I. 1990), an alimony case, the facts state that the parents had joint custody.		

Plan	Findings	Modification	Other
Optional.	Not required.	Modification of joint custody order requires change of circumstance. Inability or unwillingness to cooperate constitutes such change.	(1) Legislative policy to assure children of frequent and continuing contact with parents who have shown the ability to act in child's best interest and to encourage shared childraising. (2) Request for joint custody must be made at least 30 days before trial, except on good cause. (3) Mediation is mandatory and bifurcation of trial is discretionary to accommodate mediation. Exemptions for mediation granted for severe emotional distress. (4) Under any custody order, parents have continuing responsibility to provide addresses, phone numbers, and information regarding changes in child's health. (5) Noncustodial parent has same access as custodian to child's records.
May be required. Court services shall assist parties in developing plan when party or court requests.	Required when court declines to order joint custody despite parents agreement.	Modification to shared custody does not require change in circumstance. *Karis v. Karis,* 518 Pa. 601, 544 A.2d 1328 (1988) [& § 5301].	(1) Qualified legislative policy to assure child of reasonable and continuing contact with both parents and to encourage shared childrearing. (2) Counseling discretionary with court. (3) Each parent has same access to child's records but court may keep address confidential in situation of domestic violence.
		Change in circumstances required for modification of custody orders in general. *See, e.g., Fisher v. Miller,* 288 S.C. 576, 344 S.E.2d 149 (1986).	

State/Citation	Approach	Terminology	Parental Agreement
SOUTH CAROLINA Code of Laws of S.C. § 20-3-160 (1985).	No mention in statutes. Case law indicates divided custody and alternating custody is strongly disfavored. *Mixson v. Mixson,* 253 S.C. 436, 171 S.E.2d 581 (1969). *See also Bolick v. Bolick,* 297 S.C. 312, 376 S.E.2d 785 (S.C. Ct. App. 1989), stating that divided custody is to be avoided if at all possible and will not be approved except under exceptional circumstances.		
SOUTH DAKOTA S.D. Codified Laws Ann. §§ 25-5-7.1, 25-5-7.2, 25-5-7.3 (Supp. 1990).	Option.	*Joint Legal Custody:* Full parental rights and responsibilities with respect to child. Confer on major decisions affecting welfare of child.	
TENNESSEE Tenn. Code Ann. §§ 36-6-101, 36-6-102, 36-6-103, 36-6-104 (Supp. 1990).	Option.	*Joint Custody* or *Shared Parenting* not defined.	

Plan	Findings	Modification	Other
		Change in circumstance required to modify custody decrees in general, except when decree is based on stipulation of the parties. *Hansen v. Hansen*, 327 N.W.2d 47 (S.D. 1982).	(1) Residential parent shall decide all routine matters concerning the child. (2) Non-residential parent has same access to child's records.
		Custody decrees are subject to such changes or modifications as the exigencies of the case require. The primary consideration is the best interests of the child. *See, e.g., Woodard v. Woodard*, 783 S.W.2d 188 (Tenn. Ct. App. 1989).	(1) Copy of child's medical records and school report card equally accessible to parents.

State/Citation	Approach	Terminology	Parental Agreement
TEXAS Tex. Fam. Code Ann. §§ 14.01-.02, 14.081 (Vernon Supp. 1991).	**Mandatory** when parents agree and have filed plan satisfying statutory criteria. **Option** otherwise. **Prohibited** whenever credible evidence is presented regarding history of abuse toward parent or child or neglect of child.	*Joint Managing Conservatorship*: Sharing of rights even if the exclusive power to make certain decisions may be awarded to one party. Equal or nearly equal periods of physical possession of and access to the child not required. Ordinarily, best interest requires court to designate primary physical residence for the child.	Not required.
UTAH Utah Code Ann. §§ 30-3-10, 30-3-10.1 (1988), 30-3-10.2 (Supp. 1990), 30-3-10.3 (1988), 30-3-10.4 (Supp. 1990).	**Option** when in the child's best interest, and (1) both parents agree, or (2) both parents appear capable of implementing joint legal custody.	*Joint Legal Custody*. Sharing of rights where specified and may include exclusive authority in some matters; does not affect physical custody except as specified in order; is not based on equal or near equal physical custody as best interests often require designation of a primary residence; does not preclude designation of primary caretaker or residence.	Not required.

Plan	Findings	Modification	Other
Not required from parents but court will specify terms in decree to satisfy statutory criteria when parents have not submitted agreement. Plan/decree must address county of child's residence or which parent determines residence, support, education, and assigned/apportioned rights; dispute-resolution procedure is optional.	Courts must determine whether any plan submitted by parents meets statutory criteria. Court must also find by a preponderance after consideration of listed factors that joint award is in child's best interest.	Modification of the terms of a continuing joint managing conservatorship may be made by agreement of the parties if the agreement meets statutory criteria. The court may modify the terms of a continuing joint managing conservatorship is there are changed circumstances or the decree becomes unworkable or inappropriate and if the modification meets the best-interests standard. The court may terminate a joint managing conservatorship if (1) the welfare of the child is a matter of immediate and serious concern or there has been a substantial violation of the joint award or if there has been a material change in circumstances, *and* (2) the change to a sole award is in the child's best interests.	(1) Legislative policy to assure that children will have frequent and continuing contact with parents who have shown the ability to act in the best interest of the child and to encourage shared childrearing. (2) Court must specify joint and exclusive powers. (3) Court must specify exchange of information and, when possible, conferring on decisions. (4) Factors listed for awards when parents don't agree. Among these factors is whether each parent can encourage and accept a positive relationship between the child and the other parent. (5) Court must designate primary home for child for purposes of welfare eligibility. (6) Appointment of joint managing conservatorship does not limit court's authority to order child support, or constitute grounds for modifying a support order.
Optional.	Court must find that parents appear capable of implementing joint legal custody order, but statute does not explicitly require a *written* finding on this issue.	Need change in circumstance to modify joint legal custody award. Joint legal custody order is terminated upon both parents' filing motion to terminate.	(1) Friendly parent factor to be considered in any custody decision. (2) Factors listed for consideration in joint legal custody decision. (3) Court must inform both parties that joint custody may preclude welfare eligibility and that joint custody award is modifiable if welfare is necessary. (4) Joint custody award does not limit court's authority to order support or constitute grounds for modifying the order. (5) Court may order dispute-resolution alternative to parents.

State/Citation	Approach	Terminology	Parental Agreement
VERMONT 15 V.S.A. §§ 650 (1989), 657 (Supp. 1990), 664-670 (1989).	**Presumption** that divided or shared parent responsibilities agreed to by the parents are in the child's best interest.	*Shared Parental Rights and Responsibilities. Legal Responsibility.* Determining child's welfare other than routine daily care and control; may be sole, divided, or shared. *Physical Responsibility.* Providing routine daily care and control; may be sole, divided, or shared.	Required. If the parents cannot agree to divide or share parental rights and responsibilities, the court shall award the same primarily or solely to one parent.
VIRGINIA Va. Code Ann. §§ 20-107.2, 20-108 (1990).	Option.	*Joint Custody.* Means (1) joint legal custody where both parents retain joint responsibility regarding decision making even though child's primary residence may be with only one parent or (2) joint physical custody where both parents share physical care or (3) any combination of joint legal and joint physical custody the court deems to be in the child's best interest.	No.

Plan	Findings	Modification	Other
Optional, but when submitted, must address physical living arrangements, parent-child contact, education and medical care, travel, communication regarding child, and dispute resolving procedures.	Not required. *But see* Bissonette v. Gambrel, 152 Vt. 67, 564 A.2d 600 (1989) holding that trial court must consider all factors enumerated in § 665(b) and make findings on as many of those factors as the evidence will support.	Need change of circumstance to modify custody orders in general.	(1) Legislative policy for maximum continuing physical and emotional contact, unless direct or significant harm to the child likely to result. (2) Factors listed for consideration in custody awards; friendly parent factor included. (3) When each parent has physical custody (keeping children overnight) at least 30% of the year, total support obligations are increased 50% to reflect the cost of maintaining two households and then offset, such that obligor with greater obligation pays "difference" to the other parent. (4) Noncustodial parent has same access as custodian to records of child; access deniable if detriment to or abuse of parent. (5) Court may appoint guardian *ad litem* to represent child's interests.
Optional.	Not required.	Change of circumstance needed for modification of custody awards in general. *See, e.g., Eichelberger v. Eichelberger*, 2 Va. App. 409, 345 S.E.2d 10 (1986). Intentional withholding of visitation may constitute a change of circumstances. 1991 Va. Acts Ch. 438 (Mar. 20, 1991) (amending § 20-108).	Noncustodial parent has same access as custodian to child's records.

WASHINGTON
Wash. Rev. Code
Ann.
§§ 26.09.181,
26.09.184,
26.09.187,
26.09.191,
26.09.225,
26.09.260
(Supp. 1991).

Mandatory when parents agree to any allocation of decision-making authority. **Option** otherwise unless abandonment/refusal to parent, abuse, or domestic violence is found, then mutual decision making may not be ordered. **Option** for "substantially equal" residential periods, also.

Mutual Decision-Making Authority vs. *Sole Decision-Making Authority.* Not defined but meaning implied. [*Residence* to be determined by statutory factors, with greatest weight given to "primary caretaker." Substantially equal residential periods is discretionary with court and must be based on findings.]

Mutual decision making *cannot* be ordered over the objection of *both* parents. It *can* be ordered despite the objection of *one* parent when the court determines the objection is unreasonable based on specific criteria. Parent agreement is also not required for substantially equal residential periods if a satisfactory history of shared parenting exists and the parties are in geographic proximity. A settlement conference is mandatory where court rule provides for same.

WEST VIRGINIA
W. Va. Code
§ 48-2-15 (Supp.
1990).

No mention in statutes. Authorized by case law. *Lowe v. Lowe,* 370 S.E.2d 731 (W. Va. 1988).

Joint Custody or *Shared Custody.* Used in case law.

Required by case law. *Lowe v. Lowe,* 370 S.E.2d 731 (W. Va. 1988). However, case law permits awarding legal custody to husband while allowing wife physical custody every other week without parental agreement. *Loudermilk v. Loudermilk,* 397 S.E.2d 912 (W. Va. 1990).

Plan	Findings	Modification	Other
Proposed parenting plan is required from each party for any custody arrangement and must address dispute resolution, allocation of decision-making authority, residence, and support. Temporary parenting plan during pendency of suit is also required as basis for temporary order.	Required when substantially equal residential periods are ordered. Case law holds that, under 26.09.260 (*re* notification), it is error for court to fail to make findings as to each factor for determining whether modification is warranted. *In re Marriage of Stern*, 57 Wash. App. 707, 789 P.2d 807 (1990). *Review denied*, 115 Wash.2d 1013, 797 P.2d 513 (1990).	Need substantial change in circumstance to modify to joint custody and enactment of joint custody-legislation is not such change. Need substantial change to modify term or joint custody order. Preference for retaining ordered residence.	Factors listed for consideration of mutual decision-making awards. Each parent has the same access to child's records.
Parties "should submit . . . a joint parenting agreement." *Lowe v. Lowe*, 370 S.E.2d 731 (W. Va. 1988).		Need change of circumstance to modify custody awards in general. *See, e.g., Weece v. Cottle*, 352 S.E.2d 131 (W. Va. 1986).	

WISCONSIN
Wis. Stat. Ann.
§§ 767.001,
767.045, 767.11,
767.24, 767.325,
767.327, 767.329
(Supp. 1990).

Option only if the parents agree or one parent requests and specific findings regarding ability to cooperate are made. [Child and domestic abuse create rebuttable presumption of inability to cooperate and require clear and convincing evidence to the contrary.]

Joint Legal Custody: Both parents have equal rights regarding decision making with respect to specified decisions where one party has sole power. *Physical Placement.* Physical care and routine daily decisions not inconsistent with those made by sole or joint legal custodian.

WYOMING
Wyo. Stat.
§ 20-2-113
(Supp. 1990).

Not mentioned in statutes. Divided custody arrangements are not favored, but are allowed by case law. *See, e.g., Martin v. Martin*, 798 P.2d 321 (Wyo. 1990) (not abuse of discretion to order joint physical custody arrangement where each parent has custody for six months).

Case law uses "joint custody" without definition.

Not required by case law. *See, e.g., Feaster v. Feaster*, 721 P.2d 1095 (Wyo. 1986).

Plan	Findings	Modification	Other
	Required to support joint legal custody when one party objects. Required whenever custody or physical placement is contested or termination is opposed. Required when "joint legal custody and substantially equal physical placement decree" is modified because of parental move.	Custody orders may be modified by stipulation. Otherwise, no custody decree is modifiable within two years of entry unless showing of harm. After two years, need change of circumstance, and a rebuttable presumption favors the original terms. Decrees regarding substantially equal physical placement are modifiable on showing of best interest alone where it is impractical to continue such placement. Otherwise, decrees regarding substantially equal physical placement are modifiable on terms for general modification, above. Decrees regarding physical placement not substantially equal are modifiable on showing of best interest alone. Where decree orders joint custody and substantially equal physical placement, and one parent intends to move, any portion of legal custody or physical placement is modifiable if impractical to continue same physical arrangements. Any decree is modifiable without showing when parties agree.	(1) Factors listed for determination of physical placement allocation and for custody; friendly parent factor included. (2) One home or parent may be designated as primary for purposes of welfare eligibility. (3) Physical placement award must specify control in enough detail to allow enforcement of child-snatching laws. (4) Mediation referral mandatory where placement or custody is contested, or on request of parents agreeing to joint legal custody and physical placement. (5) 60 days advance written notice required of intent to move child more than 150 miles from other parent or to keep child out of state more than 90 days. (6) Noncustodial parent has same access as custodian to child's records. (7) Court may appoint guardian *ad litum* for minor children.
		Need change of circumstance to modify custody decrees in general. It is abuse of discretion to order automatic modification of custody order when either parent relocates. *Martin v. Martin*, 798 P.2d 321 (Wyo. 1990).	Noncustodial parent has same access as custodian to child's records.

Joint Custody Agreements and Provisions

A detailed shared-parenting agreement, with alternative clauses, is provided here. This sample custody agreement and its alternative provisions addresses only custody and support and makes no mention of property division and other matters that might be included in a complete settlement agreement. The requirements for a binding marital separation agreement, or custody and support stipulation, vary from state to state and may differ between jurisdictions within a state. Many of the sample provisions are followed by a reference source, some of which have extensive collections of marital settlement agreement forms and clauses, as well as checklists of what should be included in such agreements. Full citation to these reference sources are contained in the Bibliography. Those provisions without a reference are either the editor's or from sources which could not be identified.

IN THE _____ COURT OF THE STATE OF _____
FOR THE COUNTY OF _____
DEPARTMENT OF DOMESTIC RELATIONS

In the Matter of the Dissolution of the Marriage of

JOHN DOE	)	
Petitioner,	)	
	)	CASE NO._____
and	)	
	)	STIPULATED PARENTING AND
JANE DOE	)	CHILD SUPPORT AGREEMENT
Respondent	)	

(RECITALS)

We, John Doe, here referred to as the Father, and Jane Doe, here referred to as the Mother, are husband and wife. We have one child of our marriage, a boy, here referred to as John Jr., who is nine years old.

Irreconcilable differences have arisen between us causing the irremediable breakdown of our marriage and we have agreed to file a petition for dissolution. We have lived apart approximately two years.

(STATEMENT OF INTENT/PURPOSE/FITNESS)

We have continued to share physical and legal responsibilities for John Jr. and have cooperated in providing for his needs. He appears to have adjusted well to the existing situation. We each have a significant nurturing relationship with our child that is important to all of us.

We believe each of us to be fit parents and recognize the unique contribution each of us has to offer our child. We wish to continue to share responsibility for the care of John Jr., and each fully participate in all major decisions affecting his residence, health, education, and welfare while disrupting his life pattern as little as possible.

We intend to seek joint custody of John Jr. and propose only the most minimal necessary formality in scheduling his care, subject to consideration of schedules and the necessity of reasonable notice, in order to retain a flexible opportunity for each of us to be with John Jr. and help raise him. Our primary concern has been and shall be the best interest of our child within the reality of our marital dissolution.

(AGREEMENT)

IT IS HEREBY STIPULATED BY AND BETWEEN PETITIONER AND RESPONDENT that:

(SHARED PARENTING)

1. Mother and Father will share and participate in the joint physical and legal parenting of John Jr. Parenting of John Jr. shall be shared as set forth below.

(RESIDENCE)

2. John Jr. shall reside with each parent on an approximately equal basis. He shall reside with Mother for two weeks and then reside with Father the following two weeks, alternating between Mother and Father every other Sunday at 6 p.m. This residential arrangement is conditioned upon both parents residing in the same school district and is subject to the provisions of paragraph 10(a) regarding changed circumstances.

(SPECIAL TIMES, HOLIDAYS, AND VACATIONS)

3. (a) John Jr. shall be with the parent with whom he is not residing one evening a week commencing by 5 p.m. and be returned to where he is residing by 9 p.m.

(b) Holidays shall be spent with the parent with whom John Jr. is scheduled to reside, with the following exceptions:

Mother's Day—with Mother
Father's Day—with Father
Maternal grandparents' birthdays—with Mother
Paternal grandparents' birthdays—with Father
Week preceding Christmas through Christmas Eve—with Mother
Christmas Day from noon through following week—with Father
  (Parents alternate Christmas/Thanksgiving each year.)
Thanksgiving Eve through 2 p.m. Thanksgiving Day—with Mother
Thanksgiving Day from 2 p.m. through Thanksgiving Night—with Father
John Jr.'s birthday—with Mother, alternating years
Summer school recess—six weeks with Mother; six weeks with Father unless regular schedule prevails by mutual consent (Each March, parents will confer to review plans for John Jr.'s summer activities.)
One-day "tax holiday"—Each parent alternates years if necessary to establish Head of Household Status

(PARENTING RESPONSIBILITIES AND COOPERATION)

4. (a) The parent with whom John Jr. is residing or currently with shall be responsible for daily care and shall make necessary decisions regarding emergency medical or dental care.

(b) All major decisions regarding John Jr.'s education, religious training, cultural and artistic training, nonemergency health treatment, and general welfare shall be made by both parents together.

(c) Each parent agrees to confer on a regular basis concerning the child's needs, growth, and care, and will share and make accessible all school records and report cards.

(d) Each will permit and encourage communication by the other with teachers and school administrators regarding John Jr.'s educational progress.

(e) It is expressly understood that the above-enumerated times that each parent shall be with John Jr. and responsible for his care are subject to modifications by mutual agreement pursuant to paragraph 10.

(f) Flexibility in child-care responsibilities and involvement are to be encouraged and the terms of this Agreement are to be liberally interpreted to allow John Jr. the maximum benefit to be derived from the love, concern, and care of both Mother and Father.

(g)   Each parent agrees to promote in John Jr. respect and affection for the other parent.

(h)   Mother and Father will annually confer and review the shared custody plan as to its adequacy, feasibility, and appropriateness in consideration of John Jr.'s age and developmental progress. This review shall take place at a mutually convenient time between spring school break and summer vacation.

(CHANGE OF RESIDENCE RESTRICTION)

5. Neither parent will move John Jr.'s place of residence from the state of _____ without the written consent of the other parent. If either parent moves or attempts to move John Jr.'s residence outside of _____ without the other's written consent, then from the time of such move or attempted move, the parent remaining in the state shall be considered the sole custodial parent of John Jr. for all purposes.

(FINANCIAL SUPPORT OF CHILD)

6. Each parent shall deposit by the third day of each month, commencing _____, 199_, an amount of money for support of John Jr. in a joint checking account requiring both their signatures and restricted to payment and reimbursement of expenses incurred on behalf of John Jr. The parents will share child-support costs proportional to their gross income over $10,000 for the previous calendar year. These expenses will include food, child care, education, lessons, summer camp and activities, clothing, grooming, allowances, medical care, health insurance, travel, major gifts, and agreed-upon amounts of other expenses incurred for John Jr.'s benefit until he becomes eighteen years of age. The parents will discuss near the end of each month the expenses for that month to determine the necessary total contribution required. Such monthly total shall not, in any event, be less than $200 per month.

7. Each parent agrees to contribute to a tax-deferred annuity or trust account for the benefit of John Jr. a total of $100 each month on the same formula and condition set forth in Paragraph 6. The income and principal of this annuity or trust account is to be applied to pay to John Jr., or for his benefit, necessary amounts for his support, maintenance, books, and tuition while he is under twenty-one years of age and a student regularly attending as a full-time student a school, community college, college, or university, or regularly attending a course of vocational or technical training designed to prepare him for gainful employment. If the annuity or trust account is not used for John Jr.'s advanced education as above provided, or is not exhausted by his twenty-first birthday, then the account may be used for his benefit or paid to him as his Mother and Father may agree, or divided between the parents proportionate to each of their contributions to it.

(MEDICAL PROVISIONS)

8. Father agrees to declare John Jr. a dependent for medical insurance purposes and will include him under his employer's medical insurance program for so long as such insurance is available as an employee benefit. Additional medical expenses will be assumed by both parents on an identical ratio reflecting the child-support formula as set forth in Paragraph 6.

   (a) Both parents agree that all medical, surgical, and dental records of John Jr. will be available and accessible to both of them.

   (b) Each parent will permit and encourage communication by the other parent with doctors, clinics, and other health providers regarding John Jr.'s health and welfare.

   (c) Each parent agrees to provide advance notification to the other parent about proposed and forthcoming medical care and each will inform the other of any medical emergencies.

(LIFE INSURANCE PROVISIONS)

9. Father shall keep current insurance on his life in an amount of not less than $100,000 and Mother shall keep current insurance on her life in an amount of not less than $100,000 with John Jr. as beneficiary until he reaches the age of twenty-one, for the purposes of securing his support and expenses to that age as set forth in Paragraph 6.

(TAX PROVISIONS)

10. The parent contributing more than 50 percent of John Jr.'s child support for that calendar year shall be entitled for that year to the dependency exemption for John Jr. on federal and state income tax returns. In the event that the parents each contribute one half of the support for John Jr. in any year, the parents shall alternate claiming John Jr. as a dependent, beginning with the Mother.

(CHANGES IN CIRCUMSTANCES)

11. Should any change of circumstance occur, materially affecting the care of John Jr. or either parent's access to him, the residential care and arrangements for him shall be considered by the parents in light of then existing circumstances.

   (a) Should either Mother or Father change residences, so that he or she no longer lives in the same school district, or if either changes job patterns, every effort shall be made to facilitate the continued exercise of joint custody, so that John Jr. continues to enjoy the benefit of both parents in as close to equal time proportions as practicable, taking into consideration, among other factors, the needs and developmental stage of John Jr.

(b)   In considering future living arrangements for John Jr., Mother and Father shall have regard for his preference and the environment and care which each parent can provide.

(c)   This Agreement is intended generally not to be affected by the remarriage of either parent.

(AMENDMENTS OR MODIFICATIONS)

12. We agree that this Agreement may be modified or amended by stipulation at any time, but if changes are to be permanent or significantly affect shared parenting rights or responsibilities, they shall be reduced to writing by the parties and recorded with the court.

(DISPUTE RESOLUTION)

13. Both parents will attempt to work together to avoid any further disputes. Should any disputes arise which they cannot resolve, both parents wish to avoid the expense and acrimony of formal court proceedings. Therefore, any controversy arising out of, or relating to, this Agreement or breach of this Agreement shall first be submitted to the process of mediation through the services of a mediator on whom they mutually agree. Both parents agree to follow the process of mediation to its conclusion prior to either party's seeking further relief or modification from a court.

(CONSEQUENCES ARISING FROM DEATH OF ONE OR BOTH PARENTS)

14. Mother and Father agree that should either parent die before John Jr. becomes twenty-one years of age, the surviving parent shall assume custody and provide for his needs until John Jr. is twenty-one years of age. Should both parents die before that time without remarrying, both parents agree that John Jr.'s maternal aunt, Mary Smith, shall assume custody, acting as guardian for John Jr. according to the spirit of this stipulated Custody Agreement and the provisions in the Will of the last surviving parent. If one or both parents have remarried at the time of the death of both parents and John Jr. has developed a significant relationship with either or both stepparents, future living arrangements shall take into account, among other considerations, John Jr.'s preferences and the environment and care which his stepparent or stepparents may provide.

(ACKNOWLEDGMENTS OF RIGHTS AND OBLIGATIONS)

15. We acknowledge that each of the respective rights and obligations under this Agreement shall be deemed independent and may be enforced independently irrespective of any of the other rights and obligations set forth in the Agreement.

(BINDING EFFECT OF CUSTODY AGREEMENT)

16. We accept the foregoing as a full, final, and complete settlement of all of our custody and child-support rights arising from or growing out of our marital relationship. In consideration of the terms expressed, we release and relieve each other from any payments or obligations now or in the future regarding such custody and child-support rights, other than those specifically set forth in this stipulated Agreement, and we acknowledge and accept this Agreement as full settlement of all obligations and demands that either or both of us might or could have in any form against the other's estate on account of any matter whatsoever regarding custody and child-support rights arising from or growing out of our marital relationship.

17. We understand and agree that this stipulated Agreement will be submitted to the court for its approval and may be incorporated with full force and effect in any decree that may be entered in any proceeding for the dissolution of our marriage.

IN WITNESS WHEREOF, the parties have solemnly agreed and signed their names.

JOHN DOE	JANE DOE
Petitioner	Respondent

APPROVED AS TO FORM AND CONTENT

Attorney for Petitioner

Attorney for Respondent

DATED: _____

ALTERNATIVE CLAUSES

(RECITALS)

The parties are the parents of _____, born _____. Both parents acknowledge their concern for their minor child(ren), and have entered into this agreement for the purpose of sharing their parental responsibility for the welfare of and in the best interest of their minor child(ren). [Source: Sessums]

(STATEMENT OF INTENT/PURPOSE/FITNESS)

(Option 1)

Even though we choose to end our marriage, we are both good parents and wish to continue being actively involved in our child(ren)'s life as we were when our marriage was intact. We together can make decisions in the best interests of our child(ren) and can isolate our prior marital conflicts from our roles as parents. Shared parenting would disrupt our child(ren)'s life less than other arrangements and would allow the maximum benefit to our child(ren) of our love, concern, and care.

In agreeing to shared parental responsibility, each of us will continue having a full and active role in providing a sound moral, social, economic, and educational environment for our child(ren) and will continue that support which he/she/they has/have received to date. We will consult with each other in substantial questions relating to living arrangements, travel and transportation, religious upbringing, educational programs, financial, moral, social, recreational, and legal matters, discipline, and medical and dental care.

In accepting the broad grant of privileges conferred by this shared responsibility arrangement, we specifically recognize that these powers will not be exercised for the purpose of frustrating, denying, or controlling in any manner the social development of the other parent. We will exert our best efforts to work cooperatively in future plans consistent with the best interests of our child(ren) and in amicably resolving such disputes as any arise.

The physical placement and schedule will be decided jointly by us, and any arrangement which we decide will assure that our child(ren) has/have frequent and continuing contact with each of us.

We have conferred with each other, our child(ren), and our attorneys as to the feasibility of a shared parental arrangement and have concluded that such an arrangement is in the best interests of our newly structured family. [Source: Family Law Div., Hillsborough County, Fla.]

(Option 2)

It is our intention in agreeing to shared parental responsibility, that each of us shall continue having a full and active role in providing a sound moral, social, economic, and educational environment for the child(ren). We are both good parents and we wish to continue that support which each child has received to date.

We shall consult with one another in substantial questions relating to religious upbringing, educational programs, significant changes in social environment, and nonemergency health care of the child(ren).

In accepting the broad grant of privileges conferred by this parental responsibility arrangement upon each of the parents, we specifically recognize that these powers shall not be exercised for the purpose of frustrating, denying, or controlling in any manner the social development of the other parent. We shall exert our best efforts to work cooperatively in future plans consistent with the best interests for the child(ren) and in amicably resolving such disputes as may arise. [Source: Gaddis]

(AGREEMENT)

IN CONSIDERATION OF THE PROMISES MADE BY EACH OF US TO THE OTHER, IT IS AGREED BETWEEN US AS FOLLOWS:

(PARENTING RESPONSIBILITIES AND COOPERATION)

In connection with shared parental responsibility, we shall:

(SHARED PARENTING)

1. We both shall have shared parental responsibility and shall retain full parental rights and responsibilities with respect to the minor child(ren) subject to the following terms and conditions:

    (i) confer to exchange information and determine jointly the minor child(ren)'s well-being, education, moral-ethical-religious training, standards of conduct, supervision, travel, and nonemergency health care.

    (ii) notify the other promptly of any serious illness or accident befalling the child(ren).

    (iii) have access to records and information pertaining to the minor child(ren) including, but not limited to, medical, dental, and school records.

    (iv) be entitled to participate with and attend special activities in which the child(ren) are engaged, such as religious activities, school programs, sports events, and other extracurricular activities and programs and important social events in which the child(ren) are in or in which they may be engaged or involved.

    (v) be entitled to authorize emergency medical treatment for the minor child(ren).

    (vi) use all reasonable efforts to maintain free access and to create a feeling of affection between themselves and the minor child(ren); neither of us shall do anything to hamper the natural development of the child(ren)'s love and respect for the other party, but shall make all reasonable efforts to facilitate communication between the other party and the minor child(ren), both by telephone and through the mail.

(vii) not at any time for any reason cause the minor child(ren) to be known or identified or designated by any name other than _____ and neither shall initiate nor cause the designation of "father" or "mother" or their equivalent to be used by the minor child(ren) with reference to any person other than the parties hereto.

(viii) keep the other informed at all times of the whereabouts of the minor child(ren) when he/she/they are with either of the parties or with others. [Source: Frumkes & Sessums]

(RESIDENCE)

(Option 1)

(a) The primary physical residence of the minor child(ren) shall be in the home of _____. With respect to the geographical location of the _____ residence as a primary physical residence of the minor child(ren), _____ shall have sole responsibility for determining the location of such residence so long as such physical residence is within _____.

(b) The _____, who shall be the nonresidential parent, shall have frequent and continuing contact with the minor child(ren). [Source: Sessums]

(Option 2)

Since a "fixed residential schedule" is neither necessary or desirable at this time, and since the parents are capable of implementing a residence schedule informally, the resolution of the residence schedule will be guided by the intent of the custody agreement (decree). [Source: Cook]

(Option 3)

Exclusive of holiday and vacation periods, residence of the minor child(ren) will be alternated between parents on the basis of (insert one of the following): [See corresponding clauses below.] [Source: Cook]

—Freedom of movement by the child(ren) between two homes.
—3½ days / 3½ days.
—One week / One week.
—Two weeks / Two weeks.
—One month / One month.
—Two (Three) months / Two (Three) months.
—School year / Entire summer vacation, with equalizing weekends and "overnights."
—Workday week / weekends.
—Child(ren) remain in home and parents alternate.

3½ days / 3½ days. Each parent will have the exclusive responsibility for assuring the minor child(ren)'s schedule of school, activity, play, and rest according to the following schedule based on a time split of 3½ days / 3½ days.

The minor child(ren) will be resident with the *(mother/father)* from 12 noon, Wednesday until the following 9:30 p.m. Saturday *or* 8:00 a.m. Sunday. The minor child(ren) will be resident with the *(opposite parent)* during the alternate 3½ day period.

(Note: Three-and-a-half day schedules may also be staggered in at least two other alternatives:

(1) To provide a parent with a unified Saturday and Sunday weekend, or

(2) Provide each parent with a full, but alternate, weekend, and split residency of the five remaining week days.)

One week / One week. The minor child(ren) will be resident with the *(mother/father)* from 5:30 p.m. Friday until 5:30 p.m. Friday one week later commencing the first full week in January 19__. The minor child(ren) will be resident with the *(opposite parent)* during the alternate week.

Two weeks / Two weeks. The minor child(ren) will be resident with the *(mother/father)* from 5:30 p.m. Friday until 5:30 p.m. Friday two weeks later commencing the first full week in January 19__. The minor child(ren) will be resident with the *(opposite parent)* during the alternate two weeks.

One month / One month. The minor child(ren) will be resident with the *(mother/father)* from 9:30 p.m. on the last day of the month until 9:30 p.m. on the last day of the ensuing month commencing with the last day of December 19__. The minor child(ren) will be resident with the *(opposite parent)* during the alternate month.

Two (three) months / Two (three) months. The minor child(ren) will be resident with the *(mother/father)* from 9:30 p.m. on the last day of the month until 9:30 p.m. on the last day of the month two (or three) months hence commencing with the last day of December 19__. The minor child(ren) will be resident with the *(opposite parent)* during the alternate two (three) month period.

School year / Entire summer vacation. The minor child(ren) will be resident with the *(mother/father)* from the first day of school in the Fall until the last day of school at the conclusion of the Spring. The minor child(ren) is resident with the *(father/mother)* alternately, during the summer period. To balance the available residence time, however, during the school year the minor child(ren) will be resident with the *(father/mother)* every other weekend commencing the second week after school has opened in the Fall and the minor child(ren) shall be entitled to an additional one night a week "overnight" with the *(same parent)* during the school year.

During the holidays occurring throughout the school year, residence by the minor child(ren) will be alternated, every other year, with the *(opposite parent from the one having residence during the school year)*.

In exchange for residence with the *(father/mother)* during the summer vacation, the minor child(ren) will be resident with the *(opposite parent)* one weekend a month during the summer from 5:30 p.m. Friday until 8:30 a.m. Monday. Unless mutually agreed by both parents, the summer exchange weekend-a-month will commence on the third weekend after school has adjourned at the conclusion of the Spring school semester.

During individual one-day holidays occurring throughout the summer vacation period, residence by the minor child(ren) will be alternated, every other year, with the *(opposite parent from the one having residence during the summer vacation)*.

Workday week / Weekends. The minor child(ren) will be resident with the *(father/ mother)* during the workday week to extend from *(hour)* m. *(day)* until *(hour)* m. *(day)*. Alternately, the minor child(ren) will be resident with the *(opposite parent)* each weekend from *(5:30 p.m. Friday)* until *(8:30 a.m. Monday)*.

The *minor child(ren) will remain resident in the family home.* The parents will alternate residence in the family home and will enjoy the prerogatives of scheduling the care and responsibility for the minor child(ren) during their residence in the family home according to the following schedule. (Each parent's schedule of time available for residence in the home.)

(SPECIAL TIMES, HOLIDAYS, AND VACATIONS)

(Option 1)

It is contemplated by this agreement that _____, with whom the minor child(ren) do not maintain their primary physical residence, shall have the most liberal and frequent contact and access with the child(ren). Each of the parties shall exercise the utmost of good faith and consent to all reasonable requests of the other party in connection therewith. Not as a limitation, but as an extension of the foregoing, _____ is entitled to and may avail him/herself of at least the minimum contact and access as shall hereinafter be set forth, which may vary from time to time by mutual agreement.

The minimum contact and access to which _____ shall be entitled shall be as follows. [Source: Frumkes]

(Option 2)

During national holidays on a Friday or a Monday, with the exception of Christmas, the minor child(ren) will remain in residence for the additional one-day holiday with the parent otherwise responsible for the child(ren)'s residence during the adjoining weekend. All other holidays and events will be apportioned accordingly. [Source: Cook]

Minor child's birthday. From 8:00 a.m. on nonschool days and from 5:00 p.m. on school days, until 9:30 p.m. the minor child(ren) will be with the *(mother/father)* on even-numbered years and with the *(opposite parent)* on odd-numbered years.

Father's birthday. Mother's birthday. From 8:00 a.m. on nonschool days and from 5:00 p.m. on school days, until 9:30 p.m. the minor child(ren) will be with the respective parent during that parent's birthday.

Christmas Eve and Christmas Day. On odd-numbered years (ascertain that this is the opposite year of that pertaining to allocation of the child(ren)'s birthday) from 5:00 p.m. on Christmas Eve until 11:00 a.m. Christmas Day, the minor child(ren) will be resident with the father, and for the remainder of Christmas Day until 9:30 p.m. the minor child(ren) will be resident with the mother. The residence schedule will be reversed between the parents during even-numbered years.

Hannukah. (The court, and parents, may also find the time allocation proposed for resolution of Christmas residence to be suitable for allocation of residence during Hannukah.)

Winter vacation. On even-numbered years, from 5:00 p.m. on the day school closes for the Winter/Christmas holiday, until 11:00 a.m. Christmas Day the minor child(ren) will be in residence with the father, and thereafter during the Winter Holiday until 8:30 a.m. on the opening day of school in January the minor child(ren) will be in residence with the mother.

On odd-numbered years the Winter/Christmas holiday schedule will commence, instead, with the minor child(ren) in residence with the mother and conclude with residence with the father.

New Year's Eve and Day. (An allocation similar to that accorded to Christmas Eve and Day can also be scheduled for New Year's Eve and Day.)

Washington's Birthday. (Unless allocated as a three-day national holiday weekend with time apportioned to the parent wherein the child(ren) is/are already scheduled for residence during the adjoining weekend, the following may pertain:)

During odd-numbered years, at 5:00 p.m. on the eve prior to Washington's Birthday until 9:30 p.m. on the day of Washington's Birthday, the minor child(ren) will be in residence with the father. On even-numbered years the same residence time schedule will prevail for the mother and the minor child(ren).

Lincoln's Birthday. (Unless allocated as a three-day national holiday weekend with time apportioned to the parent wherein the child(ren) is already scheduled for residence during the adjoining weekend, the following may pertain:)

During odd-numbered years, at 5:00 p.m. on the eve prior to Lincoln's Birthday until 9:30 p.m. on the day of Lincoln's Birthday, the minor child(ren) will be in residence with the father. On even-numbered years the same residence time schedule will prevail for the mother and the minor child(ren).

Valentine's Day. During odd-numbered years, from 8:00 a.m. until 9:30 p.m. on Valentine's Day the minor child(ren) will be in residence with the father. On even-numbered years the same residence time schedule will prevail for the mother and the minor child(ren).

Spring, or Easter, School Vacation. During Spring, or Easter, school vacation, on odd-numbered years, from 5:00 p.m. on the day school closes until 8:00 a.m. on the day school reopens, the minor child(ren) will be in residence with the mother. On even-numbered years the same residence schedule will prevail for the father and the minor child(ren).

Memorial Day. (Unless allocated as a three-day national holiday weekend with time apportioned to the parent wherein the child(ren) is already scheduled for residence during the adjoining weekend, the following may pertain:)

During odd-numbered years, at 5:00 p.m. on the eve prior to Memorial Day until 9:30 p.m. on the day of Memorial Day, the minor child(ren) will be in residence with the father. On even-numbered years the same residence time schedule will prevail for the mother and the minor child(ren).

Independence Day. (Unless specially allocated as a consequence of an alternating summer vacation period, the following may be suitable:)

During odd-numbered years, from 8:00 a.m. until midnight on Independence Day the minor child(ren) will be in residence with the father. On even-numbered years the same residence time schedule will prevail for the mother and the minor child(ren).

Labor Day. (Unless specially allocated as a consequence of an alternating summer vacation period, the following may be suitable:)

During odd-numbered years, from 8:00 a.m. until midnight on Labor Day the minor child(ren) will be in residence with the father. On even-numbered years the same residence time schedule will prevail for the mother and the minor child(ren).

Halloween. During even-numbered years, from 5:00 p.m. until 10:00 p.m. the minor child(ren) will be in residence with the father. On even-numbered years the same residence time schedule will prevail for the mother and the minor child(ren).

Thanksgiving Day and Holiday. During odd-numbered years, from 5:30 p.m. on the day preceding Thanksgiving Day, until 8:30 a.m. on the Monday following Thanksgiving Holiday the minor child(ren) will be in residence with the father. On even-numbered years the same residence time schedule will prevail for the mother and the minor child(ren).

Mother's Day, Father's Day. During Mother's Day and Father's Day the minor child(ren) will be resident with the respective parent from 8:00 a.m. until 9:30 p.m.

The minor child(ren) will be resident with the *(father/mother)* for an exclusive six weeks during the summer vacation period; the period of time being selected at the convenience of the *(parent)* who is working full-time with little or no vacation flexibility is usually accorded the opportunity to set this time period upon two weeks notice to the *(other parent)*.

(Option 3)

(a) Each of the parents shall have occasion to take vacations away from home, and it is recognized that the vacationing parent may take the minor child(ren) along on vacations, consideration given to the child(ren)'s best interests.

(b) The nonvacationing parent shall have the actual care and custody of the minor child(ren) when the other parent is on vacation. [Source: Family Law Div., Hillsborough County, Fla.]

(Option 4)

The child(ren) shall stay with each parent for an extended period each calendar year to accommodate vacations and other special activities as shall be agreed upon at least 30 days in advance. This extended period may suspend the normal alternation and visitation schedule. Time with each child(ren) during birthdays and on major holidays shall be shared or alternated in relatively equal amounts as the parents may agree, regardless of which parent the child(ren) are then staying.

(Option 5)

Neither parent shall take the child(ren) out of the state without a prior 30 days' notice and subsequent consent of the other parent. [Source: Cook]

(CHANGES OF RESIDENCE RESTRICTION)

(Option 1)

The party with whom the child(ren) may, from time to time, maintain their primary physical residence will not move the child(ren)'s place of residence outside the geographical area _____ of without the express written consent of the other party (or upon order of court). Unless there is such consent (or court order) in the event the party with whom the child(ren) maintain the primary physical residence desires to reside outside the geographical areas as specified above, then the primary physical residence of the child(ren) shall be with the party who does not move his or her place of residence from said geographical area. [Source: Frumkes]

(Option 2)

Except for brief vacations, not to exceed a total of six weeks per party per year, each party is restrained from removing the minor child(ren) from _____ without the written consent of the other party or further order of court. [Source: Shear]

(Option 3)

Neither parent shall change the physical residence of the minor child(ren) outside of _____ without either the agreement of the other, or the determination by a court of competent jurisdiction that such move is in the best interest of the minor child(ren). In no event shall the minor child(ren) be removed from the continental boundaries of the United States by either party and neither party shall seek a passport for such minor child(ren).

(Option 4)

Neither parent shall move the permanent residence of the child(ren) from _____ or remove the child(ren) from this area for a period in excess of fourteen days without the prior consent of the other parent or approval by the court after prior notification to the other parent of such a court hearing.

(Option 5)

Neither parent will effectuate a superior custody position by moving their residence. [Source: Cook]

(Option 6)

Residence is an exclusive privilege and right of the child(ren) and of the respective parent with whom the child(ren) is/are residing. The alternate parent is enjoined from planning or scheduling activities for the minor child(ren) during the time period when the child(ren) is resident with the other parent without the consent, in advance, of the opposite resident parent. [Source: Cook]

(Option 7)

Although a designation of residential care of the child(ren) is made here, each of the parents, upon consulting with the other, may freely delegate or entrust to the other the care of the child(ren) during the times when he or she would otherwise have the primary responsibility. [Source: Sessums]

(FINANCIAL SUPPORT OF CHILD(REN))

(Option 1)

(a) The parties shall divide equally the costs pertaining to the minor child(ren).

(b) There will be no child support paid by either party to the other. Expenses related to the minor child(ren) will be arranged for in the following manner: each party will pay costs as they arise for food, shelter, entertainment, daily transportation, vacations taken with the child(ren), and any other costs that come up when the child(ren) are living with each party. Other costs listed below will be paid by each party in ratio to each party's base earnings. These include medical, school expenses, clothing, major gifts, college, allowance, etc. Each party will keep a record of expenses on these items and will reconcile the balance owed to each other within the first five days of the month. Base earnings mean earned wages or salary.

(c) $_____ shall be placed into an account each month. Each party with physical custody at that particular time shall be permitted to withdraw money from the account as he/she sees fit in a manner consistent with the best interests of the minor child(ren).

(d) Claims, causes of action, awards, rewards, or inheritances for or belonging to the minor child(ren) shall be handled in the following manner: any net recovery, award, reward, or inheritance in excess of $_____ shall be placed in a trust for the benefit of the minor child(ren). That sum not exceeding $_____ may be expended for the benefit of the minor child(ren).

(e) Consent of both parents shall not be required to withdraw money from the account of the minor child(ren).

(f) Child sitters shall be arranged and paid for by the parent having physical residence during that period of time. [Source: Gaddis]

(Option 2)

(a) _____ dollars shall be placed into an account each month to be used by the child(ren) and the custodial parent of that time for the support.

(b) The _____ dollars shall be contributed under the following formula: Each party shall contribute that percentage of the _____ dollars which is equal to his or her percentage of the combined income of the parties. The only income which will be considered for the purpose of determining combined gross income or the percentage thereunder is income from wages.

(c) Each party with custody at the particular time shall be permitted to withdraw money from the account as he/she sees fit in a manner consistent with the best interests of the minor child(ren) of the parties.

(Option 3)

The parties agree that no child support amount should be indicated in the dissolution decree because of the joint custody arrangement and the complications that may result from the support contributions being subject to monthly adjustments. [Source: Folberg]

(Option 4)

The parents will share child support costs based on need and ability of each parent to pay according to a formula of (% / $) by the (father/mother) and (% / $) by the (opposite parent). [Source: Cook]

(Option 5)

Child support of $_____ will be paid monthly by the (father/mother) to the (opposite parent). [Source: Cook]

(Option 6)

Child support dollar levels will be determined in accordance with the U.S. Department of Agriculture, Agricultural Research Service, Consumer and Food Economics Research Division "Cost of Raising a Child" with consideration for the appropriate geographic region, age of child, residence area, income-cost bracket, and numbers of children within a family. [Source: Cook]

(Option 7)

All school expenses for the minor child(ren) will be assumed equally by both parents until the minor child(ren) is/are *(eighteen or twenty-one)* years of age or graduates from college at the Bachelor degree level. [Source: Cook]

(OTHER CLAUSES RELATED TO FINANCIAL SUPPORT)

(TRAVEL EXPENSES)

(Option 1)

Each parent shall be responsible for all expenses in connection with his/her exercise of visitation rights including, but not limited to, travel to and from his/her place of residence to the residence of the minor child(ren) for the minor child(ren)'s travel from his/her place of residence to the parent's place of residence. [Source: Sessums]

(Option 2)

Travel costs will be apportioned based on income and ability to pay according to a formula of *(% / $)* by the *(father/mother)* and *(% / $)* by the *(opposite parent)*. [Source: Cook]

(Option 3)

The *(father/mother)* will assume travel costs of the child(ren) to fulfill residence with the opposite parent. [Source: Cook]

(Option 4)

The parent moving from the county of original residence will be required to pay the travel costs of the minor child(ren) to and from the alternate parent's residence. [Source: Cook]

The parties agree to retain in joint ownership all heirlooms listed on the attached inventory (Exhibit A) in trust for the benefit of their child(ren). They will each hold possession of the listed heirlooms in approximately equal amount, insure them, and provide in their Wills that they pass to their child(ren) in equal proportion.

(MEDICAL PROVISIONS)

(Option 1)

_____ shall maintain comprehensive medical and dental care insurance for the benefit of the child(ren) and shall be responsible for all medical, dental, and optical expenses not covered by said insurance, until the child(ren) reach the age of eighteen.

(Option 2)

In the event that employer-related medical insurance is available for the minor child(ren), the *(father/mother)* will be responsible for assuming such coverage. All medical expenses for the minor child(ren) will be assumed equally by both parents until the minor child(ren) is *(eighteen or twenty-one)* years of age.

(Option 3)

_____ shall maintain in full force and effect comprehensive policies of health and medical insurance covering and naming the minor child(ren) as the beneficiary(ies) thereon; that health and medical and dental costs and expenses not covered by insurance shall be shared as mutually agreed upon by the parties.

(Option 4)

_____ shall maintain health insurance coverage for the benefit of minor child(ren) and she/he shall pay ordinary medical and dental expenses. The parties shall pro rate any extraordinary medical, dental, or psychological expenses for the minor child(ren) on the basis of their respective adjusted gross income for the previous calendar year. [Source: Adams]

(LIFE INSURANCE PROVISIONS)

_____ shall maintain in full force and effect policies of life insurance naming as beneficiaries thereon the minor child(ren) of the parties.

(TAX PROVISIONS)

(Option 1)

The party with whom the child(ren) maintain(s) physical residence during the school year shall have the right to claim that/those child(ren) as (a) dependent(s) for tax purposes. [Source: Gaddis]

(Option 2)

The parties shall each claim *(no.)* of the child(ren) as deductions for tax purposes. [Source: Gaddis]

(Option 3)

The *(mother/father)* shall claim _____(Name)_____ as dependents for tax purposes. [Source: Gaddis]

(Option 4)

In view of the assumption and obligation of the larger dollar share of child support expenses by the *(father/mother)*, the *(same parent)* shall claim the child(ren)'s dependency exemption on federal and state income tax returns. [Source: Cook]

(Option 5)

In view of the assumption of the minor child(ren)'s expenses equally by both parents, the *(mother/father)* shall claim the dependency exemption for the minor child(ren) on federal and state income tax returns for even-numbered years and the *(opposite parent)* shall claim the exemption for the odd-numbered years. [Source: Cook]

(CHANGE IN CIRCUMSTANCES)

The current agreement with respect to their child(ren) is set forth herein. However, both parents must remain flexible. In the future, certain circumstances may require a revision or modification of this agreement. Both parents shall maintain effective communication, always acting in the best interest of the child(ren). The agreement can be changed by consent of both parents. [At this time, both parents agree that the following events would constitute a substantial change in circumstances, justifying a possible review of the current parental responsibility agreement.]

(a) One parent wanting to remove the child(ren) from the State for more than _____ days (for the following purposes: _____).

(b) Serious problems with the physical or emotional health or well-being of the child(ren).

(c) Serious physical or emotional disability or impairment of *(Name/either parent)*.

(d) Remarriage of *(Name/either parent)*.

(e) Cohabitation by *(Name/either parent)* without benefit of marriage.

(f) Change in the development or relationship needs of the child(ren). [Source: Koritzinsky]

(DISPUTE RESOLUTION)

(Option 1)

It is recognized and agreed that the terms and conditions of the joint custody arrangement set forth above shall be supplemented or changed as the needs of the minor child(ren) change and/or as the best interest of the minor child(ren) may determine. At a minimum:

(a) The parties shall determine the residence of the child(ren) for school purposes on or before (date) of each year.

(b) In no case shall the physical residence of the minor child(ren) be transferred between the parties so that the child(ren) attend more than one school in any one school year. [Source: Gaddis]

(Option 2)

In the event that the parents become irresolvably or intensely in conflict with regard to decisions affecting the minor child(ren) and his/her best interest, then in that event, the parties agree to submit such conflicts to a professional mediator. The mediator shall be appointed with the agreement of the parties or, failing agreement, by the court. Mediation shall take place and be subject to the following:

(a) An issue or conflict between the parties shall not be submitted until such time as the parties themselves have conferred and made all reasonable efforts to reach a resolution thereof.

(b) Any issue not so resolved by the parties may be submitted in writing by them to the mediator for mediation in such manner and at such times and places as shall be designated by the mediator.

(c) All decisions by the mediator shall be advisory to the parties and shall not be binding upon them. Provided, however, either party may disclose to the court the decision of the mediator in the event that such matter is later submitted to the court for its determination. [Source: Sessums]

(Option 3)

In the event that the parents alone cannot resolve a conflict, they agree to seek appropriate, competent assistance. The matter shall be referred for mediation, to a counselor, or to a professional person skilled in the area of resolution of the problems of children and their families. This procedure shall be followed to its conclusion prior to either party seeking relief from the court. While the dispute is being resolved, the parent with whom the child(ren) maintain their primary physical residence shall continue making such day-to-day decisions as are necessary, but shall take no substantial action in the area of the disagreement which would prejudice or take unfair advantage of the other parent by use of the residential status to his/her own benefit. [Source: Gaddis]

(Option 4)

If the parents are unable to resolve directly and personally any interpretation or controversy arising from the schedule and provisions as itemized in this decree (*or agreement*), the parents will:

First, seek a solution mutually by mediation, or
Second, seek a rectification and agreement by conciliation, or

Third, seek a decision by arbitration before proceeding to:
Fourth, formal litigation and resolution by the court.

The parents agree that the terms of this agreement shall become the order of the court, and shall be merged into and become a part of the interlocutory decree in the above-entitled matter. [Source: Cook]

(BINDING EFFECT OF CUSTODY AGREEMENT)

(Option 1—If Mediated Agreement)

We have reached this agreement voluntarily by the process of mediation through a neutral mediator. We understand that the mediator was not representing either or both of us and that we may each have sought a larger settlement through individual attorneys advocating our separate interests. We have each had the opportunity and have been urged by the mediator to consult with individual attorneys and other personal advisors.

(Option 2)

We both understand the legal and practical effect of this agreement in each and every respect. Our financial status has been fully explained to both parties by our respective counsel, and we both acknowledge that it is a fair agreement and that it is not the result of any fraud, duress, or undue influence exercised by either party upon the other or by any other person or persons upon either.

(Option 3)

Failure by either one of us to exercise the right to contact and access with the child(ren) on any particular occasion shall not be deemed or construed to be, nor constitute, a waiver of the right thereafter to full compliance of the provisions hereof.

(Option 4)

Notwithstanding that the parental responsibility of the minor child(ren) shall be shared, this shall bind only the parties, and all persons who deal with the parties or any one of them in reference in any way to the child(ren) or with the child(ren), need look to either one of the parties and need not get consent from, authority from, nor give notice to the other party. [Source: Frumkes]

(Option 5)

Any waiver by either of us of any provision or right of this agreement shall not be controlling. Nor shall it prevent or estop either of us from enforcing any provision, right, or option. The failure of either to insist in any one or more instances upon the strict performance of any of the terms or provisions of this agreement by the other party shall not be construed as a waiver or relinquishment for the future of any such term or provision.

(AMENDMENTS OR MODIFICATIONS)

(Option 1)

We agree that this Agreement shall not be amended or modified, except by an agreement in writing duly subscribed and acknowledged with the same formality as this Agreement.

(ACKNOWLEDGMENTS OF RIGHTS AND OBLIGATIONS)

(Option 1)

We agree that all matters affecting the interpretation of this Agreement and our rights hereto shall be governed by the laws of _____.

(Option 2)

We each acknowledge and agree that the _____(court) shall at all times have continuing and preferred jurisdiction to enforce or modify any order pertaining to custody matters.

(Option 3)

We retain the option to revise this parental access and custody agreement within two years notwithstanding the two-year provisions of the Uniform Child Custody Jurisdiction Act (UCCJA) or the "substantial and permanent" requirements of that Act or of case law.

(Option 4)

We shall share equal responsibility for any and all legal and court costs for the dissolution and for this mediated settlement agreement, including the legal fees of the attorneys.

(Option 5)

If any provision of this agreement should be held to be contrary to, or invalid under, the law of any country, state, or other jurisdiction, such illegality or invalidity shall not affect in any way the legality or validity of the remaining clauses.

References and Bibliography

Abarbanel, A., "Joint Custody Families: A Case Study Approach," Doctoral Dissertation, California School of Professional Psychology (1977).

Abarbanel, A., "Joint Custody: What Are We Afraid Of?" Unpublished paper presented at Annual Meeting of American Orthopsychiatric Association, San Francisco, CA, 1978.

Abarbanel, A., "Shared Parenting After Separation and Divorce: A Study of Joint Custody," 49 *American Journal of Orthopsychiatry* 320 (1979).

Abrahms, S., "The Joint Custody Controversy," *The New York Times Magazine*, June 18, 1978, at 47.

Achenbach, T. M., & Edelbrook, C. S., "A Typology of Child Behavioral Profile Patterns: Disputes and Correlates for Disturbed Children Aged 6–16," 8 *Journal of Abnormal Child Psychology*, 441 (1980).

Achenbach, T. M., & Edelbrock, C. S., "Behavioral Problems and Competencies Reported by Parents of Normal and Disturbed Children Aged Four Through Sixteen," 46 *Monographs of the Society for Research in Child Development* (1, Serial No. 188) (1981).

Achenbach, T. M., & Edelbrock, C. S., *Manual for the Child Behavior Checklist and Revised Child Behavioral Profile* (New York: Queen City Printers, 1983).

Adams, J., "Outline of Joint Custody Arrangements," (Sept. 1978, from editor's file).

Adler, R. E., *Sharing the Children: How to Resolve Custody Problems and Get on with Your Life* (Bethesda, MD: Adler & Adler, 1988).

Ahrons, C., "The Binuclear Family: Two Households, One Family," 2 *Alternative Lifestyles* 499 (1979a).

Ahrons, C., "The Coparental Divorce: Preliminary Research Findings and Policy Implications," in A. Milne (Ed.), *Joint Custody: A Handbook for Judges, Lawyers and Counselors* (Portland, OR: Association of Family and Conciliation Courts, 1979b).

Ahrons, C., "Divorce: A Crisis of Family Transition and Change," *Family Relations*, October 1980a, at 533.

Ahrons, C., "Joint Custody Arrangements in the Post-Divorce Family," 3 *Journal of Divorce* 189 (1980b).

Ahrons, C., "The Continuing Coparental Relationship Between Divorced Spouses," 51 *American Journal of Orthopsychiatry* 415 (1981).

Ahrons, C., "Parenting Roles and Relationships in the Binuclear Family," in *Parent–Child Relationships Post-Divorce* (Copenhagen, Denmark: Danish National Institute of Social Research, 1984).

Ainsworth, M., "The Development of Infant–Mother Attachment," in B. Caldwell & H. Ricciuti (Eds.), *Review of Child Development Research*, Vol. 3 (Chicago: University of Chicago Press, 1973).

Ainsworth, M., "Infant–Mother Attachment," 34 *American Psychologist* 932 (1979).

Alexander, J., "Defensive and Supportive Communications in Normal and Deviant Families," 40 *Journal of Consulting and Clinical Psychology* 223 (1973).

Alexander, S., "Protecting the Child's Rights in Custody Cases," 26 *The Family Coordinator* 377 (1977).

Allen, N., "Joint Custody: A Long Awaited Solution or a Mere Promise?" 22 *Conciliation Courts Review* 39 (1984).

"Alternate Managing Conservatorship Under the Family Code," 30 *Baylor Law Review* 83 (1978).

Anspach, D., "Kinship & Divorce," 38 *Journal of Marriage and the Family* 323 (1976).

Anthony, A., & Koupernik, C., *The Child in His Family: Children at Psychiatric Risk* (New York: Wiley, 1974).

Anthony, E. J., "Risk, Vulnerability and Resilience: An Overview," in E. J. Anthony & B. J. Cohler (Eds.), *The Invulnerable Child* (New York: Guilford Press, 1987).

Aries, P., *Centuries of Childhood* (New York: Random House, 1965).

Arnold, R., & Wheeler, M., *Separation and After: A Research Report* (Toronto: Ministry of Community and Social Services, 1980).

Ash, P., & Guyer, M. J., "A Followup of Children in Contested Custody Evaluations." Paper presented at the 17th Annual Meeting of the American Academy of Psychiatry and the Law, Philadelphia, PA, October 1986.

Atkin, E., & Rubin, E., *Part-Time Father* (New York: New American Library, Inc., 1977).

Atwell, A. E., Moore, U. S., Nielsen, E., & Levite, Z., "Effects of Joint Custody on Children," 12 (2) *Bulletin of the American Academy of Psychiatry and the Law* 149 (1984).

Awad, G., "Joint Custody: Preliminary Impressions," 28 *Canadian Journal of Psychiatry* 41 (1983).

"Award of Joint Custody: Perotti v. Perotti, 55 N.Y.S.2d 68," 14 *Journal of Family Law* 154 (1975).

Babbie, E. R., *Society by Agreement: An Introduction to Sociology* (Belmont: Wadsworth, 1977).

Bahr, S., "An Evaluation of Court Mediation: A Comparison in Divorce Cases with Children," 2 *Journal Of Family Issues* 39 (1981).

Bartz, K., & Witcher, W., "When Father Gets Custody," 7 *Children Today* 2 (1978).

Baum, C., "The Best of Both Parents," *The New York Times Magazine*, October 31, 1976, at 44.

Beal, E. W., "Separation, Divorce, and Single-Parent Families," in E. A. Carter & M. McGoldrick (Eds.) *The Family Life Cycle: A Framework for Family Therapy* (New York: Gardner, 1980).

Becker, G., Landes, E., & Michael, R., "An Economic Analysis of Marital Instability," 85 *Journal of Political Economy* 1141 (1977).

Belsky, J., & Steinberg, L., "The Effects of Day Care: A Critical Review," 49 *Child Development* 929 (1978).

Benedek, E., & Benedek, R., "New Child Custody Laws: Making Them Do What They Say," 42 *American Journal of Orthopsychiatry* 825 (1972).

Benedek, E., & Benedek, R., "Joint Custody: Solution or Illusion," 136 *American Journal of Psychiatry* 1540 (1979).

Benedek, R., & Benedek, E., "The Child's Preference in Michigan Custody Disputes," 7 *American Journal of Family Therapy* 37 (1979).

Benjamin, M., "General Systems Theory, Family Systems Theories, and Family Therapy: Towards an Integrated Model of Family Process," in A. Bross (Ed.) *Family Therapy: A Recursive Model of Strategic Practice* (New York: Guilford Press, 1983).

Benjamin, M., & Irving, H. H., "Research and Shared Parenting: A Critical Review," *Canadian Social Work Review '84* 13 (1985).

Benjamin, M., & Irving, H. H., "Comparison of the Experience of Satisfied and Dissatisfied Shared Parents," 14 *Journal of Divorce* in press (1989).

Berman, A., & Kirsh, D., "Definitions of Joint Custody," 5 (3) *Family Advocate*, Fall 1982, at 2.

Bernard, J., *Remarriage* (New York: Dryden, 1956).

Bienenfeld, F., *Child Custody Mediation: Techniques for Counselors, Attorneys and Parents* (Palo Alto, CA: Science and Behavior Books, 1983).

Biller, H., *Paternal Deprivation: Family, School, Sexuality and Society* (Lexington, MA: D.C. Heath, 1974).

Biller, H., "The Father and Personality Development: Paternal Deprivation and Sex-Role Development," in M. Lamb (Ed.), *The Role of the Father in Child Development* (New York: Wiley, 1976).

Biller, H. B., "The Father and Sex Role Development," in M. E. Lamb (Ed.), *The Role of Father in Child Development*, 2d ed. (New York: Wiley, 1981).

Black, M., & Jaffee, W., "Lawyer/Therapist Approach to Divorce," 16 (1) *Conciliation Courts Review*, December 1978, at 1.

Blanchard, R., & Biller, H., "Father Availability and Academic Performance Among Third-Grade Boys," 4 *Developmental Psychology* 301 (1971).

Blanding, H., "Legal Aspects of Joint Custody." Panel presentation at Conference on Joint Custody, Kelso, WA, October 14, 1977.

Block, J. H., Block, J., & Morrison, A., "Parental Agreement/Disagreement on Child Rearing Orientations and Gender Related Correlates in Children," 52 *Child Development* 965 (1981).

Bloom, B., & Hodges, W., "The Predicament of the Newly Separated," 7 *Community Mental Health Journal* 227 (1981).

Bodenheimer, B., "Progress Under the Uniform Child Custody Jurisdiction Act and Remaining Problems: Punitive Decrees, Joint Custody, and Excessive Modifications," 65 *California Law Review* 978 (1977).

Bohannon, P., "Divorce Chains, Households of Remarriage, and Multiple Divorces," in P. Bohannon (Ed.), *Divorce and After: An Analysis of the Emotional and Social Problems of Divorce* (Garden City, NY: Anchor Books, 1976a).

Bohannon, P., "The Six Stations of Divorce," in P. Bohannon (Ed.), *Divorce and After: An Analysis of the Emotional and Social Problems of Divorce* (Garden City, NY: Anchor Books, 1976b).

Bohannon, P. (Ed.), *Divorce and After: An Analysis of the Emotional and Social Problems of Divorce* (Garden City, NY: Anchor Books, 1976c).

Bottomley, A., "Resolving Family Disputes: A Critical View," in M. D. S. Freeman (Ed.), *State, Law and the Family* (London: Tavistock, 1984).

Bowerman, C., & Irish, D., "Some Relationships of Stepchildren to Their Parents," 24 *Marriage and Family* 113 (1962).

Bowman, M. E., & Ahrons, C. R., "Impact of Legal Custody Status on Father's Parenting Postdivorce," *Journal of Marriage and the Family* 481 (1985).

Brandwein, R., Brown, C., & Fox, E., "Women and Children Last: The Social Situation of Divorced Mothers and Their Families," 36 *Journal of Marriage and the Family* 498 (1974).

Bratt, C., "Joint Custody," 67 *Kentucky Law Journal* 271 (1979).

Bronfenbrenner, U., "Toward an Experimental Ecology of Human Development," 32 *American Psychologist* 513 (1977).

Bronfenbrenner, U., *The Ecology of Human Development: Experiments by Nature and Design* (Cambridge, MA: Harvard University Press, 1979).

Bross, A., & Benjamin, M., "Family Therapy: A Recursive Model of Strategic Practice," in A. Bross (Ed.) *Family Therapy: A Recursive Model of Strategic Practice* (New York: Guilford Press, 1983).

Bruch, C., "Making Visitation Work, Dual Parenting Orders," 1 (1) *Family Advocate*, Summer 1978, at 22.

Bruch, C. S., "And How Are the Children? The Effects of Ideology and Mediation on Child Custody Law and Children's Well-Being in the United States," 2 *International Journal of Law and the Family* 106 (1988).

Bumpass, L., & Sweet, J., "Differentials in Marital Instability," 37 *American Sociological Review* 754 (1972).

Burchinal, L., "Characteristics of Adolescents from Unbroken, Broken, and Reconstituted Families," 26 *Journal of Marriage and the Family* 44 (1964).

Buser, P., "A Typical Joint Custody Agreement, " 5 *Family Advocate* 26 (1982).

Caldwell, B., & Ricciuti, H. (Eds.), *Review of Child Development Research*, Vol. 3 (Chicago: University of Chicago Press, 1973).

"The California Custody Decree," 13 *Stanford Law Review* 108 (1960).

"California's Presumption Favoring Joint Child Custody: California Civil Code Sections 4600 and 4600.5," 17 *California Western Law Review* 286 (1981).

Campbell, L. E. G., & Johnston, J. R., "Multi-Family Mediation: The Use of Groups to Resolve Child Custody Disputes," in D. T. Saposnek (Ed.), *Applying Family Therapy Perspectives to Mediation* (San Francisco: Jossey-Bass, 1986).

Canacakos, E., "Joint Custody as a Fundamental Right," 23 *Arizona Law Review* 785 (1981).

Cardinal, T., & Nigro, N., "Toward a Unitary Approach to Child Custody Practice in Michigan Courts: A Procedural and Substantive Critique," 58 *University of Detroit Journal of Urban Law* 5 (1980).

Carroll, C., "Ducking the Real Issues of Joint Custody," 5 (2) *Family Advocate*, Fall 1982, at 18.

Carroll, C. N., "Ducking the Real Issues of Joint Custody Cases," in J. Folberg (Ed.), *Joint Custody and Shared Parenting* (Washington, DC: Bureau of National Affairs and Association of Family and Conciliation Courts, 1984).

Carter, E. A., & McGoldrick, M., "The Family Life Cycle and Family Therapy: An Overview," in E. A. Carter & M. McGoldrick (Eds.), *The Family Life Cycle: A Framework for Family Therapy* (New York: Gardner, 1980a).

Carter, E., & McGoldrick, M. (Eds.), *The Family Life Cycle: A Framework for Family Therapy* (New York: Gardner, 1980b).

Cassidy, R., *What Every Man Should Know About Divorce* (Washington, DC: New Republic Books, 1977).

Cath, S., Gurwit, A., & Ross, J., *Father and Child: Developmental and Clinical Perspectives* (Boston: Little, Brown and Company, 1982).

Chang, P., & Deinard, A., "Single-Father Caretakers," 52 *American Journal of Orthopsychiatry* 236 (1982).

Chapman, M., "Father Absence, Stepfathers, and the Cognitive Performance of College Students," 48 *Child Development* 1155 (1977).

Charnas, J. F., "Joint Child Custody Counseling: Divorce 1980s Style," 64 *Social Casework* 546 (1983).

Chasin, R., & Brunebaum, H., "A Model for Evaluation in Child Custody Disputes," 9 *American Journal of Family Therapy* 43 (1981).

Cherlin, A., "The Effects of Children on Marital Dissolution," 14 *Demography* 265 (1977).

Cherlin, A., "Remarriage as an Incomplete Institution," 84 *American Journal of Sociology* 634 (1978).

Chesler, P., *About Men* (New York: William Morrow & Co., 1978).

Chesler, P., *Mothers on Trial* (New York: McGraw Hill & Co., 1986).

"Children's Appointed Counsel's Joint Custody Recommendation Adopted," 3 *Family Law Reporter* 2541 (1977).

Chodorow, N. *The Reproduction of Mothering* (Berkeley: University of California Press, 1978).

Christiansen, H. (Ed.), *Handbook of Marriage and the Family* (Chicago: Rand-McNally, 1964).

Clark, H., *The Law of Domestic Relations in the United States*, 2nd Ed. (St. Paul, MN: West Publishing Co., 1988).

Clarke-Stewart, A., *Child Care in the Family* (New York: Academic Press, 1977).

Clawar, S., "Popular and Professional Misconceptions About Joint Custody," 21 (2) *Conciliation Courts Review*, December 1983, at 27.

Cleveland, M., & Irvin, K., "Custody Resolution Counseling: An Alternative Intervention," 8 *Journal of Marital and Family Therapy* 105 (1982).

Cline, D., & Westman, J., "The Impact of Divorce on the Family," 2 *Child Psychiatry and Human Development* 78 (1971).

Clingempeel, W., "Quasi-Kin Relationships and Marital Quality in Stepfather Families," 41 *Journal of Personality and Social Psychology* 890 (1981).

Clingempeel, W., & Reppucci, N., "Joint Custody After Divorce: Major Issues and Goals for Research," 91 *Psychological Bulletin* 102 (1982).

Cochran, M., "A Comparison of Group Day Care and Family Child-Rearing Patterns in Sweden," 48 *Child Development* 702 (1977).

Cochran, M., & Brassard, J., "Child Development and Personal Social Networks," 50 *Child Development* 601 (1979).

Cohen, M., "Mischievous Bill on Joint Custody," *The New York Times*, May 19, 1981, at A-14, col. 5.

Coller, D. R., "Joint Custody: Research, Theory, and Policy," 27 *Family Process* 459 (1988).

Collins, G., "'Binuclear Families' Ease Divorce Strains on Off-spring, Ex-spouses," *The Oregonian*, January 3, 1983, at C1.

Comeaux, E., "Procedural Controls in Public Sector Domestic Relations Mediation," in H. Davidson, L. Ray, & R. Horowitz (Eds.), *Alternative Means of Family Dispute Resolution* (Washington, DC: American Bar Association, 1982).

Comeaux, E., "A Guide to Implementing Divorce Mediation Services in the Public Sector," 21(2) *Conciliation Courts Review*, December 1983, at 1.

Committee on the Family Court, New York County Lawyers' Assn., *Report No. 81-A* (June 1981) (available at 14 Vesey Street, New York, NY 10007).

"Considerations Before Granting Joint Custody," 14 *Marriage and Divorce Today* 24 (1979).

"Controversial Custody Idea," 1 *Family Law Reporter* 2708 (1975).

Coogler, O., *Structure Mediation in Divorce* (Lexington, MA: Lexington Books, 1978).

Cook, J., "California Retires a Formula for Injustice in Child Custody Fights," *Los Angeles Times*, January 6, 1980a, at v.

Cook, J., "Decree or Agreement: Joint Custody Provisions and Clauses" (Los Angeles: Joint Custody Association, 1980b).

Cook, J., "Joint Custody, Sole Custody: A New Statute Reflects a New Perspective," 18 (1) *Conciliation Courts Review*, June 1980c, at 31.

Cook, S., "Children of Divorced Help Peers with Woe," *The Oregonian*, March 21, 1979.

Cooperman, C., "Does Joint Legal Custody Serve the Best Interests of the Child?" 3 *Joint Custody*, Los Angeles County Bar Family Law Section Newsletter 20 (1978).

Council of Representatives Report of the American Psychological Association, Minutes of the APA Council of Representatives Meeting, Washington, DC, January 1977.

"Court-Imposed Joint Custody Held Unworkable for Battling New York Couple," 4 *Family Law Reporter* 2302 (1978).

"Court-Ordered Joint Custody Not Feasible When Parents Embattled," 4 *Family Law Reporter* 2522 (1978).

Cox, M., & Cease, L., "Joint Custody: What Does It Mean? How Does It Work?" 1 (1) *Family Advocate*, Summer 1978, at 10.

Crouch, R., *Interstate Custody Litigation: A Guide to Use and Court Interpretation of the Uniform Child Custody Jurisdiction Act* (Washington, DC: The Bureau of National Affairs, 1981).

Crosbie-Barnett, M., "Impact of Joint vs. Sole Custody, Sex of Adolescent, and Quality of Coparental Relationship on Adjustment of Adolescents in Remarried Families." Paper presented at annual meeting of the American Orthopsychiatric Association, San Francisco, CA. March, 1988.

"Custody: Kramer vs. Reality," *Time Magazine*, February 4, 1980, at 77.

"Custody—Joint," 3 *Family Law Reporter* 2047 (1976).

Dancy, E., "Who Gets the Kids, New Solutions for the Big Dilemma," *Ms. Magazine*, September 1976, at 70.

D'Andrea, A., "Joint Custody as Related to Paternal Involvement and Paternal Self-Esteem," 21 *Conciliation Courts Review* 81 (1983).

Davidson, H., Ray, L., & Horowitz, R., *Alternative Means of Family Dispute Resolution* (Washington, DC: American Bar Association, 1982).

Derdeyn, A., "Child Custody Consultation," 45 *American Journal of Orthopsychiatry* 791 (1975).

Derdeyn, A., "Child Custody Contests in Historical Perspective," 133 *American Journal of Psychiatry* 1369 (1976a).

Derdeyn, A., "A Consideration of Legal Issues in Child Custody Contests," 33 *Archives of General Psychiatry* 165 (1976b).

Derdeyn, A. P., & Scott, E., "Joint Custody: A Critical Appraisal," 54 *American Journal of Orthopsychiatry* 199 (1984).

Despert, J., *Children of Divorce* (Garden City, NY: Doubleday, 1953).

"Developments in the Law—The Constitution and the Family," 93 *Harvard Law Review* 1156 (1980).

Diehl, M., "A Texas Father Speaks Out for Equal Rights, " 82 *Family Law Report* 10 (1982).

Dinnerstein, D., *The Mermaid and the Minotaur* (New York: Harper and Row, 1976).

27B *Corpus Juris Secundum Divorce* 308D (1959).

24 *American Jurisprudence* 2d *Divorce & Separation* 799 (1966).

"Divorcing Couples Opt for Joint Child Custody," *The Window*, March 20, 1979.

"Domestic Relations—Child Custody—Reasonable Visitation or Divided Custody?" 42 *Missouri Law Review* 136 (1977).

Drapkin, R., & Bienenfeld, F., "The Power of Including Children in Custody Mediation,"8 *Journal of Divorce* 3 (1985).

Druckman, J., & Rhodes, C., "Family Impact Analysis: Application to Child Custody Determination," 26 *The Family Coordinator* 451 (1977).

Duberman, L., "Step-Kin Relationships," 35 *Journal of Marriage and the Family* 283 (1973).

Duberman, L., *The Reconstituted Family: A Study of Remarried Couples and Their Children* (Chicago: Nelson-Hall, 1975).

Dullea, G., "Joint Custody: Is Sharing the Child a Dangerous Idea?" *The New York Times Magazine*, May 24, 1976, at 24.

Dullea, G., "Split Custody Cuts a Child in Two," *Wisconsin State Journal*, June 15, 1976.

Dullea, G., "Divorced Fathers: Who Are Happiest?" *New York Times*, February 4, 1978, and *Chicago Tribune*, March 19, 1978, 5, at 6.

Dullea, G., "Is Joint Custody Good for Children?" *The New York Times Magazine*, February 3, 1980, at 24.

Duquette, D., "Child Custody Decision Making: The Lawyer–Behavioral Scientist Interface." Paper presented at the 85th Annual Convention of the American Psychological Association, San Francisco, CA, August 26–30, 1977.

Durst, P. L., Wedemeyer, N. V., & Zurcher, L. A., "Parenting Partnership After Divorce: Implications for Practice," 32 *Social Work* 32 (1987).

Duvall, E., *Family Development*, 5th Ed. (Philadelphia: Lippincott, 1977).

Eder, V., "Shared Custody—An Idea Whose Time Has Come," 16 (1) *Conciliation Courts Review*, June 1978, at 23.

Ehrensaft, D., "When Women and Men Mother," 49 *Socialist Review* 37 (1980).

Elkin, M., "Short-Contact Counseling in a Conciliation Court," 43 *Social Casework* 184 (1962).

Elkin, M., "How the Social Worker Can Assist the Attorney in Rehabilitating Broken Marriages," in N. Kohut (Ed.), *Therapeutic Family Law* (Chicago: Family Law Publications, 1968).

Elkin, M., "The Language of Family Law Is the Language of Criminal Law," 13 (1) *Conciliation Courts Review*, September 1975, at iii.

Elkin, M., "Custody and Visitation A Time for Change," 14 (2) *Conciliation Courts Review*, December 1976, at iii.

Elkin, M., "Post-Divorce Counseling in a Conciliation Court," 1 *Journal of Divorce* 55 (1977a).

Elkin, M., "Self-Determination and Family Law," 15 (1) *Conciliation Courts Review*, September 1977b, at iii.

Elkin, M., "Reflections on Joint Custody and Family Law," 16 (13) *Conciliation Courts Review*, December 1978, at iii.

Elkin, M., "Interprofessional Cooperation and Communication Between the Law and the Behavioral Sciences: A Priority Need," 17 (2) *Conciliation Courts Review*, September 1979, at iii.

Elkin, M., "The Missing Links in Divorce Law: A Redefinition of Process and Practice," 6 *Journal of Divorce* 37 (1982).

Elkin, M., "Educational Preparation for Divorce: Another Missing Link in the Divorce Process," 21(2) *Conciliation Courts Review*, December 1983, at v.

Elkin, M., "Joint custody: A Self-Determined Structure for Shared Parenting," 22 *Conciliation Courts Review* v (1984).

Elkin, M., "Joint Custody: Affirming That Parents and Families Are Forever," 32 *Social Work* 18 (1987).

Ellsworth, P., & Levy, R., "Legislative Reform of Child Custody Adjudication," 4 *Law and Society Review* 167 (1969).

Emery, R. E., "Interparental Conflict and the Children of Discord and Divorce," 92 *Psychological Bulletin* 310 (1982).

Emery, R. E., & O'Leary, K. D., "Marital Discord and Child Behavior Problems in a Non-Clinic Sample," 12 *Journal of Abnormal Child Psychology* 411 (1984).

Emery, R. E., & Wyer, M. M., "Child Custody Mediation and Litigation: An Experimental Evaluation of the Experience of Parents," 55 *Journal of Clinical and Consulting Psychology* 179 (1987).

"Equal Custodial Time—A Revolutionary Concept," 4 *Family Law Commentator* 1 (1975).

Ernst, T., & Altis, R., "Joint Custody and Co-Parenting: Not by Law but by Love," 60 *Child Welfare* 669 (1981).

Espenshade, T. J., *Investing in Children: New Estimates of Parental Expenditures* (Washington, DC: The Urban Institute, 1984).

Espinoza, R., & Newman, Y., *Stepparenting*, DHEW Publ. (ADM) 78–579 (Washington, DC: U.S. Dept. of HEW, Center for Studies of Family Mental Health, NIMH, 1979).

Everett, W. J., "Shared Parenthood in Divorce: The Parental Covenant and Custody Law," 2 *Journal of Law and Religion* 85 (1984).

"Examining Oklahoma's Maternal Preference Doctrine: Gordon v. Gordon," 13 *Tulsa Law Journal* 802 (1978).

Eyler, D., "Divorced Parents Still Sharing Decisions in Rearing Daughter," *Oregon Journal*, April 9, 1979, at 19.

Fager, C., "Co-Parenting: Sharing the Children of Divorce," *San Francisco Bay Guardian*, February 3, 1977.

Family Law Division, Thirteenth Judicial Circuit, Hillsborough County, Florida, "Guidelines for Shared Parental Responsibility," in *Anatomy of Shared Parental Responsibility* (Tampa, FL: Florida Bar, 1982).

Fanshel, D., & Shinn, E., *Children in Foster Care: A Longitudinal Investigation* (New York: Columbia University Press, 1978).

Fast, I., & Cain, A., "The Stepparent Role: Potential for Disturbances in Family Functioning," 36 *American Journal of Orthopsychiatry* 485 (1966).

Federal Register., "Poverty Income Guidelines," *Annual Review*, 51 Fed Reg 5105 (1986).

Fein, R., "Research on Fathering: Social Policy and an Emergent Perspective," 34 *Journal of Social Issues* 122 (1978).

Feldberg, R., & Kohen, J., "Family Life in an Anti-Family Setting: A Critique of Marriage and Divorce," *The Family Coordinator*, April, 1976.

Felner, R. D., & Terre, L., "Child Custody Dispositions and Children's Adaptation Following Divorce," in L. A. Weithorn (Ed.), *Psychology and Child Custody Determinations* (Lincoln, NE: University of Nebraska Press, 1987).

Fine, S., "Children in Divorce, Custody and Access Situations: The Contribution of the Mental Health Professional," 21 *Journal of Child Psychology and Psychiatry and Allied Disciplines* 353 (1980).

Fineberg, A., "Joint Custody of Infants: Breakthrough or Fad?" 2 *Canadian Journal of Family Law* 418 (1979).

Finkelor, D., & Yllo, K., *Forced Sex in Marriage: A Preliminary Report* (New Hampshire: University of New Hampshire, Family Violence Research Program, 1980).

Finkelstein, H., Rosenthal, K., & Rosenthal, K., "Fathering After Marital Separation," 23 *Social Work* 11 (1978).

Florida Bar Continuing Legal Education Committee and the Family Law Section, *The Anatomy of Shared Parental Responsibility: Course Manual* (Tampa, FL: Florida Bar, 1982).

Folberg, J., "Facilitating Agreement—The Role of Counseling in the Courts," 12 (2) *Conciliation Courts Review*, December 1974, at 17.

Folberg, J., "Concerns About Joint Custody," in A. Milne (Ed.), *Joint Custody Handbook: A Handbook for Judges, Lawyers and Counselors* (Portland, OR: Association of Family and Conciliation Courts, 1979).

Folberg, J., "Custody Overview," in J. Folberg (Ed.), *Joint Custody and Shared Parenting* (Washington, DC: Bureau of National Affairs and Association of Family and Conciliation Courts, 1984a).

Folberg, J., "Joint Custody Statutes and Judicial Interpretations (as of January 1, 1984)," in J. Folberg (Ed.), *Joint Custody and Shared Parenting* (Washington, DC: Bureau of National Affairs and Association of Family and Conciliation Courts, 1984b).

Folberg, J., & Graham, M., "Joint Custody of Children Following Divorce," 12 (2) *University of California–Davis Law Review* 523 (1979).

Foster, H., *A Bill of Rights for Children* (Springfield, IL: Charles C. Thomas, 1974).

Foster, H., & Freed, D., *Current Developments in Child Custody* (New York: Law Journal Seminars-Press, Inc. 1978a).

Foster, H., & Freed, D., "Divorce in the 50 States: An Overview as of August 1, 1978," 4 *Family Law Reporter* 4033 (1978b).

Foster, H., & Freed, D., "Life with Father: 1978," 11 *Family Law Quarterly* 321 (1978c).

Foster, H., & Freed, D., "Joint Custody: A Viable Alternative," *New York Law Journal*, Part I, No. 90 (November 9, 1978); Part II, No. 99 (November 24, 1978); Part III, No. 119 (December 22, 1978).

Foster, H., & Freed, D., "Joint Custody: A Viable Alternative," 15 *Trial*, May 1979, at 26.

Foster, H., & Freed, D., "Joint Custody: Legislative Reform," 16 *Trial*, June 1980, at 22.

Foster, H., & Freed, D., "Family Law in the Fifty States: An Overview as of September 1982," 8 *Family Law Reporter* 4065 (1982).

Franklin, R., & Hibbs, B., "Child Custody in Transition," 6 *Journal of Marital and Family Therapy* 285 (1980).

Freedberg, L., "California's Newest Divorce Decree: Mandatory Mediation," *Ann Arbor News*, October 3, 1982.

Freud, S., *Inhibitions, Symptoms and Anxiety* (1926), Standard Edition, Vol. 20 (London: Hogarth Press, 1959).

Frumkes, M., "Negotiating and Drafting a Shared Parental Responsibility Agreement," in *Anatomy of Shared Parental Responsibility* (Tampa, FL: Florida Bar, 1982).

Furstenberg, F., "Recycling the Family: Perspectives for Researching a Neglected Family Form," 2 *Marriage and Family Review* 1 (1979).

Furstenberg, F., "Remarriage and Intergenerational Relations," in R. Fogel, E. Hatfield, S. Kiesler, & T. Shanes (Eds.), *Aging: Stability and Change in the Family* (New York: Academic Press, 1981).

Furstenberg, F., "Renegotiating Parenthood After Divorce and Remarriage." Paper presented at the 1981 Biennial Meeting of the Society for Research on Child Development, Symposium on Changing Family Patterns, Boston, April 1981.

Furstenberg, F. F., Morgan, S. P., & Allison, P. D., "Paternal Participation and Children's Well-Being After Marital Dissolution," 52 *American Sociological Review* 695 (1987).

Furstenberg, F. F., Jr., & Nord, C. W., "Parenting Apart: Patterns of Childrearing After Marital Disruption," 47 *Journal of Marriage and the Family* 893 (1985).

Furstenberg, F. F., Jr., Peterson, J. L., Nord, C. W., & Zill, N., "The Life Course of Children of Divorce: Marital Disruption and Parental Contact," 48 *American Sociological Review* 656 (1983).

Gaddis, S., "Joint Custody of Children: A Divorce Decision-Making Alternative," 16 (1) *Conciliation Courts Review*, June 1978, at 17.

Gaddis, S., "The Language of Joint Custody, " in A. Milne (Ed.), *Joint Custody: A Handbook for Judges, Lawyers and Counselors* (Portland, OR: Association of Family and Conciliation Courts, 1979).

Gaddis, S., & Bintliff, B., "Concurrent Custody: A Means of Continuing Responsibility After Dissolution," in A. Milne (Ed.), *Joint Custody: A Handbook for Judges, Lawyers and Counselors* (Portland, OR: Association of Family and Conciliation Courts, 1979).

Gaddis, S., & Sooter, S., "The New Era in Child Custody Resolution," *Washington State Bar News*, January, 1988, at 13.

Galper, M., *Co-Parenting: Sharing Your Child Equally* (Philadelphia: Running Press, 1978).

Galper, M., *Joint Custody and Co-Parenting: Sharing Your Child Equally* (Philadelphia: Running Press, 1980).

Gardner, R., *The Boys' and Girls' Book About Divorce* (New York: Jason Aronson, Inc., 1970).

Gardner, R., *Psychotherapy with Children of Divorce* (New York: Jason Aronson, Inc., 1976).

Gardner, R., "Children of Divorce—Some Legal and Psychological Considerations," 6 *Journal of Clinical Child Psychology* 3 (1977).

Gardner, R., *The Parents Book About Divorce* (New York: Bantam Books, 1979)

Gardner, R., *Family Evaluation in Child Custody Litigation* (Cresskill, NJ: Creative Therapeutics, 1982a).

Gardner, R., "Joint Custody Is Not for Everyone," 5 (2) *Family Advocate*, Fall 1982b, at 6.

Garmezy, N., Masten, A. S., & Tellegen, A., "The Study of Stress and Competence in Children: A Building Block for Developmental Psychopathology," 55 *Child Development* 97 (1984).

Gasser, R., & Taylor, C., "Role Adjustment of Single-Parent Fathers with Dependent Children," 25 *The Family Coordinator* 397 (1976).

Gavrilovich, P., "Kids Get Custody of the House in Divorce," *Detroit Free Press*, January 24, 1982.

George, V., & Wilding, P., *Motherless Families* (London: Routledge and Kegan Paul, 1972).

Gersick, K., "Fathers by Choice: Characteristics of Men Who Do and Do Not Seek Custody of Their Children." Unpublished Doctoral Dissertation, Harvard University (1975).

Gettleman, S., & Markowitz, J., *The Courage to Divorce* (New York: Baltimore Books, 1974).

Glaser, B., & Straus, A., *The Discovery of Grounded Theory: Strategies for Qualitative Research* (San Francisco: Aldine, 1967).

Glasser, P., & Navarre, E., "Structural Problems of the One-Parent Family," 21 *Journal of Social Issues* 98 (1965).

Glendon, M.A., *The Transformation of Family Law* (Chicago: University of Chicago Press, 1989).

Glick, P., "Updating the Life Cycle of the Family," 39 *Journal of Marriage and the Family* 5 (1977).

Glick, P., "Children of Divorced Parents in Demographic Perspective," 35 *Journal of Social Issues* 112 (1979).

Glick, P., "Remarriage: Some Recent Changes and Variations," 1 *Journal of Family Issues* 455 (1980).

Glick, P., & Norton, A., "Number, Timing and Duration of Marriages and Divorces in the United States: June 1975, U.S. Bureau of the Census," *Current Population Reports* (Series P-20, No. 297) (Washington, DC: U.S. Government Printing Office, 1976).

Glick, P., & Norton, A., "Marrying, Divorcing and Living Together in the United States Today," 32 *Population Bulletin* 3 (1978).

Goetting, A., "The Normative Integration of the Former Spouse Relationship," 2 *Journal of Divorce* 395 (1979).

Goldschneider, R., "Not Only on Sunday, " 49 *Parents Magazine* 40 (1974).

Goldsmith, J., "Cooperative Parenting: The Continuing Relationship Between Former Spouses." Presented at "Separation, Divorce, and Beyond," the 9th Annual Conference of The Center for Family Studies/The Family Institute of Chicago, Chicago, IL, April 24–25, 1982.

Goldstein, J., Freud, A., & Solnit, A., *Before the Best Interests of the Child* (New York: The Free Press, 1979).

Goldstein, J., Freud, A., & Solnit, A., *Beyond the Best Interests of the Child* (New York: The Free Press, 1973, 1979).

Goldzband, M. G. *Quality Time: Easing the Children Through Divorce* (New York: McGraw-Hill, 1985).

Goodman, E., "Joint Custody," *McCall's*, August 1975, at 34.

Gouge, M., "Joint Custody: A Revolution in Child Custody Law?" 20 *Washburn Law Journal* 326 (1981).

Graham, V., "Dad Who Wouldn't Give Up Soon Enjoys Joint Custody," *The Oregonian*, February 5, 1976, at Cl.

Green, D., "Joint Custody and the Emerging Two-Parent Family," 21 (1) *Conciliation Courts Review*, June 1983, at 65.

Greif, J., "Fathers, Children, and Joint Custody," 49 *American Journal of Orthopsychiatry* 311 (1979a).

Greif, J., "Joint Custody: A Sociological Study," 15 *Trial*, May 1979b, at 32.

Greif, J., & Simring, S., "Remarriage and Joint Custody, " 20 (1) *Conciliation Courts Review*, June 1982, at 9.

Grote, D., & Weinstein, J., "Joint Custody: A Viable and Ideal Alternative," 1 *Journal of Divorce* 43 (1977).

Group for the Advancement of Psychiatry, Committee on the Family, *Divorce, Child Custody and the Family* (San Francisco: Jossey-Bass Publishers, 1981).

"*Grubs v. Ross*: Oregon's New Approach to Child Custody Forum Determination," 18 *Willamette Law Review* 519 (1982).

Guidubaldi, J., & Perry, J. D., "Divorce and Mental Health Sequelae for Children: A Two-Year Follow-Up of a Nationwide Sample," 24 *Journal of the American Academy of Child Psychiatry* 531 (1985).

Gurman, S. (Ed.), *Questions and Answers in the Practice of Family Therapy* (New York: Brunner/Mazel, 1981).

Haddad, W., & Roman, M., *No-Fault Custody*, Special Report to Honorable Speaker Stanley Steingut, The Assembly of New York State, Albany, NY, July 1978.

Hagen, J. L., "Proceed with Caution: Advocating Joint Custody," 32 *Social Work* 26 (1987).

Hagen, J. L., & Hoshino, G., "Joint Custody of Children and AFDC Eligibility," 59 *Social Service Review* 636 (1985).

Haskins, R., "A Father's View," in A. J. Kahn & S. B. Kamerman (Eds.), *Child Support: From Debt Collection to Social Policy* (Beverly Hills, CA: Sage, 1987).

Haynes, J., "Managing Conflict: The Role of the Mediator," 18 (2) *Conciliation Courts Review*, December 1980, at 9.

Haynes, J., *Divorce Mediation* (New York: Springer Publishing Company, 1981).

Haynes, J., "Divorce Mediation," Paper presented at the Divorce Mediation Workshop, Community Resource Center, Macomb Community College, Warren, MI, November 12, 1982.

Henderson, R. (Ed.), *Parent–Child Interaction: Theory, Research and Prospects* (New York: Academic Press, 1981).

Hess, R., & Camara, K., "Post-Divorce Family Relationships as Mediating Factors in the Consequences of Divorce for Children," 35 *Journal of Social Issues* 79 (1979).

Hetherington, E., "Effects of Paternal Absence on Sex-Typed Behaviors in Negro and White Preadolescent Males," 4 *Journal of Personality and Social Psychology* 87 (1966).

Hetherington, E., "Effects of Paternal Absence on Personality Development in Adolescent Daughters," 7 *Developmental Psychology* 313 (1972).

Hetherington, E., "Girls Without Fathers," *Psychology Today*, February 1976, at 52.

Hetherington, E., "Divorce, A Child's Perspective," 34 *The American Psychologist* 851 (1979).

Hetherington, E., "Children and Divorce," in R. Henderson (Ed.), *Parent–Child Interaction: Theory, Research and Prospects* (New York: Academic Press, 1981).

Hetherington, E., Cox, M., & Cox, R., "Divorced Fathers," 25 *The Family Coordinator* 417 (1976).

Hetherington, E., Cox, M., & Cox, R., "The Aftermath of Divorce, " in J. Stevens, Jr., & M. Matthews (Eds.), *Mother–Child, Father–Child Relations* (Washington, DC: National Association for the Education of Young Children, 1978).

Hetherington, E., Cox, M., & Cox, R., "Family Interaction and the Social, Emotional and Cognitive Development of Children Following Divorce," in V. Vaughn & T. Brazelton (Eds.), *The Family: Setting Priorities* (New York: Science and Medicine Publishing, 1979a).

Hetherington, E., Cox, M., & Cox, R., "Play and Social Interaction Following Divorce," 35 *Journal of Social Issues* 26 (1979b).

Hetherington, E. M., Cox, M., & Cox, R., "Effects of Divorce on Parents and Children," in M. E. Lamb (Ed.), *Nontraditional Families* (Hillsdale, NJ: Lawrence Erlbaum Associates, 1982).

Hetherington, E. M., Cox, M., & Cox, R., "Long-Term Effects of Divorce and Remarriage on the Adjustment of Children," 24 *Journal of the American Academy of Child Psychiatry* 518 (1985).

Hill, R., *Informal Adoption Among Black Families* (Washington, DC: National Urban League Research Department, 1977).

Hill, R., & Rogers, R., "The Developmental Approach," in H.T. Christiansen (Ed.), *Handbook of Marriage and the Family* (Chicago: Rand-McNally, 1964).

Hingst, A., "Children and Divorce, The Child's View," 10 *Journal of Clinical Child Psychology* 161 (1981).

Hitchens, D., Martin, D., & Morgan, M., "An Alternative View to 'Child Custody' Where One Parent Is Homosexual," 17 (3) *Conciliation Courts Review*, December 1979, at 27.

Hodges, W. F., *Interventions for Children of Divorce*. (New York: Wiley, 1986).

Hodges, W. F., & Bloom, B., "Parent's Report of Children's Adjustment to Marital Separation. A Longitudinal Study," 8 *Journal of Divorce* 33 (1984).

Hodges, W. F., Buchsbaum, H. K., & Tierney, C. W., "Parent–Child Relationships and Adjustment in Preschool Children in Divorced and Intact Families," 7 (2) *Journal of Divorce* 43 (1983).

Hollingshead, A. B. *Four Factor Index of Social Status*. Unpublished manuscript (1975).

Holly, M., "Joint Custody: The New Haven Plan," *Ms. Magazine*, September 1976, at 70.

Holub, D., "The Pros and Cons of Joint Custody," in A. Milne (Ed.), *Joint Custody: A Handbook for Judges, Lawyers and Counselors* (Portland, OR: Association of Family and Conciliation Courts, 1979).

Horowitz, R., & Dodson, D., "Child Support, Custody and Visitation," in *Improving Child Support Practice* (Washington, DC: American Bar Association, 1985).

Huerta, L., "Joint Custody: Co-Parenting After Divorce," *Los Angeles Times*, January 30, 1979, IV, at 4.

Hupe, K., & Young, N., *Momma: The Source Book for Single Mothers* (New York: New American Library, 1976).

Ilfeld, F., Jr., Ilfeld, H., & Alexander, J., "Does Joint Custody Work? A First Look at Outcome Data of Relitigation," 139 *American Journal of Psychiatry* 62 (1982).

Irving, H., *Divorce Mediation: The Rational Alternative* (New York: Universe Books, 1980).

Irving, H. (Ed.), *Family Law: An Interdisciplinary Perspective* (Toronto: Carswell, 1981a).

Irving, H. H., & Benjamin, M., "Shared Parenting in Canada: Questions, Answers, and Implications," 1 *Canadian Family Law Quarterly* 79 (1986).

Irving, H. H., & Benjamin, M., *Family Mediation: Theory and Practice of Dispute Resolution* (Toronto: Carswell, 1987).

Irving, H., Benjamin, M., Bohm, P., & MacDonald, G., "A Study of Conciliation Counseling in the Family Court of Toronto: Implications for Socio-Legal Practices," in H. Irving (Ed.), *Family Law: An Interdisciplinary Perspective* (Toronto: Carswell, 1981b).

Irving, H. H., Benjamin, M., & Trocme, N., "Shared Parenting: An Empirical Analysis Utilizing a Large Data Base," 23 *Family Process* 561 (1984a).

Irving, H., Benjamin, M., & Trocme, N., "Shared Parenting: An Empirical Analysis Utilizing a Large Canadian Data Base," in J. Folberg (Ed.), *Joint Custody and Shared Parenting* (Washington, DC: Bureau of National Affairs and Association of Family and Conciliation Courts, 1984b).

Isaacs, M. B., Montalvo, B., & Abelsohn, D., *The Difficult Divorce* (New York: Basic Books, 1986).

Isaacs, M. B., "The Visitation Schedule and Child Adjustment: A Three-Year Study," 27 *Family Process* 251 (1988).

Jacob, H., *The Silent Revolution* (Chicago: University of Chicago Press, 1988).

Jacobs, J., "The Effect of Divorce on Fathers: An Overview of the Literature," 139 *American Journal of Psychiatry* 1235 (1982).

Jacobson, D., "The Impact of Marital Separation/Divorce on Children: I. Parent–Child Separation and Child Adjustment," 1 (4) *Journal of Divorce* 341 (1978a).

Jacobson, D., "The Impact of Marital Separation/Divorce on Children: II. Interparental Hostility and Child Adjustment," 2 (1) *Journal of Divorce* 3 (1978b).

Jarboe, J., "A Case for Joint Custody After the Parents' Divorce," 17 *Journal of Family Law* 741 (1979).

Jenkins, R., "Maxims in Child Custody Cases," 26 *The Family Coordinator* 385 (1977).

Johnston, J. R., & Campbell, L. E. G., "Instability in Family Networks of Divorced and Disputing Parents," 4 *Advances in Group Processes* 243 (1987).

Johnston, J. R., & Campbell, L. E. G., *Impasses of Divorce: The Dynamics and Resolution of Family Conflict* (New York: The Free Press, 1988).

Johnston, J. R., Campbell, L. E. G., & Mayes, S., "Latency Children in Post-Separation and Divorce Disputes," 24 *Journal of the American Academy of Child Psychiatry* 563 (1985).

Johnston, J. R., Gonzalez, R., & Campbell, L. E. G., "Ongoing Post-Divorce Conflict and Child Disturbance," 15 *Journal of Abnormal Child Psychology* 493 (1987).

Johnston, J. R., Kline, M., Tschann, J. M., & Campbell, L. E. G., "Ongoing Post-Divorce Conflict in Families Contesting Custody: Does Joint Custody and Frequent Access Help?" Paper presented at the 65th Annual Meeting of the American Orthopsychiatric Association, San Francisco, March 1988.

Johnston, J. R., Kline, M., & Tschann, J. M., "Ongoing Post-Divorce Conflict: Effects on Children of Joint Custody and Frequent Access," 59 *American Journal of Orthopsychiatry* 576 (1989).

"Joint Custody," 5 *Family Law Reporter* 2143 (1978).

"Joint Custody," 5 *L.A. County Bar Family Law Section Newsletter* iii (1978).

"Joint Custody Against Mother's Wishes, Ordered in New York Case," 4 *Family Law Reporter* 2043 (1977).

"Joint Custody: An Alternative for Divorced Parents," 26 *UCLA Law Review* 1084 (1979).

"Joint Custody Agreement Stands Despite Tender Years Presumption," 3 *Family Law Reporter* 2678 (1977).

"Joint Custody Awards: Toward the Development of Judicial Standards," 48 *Fordham Law Review* 105 (1979).

"Joint Custody Criticized," 9 *Family Law Reporter* 2127 (1982).

"Joint Custody: Is It Best for the Children?" *Oregon Journal* April 9, 1979, at 19.

"Joint Custody Lifestyle Grows," *Wisconsin State Journal*, April 20, 1977.

"Joint Custody Mediation Examined by Family Courts Group," 8 *Family Law Reporter* 2462 (1982).

"Joint Custody Workshop for Washington and Oregon Conciliation Courts." Panel discussion, Kelso, WA, October 14, 1977. (Available from Dr. Stanley Cohen, Department of Psychiatry, University of Oregon Health Sciences, 3181 S.W. Sam Jackson Park Road, Portland, OR 97201.)

Jones, N., "The Impact of Divorce on Children," 15 (2) *Conciliation Courts Review*, December 1977, at 25.

Kagan, I., "Family Experience and the Child's Development," 34 *American Psychologist* 886 (1979).

Kagan, J., Kearsley, R., & Zelazo, P., *Infancy: Its Place in Human Development* (Cambridge, MA: Harvard University Press, 1978).

Kalter, N., Riemar, B., Brickman, A., & Woo Chen, J., "Implications of Parental Divorce for Female Development," 24 *Journal of the American Academy of Child Psychiatry* 538 (1985).

Kapner, L., & Frumkes, M., "The Trial of Custody Conflict," 52 *Florida Bar Journal* 114 (1978).

Kehoe, M., & Salituro, P., "Making Joint Custody Work," 52 *Wisconsin Bar Bulletin* 28 (1979).

Kellogg, M., "Joint Custody," *Newsweek Magazine*, January 24, 1977, at 54.

Kelly, J., "The Visiting Relationship After Divorce: Research Findings and Clinical Implications," in I. Stuart & L. Abt (Eds.), *Children of Separation and Divorce* (New York: Van Nostrand Reinhold, 1981).

Kelly, J., "Divorce: The Adult Experience," in B. Wolman & G. Stricker (Eds.), *Handbook of Developmental Psychology* (Englewood Cliffs, NJ: Prentice Hall, 1982).

Kelly, J., "Further Observations on Joint Custody," 16 *University of California–Davis Law Review* 739 (1983).

Kelly, J., "Post-Divorce Parent–Child Relationships: The Effect of Mediation on Parental Attitudes and Visitation Plans," in *Parent–Child Relationships Post-Divorce* (Copenhagen, Denmark: Danish National Institute of Social Research, 1984a).

Kelly, J. B., "Examining Resistance to Joint Custody," in J. Folberg (Ed.), *Joint Custody and Shared Parenting* (Washington, DC: Bureau of National Affairs and Association of Family and Conciliation Courts, 1984b).

Kelly, J., & Wallerstein, J., "The Effects of Parental Divorce: Experiences of the Child in Early Latency," 46 *American Journal of Orthopsychiatry* 20 (1976).

Keniston, K., & The Carnegie Council on Children, *All Our Children: The American Family Under Pressure* (New York: Harcourt Brace, 1977).

Kent, M., & Rolf, J. (Eds.), *Primary Prevention of Psychopathology: Promoting Social Competency and Coping in Children* (Hanover, NH: University Press of New England, 1979).

Keshet, H., & Rosenthal, K., "Fathering After Marital Separation," 23 *Social Work* 11 (1978).

Keshet, J. K., & Mirkin, M. P., "Troubled Adolescents in Divorced and Remarried Families," in M. P. Mirkin & S. L. Roman (Eds.) *Handbook of Adolescent and Family Therapy* (New York: Gardner, 1985).

Kessler, S., *The American Way of Divorce* (Chicago: Nelson-Hall, 1975).

Kitson, G., & Sussman, M., "The Processes of Marital Separation and Divorce: Male and Female Similarities and Differences." Paper presented at the meeting of the American Psychological Association, NY, August 1976.

Kitson, G., & Sussman, M., "Marital Complaints, Demographic Characteristics and Symptoms of Mental Distress in Divorce," 44 *Journal of Marriage and the Family* 87 (1982).

Kitson, G. D., *Index of Attachment*. Unpublished manuscript (1979).

Klemsrud, J., ". . .And the House Gained Custody," *Milwaukee Journal*, February 12, 1978.

Klemsrud, J., "Parents Move, Children Don't Under Pact," *The Oregonian*, February 20, 1978.

Kline, M., Tschann, J. M., Johnston, J. R., & Wallerstein, J. S., "Children's Adjustment in Joint and Sole Physical Custody Families." Paper presented at the 65th Annual Meeting of the American Orthopsychiatric Association, San Francisco, March 1988.

Kloster, S., "The New Joint Custody Statute: Chrysalis of Conflict or Conciliation?" 21 *Santa Clara Law Review* 471 (1981).

Koenig, D. N., "Joint Custody: A Viable Alternative," 60 *Michigan Bar Journal* 170 (1981).

Kohut, N., *Therapeutic Family Law* (Chicago: Family Law Publications, 1968).

Kolata, G., "Child Splitting," 22 (11) *Psychology Today* 34 (1988).

Kompara, D., "Difficulties in the Socialization Process of Stepparenting," 29 *Family Relations* 69 (1980).

Koopman, E. J., & Hunt, E. J., "Child Custody Mediation: An Interdisciplinary Synthesis," 58 *American Journal of Orthopsychiatry* 379 (1988).

Koritzinsky, A., *Marital and Non-Marital Settlement Agreement Handbook* (Madison, WI: Advanced Training Seminars, 1981).

Kressel, K., Lopez-Morillas, M., Weinglass, J., & Deutsch, M., "Professional Intervention in Divorce: A Summary of the Views of Lawyers, Psychotherapists, and Clergy," 2 *Journal of Divorce* 138 (1978).

Kressel, K., *The Process of Divorce: How Professionals and Couples Negotiate Settlements* (New York: Basic Books, 1985).

Kubie, L., "Provisions for the Care of Children of Divorced Parents," in A. Wilkerson (Ed.), *The Rights of Children* (Philadelphia: Temple University Press, 1974).

Kurdek, L., Blisk, D., & Siesky, A., "Correlates of Children's Long-Term Adjustment to Their Parents' Divorce," 17 *Developmental Psychology* 565 (1981).

Kurdek, L. A., & Berg, B., "Correlates of Children's Adjustment to Their Parents' Divorces," in L. A. Kurdek (Ed.), *Children and Divorce: New Directions for Child Development* (No. 19) (San Francisco: Jossey-Bass, 1983).

Lamb, M., "Effects of Stress and Cohort on Mother– and Father–Infant Interaction," 12 *Developmental Psychology* 435 (1976a).

Lamb, M., "Interactions Between Eight-Month-Old Children and Their Fathers and Mothers," in M. Lamb (Ed.), *The Role of the Father in Child Development* (New York: Wiley, 1976b).

Lamb, M. (Ed.), *The Role of the Father in Child Development* (New York: Wiley, 1976c).

Lamb, M., "Twelve-Month-Olds and Their Parents: Interaction in a Laboratory Playroom," 12 *Developmental Psychology* 237 (1976d).

Lamb, M., "The Effects of Divorce on Children's Personality Development," 1 *Journal of Divorce* 163 (1977a).

Lamb, M., "A Reexamination of the Infant Social World," 20 *Human Development* 65 (1977b).

Langley, R., & Levy, R., *Wife Beating: The Silent Crisis* (New York: Dutton, 1977).

Langner, T., & Michael, S., *Life Stress and Mental Health* (New York: The Free Press, 1963).

Lasch, C., *The Culture of Narcissism.* (New York: Norton Books, 1979).

Lawrence, W., "Divided Custody of Children After Their Parents Divorce," 8 *Journal of Family Law* 58 (1968).

Lemon, N., "Joint Custody as a Statutory Presumption: California's New Civil Code Sections 4600 and 4600.5," 11 *Golden Gate Law Review* 485 (1981).

Levine, J., "Parents Agree to Joint Custody," *Christian Science Monitor*, May 5, 1975, at 18.

Levine, J., *Who Will Raise the Children? New Options for Fathers (and Mothers)* (New York: Bantam Books, 1977).

Levinger, G., & Moles, O. (Eds.), *Divorce and Separation: Context, Causes and Consequences* (New York: Basic Books, 1979).

Levitin, T., "Children of Divorce," 35 *Journal of Social Issues* 1 (1979).

Levy, B., & Chambers, C., "The Folly of Joint Custody," 3 *Family Advocate*, Spring 1981, at 6.

Levy, B., & Chambers, C., "The Folly of Joint Custody," 69 *Illinois Bar Journal* 412 (1981).

Lewis, M., & Weinraub, M., "The Father's Role in the Child's Social Network," in M. Lamb (Ed.), *The Role of the Father in Child Development* (New York: Wiley, 1976).

Lindey, A., *Separation Agreements and Ante-Nuptial Contracts* (New York: Matthew Bender, 1982).

Lindsley, B., "Custody Proceedings: Battlefield or Peace Conference?" 13 *Conciliation Courts Review*, September 1975, at 1.

Littner, N., "The Effects on a Child of Family Disruption and Separation from One or Both Parents." Paper delivered at Association of Family and Conciliation Courts Conference, Chicago, IL, May 1973.

Lowenstein, J. S., & Koopman, E. J., "A Comparison of Self-Esteem Between Boys Living with Single-Parent Mothers and Single-Parent Fathers," 2 *Journal of Divorce* 195 (1978).

Lowery, C., "Child Custody Decisions in Divorce Proceedings," 12 *Professional Psychology* 492 (1981).

Lowery, C. R., & Settle, S. A., "Effects of Divorce on Children: Differential Impact of Custody and Visitation Patterns," 34 *Family Relations* 455 (1985).

Luepnitz, D., "Maternal, Paternal and Joint Custody: A Study of Families After Divorce," Doctoral Dissertation, State University of New York at Buffalo (1980).

Luepnitz, D., *Child Custody: A Study of Families After Divorce* (Lexington, MA: D.C. Heath & Co., 1982).

Luepnitz, D. A., "A Comparison of Maternal, Paternal and Joint Custody: Understanding the Varieties of Post-Divorce Family Life," 12 *Journal of Divorce* 1 (1986).

Luepnitz, D. A., "A Review of Wallerstein and Kelly's *Surviving the Break-Up*," 43 *Journal of Marriage and the Family*, November 1981.

Lynn, D., *The Father: His Role in Child Development* (Belmont, CA: Wadsworth Publishing Company, 1974).

Lynn, K., "Child Custody, In Whose Best Interests?" Unpublished paper (1974).

Maccoby, E. E., Depner, C. E., & Mnookin, R. H., "Custody of Children Following Divorce," in E. M. Hetherington, & J. Arasteh (Eds.), *The Impact of Divorce, Single Parenting and Stepparenting on Children* (Hillsdale, NJ: Lawrence Erlbaum Associates, 1988).

Maidment, S., "A Look at Equal Parental Rights," 126 *The New Law Journal* 1024 (1976).

"Marriage Fails but Fatherhood's Fine, " *Milwaukee Journal*, June 18, 1979, at 12.

Martin, D., *Battered Wives* (San Francisco: Glide Publications, 1976).

McCord J., McCord, W., & Thurber, E., "Some Effects of Paternal Absence on Male Children," 64 *Journal of Abnormal and Social Psychology* 361 (1962).

McCubbin, H. I., & Figley, C. R., "Introduction," in H. I. McCubbin, & C. R. Figley (Eds.), *Stress and the Family. Volume 1: Coping with Normative Transitions* (New York: Brunner/Mazel, 1983).

McDermott, J. F., Jr., "Parental Divorce in Early Childhood," 124 *American Journal of Psychiatry* 1424 (1968).

McGready, J., *The Kitchen Sink Papers* (Garden City, NY: Doubleday, 1975).

McKie, D., Prentice, B., & Reed, P., *Divorce: Law and the Family in Canada* (Ottawa: Statistics Canada, Research and Analysis Division, 1983).

McKinnon, R., & Wallerstein, J. S., "Joint Custody and the Preschool Child," 4 (2) *Behavioral Sciences and the Law* 169 (1986).

McKinnon, R., & Wallerstein, J. S., "Joint Custody and the Preschool Child," 25 *Conciliation Courts Review* 39 (1987).

Mead, M., "Anomalies in American Postdivorce Relationships," in P. Bohannon (Ed.), *Divorce and After: An Analysis of the Emotional and Social Problems of Divorce* (Garden City, NY: Anchor Books, 1970).

Mendes, H., "Single Fathers," 25 *The Family Coordinator* 429 (1976).

"Men's Lib Movement Trains Its Guns on Divorce Courts," *U.S. News and World Report*, September 12, 1977, at 42.

Messinger, L., "Remarriage Between Divorced People with Children from Previous Marriages: A Proposal for Preparation for Remarriage," 2 *Journal of Marriage and Family Counseling* 193 (1976).

Messinger, L., "Joint Custody Conflicts," in A. S. Gurman (Ed.), *Questions and Answers in the Practice of Family Therapy* (New York: Brunner/Mazel, 1981).

Messinger, L., Walker, K., & Freeman, S., "Preparation for Remarriage Following Divorce," 48 *American Journal of Orthopsychiatry* 263 (1978).

Michigan House Judiciary Committee, "Summary Report on the Friend of Court Reform Bills," *State of Michigan House of Representatives* (1981).

Michigan House Legislative Analysis Section, "Joint Custody: Require Consideration, First Analysis," *State of Michigan House of Representatives* (1980).

Michigan House Legislative Analysis Section, "Joint Custody: Require Consideration, Second Analysis," *State of Michigan House of Representatives* (1981).

Miller, D., "Joint Custody," 13 *Family Law Quarterly* 345 (1979).

Miller, G., "Can Joint Custody Serve the Best Interests of the Child?" 9 *Bulletin of the American Academy of Psychiatry and Law* 210 (1981).

Mills, B., & Belzer, S., "Joint Custody as a Parenting Alternative," 9 *Pepperdine Law Review* 853 (1982).

Milne, A., "Custody of Children in a Divorce Process: A Family Self-Determination Model," 16 (2) *Conciliation Courts Review*, September 1978, at 1.

Milne, A. (Ed.)., *Joint Custody Handbook: A Handbook for Judges, Lawyers and Counselors* (Portland, OR: Association of Family and Conciliation Courts, 1979).

Minuchin, S., *Families and Family Therapy* (Cambridge, MA: Harvard University Press, 1974).

Mitchell, J., "Judge Gives Joint Custody No Raves," *Oregon Journal*, April 9, 1979, at 19.

Mitnick, M., "Joint Custody Information Program," 20 (1) *Conciliation Courts Review*, June 1982, at 41.

Mnookin, R., "Child Custody Adjudication: Judicial Functions in the Face of Indeterminacy," 39 *Law & Contemporary Problems* 226 (1975).

Mnookin, R., "Toward a Theory of Children's Rights," 28 *Harvard Law School Bulletin* 18 (1977).

Mnookin, R., & Kornhauser, L., "Bargaining in the Shadow of the Law: The Case of Divorce," 88 *Yale Law Journal* 950 (1979).

Moffatt, R., & Scherer, J., *Dealing with Divorce* (Boston/Toronto: Little, Brown and Company, 1976).

Molinoff, D., "After Divorce, Give Them a Father Too," *Newsday*, October 5, 1975.

Molinoff, D., "For This Father, Joint Custody Is Tough, Satisfying," *Capital Times*, October 30, 1975.

Molinoff, D., "Joint Custody: Victory for All?" *The New York Times*, March 6, 1977.

Moller, S., "Joint Custody: A Critical Analysis," 14 *Trial Lawyers Quarterly* 36 (1982).

Monahan, T., "The Changing Nature and Instability of Remarriages," 5 *Eugenics Quarterly* 73 (1958).

Moore, N., & Davenport, C., "Custody and Visitation: An Explication of Prevalent Patterns." Paper presented at the Biennial Meeting of the Society for Research in Child Development, San Francisco, CA, March 15–18, 1979.

"More Divorcees Sharing Custody," *Capital Times*, April 19, 1977.

Morgenbesser, M., & Nehls, N., *Joint Custody: An Alternative for Divorcing Families* (Chicago: Nelson-Hall, 1981).

Mulloy, W., "Domestic Relations with Tax Analysis," in E. Belsheim (Ed.), 7 *West's Legal Forms* 2d (St. Paul, MN: West Publishing Co., 1983).

Mummery, D., "Whose Child Is It Anyway? Awarding Joint Custody Over the Objection of One Parent," 15 *Fordham Urban Law Journal* 625 (1987).

Murphree, S., "Divorce: The Joint Custody Alternative," 34 *Oklahoma Law Review* 119 (1981).

National Congress for Men, Media Release, "Results of the National Congress for Men's Second Conference," Detroit, MI, August 6–8, 1982.

National Task Force on Divorce and Divorce Reform, *Task Force Report: Divorce and Divorce Reform* (Minneapolis: National Council on Family Relations, 1974).

Neely, R., "Tug of Love: The Anguish of Child Custody Cases," *Family Weekly*, October 11, 1981, at 6.

Nehls, N., "Joint Custody: An Exploration of the Issues." Unpublished paper, Social Work Class 715, University of Wisconsin—Madison (1977).

Nehls, N., "Joint Custody of Children: A Descriptive Study." Unpublished Master's Thesis, School of Nursing, University of Wisconsin Madison (1978).

Nehls, N., & Morgenbesser, M., "Joint Custody: An Exploration of the Issues," 19 *Family Process* 117 (1980).

Nelson, R., "Post-Divorce Parental Hostility, Conflict and Communication," *Journal of Divorce* (in press).

Nestor, B., "Attitudes of Child Psychiatrists Toward Homosexual Parenting and Child Custody," 17 (2) *Conciliation Courts Review*, September 1979, at 21.

Nestor, B., "Developing Cooperation Between Hostile Parents at Divorce," 16 *University of California–Davis Law Review* 771 (1983).

"New Hampshire Case: Joint Custody Presumption Is Urged by Dissenter," 5 *Family Law Reporter* 1074 (1979).

"New York Court Changes Joint Custody to Award to Father," 4 *Family Law Reporter* 2226 (1978).

Newman, G., *101 Ways To Be a Long Distance Super-Dad* (Mountain View, CA: Blossom Valley Press, 1981).

Nichols, R., & Troester, J., "Custody Evaluations: An Alternative?" 28 *The Family Coordinator* 399 (1979).

Noble, D. N., "Custody Contest: How to Divide and Reassemble a Child," 64 (7) *Social Casework* 406 (1983).

Noble, J., & Noble, W., *The Custody Trap* (New York: Hawthorn Books, 1975)

Nock, S., "The Family Life Cycle: Empirical or Conceptual Tool," 41 *Journal of Marriage and the Family* 15 (1979).

Norton, A., "The Family Life Cycle Updated: Components and Uses," in R. Winch & G. Spainer (Eds.), *Selected Studies in Marriage and the Family*, 4th Ed. (New York: Holt, Rinehart and Winston, 1974).

Norton, A., & Glick, P., "Marital Instability: Past, Present and Future," 32 *Journal of Social Issues* 5 (1976).

Nunan, S., "Joint Custody Versus Single Custody Effects on Child Development," Doctoral Dissertation, California School of Professional Psychology (1980).

Nunan, S. A., "Joint Custody Versus Sole Custody: Effects on Child Development," 41 (12B) *Dissertation Abstracts International* 4680B (1980).

Nye, I., "Child Adjustment in Broken and Unhappy, Unbroken Homes," 19 *Marriage and Family Living* 356 (1957).

Oakland County Friend of the Court, "Annual Report for 1981."

Ohlin, L., & Tonry, M. (Eds.), *Family Violence* (Chicago: University of Chicago Press, 1989).

"One Child, Two Homes," *Time Magazine*, January 29, 1979, at 61.

Orlando, F., "Mediation and Conciliation Under Section 61.21," in *Anatomy of Shared Parental Responsibility* (Tampa, FL: Florida Bar, 1982).

Orthner, D., Brown, T., & Ferguson, D., "Single-Parent Fatherhood: An Emerging Family Lifestyle," 25 *The Family Coordinator* 429 (1976).

Oshman, H., & Manosevitz, M., "Father Absence: Effects of Stepfathers Upon Psychosocial Development in Males," 12 *Developmental Psychology* 479 (1976).

Oster, A., "Custody Proceedings: A Study of Vague and Indefinite Standards," 5 *Journal of Family Law* 21 (1965).

Patterson, M., "The Added Cost of Shared Lives," 5 (2) *Family Advocate* 10 (1982).

Payne, J. D., "Co-Parenting Revisited," 2 *Family Law Review* 243 (1979).

Payne, J., "Co-Parenting Revisited," in *Payne's Digest on Divorce in Canada, 1968–1980* (Toronto: Richard DeBoo Publishers, 1980).

Payne, J. D., & Boyle, P. J., "Divided Opinion on Joint Custody," 2 (3) *Family Law Review* 163 (1979).

Payne, J., & Boyle, P., "Divided Opinions on Joint Custody, " in *Payne's Digest on Divorce in Canada, 1968–1980* (Toronto: Richard DeBoo Publishers, 1980).

Payne, J., & Kallish, K., "A Behavioral Science and Legal Analysis of Access to the Child in the Post-Separation/Divorce Family," 13 *Ottawa Law Review* 215 (1981).

Pearson, J., & Thoennes, N., *The Denver Custody Project: Report to the Piton Foundation* (Denver, CO: Center for Policy Research, 1983).

Pearson, J., & Thoennes, N., "Supporting Children After Divorce: The Conflict of Custody on Support Levels and Payments," 22 (3) *Family Law Quarterly* 319 (1988).

Pederson, F., Rubenstein, J., & Yarrow, L., "Infant Development in Father-Absent Families," 135 *Journal of Genetic Psychology* 51 (1979).

Perry, J., & Pfuhl, E., "Adjustment of Children in Solo and Remarriage Homes," 25 *Marriage and Family Living* 221 (1963).

Petterson, M., "The Added Cost of Shared Lives," in J. Folberg (Ed.), *Joint Custody and Shared Parenting* (Washington, DC: Bureau of National Affairs and Association of Family and Conciliation Courts, 1984).

Phear, W. P. C., Beck, J. C., Hauser, B. B., Clark, S. C., & Whitney, R. A., "An Empirical Study of Custody Agreements: Joint Versus Sole Legal Custody," in J. Folberg (Ed.), *Joint Custody and Shared Parenting* (Washington, DC: Bureau of National Affairs and the Association of Family and Conciliation Courts, 1984).

Plant, J., "The Psychiatrist Views Children of Divorced Parents," 10 *Law and Contemporary Problems* 807 (1944).

Podell, R., Peck, H., & First, C., "Custody—To Which Parent?" 56 *Marquette Law Review* 51 (1972).

Pojman, E. Q., "Emotional Adjustment of Boys in Sole Custody and Joint Custody Divorces Compared with Adjustment of Boys in Happy or Unhappy Marriages." Unpublished Doctoral Dissertation, California Graduate Institute, 1981.

Polikoff, N., "Why Are Mothers Losing: A Brief Analysis of Criteria Used in Child Custody Determinations," 7 *Women's Rights Law Reporter* 235 (1982).

Polikoff, N., "Custody and Visitation: Their Relationship to Establishing and Enforcing Support," 19 *Clearinghouse Review* 274 (1985).

Poll, E., "The Evolution of Joint Custody," 19 (2) *Conciliation Courts Review*, December 1981, at 53.

Porter, B., & O'Leary, K. D., "Marital Discord and Childhood Behavior Problems," 80 *Journal of Abnormal Child Psychology* 287 (1980).

Press, A., "Divorce American Style," *Newsweek Magazine*, January 10, 1983, at 42.

"Provisions for the Care of Children of Divorced Parents: A New Legal Instrument," 73 *Yale Law Journal* 1197 (1964).

"Public Act 434 of 1980: Michigan's Joint Custody Act," 60 *Michigan Bar Journal* 171 (1981).

Quinn, S., "Fathers Cry for Custody," *Juris Doctor*, May 1976, at 42.

Rabkin, J., & Johnson, M., 4 *Current Legal Forms with Tax Analysis* 10–2028.4 (New York: Matthew Bender, 1983).

Radin, N., "The Role of the Father in Cognitive, Academic and Intellectual Development," in M. E. Lamb (Ed.), *The Role of Father in Child Development*, 2nd Ed. (New York: Wiley, 1981).

Ramey, M., Stender, F., & Dunn, G., *Report of the California Women Lawyers Child Custody Project* (San Francisco, 1977).

Ramey, M., Stender, F., & Smaller, D., "Joint Custody: Are Two Homes Better than One?" 8 *Golden Gate University Law Review* 559 (1979).

Ramos, S., *The Complete Book of Child Custody* (New York: G.P. Putnam's Sons, 1979).

Raschke, H., & Raschke, V., "Family Conflict and Children's Self-Concepts: A Comparison of Intact and Single-Parent Families," 41 (2) *Journal of Marriage and Family* 367 (1979).

Reece, S., "Joint Custody: A Cautious View," 16 *University of California–Davis Law Review* 775 (1983).

Reiss, D., *The Family's Construction of Reality* (Cambridge, MA: Harvard University Press, 1981).

Ricci, I., "Dispelling the Stereotype of the 'Broken Home,'" 12 (2) *Conciliation Courts Review*, December 1976, at 7.

Ricci, I., "Divorce, Remarriage and the Schools," *Phi Delta Kappan*, March 1979, at 509.

Ricci, I., "Divorcing Family," Speech delivered at U.C.L.A., quoted in *Los Angeles Times*, January 3, 1979, at 4.

Ricci, I., *Mom's House–Dad's House* (New York: Macmillan, 1981).

Richards, C. A., & Goldenberg, I., "Joint Custody: Current Issues and Implications for Treatment." 13 *Journal of Family Therapy* 33 (1985).

Richards, C. A., & Goldenberg, I., "Fathers with Joint Physical Custody of Young Children: A Preliminary Look," 14 *American Journal of Family Therapy* 154 (1986).

Robinson, H., "Joint Custody — An Idea Whose Time Has Come," 21 *Journal of Family Law* 641 (1983).

Roman, M., "The Disposable Parent," 15 (2) *Conciliation Courts Review*, December 1977, at 1.

Roman, M., & Haddad, W., "The Case for Joint Custody," *Psychology Today*, September 1978a, at 96.

Roman, M., & Haddad, W., *The Disposable Parent* (New York: Holt, Rinehart and Winston, 1978b).

Roosevelt, R., & Lofas, J., *Living in Step* (New York: Stein and Day, 1976).

Rosen, E., "Joint Custody: In the Best Interests of the Child and the Parents," 1 *Reports of Family Law* 2d (Canada) 116 (1978).

Rosen, R., "Children of Divorce: What They Feel About Access and Other Aspects of the Divorce Experience," 6 *Journal of Clinical Child Psychology* 24 (1977).

Roth, A., "The Tender Years Presumption in Child Custody Disputes," 15 *Journal of Family Law* 423 (1975).

Rothberg, B., "Joint Custody: Parental Problems and Satisfactions," 22 *Family Process* 43 (1983).

Russell, R., "Joint Custody: Clash Over New Law," *Detroit News*, April 15, 1981.

Rutter, M., "Parent–Child Separation: Psychological Effects on the Children," 12 *Journal of Child Psychology and Psychiatry* 233 (1971).

Rutter, M., "Protective Factors in Children's Responses to Stress and Disadvantage," in M. Kent & J. Rolf (Eds.), *Primary Prevention of Psychopathology: Promoting Social Competence and Coping in Children*, Vol. 3 (Hanover, NH: University Press of New England, 1979).

Rutter, M., "Epidemiological–Longitudinal Approaches to the Study of Development," in W. A. Collins (Ed.), *The Concept of Development*, Vol. 15, Minnesota Symposia on Child Psychology (Hillsdale, NJ: Lawrence Erlbaum Associates, 1982).

Rutter, M., "Resilience in the Face of Adversity: Protective Factors and Resistance to Psychiatric Disorder," 147 *British Journal of Psychiatry* 598 (1985).

Rutter, M., & Quinton, D., "Psychiatric Disorder—Ecological Factors and Concepts of Causation," in H. McGurk (Ed.), *Ecological Factors in Human Development* (Amsterdam: North-Holland, 1977).

Sabalis, R., & Ayers, G., "Emotional Aspects of Divorce and Their Effects on the Legal Process," 26 *The Family Coordinator* 391 (1977).

Safilios-Rothschild, C., *Women And Social Policy* (Englewood Cliffs, NJ: Prentice-Hall, 1974).

Salfi, D., & Cassady, N., "Who Owns This Child? Shared Parenting Before and After Divorce, " 20 (1) *Conciliation Courts Review*, June 1982, at 31.

Salius, A., "Joint Custody," in A. Milne (Ed.), *Joint Custody Handbook: A Handbook for Judges, Lawyers and Counselors* (Portland, OR: Association of Family and Conciliation Courts, 1979).

Salius, T., "Workshop: Joint Custody," Paper delivered to Annual Conference of Association of Family and Conciliation Courts, Vancouver, British Columbia, May 20, 1978.

Salk, L., "On the Custody Rights of Fathers in Divorce, " 6 *Journal of Clinical Child Psychology* 49 (1977).

Samis, M. D. C., & Saposnek, D. T., "Parent–Child Relationships in Family Mediation: A Synthesis of Views," in D. T. Saposnek (Ed.), *Applying Family Therapy Perspective to Family Mediation* (San Francisco: Jossey-Bass, 1986).

Sandler, I., Wolchik, S. A., & Braver, S., "Social Support and Children of Divorce," in I. G. Sarason & B. R. Sarason (Eds.), *Social Support: Theory, Research and Applications* (The Hague, Netherlands: Martinus Nijhoff, 1985).

Santrock, J., "Relation of Type and Onset of Father Absence to Cognitive Development," 43 *Child Development* 455 (1972).

Santrock, J., & Warshak, R., "Father Custody and Social Development in Boys and Girls," 35 *Journal of Social Issues* 112 (1979).

Saposnek, D. T., *Mediating Child Custody Disputes: A Systematic Guide for Family Therapists, Court Counselors, Attorneys, and Judges* (San Francisco: Jossey-Bass, 1983a).

Saposnek, D. T., "Strategies in Child Custody Mediation: A Family Systems Approach," in J. A. Lemmon (Ed.), *Successful Techniques for Mediating Family Breakup* (San Francisco: Jossey-Bass, 1983b).

Saposnek, D. T., "Short-Term Psychotherapy," in N. Endler & J. McV. Hunt (Eds.), *Personality and the Behavioral Disorders*, 2nd Ed., Vol. II (New York: Wiley, 1984).

Saposnek, D. T., "What Is Fair in Child Custody Mediation?" in J. A. Lemmon (Ed.), *Making Ethical Decisions* (San Francisco: Jossey-Bass, 1985).

Saposnek, D. T., Hamburg, J., Delano, D. C., & Michaelsen, H., "How Has Mandatory Mediation Fared? Research Findings of the First Year's Follow-Up." 22 (20) *Conciliation Courts Review*, December 1984, at 7.

Schepard, A., "Taking Children Seriously: Promoting Cooperative Custody after Divorce," 64 *Texas Law Review* 687 (1985).

Schlesinger, B., "Children and Divorce in Canada: The Law Reform Commission's Recommendations," in B. Schlesinger (Ed.), *One in Ten: The Single Parent in Canada* (Toronto: Guidance Centre, Faculty of Education, University of Toronto, 1979a).

Schlesinger, B. (Ed.), *One in Ten: The Single Parent in Canada* (Toronto: Guidance Centre, Faculty of Education, University of Toronto, 1979b).

Schlesinger, B., "Marriages and Divorces: Canada, 1980, Handout Based on Statistics Canada Data" (Toronto: Faculty of Social Work, University of Toronto, 1982).

Schreiberg, R. F., "Sharing Children of Divorce: Duration and Development," 21 *Conciliation Courts Review* 53 (1983).

Schulman, J., "Who's Looking After the Children?" 5 (2) *Family Advocate*, Fall 1982, at 30.

Schwartz, S. F. G., "Towards a Presumption of Joint Custody," 18 *Family Law Quarterly* 225 (1984).

Scott, E., & Derdeyn, A., "Rethinking Joint Custody," 45 *Ohio State Law Journal* 455 (1984).

Scott, G., "Joint Custody: Does It Work?" *Ms. Magazine*, April 1983, at 77.

Sell, K., "Joint Custody and Coparenting," Paper presented at the Annual Meeting of the National Council on Family Relations, Boston, MA, August 14–18, 1979.

Sessums, S., "Sample Shared Parental Responsibility Agreement," in *Anatomy of Shared Parental Responsibility* (Tampa, FL: Florida Bar, 1982).

Sharp, S., "Modification of Agreement-Based Custody Decrees," 68 *Virginia Law Review* 1263 (1982).

Shavin, S., "Joint Parenting After Divorce: An Alternative to Traditional Child Custody," Master's Thesis, California School of Professional Psychology (1976).

Shaw, D. S., & Emery, R. E., "Parental Conflict and Other Correlates of the Adjustment of School-Age Children Whose Parents Have Separated," 15 *Journal of Abnormal Child Psychology* 269 (1987).

Shear, L., "Drafting Post-Separation Orders Allocating Parental Rights and Responsibilities." Presented at Fifth Annual Family Law Colloquium, Los Angeles, CA, 1981.

Shiller, V. M., "Joint Versus Maternal Physical Custody for Families with Latency Age Boys: Parent Characteristics and Child Adjustment," 56 *American Journal of Orthopsychiatry* 486 (1986a).

Shiller, V. M., "Loyalty Conflicts and Family Relationships in Latency Age Boys: A Comparison of Joint and Maternal Custody," 1 (4) *Journal of Divorce* 17 (1986b).

Shinn, M., "Father Absence and Children's Cognitive Development," 85 *Psychological Bulletin* 295 (1978).

Silcott, T., "Joint Custody: Who's Got the Kids?" Paper presented at the 59th Annual Meeting of the American Orthopsychiatric Association, San Francisco, CA, March 29–April 2, 1982.

Simring, S., "Joint Custody Best Alternative When Ex-Spouses Are Hostile: New Research," 9 (51) *Marriage and Divorce Today: The Professional Newsletter for Family Therapy Practitioners* 1 (1984).

Singer, J., & Reynolds, W., "A Dissent of Joint Custody," 47 *Maryland Law Review* 497 (1988).

Smith, E., "Non-Judicial Resolution of Custody and Visitation Disputes," 12 *University of California–Davis Law Review* 582 (1979).

Solomon, P., "The Father's Revolution in Custody Cases," 13 *Trial Magazine*, October 1977, at 33.

Solow, R., & Adams, P., "Custody by Agreement: Child Psychiatrist as Child Advocate," 5 *Journal of Psychiatry and the Law* 77 (1977).

Spalsbury, D., & Dilworth, J., "Custody and Visitation." Presentation at "The Divorce Adjustment Process/New Perspectives for the Family in Transition," a conference by the Family and Children's Service of Calhoun County (Michigan), Inc., July 14–15, 1981.

Spanier, G., & Anderson, E., "The Impact of the Legal System on Adjustment to Marital Separation," 41 *Journal of Marriage and the Family* 605 (1979).

Spicer, J., & Hampe, G., "Kinship Interaction After Divorce," 37 *Journal of Marriage and the Family* 113 (1975).

Spiro, H., "Joint Custody: Divorce Reform: A Medical Viewpoint." Paper presented at State Bar of Wisconsin midwinter meeting, January 27, 1978.

"Split, Divided or Alternate Custody of Children," Annot., 92 *American Law Reports* 2d 695 (1963).

Sprenkle, D. H., & Storm, C. L., "Divorce Therapy Outcome Research: A Substantive and Methodological Review," 9 (3) *Journal of Marriage and Family Therapy* 239 (1983).

Stack, C., *All Our Kin: Strategies for Survival in a Black Community* (New York: Harper and Row, 1974).

Stack, C., "Who Owns the Child? Divorce and Child Custody Decisions in Middle-Class Families," 23 *Social Problems* 505 (1976).

Stahl, P., "Joint Custody: Attitudes and Beliefs of Professionals and Joint Custody Families," Doctoral Dissertation, University of Michigan (1983).

Steil, J. M., "Marriage: An Unequal Partnership," in B. Wolman and G. Sticker (Eds.), *Handbook of Family and Marital Therapy* (New York: Plenum, 1983).

Steinman, S., "The Experience of Children in a Joint Custody Arrangement: A Report of a Study," 51 *American Journal of Orthopsychiatry* 403 (1981).

Steinman, S., "Joint Custody: What We Know, What We Have Yet to Learn and the Judicial and Legislative Implications," 16 *University of California–Davis Law Review* 739 (1983).

Steinman, S., "Joint Custody: What We Know, What We Have Yet to Learn, and the Judicial and Legislative Implications," in J. Folberg (Ed.), *Joint Custody and Shared Parenting* (Washington, DC: Bureau of National Affairs and Association of Family and Conciliation Courts, 1984).

Steinman, S. B., Knoblauch, T., & Zemmelman, S., "Children in Joint Custody: A Report of a Study of Children in Voluntary and Court-Determined Joint Custody." Paper presented at the 63rd Annual Meeting of the American Orthopsychiatric Association, Chicago, March 1986.

Steinman, S., Zemmelman, S., & Knoblauch, T., "A Study of Parents Who Sought Joint Custody Following Divorce: Who Reaches Agreement and Sustains Joint Custody and Who Returns to Court," 24 *Journal of the American Academy of Child Psychiatry* 545 (1985).

Stern, P., "Stepfather Families: Integration Around Child Discipline Issues," 1 *Issues in Mental Health Nursing* 50 (1978).

Stevens, J., Jr., & Matthews, M. (Eds.), *Mother–Child, Father–Child Relations* (Washington, DC: National Association for the Education of Young Children, 1978).

Stilley, J., "Joint Custody of Children Urged to Minimize Trauma of Divorce," *Modern Living*, November 1978, at 5.

Straus, M. A., "Measuring Intrafamily Conflict and Violence: The Conflict Tactics (CT) Scales," 41 *Journal of Marriage and the Family* 75 (1979).

Straus, M. A., "A Reevaluation of the Conflict Tactics Scale, Violence Measures and Some Measures." Unpublished manuscript, University of New Hampshire, Durham (1981).

Stuart, I., & Abt, L. (Eds.), *Children of Separation and Divorce* (New York: Van Nostrand Reinhold, 1981).

Sweeney, J., "Drop-Out Father's Tenuous Link to Child Complex," *The Oregonian*, January 3, 1983, at C1.

"Tactics Emphasized in Conference on New Developments in Custody," 5 *Family Law Reporter* 2141 (1978).

Taussig, J., & Carpenter, J., "Joint Custody," 56 *Notre Dame Law Review* 223 (1980).

Tripp, J., "Counseling Said to Avert Custody Fights," *The Oregonian*, April 11, 1979, at E8.

Trombetta, D., "Joint Custody: Recent Research and Overloaded Courtrooms Inspire New Solutions to Custody Disputes," 19 *Journal of Family Law* 213 (1980–81).

Trombetta, D., & Lebbos, B., "Co-Parenting: Everyone's Best Interest," 17 (3) *Conciliation Courts Review*, December 1979, at 13.

Tuckman, J., & Regan, R., "Intactness of Home and Behavioral Problems in Children," 7 *Journal of Child Psychology and Psychiatry* 225 (1966).

U.S. Bureau of the Census, *Current Population Reports. Number, Timing and Duration of Marriages and Divorces in the United States: June 1975* (Series P–20, No. 297) (Washington, DC: U.S. Government Printing Office, 1976).

U.S. Bureau of the Census, *Current Population Reports. Divorce, Child Custody and Child Support* (Series P–23, No. 84) (Washington, DC: U.S. Government Printing Office, 1979).

USDA, Agricultural Research Services, "Updated Estimates of the Cost of Raising Children," *Family Economics Review* 30–31 (Winter 1982).

U.S. National Center for Health Statistics, *Divorces and Divorce Rates: United States* (Vital and Health Statistics, Series 21, No. 29) (Washington, DC: U.S. Government Printing Office, 1978).

Uviller, R., "Father's Rights and Feminism: The Maternal Presumption Revisited," 1 *Harvard Women's Law Journal* 107 (1978).

Van Swearingen, C., & Choka, A., 5 *Nichols Cyclopedia of Legal Forms Annotated* 484 (Wilmette, IL: Callaghan and Co., 1983).

Vaughn, V., & Brazelton, T. (Eds.), *The Family: Setting Priorities* (New York: Science and Medicine Publishing, 1979).

"Vermont Court Takes Basically Unfavorable View of Joint Custody," 5 *Family Law Reporter* 1033 (1979).

Victor, I., & Winkler, A., *Fathers and Custody* (New York: Hawthorn Books, 1979).

Visher, E., & Visher, J., "Common Problems of Stepparents and Their Spouses," 48 *American Journal of Orthopsychiatry* 252 (1978).

Visher, E., & Visher, J., *Stepfamilies: A Guide to Working with Stepparents and Stepchildren* (New York: Brunner/Mazel, 1979).

Wald, M., "State Intervention on Behalf of 'Neglected' Children: A Search for Realistic Standards," 27 *Stanford Law Review* 985 (1975).

Walker, K., & Messinger, L., "Remarriage After Divorce: Dissolution and Reconstruction of Family Boundaries," 18 *Family Process* 185 (1979).

Walker, K., Rogers, J., & Messinger, L., "Remarriage After Divorce: A Review," 58 *Social Casework* 276 (1977).

Walker, K., & Woods, M., *A Measure of Household Production of Family Goods and Services* (Washington, DC: Center for the Family of the American Home Economics Association, 1981).

Walker, L., "Battered Women," in A. Brodsky & R. Hare-Mustin (Eds.), *Women and Psychotherapy* (New York: Guilford Press, 1980).

Wallerstein, J. S., "The Impact of Divorce on Parents and Children." Presented at "Separation, Divorce, and Beyond," the 9th Annual Conference of The Center for Family Studies/The Family Institute of Chicago, Chicago, IL, April 24–25, 1982.

Wallerstein, J. S., "Children of Divorce: Preliminary Report of a Ten-Year Follow-Up of Young Children," 54 *American Journal of Orthopsychiatry* 444 (1984).

Wallerstein, J. S., "Children of Divorce: Recent Research — Introduction," 24 *Journal of the American Academy of Child Psychiatry* 515 (1985a).

Wallerstein, J. S., "The Overburdened Child: Some Long-Term Consequences of Divorce," 30 *Social Work* 116 (1985b).

Wallerstein, J. S., "Children of Divorce: Report of a Ten-Year Follow-Up of Early Latency-Age Children," 57 *American Journal of Orthopsychiatry* 199 (1987).

Wallerstein, J. S., & Blakeslee, S., *Second Chances: Men, Women, and Children a Decade After Divorce* (New York: Ticknor & Fields, 1989).

Wallerstein, J. S., & Kelly, J. B., "The Effects of Parental Divorce: The Adolescence Experience," in J. Anthony & C. Koupernik (Eds.), *The Child in His Family: Children at Psychiatric Risk* (New York: Wiley, 1974).

Wallerstein, J. S., & Kelly, J. B., "The Effects of Parental Divorce: Experiences of the Pre-School Child," 14 *Journal of the American Academy of Child Psychiatry* 600 (1975).

Wallerstein, J. S., & Kelly, J. B., "The Effects of Parental Divorce: Experience of the Child in Later Latency," 46 *American Journal of Orthopsychiatry* 256 (1976).

Wallerstein, J. S., & Kelly, J. B., "Children and Divorce: A Review," 24 *Social Work* 468 (1979).

Wallerstein, J. S., & Kelly, J. B., "Effects of Divorce on the Visiting Father–Child Relationship," 137 *American Journal of Psychiatry* 1534 (1980a).

Wallerstein, J. S., & Kelly, J. B., *Surviving the Breakup: How Children and Parents Cope with Divorce* (New York: Basic Books, 1980b).

Ware, C., "Joint Custody: One Way to End the War," *New West*, February 26, 1979, at 42.

Ware, C., *Sharing Parenthood After Divorce* (New York: Viking Press, 1982).

Ware, C., "What a Mediator Can Do," *Ms. Magazine*, April 1983, at 79.

Watson, M., "The Children of Armageddon: The Problems of Custody Following Divorce," 21 *Syracuse Law Review* 55 (1969).

Watson, M., "Custody Alternatives: Defining the Best Interests of the Child," 30 *Family Relations* 474 (1981).

Watzlawick, P., Weakland, J., & Fisch, R., *Change: Principles of Problem Formation and Problem Resolution* (New York: Norton, 1974).

Weinman, C., "The Trial Judge Awards Custody," 10 *Law and Contemporary Problems* 721 (1944).

Weinraub, M., "Fatherhood: The Myth of the Second-Class Parent," in J. Stevens, Jr. & M. Matthews (Eds.), *Mother–Child, Father–Child Relationships* (Washington, DC: National Association for the Education of Young Children, 1978).

Weiss, E., "Divorced Women in Portland, A Report on an Inquiry," *Oregon Bureau of Labor* (1978).

Weiss, R., *Marital Separation* (New York: Basic Books, 1975).

Weiss, R., "The Adjudication of Custody When Parents Separate," in G. Levinger & O. Moles (Eds.), *Divorce and Separation: Context, Causes and Consequences* (New York: Basic Books, 1979a).

Weiss, R., *Going It Alone: The Family Life and Social Situation of the Single Parent* (New York: Basic Books, 1979b).

Weitzman, L., "Legal Regulation of Marriage: Tradition and Change," 62 *California Law Review* 1169 (1974).

Weitzman, L., "The Economics of Divorce: Social and Economic Consequences of Property, Alimony and Child Support Awards," 28 *U.C.L.A. Law Review* 1181 (1981).

Weitzman, L. J., *The Divorce Revolution: The Unexpected Social and Economic Consequences for Women and Children in America* (New York: The Free Press, 1985).

Weitzman, L., *No-Fault Divorce* (in press).

Weitzman, L., & Dixon, R., "Child Custody Awards: Legal Standards and Empirical Patterns for Child Custody," 12 *University of California–Davis Law Review* 471 (1979).

Westman, J., "Joint Custody from the Child's Point of View," in A. Milne (Ed.), *Joint Custody: A Handbook for Judges, Lawyers and Counselors* (Portland, OR: Association of Family and Conciliation Courts, 1979).

Westman, J., Cline, D., Swift, W., & Kramer, D., "Role of Child Psychiatry in Divorce," 23 *Archives of General Psychiatry* 415 (1970).

"What You Should Know About Divorce Today," 46 *Consumer Reports* 327 (1981).

Wheeler, M., *No-Fault Divorce* (Boston: Beacon Press, 1974).

White, S. W., & Bloom, B. C., "Factors Related to the Adjustment of Divorcing Men," 30 *Family Relations* 349 (1981).

Whitehead, L., "Sex Differences in Children's Responses to Family Stress: A Re-Evaluation," 20 *Journal of Child Psychology and Psychiatry* 247 (1979).

Wilkerson, A. (Ed.), *The Rights of Children* (Philadelphia: Temple University Press, 1974).

Williams, R. G., "Development of Guidelines for Child Support Orders: Final Report" (Report to U.S. Office of Child Support Enforcement) (Williamsburg, VA: National Center for State Courts, March 1987).

Wilson, K., Zurcher, L., McAdams, D., & Curtis, R., "Stepfathers and Stepchildren: An Exploratory Analysis from Two National Surveys," 37 *Journal of Marriage and the Family* 526 (1975).

Winch, R., & Spanier, G. (Eds.), *Selected Studies in Marriage and the Family,* 4th Ed. (New York: Holt, Rinehart and Winston, 1974).

Wolchik, S. A., Braver, S. L., & Sandler, I. N., "Maternal Versus Joint Custody: Children's Post-Separation Experiences and Adjustment," 14 *Journal of Clinical Child Psychology* 5 (1985).

Wolman, B., & Stricker, G. (Eds.), *Handbook of Developmental Psychology* (Englewood Cliffs, NJ: Prentice-Hall, 1982).

Women in Transition, Inc., *Women in Transition: A Feminist Handbook on Separation and Divorce* (New York: Charles Scribner's Sons, 1975).

Woods, L., "Litigation on Behalf of Battered Women," 5 *Women's Rights Law Reporter* 8, 11–13 (1976).

Woody, R., "Fathers with Child Custody," 7 *The Counseling Psychologist* 60 (1978).

Woolley, P., "Shared Custody: Demanded by Parents, Discouraged by Courts," 1 (1) *Family Advocate,* Summer 1978a, at 6.

Woolley, P., "Shared Parenting Arrangement," 1 (1) *Family Advocate* 6 (1978b).

Woolley, P., *The Custody Handbook* (New York: Summit Books, 1979).

Woolley, P., "Shared Parenting Arrangements," in J. Folberg (Ed.), *Joint Custody and Shared Parenthood* (Washington, DC: Bureau of National Affairs and Association of Family and Conciliation Courts, 1984).

Young, M., & Willmot, P., *The Symmetrical Family* (New York: Pantheon Books, 1973).

Zill, N., "Divorce, Marital Happiness, and the Mental Health of Children: Findings from the F.C.D. National Survey of Children." Paper prepared for NIMH workshop on divorce and children, Bethesda, MD, 1978.

Zill, N., "Behavior, Achievement and Health Problems Among Children in Stepfamilies: Findings from a National Survey of Child Health," in M. E. Hetherington & J. Arasteh (Eds.), *The Impact of Divorce, Single-Parenting, and Stepparenting on Children* (Hillsdale, NJ: Lawrence Erlbaum Associates, 1988).